RADICAL
POLITICAL
ECONOMY

RADICAL POLITICAL ECONOMY

Explorations
In Alternative
Economic
Analysis

VICTOR D. LIPPIT

M.E. Sharpe
Armonk, New York
London, England

Library of Congress Cataloging-in-Publication Data

Radical political economy : explorations in alternative
economic analysis / Victor D. Lippit, editor.
p.   cm.
Includes bibliographical references.
ISBN 0-87332-606-7 (alk. paper).
ISBN 0-87332-607-5 (pbk. : alk. paper).
1. Radical economics.   I. Lippit, Victor D.
HB97.7.S87   1995
330—dc20   95-16934
CIP

Printed in the United States of America

The paper used in this publication meets the minimum requirements of
American National Standard for Information Sciences—
Permanence of Paper for Printed Library Materials,
ANSI Z 39.48-1984.

⊗

BM (c)   10   9   8   7   6   5   4   3   2   1
BM (p)   10   9   8   7   6   5   4   3   2   1

For Joyce

Contents

About the Editor and the Contributors   ix

Preface   xi

Introduction
Victor D. Lippit   1

I. Labor

1.   What Do Bosses Do? The Origins and Functions of Hierarchy in Capitalist Production
Stephen A. Marglin   19

2.   Segmented Labor Markets
Richard Edwards   60

3.   Losing Touch: The Cultural Conditions of Worker Accommodation and Resistance
Stephen A. Marglin   86

II. Class

4.   An Approach to Class Analysis
Howard J. Sherman   117

5.   Power, Property, and Class
Richard Wolff and Stephen Resnick   140

III. Discrimination

6.   The Unhappy Marriage of Marxism and Feminism: Towards a More Progressive Union
Heidi I. Hartmann   165

7. Racial Inequality
    Michael Reich   197

IV. Macroeconomic Instability

8. Marxian and Post Keynesian Developments in the Sphere of
    Money, Credit and Finance: Building Alternative Perspectives
    in Monetary Macroeconomics
    Robert Pollin   205

9. Power, Accumulation, and Crisis: The Rise and Demise of the
    Postwar Social Structure of Accumulation
    David M. Gordon, Thomas E. Weisskopf, and Samuel Bowles   226

V. Economic Development

10. Theories of Finance and the Third World
    Laurence Harris   247

11. The Concept of the Surplus in Economic Development
    Victor D. Lippit   265

12. Institutional and Organizational Framework for Egalitarian
    Agricultural Growth
    Azizur Rahman Khan   287

VI. Market Socialism

13. "Market Socialism" and Its Critics
    Alec Nove   299

14. Toward a Socialism for the Future, in the Wake of the Demise
    of the Socialism of the Past
    Thomas E. Weisskopf   318

15. Socialist Economic Development in the Post-Soviet Era
    Victor D. Lippit   344

VII. The Environment

16. The Economics of the Coming Spaceship Earth
    Kenneth E. Boulding   357

17. Marxian Crisis Theory and the Contradictions of Late
    Twentieth-Century Capitalism
    Thomas E. Weisskopf   368

About the Editor and the Contributors

Kenneth E. Boulding (d. 1993) was Distinguished Professor of Economics Emeritus at the University of Colorado at Boulder.

Samuel Bowles is Professor of Economics at the University of Massachusetts, Amherst.

Richard Edwards is Dean of Social Sciences at the University of Kentucky.

David M. Gordon is the Dorothy Hirshon Professor of Economics at the New School for Social Research in New York City.

Laurence Harris is Dean of the Graduate School at the School of Oriental and African Studies at the University of London.

Heidi I. Hartmann is the Director and President of the Institute for Women's Policy Research in Washington, D.C.

Azizur Rahman Khan is Chair of the Economics Department at the University of California, Riverside.

Victor D. Lippit is Professor of Economics at the University of California, Riverside.

Stephen A. Marglin is Walter S. Barker Professor of Economics at Harvard University.

Alec Nove (d. 1994) is Emeritus Professor of Economics at the University of Glascow.

Robert Pollin is Professor of Economics at the University of California, Riverside.

Michael Reich is Professor of Economics at the University of California, Berkeley.

Stephen Resnick is Professor of Economics at the University of Massachusetts, Amherst.

Howard J. Sherman is Professor of Economics at the University of California, Riverside.

Thomas E. Weisskopf is Professor of Economics at the University of Michigan.

Richard Wolff is Professor of Economics at the University of Massachusetts, Amherst.

Preface

In teaching courses on radical political economy, I have long felt the need for a collection of essays that would reveal the breadth and analytical sophistication of the field. I believe that the importance of radical political economy lies, above all, in affording alternative means of conceptualizing critical economic issues, in affording a framework for thinking about economic issues that conventional approaches to the discipline tend to foreclose. For a number of years I have been engaged in assembling such a volume, and this book is the result.

By situating economic issues in their broader social and institutional context, and through acknowledging the impact of factors like class structure and the role of the state, radical political economy provides a fresh perspective for thinking about economics. The emphasis in this book is on exploring the insights into economic and social issues that radical political economy affords. Most of the essays are reprints of journal articles and book chapters, but several have been written especially for this volume. The resulting collection is, I believe, distinctive in both its quality and scope.

I am indebted to many people for the realization of this project. Aziz Khan and Bob Pollin read portions of the manuscript, and I benefited greatly from their critical comments. Laurence Harris and Howard Sherman were gracious enough to prepare essays especially for this volume. My colleagues at the University of California, Riverside, have helped to create an environment in which alternative approaches to economic analysis could be freely explored, and my students, both undergraduate and graduate, have provided an ongoing stimulus to fresh thinking.

Sandy Schauer and Kathy Downey, both formerly with the Economics Department office, helped to free up my time for the preparation of this volume. Among the editors at M.E. Sharpe who worked with me, I am especially indebted to Michael Weber and Eileen Gaffney. Finally, this volume would not have been possible without the love, encouragement, and constant support of my wife Joyce.

Riverside, California
October 1995

RADICAL POLITICAL ECONOMY

Introduction

Victor D. Lippit

The origins of modern economics are usually traced back to the 1776 publication of Adam Smith's *Wealth of Nations*. The full title of Smith's work—*An Inquiry into the Nature and Causes of the Wealth of Nations*—indicates the breadth of his concerns. And indeed, for about a century following the publication of Smith's seminal work, economists remained concerned with broad social issues such as the determinants of economic growth, national prosperity, and the distribution of income and wealth. For them, the question of appropriate institutional arrangements and the relation between economic and other social issues was critical. In the era of the classical economists, broadly spanning the period from Smith to Marx (who died in 1883), economists characteristically considered themselves to be political economists and their discipline political economy.

In the last quarter of the nineteenth century, marginal analysis emerged, the concept of marginal utility came to the fore, and the so-called neoclassical economics was born. The attention of economists shifted from broader social issues to more narrowly defined concerns, typically related to maximization problems in the sphere of what is currently called microeconomics. Turning away from broader social and institutional questions, economists focused on the behavior of the consumer and the firm, seeking to specify how they could allocate resources to maximize their welfare or profit. The term "political economy" was replaced by "economics." Serious concern with the economy as a whole and its broader implications for social life was not revived until the Great Depression of the 1930s reawakened consciousness that the institutional environment of the Western world could not be taken for granted.

In this context, John Maynard Keynes published (in 1936) *The General Theory of Employment, Interest and Money*. Keynes's key finding concerned the inadequacy of the neoclassical economists' comfortable assumption that economic downturns would automatically generate forces adequate to bring about recovery. Keynes showed that an equilibrium could be sustained in a capitalist

1

economy at levels far short of full employment—of people, resources, and productive capacity. He emphasized the role of aggregate demand in restoring and maintaining full employment, and of public policy in assuring that aggregate demand would be adequate. His work led to renewed concern with macroeconomic issues, which subsequently extended beyond full employment to the determinants of economic growth—or the wealth of nations.

In the 1950s and 1960s, it was not uncommon to find American economists who believed that the problems of unemployment and inflation were firmly under control. Based on the Keynesian prescription of raising aggregate demand to eliminate unemployment, or reducing aggregate demand to counter inflation, these economists believed that "fine-tuning" the economy through appropriate public policy measures could alleviate the most serious problems of capitalism. In general, the postwar period was a hopeful one in the United States. Unemployment and inflation remained low, and suburbanization and low interest rates helped sustain a great increase in home ownership. The prevailing social and economic conditions could scarcely have been less suited to the emergence of a radical critique of U.S. capitalism. And indeed, with the exception of Paul Baran, one could not find a noted radical economist on U.S. campuses in the 1950s.

The Emergence and Development of Radical Political Economy

The situation changed in the 1960s. At that time, the civil rights movement and upheavals in urban ghettos revealed a seamy underside of American prosperity. Consciousness of racism and inequality in the distribution of income and wealth rose sharply; the existence of poverty became widely recognized. In the middle of the decade, protests against the war in Vietnam began to take on national proportions. A radical intellectual life re-emerged, and in 1968 the Union for Radical Political Economics (URPE) was formed. URPE began its own journal, the *Review of Radical Political Economics,* intent on exploring a range of issues that mainstream neoclassical journals systematically ignored. By the 1970s, radical political economy attracted a growing number of serious intellectuals.

The ending of the quarter-century of postwar prosperity, the appearance of stagflation, and the increasing seriousness of recessions contributed in the 1970s to extending the range of radical political economy beyond social justice issues to theories of crisis and long-wave fluctuations in the economy. At the same time, the growing awareness of environmental deterioration spurred inquiry into its systemic sources, further extending the range and scope of radical political economy.

Perhaps the most important features distinguishing radical political economics from mainstream, neoclassical economics include a concern with social justice; a keen awareness of institutional change; a search for the systemic roots of alienation, environmental decay, and other social problems in the economic sphere;

and the incorporation of the role of the state and classes in economic analysis. Neoclassical economics has persisted in its focus on individual decision-making units, and has developed its emphasis on the scientific nature of the economics discipline into a fetish. Accordingly, mainstream economics has become ever more committed to mathematical analysis carried out in deductive form. That is, given certain assumptions, neoclassical economics typically seeks to use mathematical forms to deduce valid implications of those assumptions.

A major problem with this approach to economics lies in the fact that the original assumptions are often unreasonable, and in the fact that entire dimensions of the real world are arbitrarily excluded. There is a great irony here in that in this respect, mainstream economics developed in the West shares common ground with the crude Marxist economics developed in the Soviet Union and China in the era of Stalin and Mao. Neoclassical economics, for example, typically starts with the assumption that individuals are "utility" maximizers and firms profit maximizers.

Now if we consider the behavior of individuals, it is clear that maximizing personal benefit is indeed a prime concern. It is by no means, however, the only concern. Human motivation is more complex, and people are, after all, social beings. People act out of habit; they are constrained by institutional forces; they display altruism and concern for others; and their sense of well-being is tied closely to the state of others around them. By simplifying assumptions about human behavior, neoclassical economics makes that behavior amenable to sophisticated formal analysis, but at the same time renders that analysis only marginally relevant to behavior in the real world.

Radical political economy, by contrast, recognizing the transitional character and mutability of social institutions, seeks to develop an analysis of economic behavior that is firmly rooted in the complexity of human behavior and of the real world in which it takes place. Informed always by a concern for social justice—a world without exploitation, racism, sexism, unemployment, undue inequality, and arbitrary hierarchies—radical political economy as it has emerged in the West builds upon the formal analysis of neoclassical economics and the rich tradition of Marxian/radical analysis. In a sense, it seeks to provide a more satisfactory framework for analyzing economic behavior and economic change.

Viewed in this light, the term "political economy" is a misnomer, for it does not refer to an economics that is political—at least not in the narrow sense of the term. Rather, it refers to an economics that is social in the broadest sense of the term. It explores the relationship between people's economic activities and the social environment in which they take place, incorporating concerns ranging from the social relations of production to the meaning of economic justice in nation states (and a world) riven with racial, gender, and class divisions. Perhaps the term "social economy" would be more appropriate, but we shall stay with the more commonly used radical political economy.

Since radical political economy explores the relationships between economics and other aspects of social life, it is not surprising that people writing in this tradition often approach their study from a discipline other than economics. Thus although radical political economy is anchored in economics, it is not uncommon to find people approaching it from the perspective of such related disciplines as history, sociology, political science, anthropology, and so forth.

During the 1950s, one could count the number of prominent academic radical economists in the United States on the fingers of one hand—indeed on one finger. As we have noted, that was Paul Baran, who was hired at Stanford University before the university became aware of his radical perspective. Since Baran was hired at a tenured level, the administration could not readily dismiss him, but it did everything it could to encourage him to leave by denying him promotions and salary increases. Baran's major work, *The Political Economy of Growth,* published in 1957, represents a return to the grand tradition of classical economics in its effort to ascertain the forces generating development in part of the world and underdevelopment in the rest. The work is filled with keen insights, including the introduction of the concept of the economic surplus, although it also suffers from many defects, as an article of mine reproduced as chapter 11 in this volume—"The Concept of the Surplus in Economic Development"—makes clear. This is not at all surprising, since in many respects Baran was working in isolation, deprived of the academic intercourse with his peers that plays such a critical role in the development of scholarship; he died in 1964 at the age of fifty-four.

During the 1960s, spurred by the historical forces shaping the age, a small group of radical economists emerged in American academia. The civil rights movement early in the decade, and the popular struggle against the Vietnam War that grew in strength from the mid-1960s, led many to question the easy ideological assumptions underlying American capitalism. The poor treatment of Third World countries abroad, and of minorities, women, and workers at home—treatment widely perceived as exploitation—entered the consciousness of many graduate students and helped determine the direction of their scholarship. For the first time, studies of poverty and inequality gained an important place on the research agenda.

In the 1970s and 1980s, the number of radical political economists increased greatly, as did the range of their scholarship. At the time of this writing (1995), it is quite common to find one or two radical economists on American faculties. Discrimination persists of course, and many universities exclude them systematically while others tolerate their token representation, demanding especially strong academic qualifications for their appointment and promotion. Graduate programs emphasizing radical political economy have been systematically excluded from the older, establishment universities, but a number of such programs have emerged. The major programs emphasizing a radical political economy approach are located at the University of Massachusetts, Amherst; the University of California, Riverside; the New School for Social Research in New York City; and American University in Washington, D.C. The University of Notre Dame in South Bend, Indiana, has also placed a growing emphasis on this area.

The Distinguishing Features of Radical Political Economy

Radical political economy in the West draws on two rich traditions: the radical/Marxian tradition and conventional economics. Unlike the crude Marxian tradition, with its emphasis on deduction from revealed truths and its frequent inability to address the pressing economic issues of the real world, radical political economy is intensely concerned with explaining the real world and draws readily on empirical tools developed in mainstream economic analysis. At the same time, however, its concern with historical and social change, and with issues of social justice, and its willingness to incorporate variables like class and state into its analyses, provide a far richer theoretical framework for interpreting economic reality than that afforded by mainstream analysis.

One of the favorite myths of social science in the West is that of scholarly "neutrality," the belief that social science is a "science," and as such is divorced from ideology. Radical political economists, in contrast, typically perceive the existence of a relationship between scholarship and class interests, and understand that a given social structure tends to support its dominant class interests as much through the intellectual environment it sustains as through other means. The commitment of radical political economics to those who are disadvantaged or oppressed, a commitment that is clearly expressed in the rich body of scholarship it has produced by now, is another characteristic feature.

Within conventional economics, a field called "political economy" has also grown up over the last few decades. For the most part, it involves the application of neoclassical techniques and assumptions to a new range of economic issues. It differs from *radical* political economy, therefore, in its methodology and assumptions, as well as in the profoundly conservative thrust of its underlying direction. According to this conventional political economy, for example, racist or sexist discrimination cannot exist in a competitive economy. Since firms that engaged in such discrimination would not hire more qualified minorities or women for highly responsible positions, or would pay more to hire equally qualified white males, their labor costs would be higher than those of firms that refused to discriminate, and they would be at a competitive disadvantage. In the extreme case they would be forced out of business. The absence of women or minorities in such firms, therefore, or their absence in positions of authority, is said merely to reflect the inferior qualifications of these groups.

This interpretation of disproportionately low levels of employment for women and minorities varies sharply from the range of interpretations to be found in the radical political economy literature. While two such interpretations can be found in this collection (the essays by Heidi Hartmann and Michael Reich), it should be emphasized that these two emerge from the much broader interpretive framework that radical political economy constitutes. The essay by Reich focuses on the role discrimination plays in class conflict. Other things being equal, employers (the capitalist class) benefit when they can lower wages and benefits for a given amount of work effort. Divisions within the working class facilitate this. If, as a result of discrimination, white workers feel that they are better off than African-American workers, for example, as Reich argues, they are less likely to contest managers over their wages and working conditions. The insertion of class conflict into the analysis at the very least makes it conceivable that discrimination will enhance the profitability of capitalist enterprises. Conventional economic analysis and conservative "political economy" exclude this possibility by failing to recognize the existence of classes and class conflict.

In like fashion, divisions among the sexes may enhance profitability. In this case, however, gender-based discrimination is the underlying cause. Hartmann does not deny the existence of class conflict, but sees patriarchy—the benefit that all men as a group derive from the inferior social status of women—as an independent factor, one that preceded the establishment of the capitalist system but that continues to play a role in a new and distinctive form shaped by the dominance of that system. To the extent that white male workers are victims of the capitalist system—suffering from low wages, harsh working conditions, and fear of unemployment—they are less likely to become conscious of their status or to challenge it as long as they perceive their status to be superior to that of other groups in the society. In this context, capitalists may benefit both individually, through lower wages and higher profits than would otherwise be possible, and as a class, through the displacement of the antagonisms that work experience engenders in such a way that the capitalist system itself remains free from challenge.

While it is important to distinguish radical political economy from conventional economics and conservative "political economy" on the right, it is also important to distinguish it from the cruder forms of Marxian political economy on the left. The crude interpretations of Marx that became official doctrine in China and the Soviet Union bear little relevance to radical political economy. These crude interpretations were essentialist and reductionist (for example, incorporating the view that economic forces determine all else in society), and supported a teleological view of history as moving toward a classless society. The modern Marxian literature stands in sharp contrast to the crude "official" Marxism, as exemplified by the essays by Howard Sherman and by Richard Wolff and Stephen Resnick in this volume.

This modern, critical Marxism is a component of radical political economy but should not be regarded as identical to it. Since the primary critical tradition in economics has deep roots in the critical Marxian literature, that tradition has quite naturally influenced radical political economy deeply. Yet at the same time, the scope of radical political economy is clearly broader. One need not believe in class struggle as *the* moving force in historical change, for example, to be located properly in the field of radical political economy. What then are the determining characteristics?

Perhaps it would be appropriate to start with a critical assessment of conventional economics, with its assumptions that individuals seek to maximize personal gain while minimizing effort. Starting with the individual and treating the individual ahistorically, conventional economics fails to address a broad spectrum of issues. Individual behavior has changed historically, is shaped by institutions, and reflects broader goals and beliefs than is allowed for in conventional analysis. Individuals may attempt, consciously or unconsciously, to adhere to a tradition and set of ethics shaped by that tradition, for example, rather than seek to maximize personal benefit. In the film *The Godfather,* for example, the Godfather refuses to allow his crime family to engage in drug dealing, viewing it as immoral. In general, conventional economic analysis takes individual preferences and desires as given, refusing even to examine the social forces that underlie their expression.

Radical political economy, by contrast, questions the origins of individual preferences and takes into account the social and institutional framework within which individual decision making takes place. Thus, for example, the role of advertising and merchandising may be taken into account. If desires for goods and services are created by such means, then the individuals who satisfy such desires through their purchases may be no better off than they were before such desires were created in the first place.

Another example of how economic analysis may be influenced by taking into account institutional factors is provided by the advice Russia received from Western economists to proceed immediately with privatization after the collapse of communism. This advice neglects the fact that a set of institutions has grown up in the West over a period of two centuries that enable privately owned enterprises to function relatively smoothly and to serve, within limits, social purposes. A legal framework of commercial law and property rights, banking systems subject to the regulation of a central bank, and other institutional features contribute to the functioning of the capitalist system in the West. In the absence of such support, the change-over in the Russian ownership system has been accompanied by extremes of unemployment or underemployment, inflation, and social distress. It has also been accompanied by the emergence of a "robber baron" class able to appropriate a large part of the privatized assets at almost no cost.

Several groups of economists focus intensively on the role of institutions and the social environment in shaping economic activity. Among these we may note especially the institutionalists and the socio-economists, whose professional associations are, respectively, the Association for Evolutionary Economics (AFEE) and the Society for the Advancement of Socio-Economics (SASA). For the most part, the alternative approaches to the discipline represented by these two groups fall within the radical political economy spectrum, even though they do not display the stress on class and class conflict that is characteristically found among the critical Marxists. By treating the economics discipline as part of the social sciences, and by viewing economic behavior in its social context, all of these groups go beyond the narrow confines of conventional approaches to the discipline.

Studies in Radical Political Economy

The essays in this book have been selected with a view to illustrating the scope, richness, and depth of the radical political economy literature, as well as on the basis of their merits as individual essays. The emphasis is on introducing the reader to ways of thinking about economic issues precluded by conventional analysis. In many cases, the essays have been chosen precisely because they are provocative, challenging the reader to think about economic issues in new ways, even if the conclusions in some of the essays remain controversial.

Part I of the book focuses on labor. The two essays by Stephen Marglin, the classic "What Do Bosses Do?" and the more recent "Losing Touch" are both concerned with the origins and perpetuation of alienating labor under the capitalist system. In the first essay, Marglin questions the circumstances under which workers lost control over their own productive activity. Is the hierarchical organization of work dictated by technological imperatives, he asks, or by society? By showing that the factory system was firmly established *before* power-driven machinery was widely applied in production, Marglin demonstrates that the origins and function of capitalist hierarchy have relatively little to do with efficiency. His analysis at least leaves open the possibility of alternative forms of work organization under which work would be experienced as a deeply fulfilling part of life.

In chapter three, "Losing Touch," the second of his two essays, Marglin seeks to find the reasons underlying workers' acquiescence in a socioeconomic system (capitalism) that deprives them of meaning and satisfaction in their everyday work activity. He recognizes that individual workers lack the power to change their circumstances, but observes that this fails to explain why organized labor, through collective bargaining or other means, has focused almost exclusively on economic demands while neglecting issues of worker control and the meaningfulness of work activity. Underlying this failure, Marglin argues, is a lack of cultural support for the workers' interests.

According to Marglin, the dominant type of knowledge in Western society, *episteme,* is based on logical deduction from self-evident first principles. A second type of knowledge, *techne,* is based on experience and practice; it is the type of knowledge associated, for example, with the master craftsman. In production, the worker's knowledge is a form of *techne.* Since *episteme,* generally acquired through formal schooling, is perceived in the West to be "at the very least a superior form of knowledge, if not the *only* form of knowledge" (p. 107, below), there is no cultural support that might enable workers to resist changes in the organization of work that deprive work of intrinsic meaning; workers themselves believe their own knowledge to be inferior.

In the second essay in part I, "Segmented Labor Markets," Richard Edwards points out that in the nineteenth century, American capitalism took a labor force of varied origins and shaped it into an increasingly homogeneous body. By contrast, differentiation has characterized the twentieth century, and distinctions among workers have been increasingly institutionalized; this process has been intensified by racial and sexual discrimination. As a result, instead of there being a single labor market in the United States, there are three distinct labor markets. Edwards refers to these as the "secondary," "subordinate primary," and "independent primary" labor markets.

The secondary market consists primarily of low-skilled jobs where there are few benefits and few union or other constraints on the manner in which employers can dispose of the labor power they have purchased. These jobs typically offer low pay, little or no job security, and few prospects for advancement.

The subordinate primary market provides higher pay, more job security, and more opportunities for advancement. The unionized, mass production industries like automobiles and steel provide examples. The jobs here are distinguished from the independent primary market in that the jobs tend to involve repetitive, machine-based work, and tend to require skills that are learned in a relatively short time. Workers are characteristically subject to direct supervision, but the authority of employers to dispose of the labor power they have purchased tends to be mediated by unions and constrained by job specifications.

The independent primary market tends, by contrast, to involve greater skills, self-paced work, professional credentials, and so forth. Whereas workers in the subordinate primary market typically advance within a given firm, those in the independent primary market can move between firms with relative ease.

Edwards argues that market forces cannot account for labor market segmentation. Rather, the forces that contribute to it include (1) racial and sexual discrimination, (2) different systems of control over the labor process within firms, and (3) firm size, financial strength, and stability. For those interested in understanding the relations of production, including especially the struggles between capital and labor over control of the production process, the concept of labor market segmentation provides a critical analytical tool.

Part II of this volume addresses the question of class, a category systematically excluded from conventional economic analysis. Criticizing the starting point of neoclassical economic analysis in individual behavior, Howard Sherman defines classes by the role they play in relation to other classes in the production process. Class relations and class conflict, he argues, provide the appropriate starting point for the analysis of any class-divided society. Thus, for example, in contemporary capitalism, an understanding of the relations and conflicts between capitalists and workers provides the basis for social analysis.

The second essay in this section, written by Richard Wolff and Stephen Resnick, attempts to define class analysis in a distinctive way. In "Power, Property, and Class," Wolff and Resnick seek to clarify the concept of class so that it can be used in a more precise and meaningful fashion in carrying out economic analysis.

They argue that in the Marxist tradition various conceptions of "class" exist, resulting in inconsistent and confused analysis. Some authors, for example, locate the essence of class in property ownership, others in a differential ability to exercise power. Wolff and Resnick criticize both. They are especially critical of "essentialist" or "reductionist" interpretations of class, interpretations that identify ownership or power as the "most basic" social relationship, one that causes or determines other aspects of social behavior. Rather, they argue that society is composed of a broad range of class and nonclass processes, the interaction among which creates social reality. Each process is "overdetermined" through its interaction with all of the others.

According to Wolff and Resnick, class can be most fruitfully understood in terms of the "specific processes of producing and distributing surplus labor." That is, in all societies, direct producers consume a part of what they produce. The labor necessary to produce this part, following Marx, is called "necessary labor," necessary in the sense that it is required to sustain the livelihood and reproduction of the direct producers. Usually, the direct producers also perform labor beyond this basic or "necessary" amount; this is called "surplus labor." The "fundamental class process," according to Wolff and Resnick, is the production and appropriation of this surplus labor.

This fundamental class process does not exist in isolation from the other class and nonclass processes occurring in society. Certain other processes clearly provide necessary conditions for the fundamental class process. Thus, for example, a firm may have to hire people in its personnel department to evaluate workers, making sure that they work up to standard, or rent a building to carry out its activities. Payments of wages to the personnel department employees or of rent to the building owner are needed to enable the fundamental class process to proceed. Such "subsumed" class payments come from a redistribution of portions of the surplus labor. The initial appropriator of the surplus labor, here the firm, redistributes a portion of it to ensure that the conditions needed for the continued appropriation of surplus labor are met.

Other social activities, such as religious or cultural ones, may be nonclass in nature. The entire society, according to Wolff and Resnick, is constituted by the interaction of fundamental class processes, subsumed class processes, and nonclass processes. Individuals typically participate in more than one of these. While the analysis of class in the radical political economy literature remains highly controversial, the argument presented by Wolff and Resnick appears to be the most rigorous and theoretically sophisticated, forming a standard with which alternative theories of class will have to contend.

Part III of this volume turns to questions of sexism and discrimination. In chapter 6, Heidi Hartmann maintains that although the Marxian framework remains valid for understanding class struggles, women's struggles cannot be subsumed under or explained completely in terms of class struggles. Rather, she argues, all men benefit from the subordination of women, and the system of patriarchy that is expressed in this fact must be as much an object of feminist struggle as the unequal class relations of capitalist society.

In chapter 7, Michael Reich, who with Edwards and David Gordon is among the originators of labor market segmentation analysis, addresses the issue of racial inequality in the United States. This selection is the conclusion to his book, *Racial Inequality: A Political-Economic Analysis.* He argues that conventional economic analysis cannot account adequately for the persistence of racial inequality.

The main limitation of conventional, neoclassical analysis, according to Reich, is its tendency to focus on individual behavior to the neglect of collective action, power, and conflict. As Reich indicates, "the workplace is now understood to be a contested terrain" where capitalists seek to extract the most work for the least pay. Since maximizing profits depends on limiting collective action by workers, any divisions that capitalists can create within the labor force will serve their interests. It is within this context, Reich argues, that the institutionalization of racial inequality must be understood.

In Part IV, chapter 8, Robert Pollin introduces the insights provided by Marxian and post-Keynesian analysis in monetary economics. He places special emphasis on four key contributions. First, he notes that the two schools argue that to a considerable extent, the supply of money and credit are determined endogenously—within the financial system—and are thus in large measure independent of the supply of savings and central bank activity. Second, financial factors play a key role in the pace and direction of real investment. Third, financial fragility—an increase in the debt obligations of firms relative to their ability to service these obligations—arises repeatedly from forces generated within the contemporary capitalist system and establishes conditions conducive to financial crises. And fourth, the financial markets constitute an important site of inter- and intraclass conflict.

In chapter 9, David Gordon, Thomas Weisskopf, and Samuel Bowles attempt to analyze the forces underlying the "long waves" that have characterized the performance of capitalist economies. Business cycles have averaged four to five years in the United States over the past century and a half, but much longer periods of relative prosperity and stagnation have also been manifest, often covering intervals of fifty or sixty years. During the upswings of these long cycles, recessions still occur but are apt to be relatively mild, while during the downswings they are apt to be much more severe and prolonged. An example of a long wave upswing is to be found in the roughly quarter of a century following World War II, while the 1970s and 1980s represent a period of relative stagnation, with (labor) productivity growth falling below 1 percent and real wages stagnant.

In addressing the causes of these long waves, the authors argue that an institutional structure favorable to capitalists—and thus to capital accumulation—must be formed to sustain long wave upswings. This favorable institutional structure, which they refer to as the "social structure of accumulation" (SSA), helped to sustain the prolonged period of postwar prosperity. The key elements in it, they argue, consisted of a capital-labor accord, which ceded capitalists control over the workplace in exchange for rising real wages and benefits; "Pax Americana," in which the United States dominated the industrial world and benefited from having its currency accepted as a reserve currency throughout the world; a "capital-citizen accord," which freed companies to pursue profits with a minimum of government regulation; and limited inter-capitalist competition, both domestically and internationally.

Starting in the late 1960s, however, this favorable institutional framework began to crumble. Capital-labor conflict increased; the rise of Japan and Europe, together with the emergence of OPEC (the Organization of Petroleum-Exporting Countries), challenged U.S. economic hegemony; environmental, consumer, and other movements increased regulation and raised business costs; and intensified international and domestic competition lowered profit margins and raised uncertainty. Under these conditions, investment and innovation were discouraged and a long wave period of sluggish growth was ushered in, a period marked by stagflation in the 1970s and below-par productivity growth over the 1970s and 1980s.

Following the recession of 1990, it could be argued, a new SSA has been emerging, marked by a pick-up in productivity growth, profit rates, and investment. While the essay by Gordon, Weisskopf, and Bowles was written in the early 1980s, it provides a theoretical framework that can readily be applied to subsequent developments. Moreover, even if one remains skeptical of the importance they have attributed to some of the institutions they have singled out as playing key roles in the postwar SSA, the analytical framework they provide makes it possible to consider alternatives. The significance of their work lies primarily in providing a systematic way of thinking about the existence of long waves in capitalist economic growth, and in highlighting the importance of the institutional environment in shaping those waves via their impact on enterprise profitability and the confidence of investors.

Part V of the book turns to the economic development of Third World countries. This is a sub-field of economics that has grown up largely since the Second World War, when the rise of newly independent states, the competition of the Cold War, the revival of macroeconomics, and the emergence of growth theory all contributed to renewed interest in the very issues that concerned the classical economists—especially how to account for the wealth of nations. Since many of the assumptions concerning the functioning of markets that underlie neoclassical economic theory do not hold for Third World countries, much of the economic development literature has perforce been heterodox. The three essays included here, therefore, are but examples of the vast array of writings in the field that diverge from the orthodox path.

Chapter 10, Laurence Harris's essay "Theories of Finance and the Third World," provides a critical review of the conventional literature on development finance and an assessment of the contribution made by radical political economy in this field. Writers whom Harris situates in the Marxian tradition—but many of whom might easily be located in the broader radical political economy tradition, including both Marxian and non-Marxian elements—have created a rich conceptual framework for addressing the financial issues concerning the less developed countries. Their works cover the role of the state, the concept of original accumulation, the relation between finance and class structure, the role of finance in nations attempting socialist transition, and the role of international finance. As Harris makes clear, this alternative literature is still limited and contains unresolved disputes, but in various respects it provides insights into the issues of development finance that are not to be found in the conventional literature.

In chapter 11, "The Concept of the Surplus in Economic Development," I attempt to clarify the concept of the surplus and to indicate how it can be used, in conjunction with the analysis of class structure, in carrying out development studies. The key argument is that almost all of the less developed economies generate a surplus sufficient to provide the basis for a satisfactory development program, but whether or not such development takes place depends above all on the manner in which the dominant classes—those which dispose of the surplus—choose to allocate it.

In chapter 12, Azizur Rahman Khan examines the conditions needed for egalitarian agricultural growth, cautioning against both underestimating the difficulties in the way of successful land reform and the overzealousness in carrying out collectivization that was displayed in the communist countries. Advocates of land reform have often argued that it can promote both growth and equality, since small farms have higher land productivity than large ones (a consequence of the more intensive use of unpaid family labor). Yet Khan observes that every institutional structure of landholding is associated with a supportive institutional infrastructure and incentive systems, and changing the institutional structure will normally involve substantial costs until a new supportive structure can be set in place. In short, a trade-off between growth and equality may well be the norm, at least in the short run.

Given the social costs of land reform, Khan argues, political will is the decisive factor in carrying it out. Ironically, however, this will has usually been present only in the communist countries (except for cases where land reform was carried out by occupying powers after World War II). The irony lies in the fact that land reform in the communist countries was not ordinarily regarded as an end in itself, but as a way station on the road to an ill-advised collectivization. Collectivization, Khan maintains, does not typically promote greater equality than land reform, and by failing to address successfully the critical question of an appropriate incentive system it ends up by sacrificing both efficiency and growth.

Part VI of the book examines issues related to market socialism. The term "socialism" has long been associated with the centrally planned economies, economies whose collapse (the Soviet Union) or reform (China) has rightfully brought the central planning model into disrepute. Yet socialism has also been associated with issues of social justice, including the search for an alternative to the poverty, inequality, and alienating work experience that have been a part of the capitalist system since its inception. Moreover, since socialism has been associated with the class interests of ordinary working people, and since the dominant class in the centrally planned economies has been the bureaucracy, a group with privileged access to the power and resources of the state, the common association of central planning with socialism appears both unfortunate and inaccurate. A more appropriate term for the centrally planned economies, therefore, may be "statism," and their collapse then is a collapse of statism rather than socialism.

If this is so, the possibility of a socialism that is market-based remains open, and this possibility has been the subject of increasing exploration in the radical political economy literature. Alec Nove, a longstanding critic of Soviet economic organization and the vast inefficiencies it generates, has perhaps gone furthest in exploring the implications of a market-based socialism. In chapter 13, "Market Socialism and Its Critics," Nove responds to the arguments of Charles Bettelheim, a defender of central planning. Subsequently, Nove elaborated his position more fully in *The Economics of Feasible Socialism Revisited* (London, 1991).

In chapter 14, "Toward a Socialism for the Future, in the Wake of the Demise of the Socialism of the Past," Thomas Weisskopf considers what kinds of political-economic systems "can best make good on the socialist commitment to equity, democracy and solidarity" following the collapse of the pseudo-socialism in the Soviet Union and Eastern Europe. He counterposes market socialism to a decentralized, participatory-planning type of socialism (as opposed to the hierarchical social structures that inevitably accompany central planning), evaluating the strengths and weaknesses of the two alternatives.

In chapter 15, "Socialist Economic Development in the Post-Soviet Era," I argue that the collapse of the Soviet-type system is a collapse of statism rather than socialism. Agreeing with Nove that market socialism is indeed the only feasible form of socialism, I attempt to examine the implications of this position for economic development in the Third World. The disappearance of central planning as a viable alternative to capitalist development does not in any way negate the fact that capitalist development has historically been associated with widespread human suffering. The search for an alternative, therefore, retains its legitimacy. This essay incorporates an investigation of the type of economic policies that might properly be implemented in a market socialist framework for economic development.

The final section of the book introduces alternative perspectives on the environment. Perhaps the most fundamental aspect of radical political economy as it bears on economic analysis is the opportunity it affords to conceptualize economic issues in new ways. This process allows for insights and understanding that conventional approaches often preclude. A case in point is the commonplace stress on production and consumption as measures of how well an economy is doing. The effort to maximize growth in national income, and the use of such growth as an index of national welfare have been almost unquestioned in economic analysis, with the exception of distributional qualifications. In his striking essay "The Economics of the Coming Spaceship Earth," however, which appears here as chapter 16, Kenneth Boulding presents an alternative perspective for evaluating economic activity.

According to Boulding's argument, human beings are in the midst of a lengthy transition in the image we have of ourselves and our environment, a transition that corresponds to real changes in the state of the world. From the time of primitive human beings, the world was conceived as a virtually limitless plain, and Boulding maintains that the concept of the "open economy," without ultimate restraints on the supply of resources or the capacity to absorb wastes, corresponds to this conception of the world.

Gradually, however, we are becoming aware of the limitations that exist in the availability of resources and in the world's capacity to absorb wastes. From the massive destruction of forest resources to global warming, changes in the natural environment have promoted this transformation in human consciousness. Economic thought, however, has not even begun to adjust to the "closed economy" that is rapidly approaching. Boulding attempts in this essay to sketch in some of the conceptual changes in economic analysis that will be appropriate to "the coming spaceship earth."

In particular, Boulding notes that in the open economy—which he also calls the "cowboy economy"—the maximization of throughputs in the form of production and consumption is routinely regarded as a primary objective of economic policy. In the closed or "spaceman" economy, however, the objective will be to maximize satisfaction while *minimizing* throughputs, a reflection of the objective constraints on inputs and waste-absorbing capacity. Thus, for example, instead of seeking to maximize new house construction or clothing production, the development of a stock of housing or clothing with minimal wearing out (depreciation) would be the target of public policy, with satisfaction tied primarily to the enjoyment of an existing capital stock rather than to an increase in throughputs.

Boulding does not claim that the spaceship earth is already here, merely that we are well on our way from an open economy to a closed one, and that our economic thinking must be adjusted accordingly. He himself does not expand his analysis to take account of the impact of different economic systems. Here we might note, however, that the inherently expansive character of the capitalist system appears to be inconsistent with the requirements of a closed economy, and that its growing throughputs in the twenty-first century will constitute a major contradiction within the system, one that ultimately threatens human survival.

In chapter 17, "Marxian Crisis Theory and the Contradictions of Late Twentieth-Century Capitalism," Thomas Weisskopf examines the systemic implications of the environmental crisis. Although he shares many of Boulding's concerns about the environment, Weisskopf's starting point is quite different. He begins by asking what are the critical contradictions in late twentieth-century capitalism, where contradictions can be understood as outcomes of the normal functioning of the capitalist system that tend to undermine and ultimately preclude just such normal functioning, throwing the system into crisis and ultimately threatening its viability.

Weisskopf starts by considering and rejecting the relevance to contemporary capitalism of classical Marxian analyses of capitalist crisis. Rather, Weisskopf argues, it is the severity of the environmental and social deterioration which the capitalist system has engendered that threatens its viability. The key mechanism in this matter is the constraints imposed on profitability by the deteriorating social and natural environment, and thus on the accumulation/investment process that is at the core of a successful capitalism.

The fact that the environmental record of the centrally planned, "statist" economies was even worse does not negate this conclusion. The leaders of such economies were even more committed to economic growth (the maximization of throughputs) than those of the capitalist nations have been. Equally important, with the performance evaluation of managers within the statist system overwhelmingly based on their ability to meet plan output targets, they were systematically encouraged to neglect environmental externalities.

The collapse of the statist system and the worldwide ascendancy of capitalism, however, does not mean the problem is solved. Rather, it makes all the more important an analysis of the internal contradictions of the capitalist system. Under that system, the imperatives of profit maximization encourage an unlimited growth of throughputs, a growth that ultimately cannot be accommodated by a limited environment. Capitalism may continue to be ascendant for another century or two, during which time the environment will be subject to ongoing deterioration, but ultimately an alternative will have to be found if humanity is to survive.

The essays in this book are meant to situate economic issues in their broader social context. This, together with its social justice orientation, is precisely where radical political economy transcends the confines of conventional economic analysis. These essays present arguments that are not so much in opposition to neoclassical economic analysis as they are situated in an alternative framework or paradigm. That makes it possible to explore issues that cannot be accommodated within a conventional framework. Although many of the essays remain controversial even within the radical political economy perspective, they demonstrate the power of that perspective to introduce new ways of thinking about and, hopefully, addressing the pressing socioeconomic issues of the day.

I

Labor

1

What Do Bosses Do?
The Origins and Functions of Hierarchy in Capitalist Production

Stephen A. Marglin

I. Introduction: Does Technology Shape Social and Economic Organization or Does Social and Economic Organization Shape Technology?

Is it possible for work to contribute positively to individual development in a complex industrial society, or is alienating work the price that must be paid for material prosperity? Discussions of the possibilities for meaningful revolution generally come down, sooner or later, to this question. If hierarchical authority is essential to high productivity, then self-expression in work must at best be a luxury reserved for the very few, regardless of social and economic organization. And even the satisfactions of society's elite must be perverted by their dependence, with rare exception, on the denial of self-expression to others. But is work organization determined by technology or by society? Is hierarchical authority really necessary to high levels of production or is material prosperity compatible with nonhierarchical organization of production?

Defenders of the capitalist faith are quite sure that hierarchy is inescapable. Indeed their ultimate line of defense is that the plurality of capitalist hierarchies is preferable to a single socialist hierarchy. To seal the argument the apologist may call on as unlikely a source of support as Friedrich Engels. Perhaps it was a momentary aberration, but at one point in his career at least Engels saw authority as technologically rather than socially determined:

Originally published in *Review of Radical Political Economics,* vol. 6, no. 2, Summer 1974, pp. 60–112. Reprinted with permission.

> If man, by dint of his knowledge and inventive genius, has subdued the forces of nature, the latter avenge themselves upon him by subjecting him, in so far as he employs them, to a veritable despotism, *independent of all social organization.* Wanting to abolish authority in large-scale industry is tantamount to wanting to abolish industry itself, to destroy the power loom in order to return to the spinning wheel.[1]

Going back to the spinning wheel is obviously absurd, and if the producer must typically take orders, it is difficult to see how work could in the main be anything but alienating.

Were the social sciences experimental, the methodology for deciding whether or not hierarchical work organization is inseparable from high material productivity would be obvious. One would design technologies appropriate to an egalitarian work organization, and test the designs in actual operation. Experience would tell whether or not egalitarian work organization is utopian. But social science is not experimental. None of us has the requisite knowledge of steelmaking or cloth-making to design a new technology, much less to design one so radically different from the present norm as a serious attempt to change work organization would dictate. Besides in a society whose basic institutions—from schools to factories—are geared to hierarchy, the attempt to change one small component is probably doomed to failure. For all its shortcomings, neoclassical economics is undoubtedly right in emphasising *general* equilibrium over *partial* equilibrium.

Instead of seeking alternative designs, we must take a more round-about tack. In this paper it is asked why, in the course of capitalist development, the actual producer lost control of production. What circumstances gave rise to the boss-worker pyramid that characterizes capitalist production? And what social function does the capitalist hierarchy serve? If it turns out that the origin and function of capitalist hierarchy has relatively little to do with efficiency, then it becomes at least an open question whether or not hierarchical production is essential to a high material standard of living. And workers—manual, technical, and intellectual—may take the possibility of egalitarian work organization sufficiently seriously to examine their environment with a view to changing the economic, social, and political institutions that relegate all but a fortunate few to an existence in which work is the means to life, not part of life itself.

It is the contention of this paper that neither of the two decisive steps in depriving the workers of control of product and process—(1) the development of the minute division of labor that characterized the putting-out system and (2) the development of the centralized organization that characterizes the factory system—took place primarily for reasons of technical superiority. Rather than providing more output for the same inputs, these innovations in work organization were introduced so that the capitalist got himself a larger share of the pie at the expense of the worker, and it is only the *subsequent* growth in the size of the pie that has obscured the class interest which was at the root of these innovations. The social function of hierarchical work organization is not technical efficiency, but accumulation. By mediating between producer and consumer, the capitalist organization sets aside much more for expanding and improving plant and equipment than individuals would if they could control the pace of capital accumulation. These ideas, which are developed in the body of this paper, can be conveniently divided into four specific propositions.

I. The capitalist division of labor, typified by Adam Smith's famous example of pin manufacture, was the result of a search not for a technologically superior organization of work, but for an organization which guaranteed to the entrepreneur an essential role in the production process, as integrator of the separate efforts of his workers into a marketable product.

II. Likewise, the origin and success of the factory lay not in technological superiority, but in the substitution of the capitalist's for the worker's control of the work process and the quantity of output, in the change in the workman's choice from one of how much to work and produce, based on his relative preferences for leisure and goods, to one of whether or not to work at all, which of course is hardly much of a choice.

III. The social function of hierarchical control of production is to provide for the accumulation of capital. The individual, by and large and on the average, does not save by a conscious and deliberate choice. The pressures to spend are simply too great. Such individual (household) savings as do occur are the consequence of a lag in adjusting spending to a rise in income, for spending, like any other activity, must be learned, and learning takes time. Thus individual savings are the consequence of growth, and not an independent cause. Acquisitive societies—precapitalist, capitalist or socialist—develop institutions whereby collectivities determine the rate of accumulation. In modern capitalist society the pre-eminent collectivity for accumulation is the corporation. It is an essential social function of the corporation that its hierarchy mediate between the individual producer (and shareholder) and the market proceeds of the corporation's product, assigning a portion of these proceeds to enlarging the means of production. In the absence of hierarchical control of production, society would either have to fashion egalitarian institutions for accumulating capital or content itself with the level of capital already accumulated.

IV. The emphasis on accumulation accounts in large part for the failure of Soviet-style socialism to "overtake and surpass" the capitalist world in developing egalitarian forms of work organization. In according first priority to the accumulation of capital, the Soviet Union repeated the history of capitalism, at least as regards the relationship of men and women to their work. Theirs has not been the failure described by Santayana of those who, not knowing history, unwittingly repeat it. The Soviets consciously and deliberately embraced the capitalist mode of production. And defenders of the Soviet path to economic development would offer no apology: after all, they would probably argue, egalitarian institutions and an egalitarian (and community oriented) man could not have been created overnight, and the Soviet Union rightly felt itself too poor to contemplate an indefinite end to accumulation. Now, alas, the Soviets have the "catch-up-with-and-surpass-the-U.S.A." tiger by the tail, for it would probably take as much of a revolution to transform work organization in that society as in ours.

The following sections of this paper take these propositions one by one, in the hope of filling in sufficient detail to give them credibility.

II. Divide and Conquer

Hierarchy was of course not invented by capitalists. More to the point, neither was hierarchical production. In precapitalist societies, industrial production was organized according to a rigid master-journeyman-apprentice hierarchy, which survives today in anything like its pure form only in the graduate departments of our universities. What distinguished precapitalist from capitalist hierarchy was first that the man at the top was, like the man at the bottom, a producer. The master worked along with his apprentice rather than simply telling him what to do. Second, the hierarchy was linear rather than pyramidal. The apprentice would one day become a journeyman and likely a master. Under capitalism it is a rare worker who becomes even a foreman, not to mention independent entrepreneur or corporate president. Third, and perhaps most important, the guild workman had no intermediary between himself and the market. He generally sold a product, not his labor, and therefore controlled both product and work process.

Just as hierarchy did not originate with capitalism, neither did the division of labor. The *social* division of labor, the specialization of occupation and function, is a characteristic of all complex societies, rather than a peculiar feature of industrialized or economically advanced ones. Nothing, after all, could be more elaborate than the caste division of labor and its accompanying hierarchy in traditional Hindu society. Nor is the *technical* division of labor peculiar to capitalism or modern industry. Cloth production, for example, even under the guild system was divided into separate tasks, each controlled by specialists. But, as we have said, the guild workman controlled product and process. What we have to account for is why the guild division of labor evolved into the capitalist division of labor, in which the workman's task typically became so specialized and minute that he had no product to sell, or at least none for which there was a wide market, and had therefore to make use of the capitalist as intermediary to integrate his labor with the labor of others and transform the whole into a marketable product.

Adam Smith argues that the capitalist division of labor came about because of its technological superiority; in his view, the superiority of dividing work into ever more minutely specialized tasks was limited only by the size of the market.[2] To understand the limitations of this explanation requires clarity and precision on the meaning of "technological superiority," and the related ideas of technological efficiency and inefficiency; indeed, these ideas are central to the whole story told in this paper. We shall say, in accordance with accepted usage, that a method of production is technologically superior to another if it produces more output with the same inputs. It is not enough that a new method of production yield more output per day to be technologically superior. Even if labor is the only input, a new method of production might require more hours of labor, or more intensive effort, or more unpleasant working conditions, in which case it would be providing more output for more input, not for the same amount. It will be argued here that—contrary to neoclassical logic—a new method of production does not have to be technologically superior to be adopted; innovation depends as much on economic and social institutions—on who is in control of production and under what constraints control is exercised.

The terms "technological efficiency" and "technological inefficiency," as used by economists, have meanings that are slightly at variance with the ordinary, every-day ideas of better and worse that they evoke. A method of production is technologically efficient if no technologically superior alternative exists. It is inefficient if a superior alternative does exist. Thus more than one method of production may be—and generally is—technologically efficient if one looks only at a single product. Wheat, for example, can be efficiently produced with a lot of land and relatively little fertilizer, as in Kansas, or with a lot of fertilizer and relatively little land, as in Holland.

But if one views technological superiority and efficiency from the point of view of the whole economy, these concepts reduce, under certain circumstances, to *economic* superiority and efficiency. Under text-book assumptions of perfect and universal competition, the technologically efficient method of production is the one that costs least, and cost reduction is an index of technological superiority.[3] The relationship between minimum cost and technological efficiency is a purely logical one and does not depend at all on whether or not the world exhibits the assumptions of the model. On the other hand, the relevance of the identification of technological with economic efficiency depends absolutely on the applicability of the assumptions of the competitive model to the development of capitalism. In critical respects the development of capitalism necessarily required denial, not fulfillment, of the assumptions of perfect competition.

In a way it is surprising that the development of capitalist methods of work organization contradicts essential assumptions of perfect competition, since perfect competition has virtually nothing to say about the organization of production! Indeed, even the firm itself, a central economic institution under capitalism, plays no essential role in models of the competitive economy;[4] it is merely a convenient abstraction for the household in its role as producer and does nothing that households could not equally well do for themselves. Defenders of the faith from Wicksell to Samuelson have grandly proclaimed the perfect neutrality of perfect competition—as far as the model goes, workers could as well hire capital as capitalists workers![5] Alas, the failure of the competitive model to account for one of the most distinctive features of capitalism (and of socialism imitating capitalism)—the pyramidal work order—is for neoclassical economists a great virtue rather than a shortcoming; it is supposed to show the great generality of the theory. Generality indeed: neoclassical theory says only that hierarchy must be technologically efficient to persist, but denies the superiority of capitalist hierarchy (workers can just as well hire capital, remember!). This is to say very little, and that little, it will be argued, quite wrong.

To return to Adam Smith. *The Wealth of Nations* advances three arguments for the technological superiority of dividing labor as finely as the market will allow.

> (This) great increase of the quantity of work, which, in consequence of the division of labor, the same number of people are capable of performing, is owing to three different circumstances; first, to the increase of dexterity in every particular workman; secondly, to the saving of the time which is commonly lost in passing from one species of work to another; and lastly, to the invention of a great number of machines which facilitate labor and abridge labor, and enable one man to do the work of many.[6]

Of the three arguments, one—the saving of time—is undoubtedly important. But this argument has little or nothing to do with the minute specialization that characterizes the capitalist division of labor. A peasant, for example, will generally plow a whole field before harrowing it rather than alternating plow and harrow, furrow by furrow—in order to economize on the set-up time. But peasant agriculture is the antithesis of capitalist specialization; the individual peasant normally undertakes all the activities necessary to bring a crop from seed to marketable product. In respect of set-up time, there is nothing to differentiate agriculture from industry. To save "the time that is commonly lost in passing from one species of work to another" it is necessary only to continue in a single activity long enough that the set-up time becomes an insignificant proportion of total work time. The saving of time would require at most only that each worker continue in a single activity for days at a time, not for a whole lifetime. Saving of time implies *separation* of tasks and *duration* of activity, not *specialization*.

Smith's third argument—the propensity to invention—is not terribly persuasive. Indeed, the most devastating criticism was voiced by Smith himself in a later chapter of *The Wealth of Nations:*

> In the progress of the division of labor, the employment of the far greater part of those who live by labor, that is, of the great body of the people, comes to be confined to a few very simple operations, frequently to one or two. But the understandings of the greater part of men are formed by their ordinary employments. The man whose life is spent in performing a few simple operations, of which the effects too are, perhaps, always the same, or very nearly the same, has no occasion to exert his understanding, or to exercise his invention in finding out expedients for difficulties which never occur. He naturally loses, therefore, the habit of such exertion and generally becomes as stupid and ignorant as it is possible for a human creature to become . . .

It is otherwise in the barbarous societies, as they are commonly called, of hunters, of shepherds, and even of husbandmen in that crude state of husbandry which precedes the improvement of manufactures. In such societies the varied occupations of every man oblige every man to exert his capacity, and to invent expedients for removing difficulties which are continually occurring. Invention is kept alive, and the mind is not suffered to fall into that drowsy stupidity, which, in a civilized society, seems to benumb the understanding of almost all the inferior ranks of people.[7]

The choice does not, however, seem really to lie between stupidity and barbarity, but between the workman whose span of control is wide enough that he sees how each operation fits into the whole and the workman confined to a small number of repetitive tasks. It would be surprising indeed if the workman's propensity to invent has not been diminished by the extreme specialization that characterizes the capitalist division of labor.

This leaves "the increase of dexterity in every particular workman" as the basis of carrying specialization to the limits permitted by the size of the market. Now if Adam Smith were talking about musicians or dancers or surgeons, or even if he were speaking of the division of labor between pin-making and cloth-making, his argument would be difficult to counter. But he is speaking not of esoteric specializations, nor of the social division of labor, but of the minute division of ordinary, run-of-the-mill, industrial activities into separate skills. Take his favorite example of pin manufacture:

> . . . in the way in which this business is now carried on, not only the whole work is a peculiar trade, but it is divided into a number of branches, of which the greater part are likewise peculiar trades. One man draws out the wire, another straights it, a third cuts it, a fourth points it, a fifth grinds it at the top for receiving the head; to make the head requires two or three distinct operations; to put it on, is a peculiar business, to whiten the pins is another; it is even a trade by itself to put them into the paper; and the important business of making a pin is, in this manner, divided into about eighteen distinct operations, which in some manufactories, are all performed by distinct hands, though in others the same man will sometimes perform two or three of them. I have seen a small manufactory of this kind where ten men only were employed, and where some of them consequently performed two or three distinct operations. But though they were very poor, and therefore but indifferently accommodated with the necessary equipment, they could, when they exerted themselves, make among them about twelve pounds of pins in a day. There are in a pound upwards of four thousand pins of a middling size. Those ten persons, therefore could make among them upwards of forty-eight thousand pins in a day. Each person, therefore, making a tenth part of forty-eight thousand pins, might be considered as making four thousand eight hundred pins in a day. But if they had all wrought separately and independently, and without any of them having been educated to this peculiar business, they certainly could not each of them have made twenty, perhaps not one pin in a day . . . [8]

To the extent that the skills at issue are difficult to acquire, specialization is essential to the division of production into separate operations. But, judging from the earnings of the various specialists engaged in pin-making, these were no special skills. At least there were none that commanded premium wages. In a pin manufactory for which fairly detailed records survive from the early part of the nineteenth century, T.S. Ashton reported wages for adult males of approximately 20 shillings per week, irrespective of the particular branch in which they were engaged.[9] Women and children, as was customary, earned less, but again there appear to be no great discrepancies among the various branches of pin production. It would appear to be the case that the mysteries of pin-making were relatively quickly learned, and that the potential increase in dexterity afforded by minute division of tasks was quickly exhausted. Certainly it is hard to make a case for specialization of workmen to particular tasks on the basis of the pin industry.[10]

The dichotomy between specialization and the separate crafting of each individual pin seems to be a false one. It appears to have been technologically possible to obtain the economics of reducing set-up time *without* specialization. A workman, with his wife and children, could have proceeded from task to task, first drawing out enough wire for hundreds or thousands of pins, then straightening it, then cutting it, and so on with each successive operation, thus realizing the advantages of dividing the overall production process into separate tasks.

Why, then, did the division of labor under the putting-out system entail specialization as well as separation of tasks? In my view the reason lies in the fact that without specialization, the capitalist had no essential role to play in the production process. If each producer could himself integrate the component tasks of pin manufacture into a marketable product, he would soon discover that he had no need to deal with the market for pins through the intermediation of the putter-outer. He could sell directly and appropriate to himself the profit that the capitalist derived from mediating between the producer and the market. Separating the tasks assigned to each workman was the sole means by which the capitalist could, in the days preceding costly machinery, ensure that he would remain essential to the production process as integrator of these separate operations into a product for which a wide market existed; and specialization of men to tasks at the sub-product level was the hallmark of the putting-out system.

The capitalist division of labor, as developed under the putting-out system, embodied the same principle that "successful" imperial powers have utilized to rule their colonies: divide and conquer. Exploiting differences between Hindu and Muslim in India—if not actually creating them—the British could claim to be essential to the stability of the sub-continent. And they could, sometimes with ill-concealed satisfaction, point to the millions of deaths that followed Partition as proof of their necessity to stability. But this tragedy proved only that the British had *made* themselves essential as mediators, not that there was any inherent need for British mediation of communal differences.

Similarly, the development of an industrial system dependent on capitalist integration does not prove that the capitalist division of labor was technologically superior to integration by the producer himself. The putter-outer's peculiar contribution to production was handsomely rewarded not because of any genuine scarcity of the ability to integrate separate functions; rather the scarcity was artificially created to preserve the capitalist's role.

How could the capitalist withstand competition if his role was an artificial one? What prevented each producer from integrating his own work, and thereby coming directly into contact with a wide market? The capitalist putter-outer, who, by hypothesis, was technologically superfluous, would have been eliminated by such competition; for integrated producers would have produced pins and cloth and pottery more cheaply. Why didn't some enterprising and talented fellow organize producers to eliminate the capitalist putter-outer? The answer is that there was no profit in such a line of endeavor. If the organizer became a producer himself, he would have had to settle for a producer's wage. His co-workers might have subscribed a dinner or gold watch in his honor, but it is doubtful that their gratitude would have led them to do much more. To glean rewards from organizing, one had to become a capitalist putter-outer! The point is that no collusion was necessary between the men of talent, enterprise, and means that formed the capitalist class of putting-out days. It was in the interest of each as well as in the interest of all to maintain the system of allocating separate tasks to separate workmen. Not much wit was required to see that their prosperity, as well as their survival as mediators, depended on this system.[11]

The advantages to the mediator of standing between the producer and a wide market were apparently obvious for some time before capitalist manufacture succeeded guild manufacture. George Unwin's studies of sixteenth and seventeenth century industry suggested to him that "the various crafts were, in fact, engaged in a constant struggle as to which of them should secure the economic advantage of standing between the rest and the market."[12] And Unwin notes— but unfortunately does not elaborate the point—that "by this interlacing of the interests of dealer and craftsman the way was gradually prepared for a new form of organization, embracing both classes, which naturally sought to extend its authority as widely over the manufacture as possible."[13]

Hard evidence that "divide and conquer" rather than efficiency was at the root of the capitalist division of labor is, naturally enough, not easy to come by. One cannot really expect the capitalist, or anybody else with an interest in preserving hierarchy and authority, to proclaim publicly that production was organized to exploit the worker. And the worker who was sufficiently acute to appreciate this could, in the relatively mobile societies in which the industrial revolution first took root, join the ranks of the exploiters.

Nevertheless, an occasional glimmer of recognition does exist. One, although from a slightly later epoch, supports the divide-and-conquer view of specialization better than any forgery could. Henry Ashworth, Jr., managing partner of one of the Ashworth cotton enterprises, noted approvingly in his diary that a competitor did not allow any of his employees, not even his manager, to mix cotton, adding

> ... his manager Henry Hargreaves knows nothing about the mixing or costs of cotton so that he can never take his business away from him—all his Overlookers' business are quite separate from each other and then no one knows what is going on but himself.[14]

This story has a recent parallel. I know a man who was for a time a sandal maker. To learn the trade, he went to work for a "master" sandal maker. This worthy systematically taught him all there was to know about making sandals—except how to buy the leather. My friend could have learned this vital aspect of the trade on his own by the familiar and time-honored method of trial and error—if he had had $1000 or so to set aside for the mistakes inherent in the learning process. Lacking the capital, his boss's unwillingness to share one particular skill effectively obliged him to remain a worker as long as he remained in the trade.

One other nineteenth century comment suggests that those closer to the beginnings of industrial capitalism than ourselves were not blind to the role of division of labor in supporting a hierarchical society. *The Spectator* approved of cooperation between master and men, so long as it did not threaten capitalism. Indeed, as long as cooperation was limited to profit sharing and the like, it might strengthen capitalism for profit sharing in no way meant an end to hierarchy. By contrast, workers' cooperatives were perceived as a distinct threat, one *The Spectator* thought it necessary to exorcise before extolling the virtues of profit sharing:

> Hitherto that principle (of cooperation) has been applied in England only by associations of workmen, but the Rochdale experiments, important and successful as they were, were on one or two points incomplete. They showed that associations of workmen could manage shops, mills, and all forms of industry with success, and they immensely improved the condition of the men, but then *they did not leave a clear place for the masters.* That was a defect, for three reasons. (Emphasis added)[15]

It is of some interest to examine these reasons:

> Firstly, money in England is held in great masses in individual hands; secondly, there exists among us a vast mass of administrative or, as we call it, business ability, which is of the highest value in directing associated labor wisely, which can and does add infinitely to the value of that labor, and which is not willing to devote itself to labor in absolute or equal partnerships. It does not pay, says Mr. Brassey, to be anything but head. And lastly, cooperation among workmen is not so consonant to the national genius as cooperation between masters and men—limited monarchy having got into our bones—and

a system which harmonizes with the national genius is accepted quickly, while one which does not, even if it is superior in itself advances slowly indeed.[16]

The first—that "money . . . is held in great masses . . . in individual hands"—is a reason for hierarchical organization only if one considers the wealth distribution inviolable. Indeed, the argument is usually put the other way around: that the superiority of hierarchical production requires great wealth inequalities! The second reason—that "administrative . . . ability . . . can and does add infinitely to the value of . . . labor" but "is not willing to devote itself to labor in absolute or equal partnership"—is contradicted by the very successes claimed for the Rochdale experiments. The third—"the natural genius" for "limited monarchy"—is the last refuge of scoundrels; if one took it seriously, one could never challenge the *status-quo*.

Although the direct evidence for the divide-and-conquer view of the capitalist division of labor is not overwhelming, it is at least as impressive as the direct evidence for the efficiency view. And there is some indirect evidence too. If the specialization of workmen to tasks took place to ensure capitalist control, then where capitalist control was for other reasons beyond challenge, there is no basis, according to the divide-and-conquer hypothesis, to expect a minute specialization. And so it turns out, at least in the one case of which I have knowledge. The British coal industry offers an example of an industry in which the capitalist division of labor never took hold. Under hand-got methods, as primitive in technique as the putting-out system of manufacture, but surviving into the twentieth century, "responsibility for the complete coal-getting task rests squarely on the shoulders of a single small, face-to-face group which experiences the entire cycle of operations within the compass of its membership."[17] This group contracted directly with the colliery management and "though the contract may have been in the name of the hewer, it was regarded as a joint undertaking. Leadership and 'supervision' were internal to the group, which had a quality of *responsible autonomy*."[18] Furthermore, "each collier (was) an all-around workman, usually able to substitute for his mate. . . . He had craft pride and artisan independence. These qualities obviated status difficulties and contributed to responsible autonomy."[19] Presumably the mine owner felt no need to specialize men to tasks; the scarcity of coal seams and the institution of private property ensured that workers would not dispense with bosses.

But this is only the beginning of the story. Its most interesting chapter perhaps is the subsequent development of work organization under mechanized—longwall—conditions. As Trist and Bamforth tell the story, "need arose (with mechanization) for a unit more of the size and differentiated complexity of a small factory department."[20] On what model? "At the time the longwall method developed, there were no precedents for the adaptive underground application of machine technology. In the absence of relevant experience in the mining tradition itself, it was almost inevitable that heavy culture-borrowing (of specialization of men to tasks) should have taken place."[21]

The basic idea of the longwall system was the division of labor by shifts, each shift being responsible for a subset of the operations that move the coal from pit to ground.

> The work is broken down into a standard series of component operations that follow each other in rigid succession over three shifts of seven and a half hours each, so that a total coal-getting cycle may be completed once in each twenty-four hours of the working week. The shift spread of the 40 workmen needed on an average face is: 10 each to the first ("cutting") and second ("ripping") shifts; 20 to the third ("filling") shift.[22]

Mechanized methods did not, however, yield the fruits they seemed to promise. The problem lay in the supervision of groups of specialists each responsible for only one of the operations that constitute the whole.[23] And the solution lay in reconstituting work groups so that each shift was "responsible for task continuity rather than a specific set of tasks . . . with responsibility for coordination and control being primarily in the hands of the cycle group."[24] The distinctive features of the new system, called the "composite longwall system" were fourfold:

The Work Method

In accordance with the tradition of composite working which originated in the (hand got) system, the oncoming men on a shift were to take up the work of the cycle from the point at which it had been left by the previous shift group and continue with whatever tasks had next to be done. When the main task of a shift was completed the men were to redeploy to carry on with the next tasks whether they formed a part of the current cycle or commenced a new one.

The Workmen

In order for this task continuity to be practiced, it was necessary for the cycle group to include men who were at least competent under supervision, if not always formally qualified, to undertake the necessary tasks as they arose. It was not essential that all members of the composite team be completely multi-skilled, but only that as a team they should have sufficient skill resources available on each shift to man the roles likely to arise.

The Work Groups

The team manning the composite longwall was to be a self-selected group. The cycle group was to accept responsibility for allocating its members to the various jobs that management specified to be filled. In order to regulate the deployment, the team was to develop and operate some system for the rotation of tasks and shifts among team members.

Methods of Payment

As in (hand got) systems, there was to be a common paynote in which all members of the team were to share equally, since all members were regarded as making an equivalent contribution to the completion of the cycle.[25]

The British coal industry is one of the few places where direct comparisons of alternative methods of organizing work have been attempted. The tests are not absolutely conclusive, because the alternatives cannot be applied repeatedly to one and the same coal face. Nonetheless, the results are striking: the composite longwall method was found to produce 20 percent more coal than the conventional longwall method.[26]

Equally interesting for present purposes is the effect of reorganization on management:

> The effects of self-regulation by the cycle group on the management of the seam of which the composite longwall was a part ... was that the seam management structure was eventually simplified. *One overman was withdrawn;* it was found that there was no job for him. (Emphasis added.)

It is not hard to imagine the difficulties reorganization would have encountered had it been in the hands of the redundant overman to decide its fate.

Essential to the willingness of the overman's superiors to allow the reintroduction into the mines of self-integrating, nonspecialized, nonhierarchical work groups was the coupling of the physical scarcity of coal seams with the institution of property.[27] Had the miners been able to set up shop for themselves, management well might have found it necessary to rely, as did the capitalist putter-outer, on specialization of men to tasks as a means of keeping the worker in his "rightful" place—and thereby the boss in his.

The coal mine is to some extent typical of the stage in the development of industrial capitalism that *followed* the putting-out system, but it is, I think, wrong to ascribe primary importance to the growth in fixed capital, to the high cost of the means of production, in explaining the proletarianization of the work force. Property in machinery, like property in coal seams, was perhaps in mid-nineteenth century England as effective as specialization in insuring a role for the capitalist. Machinery was too costly for the individual workman, and the group was, for all intents and purposes, nonexistent. But before that time, machinery was not prohibitively expensive, and since then the union has become a force that might have offset the high cost of machinery—for the group if not for the individual. For some time preservation of the boss-worker hierarchy has required tacit acceptance by unions; present-day unions lack the will for change, not the strength. This is not to say that it is mere accident that unions have for the most part chosen to ignore hierarchy and its effects, and have concentrated instead on "bread-and-butter" issues. These have been the easiest to accommodate within the framework of a growing economy and agreement to limit conflict to these issues has been instrumental in muting the conflict between capitalists and workers. But the price of accommodation has been steep; unions have become another cog in the hierarchy, not the workers' defense against it.[28] It is not, however, simply a matter of reorienting priorities within the traditional framework of union leadership. Once unions were to become interested in the relationship of men to their work, they would find themselves in conflict with the very principles of capitalist organization, not merely in conflict over the division, at the margin, of the capitalist pie. No longer could labor's spokesmen be pillars of the established order.

When the absolute scarcity of natural resources limits production to a few sites, the institution of property has itself sufficed to maintain the workers in a subordinate position. Thus it is that in an extractive industry like coal mining, specialization has proved necessary under neither a hand nor a machine technology. In manufacturing industry, where nonlabor factors of production are themselves for the most part produced and, therefore, in principle accessible to groups of workers regardless of cost, specialization has continued to sustain the illusion that hierarchy is necessary for integrating the efforts of many into a marketable product.

But we get ahead of the story. At the present point in the argument, chronology suffices to refute the explanation of proletarianization of the producers by the high cost of machinery: the transformation of the independent producer to a wage laborer took place *before* machinery became expensive. It was a direct consequence of the specialization of men to component tasks that characterized the putting-out system. To be sure, capital played a role in the putting-out system; the putter-outer was after all a "capitalist." But machinery under the putting-out system was primitive; *fixed* capital was inconsequential. The capital provided by the putter-outer was predominantly working capital—stocks of goods in process—and advances against future labor.

The role played by wage advances deserves more attention than it has received, for at least in some trades it appears to have been an important means by which the capitalist maintained his hegemony.[29] Wage advances were to the capitalist what free samples of heroin are to the pusher: a means of creating dependence. It is of little moment that one was a legal and the other a physiological dependence. Both represent an addiction from which only the exceptionally strong-willed and fortunate escape.[30] The point for present purposes is that the practice of what was virtually indentured servitude (though for shorter periods of time than were customary in the British North American and African colonies) nicely complemented the specialization of men to tasks. Wage advances legally bound the worker to his master, and specialization of his activity to a small part of the whole helped to prevent the worker from circumventing his legal obligation to work for no one else (until his debt was discharged) by restricting the outlets for his production to intermediaries, a much smaller "market" than the market for a finished product. It was presumably much harder to dispose illegally of unwhitened pins than of whitened ones.[31]

The use of wage advances to maintain worker dependence and hierarchical control of production, however widespread under the putting-out system it may or may not have been, was no isolated historical phenomenon. It has been an important feature in other kinds of market economies where alternative means for subordinating the worker have not been available. Perhaps the most relevant example in the American experience was the development of agricultural organization in the post-1865 South. The problem of the post-bellum American planter was in many respects similar to the problem of the pre-factory British putter-outer: how to ensure for himself an essential role in the production process. The ex-slave was no longer legally tied to the land, and the land, like the means of industrial production in pre-factory days, was not sufficiently scarce or costly to maintain the dependency of workers on capitalists.

The problem was solved by coupling the crop-lien system of credit to the share-cropping system of farming. The planter-capitalist typically advanced credit in kind for food and other necessities of life, as well as for seed, fertilizer, and implements. These advances were secured by a lien on present and future crops, and the cultivator was legally under his creditor's thrall until the debt was repaid, which could be never since the creditor kept the books. Under the share-cropping system, the land-owner, not the tenant, controls the choice of crops,

> and he wants nothing grown except what he can sell. If the tenant takes time to keep a garden he does so at the neglect of his major interest, and, furthermore, he deprives the owner of the privilege of selling him additional groceries.[32]

Even the nominal independence of land-ownership was rarely of any value to the ex-slave. Debt was not a business arrangement, but subjugation. And the crop lien gave the capitalist virtually the same control over the cropping pattern as did land ownership. "The cropper who dared to till a truck patch was quickly warned that he was lowering his credit."[33] The result was a ruinous monoculture.

> In the greater part of the South the merchant demanded that cotton, more cotton, and almost cotton alone should be grown, because . . . the growers could neither eat it up behind his back nor slip it out for surreptitious sale.
> . . . Any attempt to sequester any of the cotton for sale elsewhere, even if beyond the amount due the storekeeper, was visited with quick retribution. In South Carolina, if the lien-holder even suspected such intent, he could get an order from the clerk of the court to have the sheriff confiscate the whole crop for sale . . .[34]

Generously assisted by the police power of the state, cotton enabled the capitalist to intervene between the producer and the market. Indeed, it is fair to conclude that cotton culture was to the capitalist planter what specialization was to the capitalist putter-outer: a choice dictated not by technological superiority but by his interest in interposing himself between the producer and the market.

III. The Rise of the Factory

The minute specialization that was the hallmark of the putting-out system only wiped out one of two aspects of workers' control of production: control over the product. Control of the work process, when and how much the worker would exert himself, remained with the worker—until the coming of the factory.

Economic historians customarily ascribe the growth of the factory to the technological superiority of large-scale machinery, which required concentration of productive effort around newly harnessed sources of energy—water and steam. The first factories, according to T.S. Ashton, arose in the beginning of the eighteenth century when *"for technical reasons,* small groups of men were brought together into workshops and little water-driven mills."[35] But the beginnings of the modern factory system are usually associated with Richard Arkwright, whose spinning mills displaced the domestic manufacture of cotton yarn. Arkwright's "water frame," it is said, dictated the factory organization of spinning: "Unlike the jenny, the frame required, for its working, power greater than that of human muscles, and hence from the beginning the process was carried on in mills or factories."[36] Other authorities agree. Thus Paul Mantoux: ". . . the use of machines distinguishes the factory from (the putting-out system), and gives its special character to the new system as against all preceeding ones . . ."[37] And, more recently, David Landes has written

> The Industrial Revolution . . . required machines which not only replaced hand labor but compelled the concentration of production in factories—in other words machines whose appetite for energy was too large for domestic sources of power and whose mechanical superiority was sufficient to break down the resistance of the older forms of hand production.[38]

These authorities, it should be said, recognize the other advantages the factory afforded, particularly a system of discipline and supervision that was impossible under the putting-out system. "It was," as Ashton says, "the need for supervision of work that led Peter Stubbs to gather the scattered filemakers into his works at Warrington."[39] Mantoux also notes the "obvious advantages from the point of view of organization and supervision"[40] of bringing together many workers into a single workshop. According to Landes the need for discipline and supervision turned "the thoughts of employers . . . to workshops where the men would be brought together to labor under watchful overseers."[41] And elsewhere Landes is even more explicit. "The essence of the factory," he writes in an introduction to a volume of essays on the development of capitalism, "is discipline—the opportunity it affords for the direction of and coordination of labor."[42]

Nevertheless, the advantages of discipline and supervision remain, in the conventional view, secondary considerations in accounting for the success of the factory system, if not for the motivation behind it. In the same breath as Mantoux notes the organizational advantages of the factory, he concludes that "the factory system . . . was the necessary outcome of the use of machinery."[43] Similarly, while identifying discipline as the essence of the factory, Landes attributes its success to technological factors: "the triumph of concentrated over dispersed manufacture was indeed made possible by the economic advantages of power-driven equipment. The factory had to beat cottage industry in the marketplace, and it was not an easy victory."[44]

The model underlying this reasoning is easy to identify: the factory survived, therefore it must have been a less costly method of production than alternatives. And in the competitive market economy, only least-cost methods are technologically efficient, provided efficiency is defined in an economy-wide sense. Hence the factory must have been technologically superior to alternatives.

However, the very mention of supervision and discipline as motivations for the factory ought to put one on guard against a too-easy identification of cost minimization with technological efficiency. In the competitive model, there is no scope for supervision and discipline except for that imposed by the market mechanism.[45] Any recognition of the importance of supervision and discipline as motivating forces behind the establishment of factories is tantamount to admission of important violations of the assumptions of perfect competition, and it follows that cost minimization cannot be identified with technological efficiency. Thus, technological superiority becomes neither necessary nor sufficient for the rise and success of the factory.

It will be argued presently that the agglomeration of workers into factories was a natural outgrowth of the putting-out system (a result, if you will, of its internal contradictions) whose success had little or nothing to do with the technological superiority of large-scale machinery. The key to the success of the factory, as well as its inspiration, was the substitution of capitalists' for workers' control of the production process; discipline and supervision could and did reduce costs *without* being technologically superior.

That the triumph of the factory, as well as the motivation behind it, lay in discipline and supervision, was clear to at least one contemporary observer. The leading nineteenth century apologist for the factory system, Andrew Ure, quite explicitly attributed Arkwright's success to his administrative prowess:

The main difficulty (faced by Arkwright) did not, to my apprehension, lie so much in the invention of a proper self-acting mechanism for drawing out and twisting cotton into a continuous thread, as in ... training human beings to renounce their desultory habits of work, and to identify themselves with the unvarying regularity of the complex automation. *To devise and administer a successful code of factory discipline, suited to the necessities of factory diligence, was the Herculean enterprise, the noble achievement of Arkwright.* Even at the present day, when the system is perfectly organized, and its labor lightened to the utmost, it is found nearly impossible to convert persons past the age of puberty, whether drawn from rural or from handicraft occupations, into useful factory hands. After struggling for a while to conquer their listless or restive habits, they either renounce the employment spontaneously, or are dismissed by the overlookers on account of inattention.

If the factory Briareus could have been created by mechanical genius alone, it should have come into being thirty years sooner; for upwards of ninety years have now elapsed since John Wyatt, of Birmingham, not only invented the series of fluted rollers, (the spinning fingers usually ascribed to Arkwright), but obtained a patent for the invention, and erected "a spinning engine without hands" in his native town . . . Wyatt was a man of good education, in a respectable walk of life, much esteemed by his superiors, and therefore favorably placed, in a mechanical point of view, for maturing his admirable scheme. But he was of a gentle and passive spirit, little qualified to cope with the hardships of a new manufacturing enterprise. *It required, in fact, a man of a Napoleon nerve and ambition, to subdue the refractory tempers of workpeople accustomed to irregular paroxysms of diligence* . . . Such was Arkwright.[46] (Emphasis added.)

Wyatt's efforts, and his ultimate failure, are shrouded in mystery. Indeed, it is impossible to sort out his contribution from the contribution of his collaborator, Lewis Paul. No model of the Wyatt-Paul machine survives, but Mantoux supports Ure's judgment that Wyatt and Paul anticipated Arkwright in all technical essentials. Arkwright's machine, according to Mantoux, "differs from that of Wyatt only in its details. These trifling differences cannot explain Arkwright's triumphal success."[47]

Contemporary evidence suggests that the problems of organizing the work force played a substantial part in the failure of the Wyatt-Paul enterprises. The correspondence between the principals and their officer suggest a continuing preoccupation with discipline. Edward Cave, a financial backer as well as a licensee, set up shop with hand-powered equipment in anticipation of finding a suitable water mill. Early on he wrote to Paul: "I have not half my people come to work today, and I have no great fascination in the prospect I have to put myself in the power of such people."[48] Discipline did not improve once the Cave factory became mechanized. When Wyatt visited the new spinning mill at Northampton in 1743 he found that "only four frames were regularly at work, since there were seldom hands enough for five."[49] The search for new methods of discipline continued. A month later, Cave's lieutenant wrote Wyatt:

I think they (the workers) have done as much in four days this week as they did in a week when you were here . . . There were not hands enough to work all five engines but four is worked complete which did about 100 skeins a day one with another, nay some did 130. One reason for this extra advance is Mr. Harrison (the mill manager) bought 4 handkerchiefs one for each machine value about 1/2p. each and hung them over the engine as prizes for the girls that do most . . . [50]

These crude attempts to "subdue the refractory tempers of work-people" by judicious use of the carrot apparently came to nought. One of the few indisputable facts about the Wyatt-Paul attempts is that they failed. And between Wyatt and Arkwright no one managed to bring Wyatt's invention to a successful conclusion, a remarkable failure indeed if the defects of machine spinning were primarily technological in nature.

There is additional evidence for the assertion that factory spinning did not depend for its success on a superior machine technology. Factory spinning took hold in the woolen industry as well as in cotton, and its success in the wool trade could only have been for organizational reasons. The technology of wool-spinning for many years after the factory made its appearance was the same in factory as in cottage; in both the "spinning jenny" was the basic machine well into the nineteenth century.[51] The Hammonds suggest that factory spinning dominated by the beginning of the century:

> By 1803 the transformation was practically complete. The clothiers had one by one introduced the system of "spinning houses" on their own premises, and the weavers were filled with apprehension lest they too should be forced to work under their employer's roof.[52]

At some places water power may have been used for working the jennies,[53] but this does not appear to have been the general case. Benjamin Gott, called by Mantoux the "first of the great Yorkshire spinners"[54] never used power in his spinning (or weaving) rooms during his quarter-century career as factory master and nevertheless appears to have made a satisfactory profit.[55] Certainly Gott never abandoned spinning and weaving to domestic workshops, although these hand-powered activities could have been carried on separately from the operations to which Gott applied steam power—scribbling and fulling. Indeed, the customary practice when Gott began his factory in 1793 was for scribbling and fulling to be a trade distinct from spinning and weaving.[56]

In weaving the case is even clearer than in spinning. Gott's handloom weaving sheds were not unique. Long before the powerloom became practicable, handloom weavers were brought together into workshops to weave by the same techniques that were employed in cottage industry. Clearly, the handloom shops would not have persisted if it had not been profitable for the entrepreneur, and just as clearly the source of profits could not have been in a superior technology. There is no evidence that the handloom in the capitalist's factory was any different from the one in the weaver's house.

I have found no comprehensive quantitative estimates of the relative importance of handloom factories, and it would probably require a major research effort to make even a reasoned guess.[57] A recent study of the history of cotton handloom weaving concludes that "although (the handloom weaving shed) was never anything like the predominant form of organization in cotton weaving, it was not negligible, nor was it confined . . . to fancy goods only."[58] The author of this study continues:

> According to the historian of Rossendale, in the period 1815–1830, when "the trade of cotton weaving on the handloom was at its briskest, there were at the lowest computation thirty weaving shops, apart from the looms in dwelling

houses, in the forest of Rossendale." The distinguishing feature of the sheds was that they employed a number of weavers on handlooms outside their own homes and families; they were substantially larger than the small shops of four or six (looms) run by a master weaver and apprentices in some of the more specialized lines at Bolton or Paisley. Isolated cases have been found with as many as 150 or 200 handlooms, quite a few with between 50 and 100, and a considerable number with 20 or more. Such sheds were to be found in town and country throughout the weaving area.

. . . For both employers and workers, the handloom shed represented a transitional stage in the organization of cotton weaving between the true domestic system and the power driven factory. It does not necessarily follow, however, that the handloom shed was a comparatively late development in cotton, or that it was a conscious imitation of the powerloom factory. With the coming of the dandyloom (an improved handloom) in the late 1820s, there was a probable increase in the number of such sheds, but there is some evidence from notices in the local newspapers for their existence in the 1780s and 1790s.[59]

Even as late as 1838, the weaver's animosity might, as in the case of Thomas Exell of Gloucestershire, be directed against the handloom shop and its owner, not against the powerloom. "Exell was," according to Wadsworth and Mann, "lamenting . . . the concentration of handlooms and jennies in the clothier's shop" when he wrote "They have driven us away from our houses and gardens to work as prisoners in their factories and their seminaries of vice."[60]

The early years of the nineteenth century saw the concentration of outworkers into workshops in other trades too. Supervision appears to have provided not only the motivation for "Peter Stubbs to gather the scattered filemakers into his works at Warrington," but a sufficient economic rationale for maintaining a factory-like organization in place of the putting-out system. Ashton's careful study of the Stubbs enterprise[61] does not suggest any technological argument for bringing the filemakers together, at least none he considers to be compelling. Nor does Ashton suggest that the new method of organizing work was ever abandoned. On the contrary: some of the original workshops were still standing in his own day.[62]

None of this is to deny the importance of the technological changes that have taken place since the eighteenth century. But these changes were not independent causes of the factory. On the contrary, the particular forms that technological change took were shaped and determined by factory organization. It is not accidental that technological change atrophied within the putting-out system after Hargreaves's jenny but flourished within the factory. On the demand side, the capitalist provided the market for inventions and improvements, and his interest lay—for reasons of supervision and discipline—with the factory. The supply side was only slightly more complex. In principle, an inventor might obtain a patent and license the use of his inventions to putter-outers or, indeed, to independent producers. In practice, as long as production took place in scattered cottages, it was difficult if not impossible to detect and punish piracy of patent rights. It was much easier to enforce patent rights with production concentrated into factories, and this naturally channeled inventive activity into the more remunerative market. And of course many improvements were by their very nature nonpatentable, and their benefits were under capitalist economic organization capturable only by entrepreneurs.

This argument may be thought to imply a *dynamic* technological superiority for the factory system, for it may fairly be interpreted as suggesting that the factory provided a more congenial climate for technological change. A more congenial climate for innovation does not, however, imply technological superiority, dynamic or static. For the factory superiority in this domain rested in turn on a particular set of institutional arrangements, in particular the arrangements for rewarding inventors by legal monopolies vested in patents. An invention, like knowledge generally, is a "public good": the use of an idea by one person does not reduce the stock of knowledge in the way that consumption of a loaf of bread reduces the stock of wheat. It is well understood that public goods cannot be efficiently distributed through the market mechanism; so patents cannot be defended on efficiency grounds.

Indeed, the usual defense of patents is in terms of the incentives afforded for invention. But the argument is hardly compelling. There is no *a priori* reason why society might not reward inventors in other ways. In the eighteenth century, for example, Thomas Lombe was voted £14,000 in lieu of a renewal of his patent for silk-throwing machinery, a small amount in proportion to the £120,000 he earned during the fourteen year term of his patent, but a tidy sum nevertheless, presumably enough to coax out the secrets of all but the most diffident genius.[63] To be sure, as it was practiced in Great Britain at least, the public reward of inventors was a fitful and unreliable arrangement, but this does not mean that a way could not have been found to make the system workable had the will existed. Had the patent system not played into the hands of the more powerful capitalists, by favoring those with sufficient resources to pay for licenses (and incidentally contributing to the polarization of the producing classes into bosses and workers), the patent system need not have become the dominant institutional mode for rewarding inventors.

There remains one loose end in this account of the rise of the factory: why did the market mechanism, which has been supposed by its defenders from Adam Smith onwards to harness the self-interest of the producer to the public interest, fail to provide adequate supervision and discipline under the putting-out system? Discipline and supervision, it must be understood, were inadequate only from the point of view of the capitalist, not from the point of view of the worker. And though it is true that in a sufficiently abstract model of perfect competition, profits are an index of the well-being of society as a whole as well as capitalists' well-being, this identity of interests does not characterize any real capitalist economy, no more the "competitive" capitalism of Adam Smith's day than the monopoly capitalism of our own. In the perfectly competitive model, there are no capitalists and no workers, there are only households that dispose of different bundles of resources, all of which—labor included—are traded on markets in which no one possesses any economic power. For this reason, laborers can equally well be thought to hire capital as capitalists labor, and the firm plays no significant role in the analysis. By contrast, the hallmark of the putting-out system was a specialization so minute that it denied to the worker the relatively wide (competitive!) market that existed for products, replacing the product market with a narrow market for a sub-product that, in a limited geographical area, a few putter-outers could dominate.[64] This perversion of the competitive principle, which lies at the heart of the capitalist division of labor, made discipline and supervision a class issue rather than an issue of technological efficiency; a lack of discipline and supervision could be disastrous for profits without being inefficient.

The indiscipline of the laboring classes, or more bluntly, their laziness, was widely noted by eighteenth century observers.

> It is a fact well known (wrote a mid-century commentator) . . . that scarcity, to a certain degree, promoted industry, and that the manufacturer (worker) who can subsist on three days work will be idle and drunken the remainder of the week . . . The poor in the manufacturing counties will never work any more time in general than is necessary just to live and support their weekly debauches . . . We can fairly aver that a reduction of wages in the woolen manufacture would be a national blessing and advantage, and no real injury to the poor. By this means we might keep our trade, uphold our rents, and reform the people into the bargain.[65]

Indiscipline, in other words, meant that as wages rose, workers chose to work less. In more neutral language, laziness was simply a preference for leisure! Far from being an "unreasonable inversion of the laws of sensible economic behavior,"[66] a backward bending labor-supply curve is a most natural phenomenon as long as the individual worker controls the supply of labor.

At least no devotee of the conventional indifference-curve approach to leisure-goods choices would dare argue that there is anything at all peculiar about a backward bending labor-supply curve.[67] Central to indifference-curve analysis of consumption choices is the separation of substitution and income effects. A rising wage makes leisure relatively more expensive to the worker, to be sure. But against this negative "substitution" effect must be considered the "income" effect; besides changing the terms of trade between leisure and goods, a rising wage is like a windfall that makes the worker able to afford more leisure. As long as leisure is a "normal" good (one for which the income effect is positive), substitution and income effects work in opposite directions. And the outcome is unpredictable; certainly no neoclassical economist worth his salt would argue that the substitution effect must be stronger than the income effect.[68]

In a competitive market, however, the shape of the labor-supply curve in the aggregate is of little moment. By definition, any individual capitalist can hire as many workers as he likes at the going wage. And the wage he pays is reflected in the market price of his product. He earns the competitive rate of profit, whether the going wage is low or high. But for the oligopsonistic putter-outers, the fact that higher wages led workers to choose more leisure was not only perverse, it was disastrous. In 1769, Arthur Young noted "the sentiment universal" among the cotton manufacturers of Manchester "that their best friend is high provisions."[69]

Thus the very success of pre-factory capitalism contained within it the seeds of its own transformation. As Britain's internal commerce and its export trade expanded, wages rose and workers insisted in taking out a portion of their gains in the form of greater leisure. However sensible this response may have been from their own point of view, it was no way for an enterprising capitalist to get ahead. Nor did the capitalist meekly accept the workings of the invisible hand.

His first recourse was to the law. In the eighteenth century, Parliament twice enacted laws requiring domestic woolen workers to complete and return work within specified periods of time. In 1749 the period was fixed at twenty-one days, and in 1777 the period was reduced to eight days.[70] But more direct action proved necessary. The capitalist's salvation lay in taking immediate control of the proportions of work and leisure. Capitalists' interests required that the worker's choice become one of whether or not to work at all—the only choice he was to have within the factory system.

To a great extent, supervision and discipline meant the same thing in the factory. Under the watchful eye of the foreman, the worker was no longer free to pace himself according to his own standards. But supervision was important for another reason: under the putting-out system materials inevitably came under the control of the workman during the process of manufacture. This created a variety of ways for the workman to augment his earnings; in the woolen trade a worker might exchange poor wool for good, or conceal imperfections in spinning, or wet the wool to make it seem heavier.[71] Above all, there was the possibility of outright embezzlement. It seems likely that these possibilities multiplied as trade developed and grew, for disposing of illegally-gotten goods would appear to have been easier as the channels of trade multiplied and expanded. In any event, capitalists increasingly utilized the legislative, police, and judicial powers of the state to prevent workers from eroding their profits during the course of the eighteenth century.[72] Indeed, even the traditional maxim of English justice—that a man was innocent until proven guilty—counted for little where such a clear and present danger to profits was concerned. A Parliamentary Act of 1777 allowed search of a workman's home on mere suspicion of embezzlement. If suspicious goods were found on his premises, it was up to the worker to prove his innocence. Otherwise he was assumed to be guilty—even if no proof were forthcoming.[73]

The worker's "dishonesty," like his "laziness," could not be cured by recourse to the law, however diligently Parliament might try to serve the interests of the capitalist class. The local magistrates might not be sufficiently in tune with the needs of the master manufacturers,[74] particularly one would imagine, if they were members of the landed gentry. In any event, enforcement of the law must have been cumbersome at best, especially where manufacturing was dispersed over a relatively wide geographical area. It is no wonder that, as Landes says, "the thoughts of employers turned to workshops where the men would be brought together to labor under watchful overseers." As late as 1824, a correspondent of the *Blackburn Mail* specifically urged the factory system as a means of combating embezzlement:

> It is high time ... that we should have a change either to powerlooms or to (hand) loom shops and factories, when at least one sixth part of the production of cotton goods is affected by (embezzlement).[75]

It is important to emphasize that the discipline and supervision afforded by the factory had nothing to do with efficiency, at least as this term is used by economists. Disciplining the work force meant a larger output in return for a greater input of labor, not more output for the same input.[76] Supervising—insofar as it meant something different from disciplining—the work force simply reduced the real wage; an end to embezzlement and like deceits changed the division of the pie in favor of capitalists. In the competitive model, innovation to improve the position of one individual or group at the expense of another may not be feasible. But the history of employer-worker relations under the putting-out system belies the competitive model. Embezzlement and other forms of deceit were exercises in "countervailing power," and pitifully weak ones at that.[77] The factory effectively put an end both to "dishonesty" and "laziness."

The factory system, then, was not technologically superior to the putting-out system, at least not until technological change was channeled exclusively into this mould. But was it in any event efficient? Was it no better than available alternatives not only for the capitalist, but for the factory worker as well, however severe the consequences (mere "pecuniary diseconomies" in technical language) for those who persisted in cottage industry? After all, nobody was legally compelled to work in a factory. The worker, no less than the capitalist, "revealed" by the very act of entering the factory a "preference" for factory organization, or at least for the combination of factory organization and factory pay[78]—or so neoclassical logic goes.

How applicable is this logic in fact? First of all, it is a strange logic of choice that places its entire emphasis on the absence of legal compulsion. Judging from the sources from which factory labor was originally drawn, the workers had relatively little effective choice. According to Mantoux

> In the early days factory labor consisted of the most ill-assorted elements: country people driven from their villages by the growth of large estates (that is,

by the enclosure movement), disbanded soldiers, paupers, the scum of every class and of every occupation.[79]

The question is not so much whether or not factory employment was better for workers than starving—let us grant that it was—but whether or not it was better than alternative forces of productive organization that would have allowed the worker a measure of control of product and process, even at the cost of a lower level of output and earnings.[80] But to grow and develop in nineteenth century Britain (or in twentieth century America) such alternatives would have had to have been profitable for the organizer of production. Since worker control of product and process ultimately leaves no place for the capitalist, it is hardly surprising that the development of capitalism, while extending the sway of the market in labor as well as goods, and extending the range of occupations, did not create a long list of employment opportunities in which workers displaced from the traditional occupations of their parents could control product and process.

Where alternatives to factory employment were available, there is evidence that workers flocked to them. Cottage weaving was one of the few, perhaps the only important, ready alternative to factory work for those lacking special skills. And despite the abysmally low level to which wages fell, a force of domestic cotton weavers numbering some 250,000 survived well into the nineteenth century. The maintenance of the weavers' numbers is, in the light of attrition caused by death and emigration, convincing evidence of persistent new entry into the field.[81] However, the bias of technological change towards improvements consistent with factory organization sooner or later took its toll of alternatives, weaving included.[82] The putting-out system, with its pitiful vestiges of worker control, virtually disappeared in Great Britain by mid-century. And weaving was about the last important holdout of cottage industry. Where this alternative was not available, the worker's freedom to refuse factory employment was the freedom to starve.

And even where the adult male had a real choice, so that the logic of "revealed preference" is conceivably more than formally applicable,[83] his wife and children had no such prerogatives. Women and children, who by all accounts constituted the overwhelming majority of factory workers in the early days,[84] were there not because they chose to be but because their husbands and fathers told them to be. The application of revealed preference to their presence in the factory requires a rather elastic view of the concept of individual choice.

In the case of pauper children, no amount of stretching of the logic of revealed preference will do. Sold by parish authorities as "factory apprentices" for terms of service up to ten or more years in order to save the local taxpayer the cost of food, clothing, and shelter, these poor unfortunates had no choice whatsoever, legal or otherwise. Apprenticeship itself was nothing new, nor was the binding over of pauper children to masters by parish authorities. But by the end of the eighteenth century, the institution of apprenticeship was no longer a means of limiting entry into the various crafts and trades and of ensuring the maintenance of quality standards. It had become, in accordance with the exigencies of capitalist enterprise, a system of indentured servitude.[85] As factories became prominent features of the industrial landscape, an enterprising capitalist might seize upon an advertisement like this one:

> To Let, The Labor of 260 Children
>
> With Rooms and Every Convenience for carrying on the Cotton Business. For particulars, enquire of Mr. Richard Clough, Common Street, Manchester.[86]

Mantoux goes so far as to claim that in the factory's early days, no parents would allow their own children inside, so that pauper apprentices were "the only children employed in the factories."[87] But despite the contemporary evidence Mantoux cites to support his claim, it may be a bit exaggerated. The Oldknow mill at Mellor appears to have relied primarily upon family groups (mothers as well as children), and Unwin suggests that the provision of employment to fathers of these families—outside the mill in general—was a continuing concern of Samuel Oldknow. But pauper apprentices were nevertheless a significant part of the work force at Mellor, reaching a maximum of perhaps twenty-five percent at the end of the eighteenth century.[88]

It is not directly relevant to the purposes of this paper to enter into a moral discussion of child labor generally or pauper apprenticeship in particular.[89] Given the factory, child labor was very likely a necessary evil, at least in the early days. As Ure wrote,

> . . . it is found nearly impossible to convert persons past the age of puberty, whether drawn from rural or from handicraft occupations, into useful factory hands. After struggling for a while to conquer their listless or restive habits, they either renounce the employment spontaneously, or are dismissed by the overlookers on account of inattention.

This is not, as history has shown, to remain a permanent state of affairs; the factory did, after all, survive the abolition of child labor. Not surprisingly, recruiting the first generation of factory workers was the key problem. For this generation's progeny the factory was part of the natural order, perhaps the only natural order. Once grown to maturity, fortified by the discipline of church and school, the next generation could be recruited to the factory with probably no greater difficulty than the sons of colliers are recruited to the mines or the sons of career soldiers to the army.

The recruitment of the first generation of workers willing and able to submit to an externally determined discipline has been a continuing obstacle to the expansion of the factory system. Even mid-twentieth century America has had to face the problem, and here too the lack of alternatives has had an important role to play in aiding the market mechanism. Just after World War II, General Motors introduced machine-paced discipline to Framingham, Massachusetts, in the form of an automobile assembly plant. Over eight-five percent of a sample[90] of workers interviewed by a team of sociologists under the direction of Charles Walker and Robert Guest had previously worked on jobs where they themselves had determined their own work pace. When interviewed by the Walker-Guest team in 1949, half the sample cited the lack of alternatives—termination of previous jobs or lack of steady work—as the reason for joining GM. And about a quarter said that they would be willing to take a cut in pay, if they could only find another job.[91] Said one:

> I'd take almost any job to get away from there. A body can't stand it there. My health counts most. What's the use of money if you ruin your health?[92]

If the problems of discipline and supervision—not the lack of a suitable technology—were the obstacles to the agglomeration of workers, why did the factory system emerge only at the end of the eighteenth century? In fact, the factory system goes back much farther, at least to Roman times. The factory, according to Tenny Frank, was the dominant means of organizing the manufacture of at least two commodities, bricks and red-glazed pottery.[93] Interestingly for our purposes, Roman factories appear to have been manned almost exclusively by workers who had the same degree of choice as pauper children in eighteenth century England—that is to say, by slaves. By contrast, factories were exceptional in manufactures dominated by freedmen. Frank lists several—clay-lamps, metal wares, jewelry, and water pipes—in which slaves were relatively uncommon; all were organized along small-scale craft lines.[94] This dualism is not so surprising after all. Independent craftsmen producing directly for the market offer no scope for supervision, whereas slave labor is obviously difficult to mobilize without supervision. The factory offered the ancient as well as the modern world an organization conducive to strict supervision.[95]

The surviving facts may be too scanty to prove anything, but they strongly suggest that whether work was organized along factory or craft lines was in Roman times determined, not by technological considerations, but by the relative power of the two producing classes. Freedmen and citizens had sufficient power to maintain a guild organization. Slaves had no power—and ended up in factories.

This reasoning bears on the development of capitalism in modern times. Guild organization of production and distribution eventually gave way to the putting-out system for two reasons: it was more profitable to the class that was able to interpose itself between the producer and the market, and, equally important, profits provided the nascent capitalist class with the political power to break down the institutional arrangements of guild organization—strict rules of apprenticeship, strict association of production with marketing, and the like—and replace them with institutional arrangements favorable to the putting-out system—the free market in labor as well as commodities, buttressed by strict rules of industrial discipline, with harsh penalties for embezzlement and other infractions. Until the political power of the small master and journeyman was broken, the putting-out system could not flourish, for the division of labor that formed the essence of the putting-out system denied both the orderly progression of apprentice to master and the union of producer and merchant in the same person.

At the same time, the putting-out system was necessarily transitional. Once a free market in labor was brought into existence, it was only a matter of time until the employer took to the factory as a means of curbing those aspects of freedom that depressed profits. Legal arrangements carefully set up to buttress the employer against the worker's "laziness" and "dishonesty" were, as we have seen, never enforceable to the capitalist's satisfaction.

The factory likely would have made its appearance much sooner than it in fact did if the small master and journeyman, fighting the battle of the guild against capitalism, had not been able for a time to use for their own ends the strategy of divide and conquer. Taking advantage of divisions between more powerful classes, the small master and journeyman were able to forge temporary alliances that for a time at least were successful in stalling the advent of the factory. For example, the alliance of the small cloth-making master with the large merchant not engaged in production maintained strict controls on apprenticeship well into the seventeenth century.[96]

A more striking, perhaps the most striking, example of successful alliance with more powerful interests had as outcome a Parliamentary prohibition against the loom shop. Thus runs the Weavers' Act of 1555, two hundred years before Arkwright:

> Forasmuch as the weavers of this realm have, as well at the present Parliament as at divers others times, complained that the rich and wealthy clothiers do in many ways oppress them, some by setting up and keeping in their houses divers looms, and keeping and maintaining them by journeymen and persons unskillful, to the decay of a great number of artificers who were brought up in the said art of weaving . . . it is therefore, for remedy of the premises and for the averting of a great number of inconveniences which may grow if in time it be not foreseen, ordained and enacted by authority of this present Parliament, that no person using the mystery of clothmaking, and dwelling out of a city, borough, market town, or incorporate town, shall keep, or return, or have in his or their houses or possession more than one woolen loom at a time . . .[97]

The main purpose of this Act may have been, as Unwin suggests, "to keep control of the industry in the hands of the town employers (who were exempted from its coverage) by checking the growth of a class of country capitalists."[98] It was precisely by riding the coattails of more powerful interests that the small master and journeyman were able to hold their own as long as they did.

Indeed, the important thing about the 1555 Act is not the precise alignment of the forces for and against, but its very existence at such an early date. Where there was so much smoke there must have been some fire, and some powerful motivation to the agglomeration of workers—long before steam or even water power could possibly have been the stimulus. Witch hunts apart, important legislative bodies are not in the habit of enacting laws against imaginary evils. To be the occasion of parliamentary repression, the loom shop must have been a real economic threat to the independent weavers even in the sixteenth century. By the same token, there must have been a class that stood to profit from the expansion of factory organization. The difference between the sixteenth and later centuries was in the relative power of this class and the classes that opposed the development of capitalist enterprise.

Industrial capitalism did not gain power suddenly; rather it was a fitful and gradual process, as a history like Unwin's makes clear.[99] But by the end of the eighteenth century the process was pretty well complete. The outright repeal of statutes limiting apprenticeship or otherwise regulating capitalists only reflected the new realities. By this time the process of innovation towards the form of work organization most congenial to the interests of the capitalist class was in full sway. The steam mill didn't give us the capitalist; the capitalist gave us the steam mill.

IV. Variations on a Theme

The resort of economically and politically powerful classes to innovation in order to change the distribution of income in their favor (rather than to increase its size) was not unique to the industrial revolution. Marc Bloch's "Advent and Triumph of the Water Mill" tells a fascinating story of a similar phenomenon in feudal times.[100] The dominance of water-powered flour mills may reasonably be thought to be a consequence of their technological superiority over handmills. But Bloch's article suggests another explanation: water mills enabled the feudal lord to extract dues that were unenforceable under a handmilling technology.

What is the evidence for the assertion that the water mill was inspired by distributional rather than technological considerations? First grinding at the lord's mill was obligatory, and the milling tolls varied inversely with the status of the owner of the grain. Justice Fitzherbert's *Boke of Surveying* (1538) noted the systematic variations:

> There be many divers grants made by the lord: some men to be ground to the twentieth part (a toll in kind of 1/20 of the quantity ground) and some to the twenty-fourth part; tenants-at-will to the sixteenth part; and bondsmen to the twelfth part.[101]

In extreme cases, the toll on grain grown on the lord's manor was as high as one-third,[102] which suggests that the obligation to grind at the lord's mill (the milling "soke") was in the extreme merely a device for ensuring that the peasant not evade what was actually a payment for the use of the lord's land, by secretly harvesting and sequestering grain due the lord. The close relationship in the minds of contemporaries between the milling soke and land rent is indicated by an extensive controversy over the application of the milling soke to bought grain.[103] Despite the obvious possibilities for evasion of dues on home-grown grain that an exemption for purchased grain would have provided, Justice Fitzherbert came down firmly for limiting the soke:

> To the corn mills, to the most part of them, belongeth Socone (soke)—that is to say, the custom of the tenants is to grind their corn at the lord's mill; and that is, me-seemeth, all such corn as groweth upon the lord's ground, and that he (the tenant) spendeth in his house. But if he buy his corn in the market or other place, he is then at liberty to grind where he may be best served.[104]

Whether the obligation to grind grain at the lord's mill (coupled with confiscatory tolls) was a more enforceable version of a land rent, or whether it was an additional device for enriching the landlord at the expense of the tenant may not be terribly important for present purposes. Both hypotheses are consistent with the proposition that distributional rather than technological considerations dominated the choice of milling technique. In arguing for this proposition Bloch finds it significant that "All the (water) mills whose history we can more or less follow were in fact seignorial in origin."[105]

> . . . where—as in Frisia—the community was exceptional in managing to avoid being stifled by seignorial authority, the peasants only took advantage of their liberty to remain obstinately faithful to their own individual mills. They were not prepared to come to a friendly agreement with one another and adapt technical progress to their own requirements.[106]

Presumably the lord, as he gained power, would have been content to allow peasants to continue with their handmills if he could have extracted milling dues independently of milling technique. Thus, at certain places and times, the lords "did not so much claim to suppress (handmills) as to make the use of them subject to the payment of a due."[107] But enforcement must have posed the same problems it later did for the putting-out master. It must have been extremely difficult to prevent the peasant from "embezzling" the lord's "rightful" portion of grain if the milling operation took place within the peasant's own house. Bloch mentions the "lawsuits which grimly pursued their endless and fruitless course, leaving the tenants always the losers"[108]—but at great expense of time, effort, and money to the lord as well. Moreover,

> In the countryside, seignorial authority, harassing though it was, was very poorly served. It was therefore often incapable of acting with that continuity

which alone would have made it possible to reduce the peasants, past masters in the art of passive resistance, to complete submission.[109]

Just as later the master manufacturer's "thoughts turned to workshops where the men could be brought together to labor under the eyes of watchful overseers," so must the feudal lord's thoughts have turned to a centralized water mill where grain would be ground under the watchful eyes of his bailiffs. Essential therefore to the triumph of the water mill was not only a monopoly of the sources of water power, but an absolute prohibition against the use of handmills—the establishment of the soke.

> A very great piece of luck enables us to see the monks of Jumierges, in an agreement dated 1207, breaking up any handmills that might still exist on the lands of Viville. The reason is no doubt that this little fief, carved out of a monastic estate for the benefit of some high-ranking *sergent* of the abbot, had in fact escaped for a long period the payment of seignorial dues. The scenes that took place in this corner of the Norman countryside under Philip Augustus must have had many precedents in the days of the last Carolingians or the first Capetians. But they escape the meshes of the historian's net.[110]

At about the same time the milling soke was being explicitly incorporated into English milling rights. "'The men shall not be allowed to possess any handmills'—such was the clause inserted by the canons of Embsay in Yorkshire between 1120 and 1151, in a charter in which a noble lady made over to them a certain water mill."[111]

The struggle between the lord and peasant was hardly an equal one, and the history of grain-milling reflects this asymmetry: the handmill gradually disappeared from the scene. But when the peasant temporarily gained the upper hand, one of the first casualties was the lord's monopoly on grain-milling—and maybe the lord and the water mill for good measure. After recounting a half century of intermittent struggle between the people of St. Albans and the abbot who was their lord, Bloch nears the end of what he calls, without exaggeration a "veritable milling epic":[112]

> . . . when in 1381 the great insurrection of the common people broke out in England and Wat Tyler and John Ball emerged as leaders, the people of St. Albans were infected by the same fever and attacked the abbey . . . The deed of liberation which they extorted from the monks recognized their freedom to maintain "hand-mills" in every home. The insurrection however proved to be like a blaze of straw that soon burns itself out. When it had collapsed all over England, the charter of St. Albans and all the other extorted privileges were annulled by royal statute. But was this the end of a struggle that had lasted over a century? Far from it. The (monastic) chronicler, as he draws to the close of his story, has to admit that for malting at any rate the detestable hand-mills have come into action again and have been again forbidden.[113]

What lessons do we draw from Bloch's account of the conflict between alternative milling techniques? Most important, it was not technological superiority, but the nature of feudal power and the requisites of enforcing that power that determined the replacement of handmills by water mills. It was not the handmill that gave us feudalism, but the feudal lord that gave us the water mill.

A model of feudalism that assumes a given distribution of power between master and man would naturally suggest that milling techniques should have been chosen on the basis of technological efficiency. But such a model implicitly ignores the dynamic conflict between classes and the need of the controlling class to choose technologies that facilitate the exercise of its power. A static analysis of the choice between handmill and water mill, or of feudalism generally, is as far off the mark as an analysis of the choice between domestic and factory production, or of capitalism generally, based on the neoclassical model of perfect competition. The key roles played by supervision and discipline—or, more generally, the exercise of power—in the determination of technology require models that are grounded in the challenge-response mechanism of class conflict, models at once dynamic and dialectic.

The collectivization of Soviet agriculture makes clear that efficiency is not necessarily the determinant of technology under socialism any more than under feudalism or capitalism. Stalin's arguments, to be sure, stressed the technological superiority of collective farming:

> The way out (of the difficulties of the twenties) is to turn the small scattered peasant farms into large united farms based on the common cultivation of the soil, to introduce collective cultivation of the soil on the basis of new and higher technique. The way out is to unite the small and dwarf peasant farms gradually and surely, not by pressure but by example and persuasion, into large farms based on common cooperative cultivation of the soil, with the use of agricultural machines and tractors and scientific methods of intensive agriculture.[114]

A different rationale emerges from the account of even the most sympathetic of outside observers—for example, Maurice Dobb.[115] The difficulty from which a way out was most urgently needed was not low agricultural output, but the mobilization of enough surplus grain to permit the Government both to maintain the level of real wage rates in industry and at the same time to launch an ambitious program of capital accumulation, which would require both exports to pay for imported machinery and expansion of employment in capital-goods producing industries. Under the New Economic Policy of the twenties, the Soviet Government's ability to impose on the peasants its own conception of the size of the agricultural surplus was limited to its control over the terms on which grain would be exchanged for industrial products.

Inadvertently, the Revolution had exacerbated the problem of mobilizing the agricultural surplus. In sharp contrast with the methods followed in reorganizing large-scale industry, the Revolution broke up large landholdings and maintained the principle of private property in agriculture.[116] Until the collectivization drive at the end of the 1920's, grain production was overwhelmingly in the hands of *kulaks, sredniaks,* and *bedniaks*—rich, middle, and poor peasants. So when the dislocations of civil war were surmounted and production restored to pre-war levels, peasant producers controlled the allocation of grain between on-farm consumption and market sales. And just as the British workman of the eighteenth century wanted to take a significant portion of any increase in real income in the form of leisure, so the Russian peasant of the twentieth chose to eat better as he became the master of the grain formerly due the landlord. However desirable this was for the peasant, the results were disastrous for the rest of the economy. Grain production "was (in 1925–26) nearly nine-tenths of 1913; but the marketed surplus was less than one-half of the pre-war amount."[117]

Of course, the Soviet Government could and did levy taxes upon the peasant, but there remained the age-old problem of enforcement. Moreover the civil war had made the peasant-worker alliance politically essential, which, as Lenin told the Tenth Party Congress in 1921, posed certain constraints on agricultural policy:

> The interests of these classes do not coincide: the small farmer does not desire what the worker is striving for. Nevertheless, only by coming to an agreement with the peasants can we save the socialist revolution. We must either satisfy the middle peasant economically and restore the free market, or else we shall be unable to maintain the power of the working class.[118]

As long as the market remained the principal means of mobilizing an agricultural surplus out of the countryside, the Government could do little more than manipulate the terms of trade. The debate that ensued between the proponents of high prices for agricultural goods (to coax out the surplus) and those who favored low prices (to minimize the costs in terms of industrial goods of mobilizing the surplus) was, alas, largely beside the point. Against the argument for high prices was first of all the possibility that *no* price policy would have coaxed out enough grain both to maintain the urban real wage and to launch an ambitious program of capital accumulation. The supply curve for grain under small-holder agriculture could, like the supply curve of labor under the putting-out system, have both forward-sloping and backward-bending ranges; there may simply have been no terms of trade at which the peasant would have freely parted with enough grain to allow the Government both to pay for imports and to feed a work force swelled by the addition of workers building machines and factories, dams and highways—without sharply reducing the real wages of all workers. But even if sufficiently high relative prices would have coaxed out adequate supplies of grain, the cost in terms of industrial consumer goods, domestic or imported, would probably have made capital accumulation all but impossible— save by a reduction in the real wage. Low agricultural prices were no solution, however. For, beyond a certain point at least, lower prices would simply encourage peasants to eat more and sell less.

Faced with this dilemma, the Soviet authorities could have sacrificed either capital accumulation or the real wage. But in the twenties, at least, the Revolution was not sufficiently secure to permit a conscious policy of reducing real wages, whatever the convictions of the leaders.[119] As a result, capital accumulation suffered. Thus it was that

> the apparent gap in urban consumption which (the) shortage of marketed grain supplies occasioned was met by reducing the export of grain, which even in the peak year of the post-war period did not exceed a third of its pre-war quantity.[120]

And thus it was that "in the middle and late '20's, unemployment (skilled and unskilled) was large and was tending to increase."[121]

The decision, towards the end of the decade, to double or triple the rate of capital accumulation over a period of five years—the goal of the "minimal" and "optimal" variants of the First Five Year Plan[122]—required either a policy aimed at reducing the industrial wage rate (though not the wage *bill*) or a policy designed to reduce total consumption in the countryside.[123] To reduce industrial wages would have undermined the support of the most revolutionary class—the proletariat. Besides, such a policy would surely have made it more difficult to recruit new entrants to the industrial labor force once the initial backlog of unemployment had been overcome.[124] This left no choice but to break the peasants' control over the disposition of agricultural production. It is hard not to agree with Dobb's conclusion: "Collective farming was (an) expedient for solving the difficulty of supplying agricultural produce to an expanding (industrial) population."[125] With collectivization, the Government at last determined not only the terms of trade, but the *quantities* of agricultural and industrial products flowing between the countryside and the city.

The economic problem posed by peasant ownership of land was, in short, not one of insufficient production, and not necessarily one of a surplus insufficient for feeding the nonagricultural population. It was rather that land ownership gave the peasants too strong a voice in determining the rate of capital accumulation. "New and higher technique" was no more the basis of collective farming than it was, centuries earlier, of the water mill. Had technological superiority rather than control of the surplus really been the basis of collectivization, the Soviet Government would have had no more reason to renege on Stalin's promise to rely on "example and persuasion" to bring the peasants aboard [126] than the feudal lord had to outlaw the handmill in order to ensure the success of the water mill.

A due regard for the role of economic power and the institutional constraints on the use of power are as important to understanding socialist economic development as to understanding the development of earlier economic systems. Under socialism (at least in its Soviet strain), no less than under feudalism and capitalism, the primary determinant of basic choices with respect to the organization of production has not been technology—exogenous and inexorable—but the exercise of power—endogenous and resistible.

Notes

1. F. Engels, "On Authority," first published in *Almenacco Republicano,* 1894; English translation in Marx and Engels, *Basic Writings in Politics and Philosophy,* L. Feuer (ed.), Doubleday and Co., Garden City, New York, 1959, p. 483. Emphasis added.

2. The attribution of the division of labor to efficiency antedates Adam Smith by at least two millenia. Plato, indeed, argued for the political institutions of the Republic on the basis of an analogy with the virtue of specialization in the economic sphere. Smith's specific arguments were anticipated by Henry Martyn three quarters of a century before the publication of the *Wealth of Nations.* See *Considerations Upon the East-India Trade,* London, 1701.

3. For a concise and elegant discussion of the relationship between technological efficiency and least-cost methods of production, see Tjalling Koopmans, *Three Essays on the State of Economic Science,* McGraw-Hill, New York, 1957, essay 1, especially pp. 66–126.

4. At least in the constant-returns-to-scale version of the competitive economy. Any other version implies the existence of a factor of production (like "entrepreneurial effort") that is not traded on the market, and with respect to which the model is therefore noncompetitive.

5. "We may, therefore, assume either that the landowner will hire laborers for a wage . . . or that the laborers will hire the land for rent." Knut Wicksell, *Lectures on Political Economy* (translated by E. Classen), Routledge and Kegan Paul, London, 1934, vol. I, p. 109.

"Remember that in a perfectly competitive market it really doesn't matter who hires whom; so have labor hire 'capital' . . . ," Paul Samuelson, "Wage and Interest: A Modern Dissection of Marxian Economic Models," *American Economic Review,* December, 1957.

6. A. Smith, *The Wealth of Nations* (Cannan edition), Random House, New York, 1937, p. 7.

7. Smith, *op. cit.,* pp. 734–735.

8. Smith, *op. cit.,* pp. 4–5.

9. T.S. Ashton, "The Records of a Pin Manufactory—1814–21," *Economica,* November, 1925, pp. 281–292.

10. For another example, cotton handloom weaving, though described by J.L. and Barbara Hammond in a volume entitled *The Skilled Laborer,* Longmans Green, London, 1919, was apparently a skill quickly learned (p. 70). A British manufacturer testified before a parliamentary committee that "a lad of fourteen may acquire a sufficient knowledge of it in six weeks." Duncan Bythell's *The Handloom Weavers,* Cambridge University Press, Cambridge, England, 1969, which is my immediate source for the manufacturer's testimony, is quite explicit: "Cotton handloom weaving, from its earliest days, was an unskilled, casual occupation which provided a domestic by-trade for thousands of women and children . . ." (p. 270)

The apparent ease with which, according to the Hammonds, women replaced male woolen weavers gone off to fight Napoleon suggests that woolen weaving too was not such a difficult skill to acquire (*op. cit.,* pp. 60–162). Indeed the competition of women in some branches of the woolen trade was such that in at least one place the men felt obliged to bind themselves collectively "not to allow any women to learn the trade" (*ibid.,* p. 162), an action that would hardly have been necessary if the requisite strength or skill had been beyond the power of women to acquire. The role of war-induced labor shortages in breaking down artificial sex barriers, and the subsequent difficulties in reestablishing these barriers is reminiscent of American experience in World War II.

11. This is not to say that the putter-outer, or "master manufacturer" never contributed anything of technological importance to the production process. But where the capitalist did contribute a useful technological innovation, he could effectively appropriate to himself the gains (of what in economic terms is a "public good") by preventing others, particularly his workers, from learning and imitating his trade secrets. What better way to achieve secrecy than to insist that each worker know only a part of the whole? The patent system was notoriously ineffective, and the benefactions of a grateful nation all too haphazard to rely upon, especially for the marginal improvements that are the most all but a handful of innovators could possibly achieve.

12. George Unwin, *Industrial Organization in the Sixteenth and Seventeenth Centuries,* first published by the Clarendon Press, Oxford, England, 1904 and republished by Cass, London, 1957, p. 96.

13. *Ibid.,* p. 96.

14. Quoted in Rhodes Boyson, *The Ashworth Cotton Enterprise,* Oxford University Press, Oxford, England, 1970, p. 52.

15. *The Spectator,* London, May 26, 1866, p. 569.

16. *Ibid.,* p. 569.

17. E.L. Trist and K.W. Bamforth, "Some Social and Psychological Consequences of the Longwall Method of Coal-Getting," *Human Relations,* Vol. IV, No. 1, 1951, p. 6.

18. *Ibid.,* p. 6.

19. Trist and Bamforth, *op. cit.,* p. 6.

20. *Ibid.,* p. 9.

21. *Ibid.,* p. 23–24.

22. *Ibid.,* p. 11.

23. As we shall see, supervision was a problem endemic to the specialization of men to tasks under the putting-out system. The factory system was a solution to this problem, one, it will be argued, that reflected capitalists' interests rather than a supposed technological superiority.

24. Harvard Business School Case Study, "British Coal Industries (C)," prepared by Gene W. Dalton under the direction of Paul R. Lawrence, and based on E.L. Trist and H. Murray, "Work Organization at the Coal Face," No. 506, Tavistock Institute, London, England.

25. Harvard Business School Case Study, "British Coal Industries (B)," prepared by Gene W. Dalton under the direction of Paul R. Lawrence, and based on E.L. Trist and H. Murray, "Work Organization at the Coal Face," Doc. No. 506, Tavistock Institute, London, England.

26. "British Coal Industries (C)," *op. cit.*

27. Nationalization did not change the concept of property; it merely transformed title of the mines to the state.

28. Paul Jacobs's is a voice crying out in the wilderness:

> If unions are going to survive and grow in the coming period, they have to break with their old patterns. First of all, they have to break with their pattern of not thinking about *work,* the nature of work, their relationship to work, and what they can do about work. What do we do about work now? Well, we say we're going to fix the wages, we're going to try to establish what we think ought to be minimal working conditions, we're going to slow down the line, we're going to argue about the speed of the line. But do we ever say: Hey, the whole concept of production of an automobile on a line stinks; the whole thing is wrong; what we ought to be doing is figuring out new ways of looking at the problem of work? No, these are questions from which every union withdraws.
>
> I heard the vice-president of Kaiser explain their new agreement with the Steelworkers Union, and he was asked what the union would have to say about the nature of work processes in the plant. "Nothing," he said. "My goodness, the Steelworkers Union wouldn't ever dream of venturing into this area . . ."

(Center for the Study of Democratic Institutions, *Labor Looks at Labor,* Fund for the Republic, Santa Barbara, California, 1963, pp. 14–15).

29. See T.S. Ashton, *An Eighteenth Century Industrialist,* Manchester University Press, Manchester, 1939, chapters 2–3, for an account of the importance of wage advances in the metal trades. Advances to weavers were common in the putting-out enterprise run by Samuel Oldknow. However, the amounts were relatively small, of the order of a week's wages. (G. Unwin and others, *Samuel Oldknow and the Arkwrights,* Manchester University Press, Manchester, 1924, p. 49.) If, in fact, wage advances were an important instrument of capitalist control only in the metal trades, it would be interesting to know why. George Unwin gives one instance of a debt-employment nexus in the cloth industry as early as the reign of Henry VIII. (*Industrial Organization in the Sixteenth and Seventeenth Centuries,* p. 52).

30. It is of equally little moment that the worker's dependence was "freely" entered into, any more than the pusher's enticement of the unwary is any less destructive because one has the right to refuse the come-on.

31. Though presumably not impossible. Embezzlement was a continuing problem under the putting-out system, and it will be argued presently that the chief advantage of the factory system in its early days was the ability to provide the supervision necessary to cure this and other ills.

32. Fred Shannon, *The Farmer's Last Frontier,* Holt, Rhinehart and Winston, New York, 1945, p. 88.

33. *Ibid.,* p. 92.

34. *Ibid.*

35. T.S. Ashton, *The Industrial Revolution 1760–1830,* Oxford University Press, London, 1948, p. 33 (emphasis added).

36. *Ibid.,* p. 72.

37. P. Mantoux, *The Industrial Revolution in the Eighteenth Century,* Harper and Row, New York, 1962, p. 39. (First English edition published in 1928).

38. D.S. Landes, *The Unbound Prometheus,* Cambridge University Press, Cambridge, England, 1969, p. 81.

39. *The Industrial Revolution, op. cit.,* p. 109. See also Ashton, *An Eighteenth Century Industrialist,* p. 26.

40. *The Industrial Revolution in the Eighteenth Century, op. cit.,* p. 246.

41. Landes, *op. cit.,* p. 60.

42. D.S. Landes (editor), *The Rise of Capitalism,* Macmillan, New York, 1966, p. 14.

43. Mantoux, *op. cit.,* p. 246.

44. *Ibid,* p. 14. Cf. Herbert Heaton, *The Yorkshire Woolen and Worsted Industries,* Oxford University Press, Oxford, 1920: "the major part of the economic advantage of the factory springs from the use of machinery capable of performing work quickly, and the use of power which can make the machinery go at high speed." p. 352.

45. Ronald Coase appears to be unique in recognizing that the very existence of capitalist enterprise is incompatible with the reliance of perfect competition on the market mechanism for coordinating economic activity. Coase, however, sees the capitalist firm as the means not for subordinating workers but for saving the costs of the market transactions:

> . . . a firm will tend to expand until the costs of organizing an extra transaction within the firm become equal to the costs on the open market or the costs of organizing in another firm.

See "The Nature of the Firm," *Economica* vol. IV, 1937, pp. 386–405, reprinted in Stigler and Boulding (eds.), *Readings in Price Theory,* Irwin, Chicago, Illinois, 1952, pp. 331–351. The quotation is from p. 341 of Boulding and Stigler.

46. A. Ure, *The Philosophy of Manufacturers,* Charles Knight, London, 1835, pp. 15–16. Military analogies abound in contemporary observations of the early factory. Boswell described Mathew Boulton, Watt's partner in the manufacture of steam engines, as "an iron captain in the midst of his troops" after a visit to the works in 1776. (Quoted in Mantoux, *op. cit.,* p. 376).

47. Mantoux, *op. cit.,* p. 223. Wadsworth and Mann differ. See Alfred P. Wadsworth and Julia DeLacy Mann, *The Cotton Trade and Industrial Lancashire,* Manchester University Press, Manchester England, 1931, pp. 482–483.

48. Quoted in Julia DeLacy Mann, "The Transition to Machine-Spinning" in Wadsworth and Mann, *op. cit.,* p. 433.

49. *Ibid.,* p. 436.

50. *Ibid.,* p. 437.

51. "Up to the close of the period (1820), and probably until after 1830, when Crompton's mule had been made 'self-acting,' it made no headway in the woolen industry." W.B. Crump, *The Leeds Woolen Industry 1780–1820,* Thoresby Society, Leeds England, 1931, p. 25.

52. J.L. Hammond and Barbara Hammond, *op. cit.,* p. 146.

53. *Ibid.,* p. 148.

54. Mantoux, *op. cit.,* p. 264.

55. Crump, *op. cit.,* esp. pp. 24–25, 34.

56. *Ibid.,* p. 24.

57. Albert P. Usher, *An Introduction to the Industrial History of England,* Houghton Mifflin, Boston, 1920, reports some statistics for 1840, but does not give his source: "In the Coventry ribbon district, there were 545 handlooms in factories, 1264 handlooms employed by capitalists outside the factories, and 121 looms in the hands of independent masters. At Norwich 656 handlooms were in factories out of a total of 3398 for the district as a whole." (p. 353.)

58. D. Bythell, *op. cit.,* p. 33.

59. *Ibid.,* pp. 33–34.

60. Wadsworth and Mann, *op. cit.,* p. 393.

61. *An Eighteenth Century Industrialist.*

62. *Ibid.,* p. 26.

63. Mantoux, *op. cit.,* pp. 195–196. In the case of Lombe and his brother, genius, apart from organizing talent, consisted in pirating an Italian invention.

64. On the power of bosses over workers see, among others, Landes, *op. cit.,* p. 56; E.P. Thompson, *The Making of the English Working Class,* Random House, New York, 1963, chapter 9, especially the quotations on pp. 280, 297. Adam Smith was quite explicit: "Masters are always and everywhere in a sort of tacit, but constant and uniform combination, not to raise the wages of labor above their actual rate. To violate this combination is everywhere a most unpopular action, and a sort of reproach to a master among his neighbors and equals. We seldom, indeed hear of this combination, because it is the usual, and one may say, the natural state of things which nobody hears of." *The Wealth of Nations, op. cit.,* Book I, Chapter 8, pp. 66–67.

65. J. Smith, *Memoirs of Wool* (1747); quoted in E.P. Thompson, *op. cit.,* p. 277.

66. The characterization is Landes's, *Unbound Prometheus,* p. 59.

67. Contrary to Landes's implication, "a fairly rigid conception of what (is) felt to be a decent standard of living" (*ibid.,* p. 59) is not required for a backward bending supply curve of a good or service that (like time) affords utility to the seller.

68. It may be slightly ironic that an important necessary condition for the indifference-curve model to be applicable to one of the most fundamental problems of economic choice is inconsistent with capitalism. For the indifference-curve model to be applicable

to goods-leisure choices, control of the hours of work must rest with the worker. But this is inconsistent with capitalist control of the work process, and hence with capitalism itself.

69. A. Young, *Northern Tour;* quoted in Wadsworth and Mann, *op. cit.,* p. 389.

70. Heaton, *op. cit.,* p. 422. These laws had historic precedents. Unwin reports a municipal order dating from 1570 in Bury St. Edmunds requiring spinsters to work up six pounds of wool per week. Employers were to give notice to the constable in the event any one failed to obey the order (*op. cit.,* p. 94).

71. Heaton, *ibid.,* p. 418.

72. See Heaton, *ibid.,* pp. 418–437 for an account of the woolen industry, Wadsworth and Mann, *op. cit.,* pp. 395–400 for the cotton industry.

73. Heaton, *op. cit.,* p. 422.

74. Heaton, *ibid.,* p. 428.

75. Quoted in Bythell, *op. cit.,* p. 72.

76. In technical terms, the shift from workers' control of goods-leisure choices to capitalists' control meant a shift *along* a given production function not a shift in the function itself.

77. Any comment on the alleged immorality of these defenses is probably superfluous. This was after all an era in which unions were illegal "combinations," proscribed under common law of conspiracy (and later, by statute).

78. Factory wages for handloom weaving were higher than wages earned for the same work performed in the worker's cottage—presumably the reward both for longer hours and for submitting to the factory supervision and discipline. See Bythell, *op. cit.,* p. 134.

79. Mantoux, *op. cit.,* p. 375.

80. "Better" is used here in a broader sense than it is conventionally used by economists when comparing different bundles of commodities even when they bother to count leisure as one of the goods. Integrity—personal and cultural—can hardly be represented on an indifference curve. For a discussion of the effects of economic change on cultural integrity, see Karl Polanyi, "Class Interest and Social Change" originally published in *The Great Transformation,* Rinehard, New York, 1944; reprinted in *Primitive, Archaic and Modern Economies,* edited by George Dalton, Doubleday, Garden City, New York, 1968, pp. 38–58.

81. On the size of the labor force in domestic cotton weaving, see Landes, *op. cit.,* pp. 86–87; Bythell, *op. cit.,* pp. 54–57. On wages, see Bythell, *ibid.,* chapter 6 and appendices; Sydney J. Chapman, *Lancashire Cotton Industry,* Manchester University Press, Manchester, England, 1904, pp. 43–44.

82. The amazing thing is that the cottage weavers held out as long as they did, testimony as Landes says, "to the obstinacy and tenacity of men who were unwilling to trade their independence for the better-paid discipline of the factory." (*Unbound Prometheus,* p. 86).

The reluctance of cottage weavers to submit to factory discipline was widely commented upon by contemporaries. As late as 1836, a noted critic of the factory, John Fielden, wrote "they will neither go into (the factories) nor suffer their children to go." (Quoted in Bythell, *op. cit.,* p. 252). Another critic testified to a Select Committee of Parliament that a cottage weaver would not seek factory employment because "he would be subject to a discipline that a handloom weaver can never submit to." (Select Committee on Handloom Weavers' Petitions, 1834; quoted in E.P. Thompson, *op. cit.,* p. 307.)

Whether the cottage weavers' inadaptability to the factory was a matter of taste or of the lack of psychological attitudes essential to factory discipline is a question of present as well as historical significance. (Ure, for what his opinion is worth, clearly sides with the view that the cottage weaver *could* not adapt as opposed to the view that he *would* not.) For the argument that the role of schools is precisely to inculcate attitudes conducive to labor discipline see Herbert Gintis, "Education, Technology, and the Characteristics, of Worker Productivity," *American Economic Review,* May, 1971.

83. For men, factory employment could be quite attractive. Agglomeration of workers did not by this one fell swoop solve all problems of discipline. In spinning mills, for example, adult males formed a corps of noncommissioned officers; women and children were the soldiers of the line. And factory employment was relatively attractive for these "labor aristocrats." To quote Ure,

> The political economist may naturally ask how . . . the wages of the fine spinners can be maintained at their present high pitch. To this question one of the best informed manufacturers made me this reply: "We find a moderate saving in the wages to be of little consequence in comparison of contentment, and we therefore keep them as high as we can possibly afford, in order to be entitled to the best quality of work. A spinner reckons the charge of a pair of mules in our factory a fortune for life, he will therefore do his utmost to retain his situation, and to uphold the high character of our yarn."

Ure, *op. cit.*, p. 366.

84. For example, in the Oldknow spinning mill at Mellor, only ten percent of the workers were male heads of families, even excluding child apprentices. G. Unwin and others, *Samuel Oldknow and the Arkwrights,* Manchester University Press, Manchester, England, 1924, p. 167.

85. See Ashton, *An Eighteenth Century Industrialist,* p. 28 who cites as his authority O.J. Dunlop, *English Apprenticeship and Child Labor,* p. 196. See also Bythell, *op. cit.,* p. 52; Wadsworth and Mann, *op. cit.,* pp. 407–408.

86. *Wheelers Manchester Chronicle,* August 7, 1784. Quoted in Wadsworth and Mann, *op. cit.,* p. 408. If inclined to business on a more modest scale, one might be tempted by a package offer of a factory of sixteen looms and the labor of twelve apprentices. *Manchester Mercury,* December 1, 1789. Quoted in Bythell, *op. cit.,* p. 52.

87. Mantoux, *op. cit.,* p. 411.

88. G. Unwin and others, *Samuel Oldknow and the Arkwrights,* pp. 166–175.

89. The evils speak for themselves, and it will suffice perhaps to note that a man like Unwin reveals more than anything else the poverty of his own imagination when, in bending over backwards to be fair and objective, he defends the system (*ibid.,* pp. 170–175) on the grounds that it was superior to the alternative of the workhouse.

90. The sample was just over one-fifth of all the production workers.

91. Charles R. Walker and Robert H. Guest, *The Man on the Assembly Line,* Harvard University Press, Cambridge, Mass., 1952, chapter 6. A follow-up survey of worker attitudes would be fascinating: To what extent did those who initially resisted and resented the dehumanizing aspects of assembly-line work come to accept them—in return for relatively high pay and job security? What was the process by which workers' values and tastes changed in response to their employment at GM? To what extent did they eventually seek more congenial work?

92. *Ibid.,* p. 88. Sometimes, it would appear, the problem of recruiting a suitable labor force is resolved in ways that inhibit rather than foster the work attitudes necessary for expansion of industrial capitalism. The abundance of unemployed and underemployed workers in India, for example, appears to have permitted foreign and Indian entrepreneurs to graft an alien factory system into indigenous society without developing the discipline characteristic of Western factory labor. Indian workers are much freer than their Western counterparts to come and go as they please, for a contingent of substitute workers stands ready to fill in as needed. See A.K. Rice, *Productivity and Organization: The Amhedabad Experiment,* Tavistock, London, 1958, pp. 79, 118 for incidental support of this hypothesis.

93. Tenney Frank, *An Economic History of Rome,* Second Revised Edition, Johns Hopkins University Press, Baltimore, 1927, chapter 14.

94. *Ibid.,* chapter 14.

95. Freedmen, it should be noted, did apparently work for wages, though not in factories.

The existence of a proletariat seems beyond dispute. *Ibid.,* pp. 269–270 and chapter 17.

96. Unwin, *Industrial Organization in the Sixteenth and Seventeenth Centuries,* p. 199.

97. [Weavers' Act of 1555], 3 & 4 Philip and Mary, c.11. Quoted in Mantoux, *op. cit.,* pp. 34–35.

98. Unwin, *Industrial Organization in the Sixteenth and Seventeenth Centuries,* p. 93.

99. *Ibid.*

100. Reprinted in Marc Bloch, *Land and Work in Medieval Europe,* (translated by J. E. Anderson), Harper and Row, New York, 1969, pp. 136–168.

101. Quoted in Richard Bennett and John Elton, *History of Corn Milling,* vol. III, Simpkin, Marshall and Company, London, 1900, p. 155.

102. *Ibid.,* pp. 221, 253.

103. *Ibid.,* chapter 9.

104. Quoted in Bennett and Elton, *op. cit.,* p. 242. By the time of Henry VIII, feudal institutions had begun to decay and it is hard to decide between the hypothesis that the learned justice's remarks reflects this decay and the hypothesis that the milling soke was bound up with land rent.

105. Bloch, *op. cit.,* p. 151.

106. *Ibid.,* p. 151.

107. Bloch, *op. cit.,* p. 156.

108. Bloch, *op. cit.,* p. 157.

109. *Ibid.,* p. 155.

110. *Ibid.,* p. 154.

111. Bloch, *op. cit.,* p. 157. Bennett and Elton devote a whole chapter to the institution of soke. *Op. cit.,* chapter 8.

112. Bloch, *op. cit.,* p. 157.

113. *Ibid.,* p. 158.

114. Report to the Fifteenth Congress of the Communist Party of the Soviet Union, December 1927. Quoted in Maurice Dobb, *Soviet Economic Development Since 1917,* Fifth Edition, Routledge and Kegan Paul, London, 1960, p. 222.

115. *Ibid.,* especially chapter 9.

116. According to official Soviet figures, less than two percent of total grain production was accounted for by state and collective farms in 1926–27, *ibid.,* p. 217.

117. *Ibid.,* p. 214.

118. Quoted in Dobb, *ibid.,* p. 130.

119. Abram Bergson quotes a study based on Soviet statistics to the effect that real wages rose by eleven percent between 1913 and 1928. *The Structure of Soviet Wages,* Harvard University Press, Cambridge, 1944, p. 203.

120. Dobb, *op. cit.,* p. 214.

121. *Ibid.,* p. 189.

122. *Ibid.,* p. 236.

123. It was not necessary to reduce the *average* standard of living, as the Plan's provision for increased total consumption makes clear. That part of the labor force that was unemployed or underemployed in the twenties would receive employment and wages as a result of the expansion envisioned in the Plan, and the improvement in their standard of living could more than make up for the deterioration of the standard of living imposed on everybody else, both in terms of distributive justice and statistical averages.

124. Whatever reductions in real wages accompanied the First Five Year Plan were probably, as Dobb says, the unforeseen result of the resistance of peasants to collectivization and the consequent reduction in agricultural output. *Ibid.,* p. 237.

125. Dobb, *op. cit.,* p. 225.

126. Compare Dobb, *ibid.,* pp. 228–229.

2

Segmented Labor Markets

Richard Edwards

Structural control has cast a longer shadow than is visible from within the firm itself. The new system of control has contributed to the redivision and segmentation of the American working class. Both exogenous divisions (especially racial and sexual ones) and new distinctions of capitalism's own making have become embedded in the economic structure of society. And the divisions within the working class have distorted and blunted the class opposition to capitalism, making for a weak socialist movement and a long period of relative stability within the regime of monopoly capitalism.

This marks a clear reversal of the tendency dominant in the nineteenth century. During American capitalism's first century it inherited and recruited a highly heterogeneous labor force, but it reshaped its wage laborers into an increasingly homogeneous class. In the twentieth century, the economic system has attracted groups as divergent as before, but capitalist development has tended to institutionalize, instead of abolish, the distinctions among them. In particular, the dichotomizing of the economy into core and periphery has introduced a new structural division in the conditions of employment. The rise of the large administrative staff, with its middle position between employers and manual workers, has further fractured the common class basis. Moreover, institutionalized racial and sexual discrimination has served to deepen the splits within the working class. In all these cases, capitalist development has not only splintered the working class, it has also institutionalized the divisions. It has created distinct and enduring "fractions."[1]

The various lines of division can be seen in the operation of labor markets. Just as with other commodities, so with labor power, conditions in the market

Originally published in Richard Edwards, *Contested Terrain: The Transformation of the Workplace in the Twentieth Century.* New York: Basic Books, 1979, pp. 163–183.

determine the circumstances of its *sale* (including the price received and the allocation of the commodity among various potential buyers). On the other hand, the way in which any purchased commodity is *consumed* depends upon the use to which it is put by its buyer after purchase; in the case of labor power, its consumption occurs in the labor process, the control of which has been the subject of ... analysis. ... The distinction between sale (through labor markets) and consumption (in the labor process) permits us to assess the role labor markets play in segmenting the working class.

Labor markets constitute the principal means of segmenting the working class, because it is through labor market processes that workers are hired into their various jobs. We can see the differential treatment of labor force groups as the operation of distinct markets—the job market for factory operatives being quite distinct, for example, from the job market for middle-level administrative staff. Thus, the way the working class is segmented is clear: it is segmented through the operation of segmented labor markets.

Why segmented markets exist is a deeper question, however. In theory, labor markets could be segmented because buyers with great market power (*monopsonists*) can achieve a more profitable overall settlement by bargaining separately with distinct groups in the market than if they treat everyone similarly.[2] In this case, segmentation can be explained as an attempt to lower the overall price (wage) that the buyer has to pay.

While employers would undoubtedly wish to act as monopsonists and reduce the wages they are forced to pay, this explanation for segmentation is distinctly unlikely for one important reason: there exist many employers, and few have monopsony power. With relatively minor exceptions, employers cannot act as monopsonists.

Similarly, labor markets could be segmented because some workers are able to act as monopolists in the sale of particular types of labor power, establishing barriers to entry into some occupations and closing off these occupations to other workers. Here again, the issue is not so much whether workers might *want* to achieve such protection from wider competition (undoubtedly they do) but rather whether they are *able* to do so. With a few noteworthy exceptions, competition also prevails on the supply side of the labor market, and so the notion of worker-enforced segmentations does not seem plausible. Perhaps a few of the stronger craft unions can act to limit the number of new entrants into their occupations (although their power to do so seems quite suspect), but such power is clearly absent in most occupations.

All this suggests that segmentation arises not from market forces themselves but rather from the underlying uses of labor power. If this is true, it means that to understand why segmentation occurs, we must look to how labor power is consumed in the labor process.

This chapter will describe one feature of the redivision of the American working class: segmented labor markets.[3] . . .

The Three Labor Markets

The idea that labor markets treat groups differently needs little new justification.[4] Most people know, even if too few care, that the unemployment rate of blacks regularly runs at least double that of whites. At the other end of the spectrum, new Harvard Business School graduates can on average look forward to an annual income of $50,000 (or is it now $65,000?) within five years. Women's earnings, despite antidiscrimination legislation, have remained steady (within a few points) at 60 percent of male earnings throughout the postwar period. Between a third and a half of teenage black job-seekers normally cannot find work.

More novel is the notion that the various groups and the cross-cutting and overlapping divisions in the labor market can reasonably be arranged into a limited number of labor market segments. But this conclusion emerges from research on segmented labor markets that began in the 1960s with studies of urban labor markets by Barry Bluestone, David Gordon, Peter Doeringer and Michael Piore, and others, who observed that urban blacks and other working poor people appeared to be operating in a labor market distinct from that of urban white males.[5] It was not just that blacks and others in what was labeled the "secondary labor market" were paid less; the labor market itself seemed to work differently for them. Education, for example, seemed to provide very little return for secondary workers, whereas it provided a substantial return in the other segment, the "primary market." Similarly, jobs in the secondary market did not seem to lead to better jobs, unlike the primary market where each job was potentially a stepping-stone to a better position. Observers could point to many other differences as well in the way the markets operated.

However, such observations remained largely unverified until David Gordon devised an empirical test. Taking some forty-seven measures of employment characteristics, Gordon used a statistical procedure that clearly revealed distinct clusters of jobs, with very different labor market outcomes (wage rates, frequency of unemployment, and so on) associated with each.[6] In short, his analysis provided support for the theory of segmented labor markets.

Several subsequent studies have further strengthened the case for the segmented market approach. In general, these studies not only show that the market *outcomes* are different by segment, but more importantly they provide evidence that the market *processes* also differ by segment.[7] But this research has suggested some reformulations in the original "dual market" theory. For one thing, because it is less riveted to the problems of poor and minority workers, the new research has argued persuasively for distinctions among not two but three labor market segments—the "secondary" market, the "subordinate primary" market, and the "independent primary" market. Moreover, while the earlier work emphasized a very small, "abnormal" secondary market, it now seems clear that the three segments are of about equal size. Widely varying estimates suggest that each represents between a quarter and a third of the total labor force, the remaining portion being accounted for by self-employed persons, employers, and high-level managers.[8]

Unlike the earlier work, which tended to focus on differences among workers, subsequent analysis has also suggested that the fundamental differences are not so much among the workers as among the jobs that workers hold. At any point in time, of course, differences do exist in both the workers and their jobs. Yet the research seems to say that if we are to understand the historical forces that established and maintain the divisions, we must look to the job structure.

One problem that has not been solved by recent research is precisely how to define the segments. Anecdotal observation like Doeringer and Piore's and empirical forays like Gordon's suggested that the segments should be defined as a cluster of characteristics, with no single characteristic being fundamental or invariably decisive.[9] What cluster of characteristics, then, defines a secondary job, a subordinate-primary job, or an independent-primary job? Research continues on this issue, but the main dimensions of the answer are already apparent, and probably only minor modification will be added by more precise quantitative criteria. Accepting the hazards of anticipating ongoing research, then, we can suggest the main differences distinguishing the segments.

The Secondary Market

One segment, the secondary market, is the preserve of casual labor—"casual," that is, not in the sweat required of the workers but rather in the lack of any worker rights or elaborate employer-imposed work structures. Here labor power comes closest to being treated simply as a commodity unfettered and unencumbered by any job structure, union, or other institutional constraints.

The secondary market includes many different types of jobs, and spans both production and nonproduction work. Low-skill jobs in small, nonunion manufacturing concerns constitute one part of this market. "Service" employment—the jobs of janitors, waiters and waitresses, hospital orderlies, deliverymen and messengers, attendants, guards, personal care workers, and others—represents a second major component. Another group consists of the lower-level positions in retail and wholesale trade: slots filled by sales clerks, order-takers, check-out clerks, inventory stockers, and so forth. The secondary market also includes increasing numbers of the lowest-level clerical jobs, those typing, filing, key-punching, and other positions that have become part of the large typing (or records-filing and retrieval or key-punching) pools. Finally, we must add migrant agricultural labor, seasonal employment required for the peak periods of planting and especially harvesting. Although other jobs such as part-time teaching or textile work in the South also fall into the secondary-market segment, the above categories contain the mass of secondary employment. . . .

What marks these jobs as secondary is the casual nature of the employment. The work almost never requires previous training or education beyond basic literacy. Few skills are required and few can be learned. Such jobs offer low pay and virtually no job security. They are, in other words, typically dead-end jobs, with few prospects for advancement and little reward for seniority in the form of either higher pay or a better job. With little incentive to stay, workers may move frequently, and turnover in these jobs tends to be high. The only thing that a worker brings to a secondary job is labor power; the worker is treated and paid accordingly.

From the research that has been done, it is possible to give some indication of the characteristics of secondary employment and of the order of magnitude of the differences between segments. All the studies whose results are reported below were based on samples of male workers, so caution is required if we are to generalize. Moreover, the studies employed quite different techniques for categorizing into segments, and the samples reflect quite different underlying populations. Nonetheless, the results seem impressively similar. Consider pay, for example. In Paul Osterman's study, secondary workers' annual earnings in 1967 averaged only 69 percent of the average earnings of primary workers. Martin Carnoy and Russell Rumberger found that secondary workers' annual earnings ($5,690 in 1970) averaged 70 percent of the mean annual earnings of independent primary workers. Samuel Rosenberg found that the average hourly wage in secondary jobs ranged from 78 to 84 percent of the average hourly wage in primary jobs, while average annual income of secondary workers fell between 74 to 80 percent of the average for primary workers. In David Gordon's original study, hourly pay and annual incomes in the secondary market averaged 86 percent of pay and income in the primary market. Robert Buchele, in what is probably the most careful study to date, did not use pay as a criterion for categorizing jobs; instead he looked at intrinsic characteristics of the work itself. He found that among white middle-aged males, secondary workers' annual earnings averaged 81 percent of the earnings of subordinate primary workers and between 53 and 76 percent of the earnings of independent primary workers.[10]

From all these studies it appears that the wages associated with secondary work range from two-thirds to four-fifths of the wages for primary jobs. The finding that secondary workers earn less than primary workers is hardly news, since having a low wage was frequently among the criteria defining secondary status in the first place. What this research does do, however, is indicate the extent of the wages differential, one of the job characteristics included in the cluster that defines the segment.

Similarly, we can consider job tenure. One way of measuring tenure differences is to compare job tenure rates among groups heavily represented in the primary market (essentially white males) with those in the secondary markets (teenagers, black males, black females, all females over 25). Leaving aside the necessarily low job tenure among all categories of teenagers, we find that white males starting at age 25 have consistently longer job tenure than members of any of the other groups and that the absolute gap increases with age. In 1968 among workers 50 to 54 years old, for example, white males had occupied their current jobs for 12.8 years, compared to only 6.2 years for women and 10.1 years for nonwhite males.[11] But this test is only indirect, since demographically defined groups must be used as proxies for market-segmented categories. A more direct test can be inferred from data reported by David Gordon, since his analysis places workers in primary or secondary jobs. Both first-job tenure and present-job tenure were significantly higher for primary than for secondary workers in his samples. In Robert Buchele's sample of middle-aged white males, workers in secondary jobs were found to have significantly lower tenure (11.3 years) than either subordinate primary workers (13.8 years) or independent primary supervisory workers (15.2 years).[12] Gordon's analysis of other measures of employment stability—weeks worked per year, whether or not the worker looked for work during the year, and several stability-related personal background variables (such as marital status, whether the worker was a head of household, years in labor force, and so on)—further supports the idea that employment stability constitutes a significant difference between segments. Similarly, Samuel Rosenberg found that when occupations were classified into secondary and primary markets, workers in primary jobs had greater seniority than secondary workers in all four of the cities he studied. These results offer confirmation of the results obtained from looking at tenure differences among demographically defined groups; secondary employment seems to be associated with much more frequent job changes.[13]

Yet, as Samuel Rosenberg has also argued, the average tenure even for secondary workers is several years, suggesting that at least some secondary workers stay at their jobs for relatively long periods and are not perpetual job-changers. Robert Buchele also found that secondary workers had relatively high tenure. These findings reinforce the view that it is the lack of job security and the ever-present possibility of immediate replacement by others from the reserve army that marks a secondary job. If some secondary workers (especially those studied by Doeringer and Piore) respond to this situation by choosing to change jobs frequently, others (those studied by Rosenberg and Buchele) assess their chances differently and remain at a single job. All secondary workers, however, experience the lack of job protection and the immediate possibility of replacement.[14]

Recent research has also helped flesh out other aspects of secondary employment. For example, Carnoy and Rumberger found definite evidence that secondary jobs are dead-end employment in the sense that additional experience does not lead to higher earnings. Thus, in their sample the age-wage profit—the curve showing how much wages rise with increasing age—is flat, showing no wage increase for black secondary workers from the worker's late twenties until about sixty years of age, and for white secondary workers until about fifty years of age (thereafter wages tend to fall); in contrast, primary workers' wages tend to rise substantially with age. This finding is reproduced in both Buchele's and Osterman's studies, where labor force experience (or age) contributes so little to earnings that it is statistically insignificant. And David Gordon found that among black males in the secondary market, the age-wage profile is entirely flat, while among primary workers, wages rise with age.[15]

Another characteristic of secondary jobs that is well supported in these studies is the small return to education. Buchele found that for workers with less than a high school education, there was a slight benefit for each year of schooling achieved, but secondary workers got no additional return for any further schooling, although occupational training did help. In Osterman's sample, the effect of education in increasing earnings was four to six times greater for primary workers than for secondary workers; in fact, the return that secondary workers obtained from an extra year of education was so slight that statistically we cannot be sure it is different from zero, and the findings applied to all secondary males, whether white or black. Similar results, though stronger for black secondary workers, were obtained by Gordon and by Carnoy and Rumberger.[16]

Thus, labor market research seems to bear out the conclusion that the secondary market is indeed a distinct market, characterized both by different market outcomes and different market processes. It contains low-paying jobs of casual labor, jobs that provide little employment security or stability and for which the links between one job a worker may hold and the next are slight. These are dead-end jobs offering little opportunity for advancement, requiring few skills, and promoting relatively high voluntary turnover. Neither seniority nor education seems to pay off. And since employers have little investment in matching workers and their jobs, they feel free to replace or dismiss workers as their labor needs change.

The Subordinate Primary Market

In contrast to the secondary jobs, primary jobs offer some job security, relatively stable employment, higher wages, and extensive linkages between successive jobs that the typical worker holds. While the particular mechanisms providing security and stability and the nature of the actual linkages differ between the two tiers of the primary market, all primary jobs share the characteristic of offering well-defined occupations, with established paths for advancement.

The subordinate and independent jobs diverge, however, because of other characteristics, and again no single dimension emerges from labor market behavior as the defining criterion. The subordinate primary market has within it both production and nonproduction jobs.[17] The biggest group includes the jobs of the traditional industrial working class—production jobs in the unionized mass-production industries: plant jobs in auto assembly, steelmaking, rubber and tire manufacturing, electrical products construction, farm implements production, machinery manufacture, metal fabrication, camera and other consumer products assembly, home appliance manufacture, and the like. The other large group of subordinate primary jobs includes the positions of unionized workers in lower-level sales, clerical, and administrative work, found mostly in the major retailing, utilities, and manufacturing corporations. Other subordinate primary jobs include the production-type positions in core firms in transportation (railroad engineers, interurban and transit system bus drivers, and airline maintenance personnel), in retailing and wholesaling (warehousemen) and in utilities and other sectors of the core economy.

These jobs are distinguished from the casual-labor jobs of the secondary market most fundamentally (though not invariably) by the presence of unions. The jobs are better-paying than secondary employment, and they generally involve long-term, stable work with prospects for advancement and some job guarantees. In the case of unionized workers, the steps for advancement and the employment guarantees are contained in union seniority clauses; for non-unionized workers, both the promotional paths and the guarantees are less clear and are based only on employer practices, but they do exist. These are permanent, rather than temporary or casual, jobs.

A recent study by Lawrence Kahn makes clear the role of unions in the subordinate primary market. Kahn studied longshoremen in San Francisco (where a militant union was established in the mid-1930s) and in New York (where no union existed). He found that the labor processes in New York and in San Francisco prior to the formation of the union were basically similar. The volume of work fluctuated with the more or less random arrival of ships to be unloaded and loaded; the work tasks themselves required great effort but little skill; and job conditions were often hazardous. Not surprisingly, a system of casual labor prevailed, with low wages, arbitrary hiring procedures that encouraged favoritism, and not only no job security but also the need to be rehired every day in the daily "shape-up." These secondary-market conditions persisted into the 1950s in New York, but in San Francisco they did not survive the 1930s. The International Longshoremen's Association led a series of strikes and job actions from 1934 to 1936 that effectively ended the old system by instituting a union-run hiring hall, preferential hiring for union members, regular hours, grievance machinery, substantially higher wages, and regulation of the work load. In short, the union forced the establishment of the subordinate primary pattern. This settlement became the model when workers organized elsewhere (New York in the 1950s).[18]

On the other side, subordinate primary jobs are distinguished from independent primary jobs in that their work tasks are repetitive, routinized, and subject to machine pacing. The skills required are learned rather quickly (within a few days or weeks), and they are often acquired on the job. The jobs provide little opportunity for workers to have any control over their own jobs.

The job ladders that link one job with subsequent ones in the same occupation may derive either from the employing firm (as is generally the case with nonproduction jobs) or from industrial union rules (for production jobs), but in either case they tend to be firm-specific. That is, the path for advancement almost always depends on seniority within the firm, and indeed such seniority becomes, in this internal labor market, the necessary admission ticket to the better-paying positions higher on the job ladder. Workers have a big incentive to remain with one employer, and they show markedly lower turnover rates than secondary workers.

This picture of subordinate primary employment has been substantially confirmed in some detailed research. In addition to the evidence already cited in our discussion of the secondary market (which shows the higher pay and greater tenure of primary workers), we also have evidence more particularly focused on subordinate primary jobs. Consider, for example, the economic return to age or experience—which is a statistical way to determine whether jobs are dead ends or whether they are part of a "career ladder." In the secondary market, as we saw, the lack of any return to age or experience meant that little advancement was possible within a job and that experience did not qualify the worker for a better job. But in subordinate primary employment, all this changes.

Subordinate primary jobs offer substantial returns to age and experience. According to Paul Osterman's results, for example, workers thirty-one years old earned about $1,150 less per year than those who were forty-one; in other words, the extra decade's experience raised the older workers' wages by roughly 18 percent. (By contrast, the average secondary worker would get only $218 more than a secondary worker with ten year's less experience, roughly a 4 percent raise.) Other studies have also reported large returns to experience.[19]

Similarly, schooling (at least through high school and the first few years of college), also seems to pay off for subordinate primary workers. Osterman found that each year of schooling gives the average subordinate primary worker a bonus of $459 per year, or more than a 6 percent raise. (Again, the best estimate of the return for a secondary worker is $76, a mere 1½ percent increase.) Buchele found that each of the first three years of college returned over $1,000 per year in higher income, although after that the return seems to fall off. Large returns to schooling for subordinate primary workers at least through high school, and for white males even beyond, were also reported by Carnoy and Rumberger.[20]

Subordinate primary jobs may carry with them substantial risks of unemployment, but the risks are of a quite different sort from those present in secondary jobs. Secondary workers face dismissal even during boom times for disciplinary or other arbitrary reasons, but subordinate primary workers usually enjoy at least some employment protection against such firings, most importantly through unions.[21] The main danger for subordinate primary workers comes from business depressions, since these workers have little protection against being laid off or furloughed when production exceeds demand. High rates of unemployment may prevail, as the experience of the 1970s demonstrates, but even in these circumstances subordinate primary workers face prospects different from those facing secondary workers. Subordinate primary workers are generally laid off in order of least seniority, so high seniority may insulate a worker from all but the most severe layoffs. Unlike secondary workers, who are simply dismissed and cut adrift when business gets bad, subordinate primary workers usually continue some association with their union, perhaps receive union-negotiated supplemental unemployment benefits, and can be called back to work in order of seniority when business picks up. A worker laid off at the auto plants remains an (unemployed) auto worker, rather than simply joining the ranks of the anonymous unemployed.

The subordinate primary market, then, contains the jobs of the old industrial working class, reinforced by the lower-level jobs of unionized clerical employees. In these routinized, typically machine-operative positions, workers find that by staying on the job ladder they can progress to significantly higher wages and perhaps to better jobs. Schooling also pays off, especially, it appears, at the level of high school and the first few years of college. Cyclical unemployment is a not-uncommon feature in subordinate primary work, particularly in production or blue-collar positions; but even during spells of layoffs, subordinate primary positions display their distinctiveness from secondary work by the continuing connections between laid-off workers and their jobs.

The Independent Primary Market

Jobs in the independent primary market, like jobs in the subordinate primary market, offer stable employment with considerable job security, established patterns of career progression, and relatively high pay. But they differ from subordinate primary jobs in that they typically involve general, rather than firm-specific, skills; they may have career ladders that imply movements between firms; they are not centered on operating machinery; they typically require skills obtained in advanced or specialized schooling; they often demand educational credentials; they are likely to have occupational or professional standards for performance; and they are likely to require independent initiative or self-pacing.

Three groups of jobs dominate the independent primary market.[22] The first fills the middle layers of the firm's employment structure and consists of jobs for long-term clerical, sales, and technical staff, foremen, bookkeepers, personal and specialized secretaries, supervisors, and so on. A second group of independent primary jobs grows out of craft work that employs electricians, carpenters, plumbers, steam-fitters, and machinists. A third large group of independent primary jobs includes the professional positions—accountants, research scientists, engineers, registered nurses and doctors, lawyers and tax specialists, and others. As the jobs in these three groups indicate, the independent primary market, like the other segments, spans both blue-collar and white-collar work.[23]

Another characteristic of the independent primary market is the greater role played by the public sector. For professional and technical workers in particular, the state's share of employment has steadily advanced over the last three decades, to the point where the state now employs between 35 and 45 percent of all professional and technical workers. Teachers, social welfare workers, nurses, doctors, other health professionals, accountants, lawyers, engineers, and others have been hired in great numbers to carry out the state's permanent new functions in welfare, warfare, and regulation. Overall, the state sector appears to account for between a fifth and a third of all independent primary employment.[24]

The average level of pay in independent primary jobs is, of course, significantly higher than in the other segments. In Robert Buchele's study, for example, mean annual earnings ranged from 106 percent to 152 percent of subordinate primary earnings. Paul Osterman's estimate, again for average annual earnings, was 172 percent. Martin Carnoy and Russell Rumberger found independent primary earnings to be 132 percent of subordinate primary earnings.[25]

Moreover, earnings in independent primary jobs show much greater increases in response to experience or age than in the other segments, confirming the existence of important promotional or career ladders linking prior employment with subsequent jobs. In Paul Osterman's study, workers thirty-two years old earned roughly $9,550 on average; workers identical in other characteristics but having the additional experience, seniority, or whatever is implied by being ten years older, received $12,808—a whopping $3,258 or 34 percent raise, as compared to 4 percent and 18 percent respectively for secondary and subordinate primary workers. Carnoy and Rumberger also found greater returns on age for this segment than for the other segments, especially for white males, and the seniority bonus extended longer—right up to the retirement age, in fact.[26]

Similarly, formal education plays a much greater role in independent primary jobs. In Paul Osterman's study, each year of schooling boosted the average worker's annual earnings by $1,224, nearly a 10 percent raise (compared to 1½ percent and 6 percent increases in secondary and subordinate primary workers' incomes). Large returns to schooling for independent primary workers show up in other studies as well; Buchele found that each year of schooling after college provided supervisory workers with an extra $3,000 in income. Large returns were present at other levels (especially college) as well, and for all categories of independent primary workers. Carnoy and Rumberger found equally large returns for educational attainment.[27]

Despite these similarities, independent primary jobs also differ from each other, and the differences are especially pronounced in the patterns of unemployment and in movement up the job ladder. For supervisory and other administrative employees, the future lies in sticking with the company; they have the highest "tenure in present jobs" of all workers, the lowest overall unemployment rate, the fewest spells of unemployment, the lowest probability of having quit their jobs, the lowest number of jobs held during a given year, the highest probability of having received company training, and a very low probability (second only to that of professional workers) of having been laid off. Moreover, they are the only workers for whom having more than thirty years' experience contributes positively to earnings. In short, supervisory work fosters long tenure and little voluntary turnover, and it carries slight risks of unemployment. Once in a supervisory job, a worker tends to stay.[28]

Professional and craft employment, on the other hand, tends to establish promotional paths through professional or craft standards as well as through employer-imposed job structures. The result is a pattern of job movement that, measured in terms of the number of moves, more clearly resembles the secondary market. For example, in Buchele's study, the "years of tenure in present job" for professional and craft workers (11.7 and 11.6 respectively) was comparable to that for secondary workers (11.3) and much less than that for either subordinate primary workers (13.8) or independent primary supervisory workers (15.2). Similarly, the probability of having quit in any year and the average number of jobs held during the year were considerably higher for professional and craft workers than for other independent primary workers or for subordinate primary workers, and closest to statistics for secondary workers.[29]

But while the extent of job switching in professional and craft work approaches that in secondary jobs, its meaning is quite different. When workers change jobs in the secondary market, their moves generally do not lead to any advancement or any natural next jobs, and so secondary workers follow the random pattern of job switching described earlier. In professional or craft work, job changes mean movement from one employer to another but still within the occupational job ladders. The fact that professional workers earn a substantial return to experience through the first nineteen or so years of working, while secondary workers get no return, means that when professional workers move to new jobs and gain experience, they continue to increase their earnings.[30]

For craft workers, job switching does not imply progress (like secondary workers, craft workers get little return [from] greater experience), but it serves as a method for continuing employment in occupations that pay a premium (30 percent in Buchele's sample) over casual labor.

Increased voluntary turnover creates the statistical effect of higher unemployment rates, and so (in Buchele's study, for example) professional workers have a higher overall unemployment rate than supervisory workers, despite a *lower* probability of being laid off. In craft work, however, it is clear that involuntary unemployment looms much larger than in other independent primary jobs, or indeed in any other work. Craft workers suffer nearly as many spells of unemployment, a higher overall unemployment rate, and a much greater chance of being laid off than even secondary workers. Yet like subordinate primary workers (who, when unemployed, retain ties to their jobs, their unions, and their occupations while they wait to be recalled), craft workers have an even stronger bond to their occupation and, when laid off, remain (unemployed) craft workers rather than simply joining the ranks of those looking for any kind of work. Moreover, despite their higher unemployment rates, craft workers on average continue to earn substantially higher annual incomes than secondary workers.[31]

Independent primary jobs, then, constitute the third market segment. Like other primary jobs, independent primary employment creates well-defined occupations with job ladders and established patterns of movement between jobs. The jobs in this segment are skilled jobs, requiring relatively high levels of schooling or advanced training. As Michael Piore has noted, formal education (or craft union membership or licensing) is an essential requisite for employment; while educational requirements are often not taken seriously in the other segments and are more or less rigorously enforced depending on how tight the labor market is, in independent primary jobs the credentials become nearly absolute requirements for entry. Large returns accrue to both additional schooling and experience. Independent primary jobs, especially the professional and craft positions, have professional or occupational standards that govern performance, and so mobility and turnover tend to be both high and associated with advancement. Except for craft work, these jobs carry slight overall chances of layoffs. Most strikingly, all independent primary jobs foster occupational consciousness; that is, they provide the basis for job-holders to define their own identities in terms of their particular occupation.

Systems of Control and the Three Labor Markets

If, as this research suggests, the labor market is segmented into three parts, what forces account for the division? I have already suggested that market behavior itself cannot answer this question. After all, labor markets are but mechanisms bringing employers' needs for productive labor together with the available supplies of workers. Unless a high degree of market power exists (an implausible assumption for labor markets), labor markets constitute a means of mediation; they reflect the underlying forces in production and in the laboring population.

Racial and sexual discrimination provide one set of forces leading to labor market segmentation. Blacks and women were pushed into particular race- or sex-stereotyped jobs, jobs that were consistent with the broader social evaluation of each group. Blacks were hired into the dirtiest, most physically demanding, and lowest-skilled occupations, while women were pushed toward "helping" occupations, especially clerical work. Moreover, both groups, especially blacks, were intentionally recruited for particular occupations as a way for management to divide and thereby rule the firm's workforce. Blacks and women had little bargaining power and few alternate job possibilities, facts which ensured that their work would remain low-paying and with few job rights.

Intentional discrimination remains important, but increasingly it has been supplanted by institutional discrimination. And institutional discrimination, in addition to appearing in the form of segregated schooling and culturally biased tests, occurs through segmented labor markets. Thus, in probing the causes of segmented labor markets, we seek in part to understand how racial discrimination and sexual discrimination have become incorporated in the institutional processes of labor markets.

But the analysis of the preceding chapters provides yet another key to the origins of segmented labor markets; let me state it baldly before introducing the necessary qualifications. Labor markets are segmented because they express a historical segmentation of the labor process; specifically, a distinct system of control inside the firm underlies each of the three market segments. The secondary labor market is the market expression of workplaces organized according to simple control. The subordinate primary market contains those workplaces (workers and jobs) under the "mixed" system of technical control and unions. And the independent primary market reflects bureaucratically controlled labor processes. Thus, the fundamental basis for division into three segments is to be found in the workplace, not in the labor market; so to define the three market segments we now have a single criterion—the type of control system—rather than simply a cluster of market behavior characteristics.[32]

It should be clear that the relationship between types of control and labor market segments is not perfect or exhaustive. Anomalies appear and, more importantly, development occurs such that any static typology can never adequately capture all the transitional and developmental situations. The accompanying chart [see page 74] asserts that most jobs are concentrated in the diagonal cells (numbered I, II, and III) and that the off-diagonal cells are of minor importance. Yet certainly some jobs fall in the off-diagonal cells, and examples are listed in the chart. Nonetheless, the corresponding (diagonal) types of control and labor market segments appear to be poles of great magnetic force, attracting the majority of jobs.[33]

The system-of-control approach leads to a somewhat different understanding of the role of job skills, schooling, on-the-job training, experience, and other technical characteristics of labor. These characteristics are usually thought to create different types of labor (and so they do), and therefore to be the basis themselves of different treatment in the labor market. The relevance of these technical attributes, even their preeminence in certain cases, cannot be denied. However, the analysis presented here suggests that it is the system of control that creates the context within which experience, training, schooling, skills, and other attributes assume their importance. Rather than ignoring the technical relations of production, such an approach emphasizes that considerable choice surrounds the selection of any productive technique. In most industries, a range of techniques is already available. Even in those production processes where little choice exists, the decision whether to use high-skill or low-skill labor, for example, essentially depends on whether the firm finds it profitable to undertake the research and development necessary to convert high-skill production to low-skill production.[34] Whether it is profitable depends in turn not only on the relative wage costs but also on the rate at which labor power is transformed into labor— that is, on the organization of the labor process itself. Thus, the reason experience and schooling are unimportant for explaining secondary workers' incomes but are crucial for explaining subordinate primary workers' incomes derives not

The Correspondence between Systems of Control and Labor Market Segments for Sample Jobs

Market Segment (Jobs)	System of Control		
	Simple Control	Technical Control	Bureaucratic Control
Secondary	I. • Small manufacturing jobs • Service jobs • Retail sales •Temporary and typing-pool office work	Southern textile jobs	Part-time academic jobs
Subordinate primary	Unionized garment workers	II. • Jobs in auto and steel plants • Assembly-line production work • Machine-paced clerical work	Personal secretary jobs
Independent primary	Jobs in small consulting firms	Technicians' jobs monitoring chemicals production	III. • Jobs at IBM, Polaroid • Craft work • Nonproduction staff jobs

so much from invariant differences in the nature of the products being produced and in the accompanying inherent skill requirements as from the consistently different ways of organizing the labor process. Secondary work is organized so as to minimize the need for experience and schooling, whereas subordinate primary work is organized so as to build upon these factors. The technical processes of production place certain limits on the range of organizational possibilities, of course, but in practice these limits tend to provide considerable flexibility.[35]

This perspective, then, leads us to investigate the relationship between the labor process and labor markets. Indeed, structural forms of control (technical control and bureaucratic control) emerged out of the core firm's attempts to turn the tide of conflict on the shop and office floor decisively in its favor, and these efforts carried implications (not always foreseen) for the way the core firm's workforce would be recruited, paid, and reproduced.

Technical control at first seemed to require no alteration in the way the firm obtained its labor. Indeed, the early days of the Ford plants appeared to provide capitalists with that happy prospect of the unification of the potency of the reserve army outside the plant walls and the rigid internal discipline of technical control inside. Turnover was extremely high—certainly as high as in the secondary market today—and job security was nil.

Technical control united with secondary market-type casual labor lasted until the great CIO organizing drives of the 1930s. The success of the auto workers, steelworkers, electrical workers, rubberworkers, and others in building industrial unions doomed that combination and put in its place the configuration represented by cell II in the chart, technical control inside the firm matched with primary labor market–type job security, stability, and (through union seniority) promotional prospects. This configuration has characterized the traditional mass-production industries throughout the postwar period.

In effect, the agreement that was worked out amounted to the establishment of an internal labor market. An internal market is simply a set of procedures contained wholly within the firm for performing the functions of the external market: the allocation and pricing of labor. Unions, as at U.S. Steel, for example, won for their members the rights to fill vacancies based on seniority and to have outside hiring done only at lower-paying, entry-level jobs. Union scales governed each job's pay.

Technical control, then, does not directly require primary market job rights, and the relation between them is not invariable. Certainly, the advantages of technical control and casual labor markets have motivated the corporations' investments in Brazil, South Korea, and other repressive countries where workers cannot establish unions or win job rights. Similarly, the attempt by core firms (most conspicuously GM) to move production facilities to the South indicates that at least some employers think that old-time benefits of technical control and secondary labor are possible even within the United States. GM may have thought it could horn in on the turf of J.P. Stevens and other textile manufacturers, who long ago discovered that technical control and nonunion labor were possible because of the South's peculiar blend of antiunion law and local custom.

Yet what was possible for an isolated textile industry does not appear possible generally. GM has experienced its first successful union drive in its southern plants, and even J.P. Stevens is the target of a growing union struggle. The AFL-CIO has targeted the whole South as the arena for its first serious organizing efforts in many years. The unions have pushed labor law reform primarily to overcome the tactics of antiunion southern employers like Stevens. Local organizations, like those in North Carolina organized around the brown-lung dangers of the cotton mills, create incipient possibilities for militant resistance. Such efforts are still in their early stages and victory is by no means inevitable, yet they indicate that firms like GM and others will most likely be denied the advantages of technical control and secondary labor.

Technical control in the core firms brings unionization in its wake, and through unionization, the characteristics of primary-market employment.[36] Here seniority provisions and other union contract rules govern the allocation of workers to jobs, the wages to be paid, the relative vulnerability to layoff, and the protections and appeals from discipline and dismissal. The middle cell of the chart, then, must be understood as possessing the labor market characteristics that have emerged from a historic compromise—a bargain between core firms and industrial unions that leaves the management of the business in the employers' hands but guarantees to workers primary-market job rights.

Bureaucratic control also moved the firm out of secondary-market employment, not because of any compromise with workers but rather due to employers' efforts to avoid the need for such compromise. Bureaucratic control reversed the first-resort dependence on reserve-army discipline, and firms intentionally put in its place the greater job security, promotion prospects, and assumption of long-term employment that characterize primary-market jobs. But more than eliminating secondary employment, bureaucratic control pushed the firm specifically toward independent primary employment, with its emphasis on occupational or professional standards, incentives for identifying with the job, importance of schooling, and high return for experience. In the first place, bureaucratic control emerged out of those workplaces that tended to employ educated workers: the offices, shops, and labs of the white-collar staff, technical and professional workers, and so on. It was natural, then, that the new form of control, based on exploiting status differences among workers, should focus upon differences in the attainment of schooling and make them central to translating the workplace hierarchy into usable labor-market hiring criteria. This happy correspondence can be seen in the eagerness with which early employers seized upon educational credentials as convenient (and legitimizing) ways of screening workers, and the diligence with which educational reformers have sought to remold schools to fit the changing demands of work.[37]

More directly, the way bureaucratic control functions tends to require and reinforce independent primary patterns. For example, Polaroid, like other bureaucratically controlled firms, establishes promotion ladders and an internal market. New workers are recruited from the external labor market only for the bottom-rung jobs, the entry-level jobs within each skill category. Polaroid's job ladder for engineers is as follows:

Job Title	Years of Experience
Associate Engineer	0 – 2
Engineer	2 – 5
Senior Engineer	4 – 10
Principal Engineer	10 – 18
Senior Principal Engineer	over 15

When a vacancy occurs, Polaroid engineers can bid for the job. The actual decision is based in part on applicants' experience, which in practice means seniority gained while in Polaroid's employ. But, in addition, for all but the bottom-rung jobs on each ladder, the applicants' work records and recommendations from company supervisors, as well as formal training and skills, determine who gets promoted to the various openings.

Thus with regard to recruiting and reproducing the firm's workforce, bureaucratic organization operates as an internal labor market. As such, it must accommodate two quite different market processes: it must select, from among all workers, those who will be appropriate for bureaucratically controlled work; then it must allocate the selected workers, over the course of their careers, to higher-paying jobs through internal market mechanisms. In the context of bureaucratic control both of these tasks tend to foster independent primary employment patterns.[38]

Bureaucratic control, then, moves the firm toward independent primary employment patterns. It establishes the apparatus for the employer's model (rather than the compromise version) of the internal labor market, and it creates the incentives for high tenure, the importance of schooling, occupational consciousness, and the other characteristics of independent primary employment. The advantage for employers is simply the greater flexibility they enjoy in instituting productivity-enhancing internal market procedures.

If technical control leads to subordinate primary employment and bureaucratic control to an independent primary market, simple control results in secondary-type jobs; in this case, both the labor process and the accompanying labor market are distinguished by the *lack* of elaborate structural or institutional features. The essence of simple control, in either its entrepreneurial or hierarchical form, is the arbitrary power of foremen and supervisors to direct work, to monitor performance, and to discipline or reward workers. Almost by definition, the workers in such a system can have little job security. More subtly, the absence of a structurally based control system provides little avenue or incentive for worker promotion, so secondary jobs turn into dead ends.

Secondary employers generally do not have the scale, the volume of profits, or the stability to make the long-term commitments necessary to establish primary-market employment. For example, guarantees of employment security and benefits and privileges rising with seniority typically require contractual obligations extending considerably into the future.[39] Similarly, the administrative apparatus associated with formal periodic review of workers' performance, grievance appeals, and the like, requires a further long-term commitment of resources. The core firm, with its huge scale and extensive market power, plans for the long-term in all its operations, including the organization of its labor force; the periphery firm cannot.

The result of the great changes in work organization inside core firms, then, has been reflected in a corresponding change in labor markets. Systems of control in the core firms now differ from those in the firms of the competitive periphery, and in turn labor markets have become segmented. The different systems of control are not the only force pushing toward labor segmentation, but they surely are one of the most important.[40] This view of the aggregate job structure leads directly to an analysis of the labor force—that is, to the parts or fractions of the working class.

Notes

1. In each period there have been pressures toward both homogenization and segmentation, as, for example, capitalists played upon ethnic divisions in the last century to break up working class solidarity, and they have integrated black auto workers into the mainstream white male labor force in this century. But the dominant trend in the last century was homogenization, and, in this century, redivision.

2. Similarly, utility companies as monopolists segment their service markets, selling at different rates to residential and commercial buyers, thereby achieving higher profits than they could attain by selling to all at the same rate.

3. See R. Edwards, M. Reich, and D. Gordon (1975) and D. Gordon, R. Edwards, and M. Reich (forthcoming). This chapter owes much to that joint work. In describing different segments as separate markets, we are, of course, simultaneously specifying a certain level of analysis—that of the internal structure of the working class. Seen from a higher level of abstraction—the relation between working class and capitalist class, for example—the differences among the segments do not appear so great. For example, one of the central differences to emerge is the greater employment security of primary workers, especially independent primary workers, in contrast to secondary workers. Yet in capitalist society *all* workers are dependent upon capital for their employment, and while some workers have relatively greater guarantees than others of not being fired, no workers have complete job security, a truth some highly paid managers learned in the last recession when they lost their jobs. The analysis that follows, then, is aimed at understanding the composition and development of the working class and its sources of heterogeneity, rather than at suggesting the emergence of new classes.

4. Neoclassical economists, especially human capital theorists, remain committed to their ideal of the individual as economic agent. They have not been able to square this view with the facts, however, and sex and race continue to be important explanations in wage or income analysis; see, for example, Zvi Griliches and William Mason (1972).

5. Michael Piore (1969); Barry Bluestone (1970); Barry Bluestone, et al. (1973); David Gordon (1971); Peter Doeringer and Michael Piore (1971). For a different argument making much the same point, see Paul Sweezy (1972).

6. David Gordon (1971), Chapter 4. The variables are quite diverse, including monetary and status measures, demographic variables, education and training indexes, employment stability measures, industry and job characteristics variables, migration measures, labor market search variables, occupational mobility variables, and attitudinal scales Gordon's analysis was based on the two-segment or dual-market model.

7. Paul Osterman (1975, p. 513), for example, arbitrarily classified jobs as secondary if, as dual-market theory suggested, they were "characterized by low wages, instability of employment, and similar factors." By comparing the factors explaining wage variation *within* the secondary and primary segments, he was able to show that the "wage-setting process does differ substantially [between] the segments." Similarly, Martin Carnoy and Russell Rumberger (1975, p. 53) studied data for 1965 and 1970. After dividing jobs into market segments according to various dual-market characteristics (training required, job-holder's relation to other people during work, and so on), they compared the processes generating various market outcomes: mobility between and within segments, the return to

education and seniority within segments, and so forth. Their research concluded that the relationships among education, work experience, earnings, and other variables differed significantly between segments. Robert Buchele (1976), in a careful study of middle-aged white males, discovered large differences between the market segments in annual earnings, likelihood of unemployment, and eight other labor market outcomes. More than that, however, he showed that a large proportion of each of these differences could not be explained by "human capital" variables (education, experience), and that the differences in fact resulted from segmented markets themselves. See, in addition to the essays cited above and in Note 5, Barry Bluestone (1974); David Gordon (1972a, b); Samuel Rosenberg (1975); Lawrence Kahn (1975); Francine Blau (1975); Michael Piore (1975); Martin Carnoy and Russell Rumberger (1975); Bennett Harrison (1972); and Edna Bonacich (1976). For dissenting views, see Paul Andrisani (1973), Michael Wachter (1974), and Glen Cain (1976).

8. The most careful estimates of the overall size of each segment in the national labor force will be published by David Gordon (forthcoming), and the one-quarter to one-third estimates given in the text for each segment are compatible with his preliminary results. Harry Braverman's (1974, pp. 379, 403–404) discussion can be interpreted as placing the combined secondary and subordinate primary workforce at two-thirds to three-quarters and the independent primary at over 15 but less than 20 percent of the total labor force. Erik Wright (1976, p. 37) would seem to estimate the former (combined) group at 40 to 50 percent, the latter at 25 to 37 percent. Martin Carnoy and Russell Rumberger (1975, Tables 2 and 3) estimate the relative sizes (not allowing for self-employed) of the segments as secondary, 17 percent; subordinate primary, 47 percent; independent primary, 36 percent.

9. Analytically, it seemed essential to find clear differences among segments on one or two fundamental dimensions, in order to provide an objective and replicable method of determining market boundaries. Yet early attempts to develop such "definitional" dimensions (Richard C. Edwards, 1975b) fell short of the mark. Moreover, the anecdotal evidence suggested that such definition would be artificial and the resulting categories would not represent what was actually being observed. Below it is suggested that such a criterion does exist, but that it is a characteristic of the labor process, not of labor markets. This point has caused much confusion among those who have written on segmentation, because as they searched for a clean and decisive criterion for dividing occupations and/or workers, they have understandably come to different conclusions. Similarly, the critics of segmentation theory have criticized the approach for its failure to come up with a market dimension as a clear means of division. But such a criterion is impossible, since the market segments but reflect divisions in the "sphere of production," and so we must look to the labor process for the roots of segmented markets. At the level of labor markets, then, the segments appear as clusters of characteristics, and *at the level of labor market analysis* we cannot choose any particular determining dimension.

10. Calculated from Paul Osterman (1975), p. 516. Martin Carnoy and Russell Rumberger (1975), Table 16. Calculated from Samuel Rosenberg (1975), Tables 3-11 and 3-12. The range for annual incomes was lower than the range for hourly wages because secondary workers on average are employed for fewer weeks per year. Calculated from David Gordon (1971), p. 385. Calculated from Robert Buchele (1976), Table 23. Whenever Buchele's results are reported below, his occupational classes 1 to 3 (professional, supervisory, and craft jobs) are cited as "independent-primary," his class 4 (subordinate) as "subordinate-primary," and his class 5 (menial) as "secondary." His sample is the National Longitudinal Survey Pre-Retirement Years data.

11. *Monthly Labor Review*, September, 1969, p. 18, Table 1.

12. Robert Buchele (1976), Table 22; occupational classes 1 (professional) and 3

(craft) had tenure rates comparable to secondary workers, as Michael Piore (1975), among others, had hypothesized.

13. David Gordon (1971), Samuel Rosenberg (1975), Table 3-10.

14. In Buchele's study, for example, the lower tenure rate among secondary workers *cannot* be attributed to less workforce experience or less education, since, after correcting for these factors, a large difference remains; Robert Buchele (1976), Table 22.

15. Martin Carnoy and Russell Rumberger (1975), pp. 40–41. Robert Buchele (1976), Table 23; Paul Osterman (1975), Tables 4, 5, and 6. David Gordon (1971), pp. 416–418. Gordon did find that among white secondary males there is a return on age, but he notes that this effect may well be due to younger whites moving out of the secondary market. This interpretation is strengthened by evidence that white males begin employment in the secondary market (during college and before deciding on a career), but then move on to primary jobs with experience; see Samuel Rosenberg (1975), Table 5-1.

16. Robert Buchele (1976), Table 23. Paul Osterman (1975), Tables 4, 5, and 6. David Gordon (1971), Table V-6; Martin Carnoy and Russell Rumberger (1975), pp. 41–42.

17. Perhaps at one time "blue-collar" was an effective shorthand term for this market segment, but as many observers (David Gordon, 1972b; Paul Osterman, 1975; Harry Braverman, 1974) have noted, the blue- versus white-collar distinction has lost most of its persuasiveness. For one thing, many blue-collar jobs have achieved the pay, independence, mental labor components, and privileges formerly associated with white-collar status; more significantly, the machine-pacing, low pay, lack of privileges, and manual-labor job activities formerly thought to characterize only blue-collar employment have increasingly come to dominate at least the lower rungs of white-collar jobs. The old distinctions, which may well have been inaccurate for the past, become positively mystifying for the present, hence the need for new categories.

18. Lawrence Kahn (1975), Chapter III. In New York, organized-crime figures dominated the longshoremen's union, and the 1950s reorganization of work followed the (temporary) breaking of their corrupting grip.

19. Calculated from Paul Osterman (1975), Tables 2 and 4. The earnings-generating function in Osterman's study, as is usual, contains a single term for schooling but a quadratic term (age and age squared) for age or experience. This form implies that every year of schooling is of equal benefit to any other year, but that the return on age is different at different ages. Hence in calculating the age return, we must always specify a particular age interval (the intervals cited in the text are always for the mean-minus-ten-years to the mean age or experience. See also David Gordon (1971), Tables V-6 and V-7, especially for white males; Martin Carnoy and Russell Rumberger (1975), Tables 16 and 17 and pp. 41–44. Robert Buchele (1976, Table 23) did not find a significant experience return.

20. Calculated from Paul Osterman (1975), Tables 2 and 4; Robert Buchele (1976), Table 23; Martin Carnoy and Russell Rumberger (1975), Tables 16 and 17.

21. This characteristic shows up strongly in Robert Buchele's analysis (1976, Tables 6, 7, 9, 18, and 20) of the probability of having been laid off. Craft workers had the highest probability, but subordinate workers in Buchele's sample experienced a probability even higher than secondary workers. Similarly, craft workers and subordinate primary workers suffered a higher overall unemployment rate than secondary workers. However, when the data are corrected for employment by core versus periphery firm (as should have been done in *defining* market segments), the secondary-market peripheral-firm worker has a substantially higher overall unemployment rate, frequency of unemployment, and probability of having been laid off than subordinate primary-market core-firm workers.

22. The relative size of these three occupational groups is subject to some dispute. For

example, in Robert Buchele's (1976, Table 3) sample, craft work was the largest category; however, his inclusion of auto mechanics, repairmen, and electrical technicians—workers with few craft protections—inflates the size of his craft category.

23. Because a research focus on the primary market is more recent, less agreement exists as to who should be included in the independent primary segment. Michael Piore (1975), for example, leaves out craft workers; Robert Buchele (1976) treats professional, supervisory, and craft workers as three distinct "occupational classes."

24. Various estimates exist of the importance of public jobs in the independent primary market, and the only real point of consensus is that the biggest impact occurs in the professional occupations. Martin Carnoy and Russell Rumberger (1975), Tables 5 to 8, put the figure at slightly over 20 percent, an estimate that seems to coincide with that given by Robert Buchele (1976), Table 3.

25. Calculated from Robert Buchele (1976), Table 23; Paul Osterman (1975), Table 2; Martin Carnoy and Russell Rumberger (1975), Table 16.

26. Calculated from Paul Osterman (1975), Tables 2 and 4 and Martin Carnoy and Russell Rumberger (1975), Tables 16 and 17. For black males, the return to age may be greater in the subordinate primary sector, but their sample of black independent primary workers is very small. Robert Buchele (1976, Table 23) found a positive return for professional employees during the first nineteen years of experience, and a positive return for supervisory employers who had more than thirty years experience; other experience returns for independent primary workers were insignificantly different from zero.

27. Calculated from Paul Osterman (1975), Tables 2 and 4; Robert Buchele (1976), Table 23, Martin Carnoy and Russell Rumberger (1975), Tables 16 and 17.

28. Robert Buchele (1976), Tables 6, 7, 9 to 13, and 23; the coefficient—the best estimate—for "more than 30 years' experience" is positive but not statistically significantly different from zero. The coefficients for the other categories of independent workers are negative.

29. Robert Buchele (1976), Tables 6, 7 and 9 to 13.

30. Ibid., Table 23.

31. Ibid., Tables 6, 7, 9, and 23.

32. The observation that each market segment seems to have a characteristic form of organizing work associated with it is not new. Michael Piore (1970, pp. 55, 57), for instance, has described discipline in secondary jobs as "harsh and often arbitrary" and has observed that "reward and punishment in the [secondary] workplace are continually based upon personal relationships between worker and supervisor."

Yet earlier observers focused only on markets and specifically on the pathology of secondary employment (in contrast to what was seen as the more normal patterns of primary work); as a result, the relationship between organization in the labor process and patterns in labor markets appeared to be *ad hoc,* and the emergence of the secondary market was without historical reasons or rationale. Arbitrary control became but one more of the characteristics in the cluster that defined the secondary market. Instead, as the analysis here shows, it is the primary markets that have emerged as new on the scene, and their appearance is a direct product of the internal transformation of the core firm.

33. The secondary market includes periphery-sector manufacturing firms that have made increasing use of technical or mechanical methods of control, especially time and motion study and machine-pacing of individual jobs. These firms in general still retain simple control (arbitrary power of foremen and supervisors) as their basic organization of power, reinforced by these mechanical means; most revealingly, the enforcement of machine paces is achieved through bullying and other personal tactics aimed at the worker. Nonetheless, the peripheral sector (containing all enterprises except core firms) displays great diversity, and so do its workplaces.

34. For one interesting and persuasive study of the impact of type of organization on the importance of experience, see Paul Ryan's (1977) study of the welders at a Quincy, Massachusetts shipyard. For an excellent description of the process of transforming high-skill production into low-skill production, drawing evidence from a broad range of industries, see Harry Braverman (1974), Parts II and IV.

35. In the human capital version, only the technical characteristics matter, and they do not give rise to distinct markets but rather simply to different market outcomes because of people's different endowments of human capital; see Jacob Mincer (1974). In the dual labor market version, general versus specific skills, on-the-job learning versus lack of it, and so on become the causes of market segmentation; see Peter Doeringer and Michael Piore (1971). The statement here is equivalent to saying that within the range of possible techniques, there is sufficient choice to permit selection based on compatibility with different forms of work organization. The firm's choice cannot be described as "efficient," since this concept cannot be defined once we admit the distinction between labor and labor power, but it certainly is the most profitable.

36. Note that the success of industrial unions in pushing mass-production core firms to subordinate primary-employment patterns does not in general derive from their ability to exclude other workers; instead, the unions' power derives from their ability to mobilize all those in the industry. In this sense segmentation results from the struggle over control of the labor process rather than through market exclusion.

37. See Loren Baritz (1960); Ivar Berg (1971); and Samuel Bowles and Herbert Gintis (1975).

38. We can see how these two processes foster independent-primary employment. . . . Consider first the independent-primary characteristic of long tenure. Bureaucratic control relies on directing tasks by means of work criteria, and its incentive system is based on periodic evaluation and institutionalized rewards through promotion. All of these components presuppose lengthy employment for their functioning and their effect. At the lowest levels, employers try to screen out workers who show up for work irregularly, have high turnover, and manifest the other unstable work characteristics dysfunctional for bureaucratic employment. . . . [W]ork at these levels is organized and controlled through explicit rules and well-developed and routinized procedures. Workers who do not follow the rules are penalized by no advancement and, perhaps, eventual dismissal. Central to this method of work direction is an incentive structure that rewards workers who obey these rules and who work reliably and dependably.

For new workers, explicit rules are the principal work criteria, and new workers are in a sense on probation, while they learn the rules and demonstrate that they have mastered proper rules orientation; hence, workers in low-level jobs find that learning to follow rules is a necessary trait for keeping one's job and for gaining the supervisor's approval.

The importance of rules orientation in predicting supervisors' ratings in the lower-level jobs seems to capture the importance of this trait in the first process (in distinguishing inappropriate or nonindependent primary-type workers); in this process the supervisor's evaluation is crucial. On the other hand, rules orientation was found to be insignificant in predicting pay differences in these jobs. This result is consistent with its insignificance in predicting either supervisors' ratings or pay in higher-level jobs: rules orientation is simply not important in the second internal-market process (allocating workers).

At higher levels in the hierarchy, the second process becomes the basis for the reward structure. The organization of work at these levels depends more on implicit rules, expectations, and self-motivation or self-control. Obeying rules by itself is insufficient here and is neither highly rewarded within a group nor used as the basis for advancement to or through the higher levels. Instead, access to and success in these levels is predicated on developing reliable and dependable work habits and (especially) an outlook similar to that of the higher-echelon management of the enterprise—in a sense, on becoming an "organization person." This conclusion is suggested by our finding that the trait "habits of dependability and predictability" was rewarded at middle levels and the "internalization of enterprise's goals" trait was most highly rewarded at higher levels. Importantly, the latter trait is the most significant one for achieving higher pay; the [internalization] trait appears to be the path to advancement. Indeed, all three modes of compliance might well be interpreted as successively more sophisticated stages of accepting and internalizing the firm's goals.

The effect of this mode of control on job tenure should be clear. Consider the problem the firm has when hiring a worker who is new to that firm. The employer cannot easily determine whether or not this worker has those behavior traits they find important in their workers. Despite millions of dollars and forty years of research, no psychological test exists that can be given to new workers to predict job success reasonably well. So personnel managers use psychological tests that admittedly predict very little; they fall back on educational credentials as screening devices on the (not unwarranted but imprecise) assumption that diligence at work depends on the same characteristics as success in schooling (see Richard C. Edwards, 1977; Samuel Bowles, Herbert Gintis, and Peter Meyer, 1975; and Samuel Bowles and Herbert Gintis, 1973); and they rely heavily on recommendations from previous employers and on the applicant's work record, though it is usually difficult to evaluate the context of previous work experience. But in the final analysis, the firm can only learn whether a worker has the appropriate traits through a long process of actual experience with the worker on the job, and to do so it must keep workers long enough to make its assessment.

Similarly, when the firm attempts to fill its higher slots with workers who are predictable and dependable and have internalized the enterprise's goals, no simple tests, no demonstration or certification of skills can suffice. Again, the only sure test is the firm's own experience with the worker as its employee, the record of which is its file of supervisors' evaluations of the worker's performance. Bureaucratic control again fosters long tenure.

Another independent-primary characteristic that grows out of bureaucratic control is the "occupational consciousness" of independent primary workers. As indicated in the last chapter, bureaucratic control directly reinforces identifying with the job and internalizing the firm's goals. These behaviors among supervisors and middle-layer workers typically produce an overall identification with the firm itself, as the worker's occupation becomes indistinct from employment with the firm. Among craft or professional workers, with the reinforcing weight of craft tradition or professional association, the bureaucratic incentives typically produce a strong identification with the worker's occupation. In all three cases, bureaucratic control fosters the strong sense of identity with one's work.

39. Viewed from the worker's perspective, such obligations seem less permanent, since they can be jettisoned through bankruptcy proceedings or lost through company mergers, and many workers experience the loss of retirement benefits despite contractual rights. Nonetheless, for the small company, such measures, while eagerly accepted *in extremis*, are naturally not viewed as normal ways to run a profitable business.

40. Other sources are racism and sexism, the conscious efforts of employers to split the working class, and more diverse "cultural" factors involving family structure and schooling. See David Gordon, Richard Edwards, and Michael Reich (forthcoming).

References

Andrisani, Paul. *An Empirical Analysis of the Dual Labor Market Theory.* Unpublished Ph.D. thesis, Ohio State University, Columbus, 1973.

Baritz, Loren. *The Servants of Power.* Middletown, Conn.: Wesleyan University Press, 1966.

Berg, Ivar. *Education and Jobs: The Great Training Robbery.* Boston: Beacon Press, 1971.

Blau, Francine. *Pay Differentials and Differences in the Distribution of Employment of Male and Female Office Workers.* Unpublished Ph.D. thesis, Harvard University, Cambridge, Mass., 1975.

Bluestone, Barry. *The Tripartite Economy: Labor Markets and the Working Poor. Poverty and Human Resources,* July–August, 1970.

———. "The Personal Earnings Distribution: Individual and Institutional Determinants." Unpublished Ph.D. thesis, University of Michigan, Ann Arbor, 1974.

———; Murphy, William M.; and Stevenson, Mary. *Low Wages and the Working Poor.* Ann Arbor, Mich.: The Institute of Labor and Industrial Relations, 1973.

Bonacich, Edna. "Advanced Capitalism and Black/White Race Relations in the United States: A Split Labor Market Interpretation." *American Sociological Review,* 1976.

Bowles, Samuel and Gintis, Herbert. "I.Q. in the United States Class Structure." *Social Policy,* January–February, 1973.

———. *Schooling in Capitalist America.* New York: Basic Books, 1975.

———, and Meyer, Peter. "Education and Personal Development: The Long Shadow of Work." *Berkeley Journal of Sociology,* Fall, 1975.

Braverman, Harry. *Labor and Monopoly Capital.* New York: Monthly Review Press, 1974.

Buchele, Robert. *Jobs and Workers: A Labor Market Segmentation Perspective on the Work Experience of Middle-Aged Men.* Unpublished paper submitted to the Secretary of Labor's Conference on the National Longitudinal Survey of the Pre-Retirement Years, Boston, 1976.

Cain, Glen. "The Challenge of Segmented Labor Market Theories to Orthodox Theory: A Survey." *Journal of Economic Literature,* December, 1976.

Carnoy, Martin and Rumberger, Russell. *Segmented Labor Markets: Some Empirical Forays.* Palo Alto, Calif.: Center for Economic Studies, 1975.

Doeringer, Peter and Piore, Michael, *Internal Labor Markets and Manpower Analysis.* Lexington, Mass.: D.C. Heath, Lexington Books, 1971.

Edwards, Richard C. "The Social Relations of Production in the Firm and Labor Market Structure." *Politics and Society,* 1975.

———. "Personal Traits and 'Success' in Schooling and Work." *Educational and Psychological Measurement,* Spring, 1977.

———; Reich, Michael; and Gordon, David, eds. *Labor Market Segmentation.* Lexington, Mass.: D.C. Heath, 1975.

Gordon, David. *Class, Productivity, and the Ghetto: A Study of Labor Market Stratification.* Unpublished Ph.D. thesis, Harvard University, 1971.

———. *Theories of Poverty and Underemployment.* Lexington, Mass.: D.C. Heath, Lexington Books, 1972a.

———. "From Steam Whistles to Coffee Breaks." *Dissent,* Winter, 1972b.

———. "Methodological and Empirical Issues in the Theory of Labor Market Segmentation." Forthcoming.

———; Edwards, Richard C.; and Reich, Michael. "Labor Market Segmentation in American Capitalism." Forthcoming.

Griliches, Zvi and Mason, William. "Education, Income and Ability," *Journal of Political Economy,* May–June, 1972.

Harrison, Bennett. *Education, Training, and the Urban Ghetto.* Baltimore: Johns Hopkins Press, 1972.

Kahn, Lawrence. *Unions and Labor Market Segmentation.* Unpublished Ph.D. thesis, University of California, Berkeley, 1975.

Mincer, Jacob. *Schooling, Experience and Earnings.* New York: Columbia University Press, 1974.

Osterman, Paul. "An Empirical Study of Labor Market Segmentation." *Journal of Industrial and Labor Relations,* 1975.

Piore, Michael. "On-the-Job Training in the Dual Labor Market." In *Public-Private Manpower Policies* by Arnold Weber et al. Madison, Wisc., Industrial Relations Research Association, 1969.

————. "Manpower Policy." In *The State and the Poor,* by S. Beer and R. Barringer. Cambridge, Mass.: Winthrop Publishing Company, 1970.

————. "Notes for a Theory of Labor Market Stratification." In *Labor Market Segmentation,* by Richard C. Edwards, Michael Reich, and David Gordon. Lexington, Mass.: D.C. Heath, 1975.

Rosenberg, Samuel. *The Dual Labor Market: Its Existence and Consequences.* Unpublished Ph.D. thesis, University of California, Berkeley, 1975.

Ryan, Paul. *Job Training.* Unpublished Ph.D. thesis, Harvard University, 1977.

Sweezy, Paul. "Marx and the Proletariat." In *Modern Capitalism and Other Essays,* by Paul Sweezy, New York: Monthly Review Press, 1972.

Wachter, Michael. "Primary and Secondary Labor Markets: A Critique of the Dual Approach," *Brookings Papers on Economic Activity,* 1974.

Wright, Erik. "Class Boundaries in Advanced Capitalist Societies." *New Left Review,* July–August, 1976.

3

Losing Touch

The Cultural Conditions of Worker Accommodation and Resistance

Stephen A. Marglin

1. Introduction

This chapter continues a series of enquiries (Marglin 1974, 1979, 1984) which have focused on the role of profitability and capitalist class interest, as distinct from efficiency[1] in shaping the organization of work. At issue here is the workers' side of the story, specifically the cultural underpinnings of resistance and accommodation to the capitalists' project of domination.

The argument is built up from several separate propositions. The first is that cultural variables are central to the outcome of conflict over the organization of work. What people value, how they know—both systems of values and systems of knowledge—affect whether, how, and with what degree of commitment people will defend themselves and their work against the capitalist (or the commissar, for that matter). Indeed, this chapter, although it assumes the importance of class struggle in determining the organization of work, asserts equally strongly that the parameters of class are determined by cultural values. Even class itself is not born of economics alone, but of the union of economic interest and cultural justification. Classes act in history only when they are armed and legitimized by cultural values which are generally and widely held throughout the society. And culture not only empowers, it sets limits to class conflict. People struggle only to the extent that their common cultural heritage permits of different interpretations.

Reprinted by permission from *Dominating Knowledge: Development, Culture, and Resistance,* ed. Frédérique Apffel Marglin and Stephen A. Marglin (Oxford, England: Clarendon Press, 1990), pp. 217–225, 231–37, 243–53, and 277–82.

The first concrete application of this idea is that the tenacity with which workers defend their work arrangements depends on the meaning that they attach to their work. This meaning can take one of two forms, *holistic* or *individualistic*. Holistic meaning attaches significance to one's work because it is an integral part of a whole which commands the allegiance and assent of the community; *individualistic* meaning, by contrast, is a significance that one creates oneself through work.

The preconditions of holistic and individualistic meaning differ. Holistic meaning requires that work be embedded in the cultural fabric, that it be an expression of one's relationship to the cosmos rather than simply a matter of earning one's daily bread. Individualistic meaning requires that one be in control of process and product, without which the very project of *creating* meaning becomes unthinkable.

The problem for workers has been twofold, for Western culture fosters neither holistic nor individualistic meaning for most forms of work. First, the Judaeo-Christian and the Greek traditions disembed most work from a context that might make it meaningful. Second, starting with Plato and Aristotle, one system of knowledge has become hegemonic. The problem is that workers' knowledge is generally organized in terms of other, "inferior" systems, with the result that it becomes the inferior knowledge of inferior people. The culture thus undermines workers' attempts to defend their control of work.

These arguments are developed in the sections that follow. After a sketch of the relevant background (Sections 2–4), we shall turn to the main ideas, the disembeddedness of work (Section 5) and the devaluation of workers' knowledge systems (Sections 6–10) in the West. Sections 11–13 highlight these ideas by contrasting the conception of work in Hindu culture as revealed by a case-study of a weaving community.

2. Meaning—Holistic and Individual

Work is, and undoubtedly will remain, a core element in establishing a sense of purpose and accomplishment, a sense of significance for one's entire life. Even to speak of the meaning of work is therefore necessarily to speak of the meaning of life, and to oppose the nihilism of Macbeth ("[Life] . . . is a tale/Told by an idiot, full of sound and fury,/Signifying nothing") or the utilitarianism of Freud ("What decides the purpose of life is the . . . pleasure principle" [1961: 23]).

Notwithstanding the scepticism, and indeed downright hostility, of the modern, secular West to any attempt to invest life with meaning—"human presumptuousness" Freud called it (1961: 22)—human beings expend considerable energy to disprove Macbeth. Our loves, our friendships, our relations with parents and children, *our work*, are at least partially a function of a deep-seated drive to make our lives signify something. Certainly Freud's pleasure principle falls well short of explaining attitudes towards work and love, which Freud himself is supposed to have made the measure of successful psychological adjustment.

Social organization may facilitate or hinder the search for meaning. In non-individualistic, "holistic" societies, the meaning of work is a cultural given, but this is the case only exceptionally in individualistic societies. When one is part of a "cause"—the last one which commanded broad allegiance in the United States was the cause of defeating Germany and Japan during World War II—it is much like being part of the effort to build a cathedral in the non-individualistic Middle Ages: the particular job can be subordinated to the whole and derive its meaning from the meaning of the whole.

But the general situation of modern individualistic society is that there is no such transcendent cause. Instead, one must be both playwright and leading actor; we each must create our meaning both through the roles we write for ourselves and the way we act them. Doubtless it was much easier when parts in the theatre of life were socially given, and all one had to do was to interpret one's part.

There are thus two kinds of meaning that attach to work, or perhaps it is more accurate to speak of two separate paths through which work feeds into the meaning people attach to human existence. The first is a *holistic* meaning, with significance and purpose assigned to work by the common consent of the community. The glory of God or the defence of democracy, or for that matter the construction of socialism, all exemplify transcendent causes that have invested work with meaning at some places and times.

The second form of meaning is *individualistic,* a significance and purpose that the worker herself creates and asserts through her work. "Symbolic immortality," to borrow a term from Robert Jay Lifton (1983: 21), "something to point to" in the words of a steelworker whose story is the preface to Studs Terkel's *Working* (1972).[2] The achievements of work, more than the result of any other activity we undertake, give us grounds for believing that we might transcend our physical mortality, a belief already implicit in holistic meaning.

Control over process and product becomes central to any discussion of the meaning of work once we recognize the absence of a holistic meaning in contemporary Western society. For control is a necessary, if hardly sufficient, condition for investing one's work with individualistic meaning. But individual or even collective control by workers clashes with the capitalist project of domination. The central proposition of my first paper on work organization (Marglin 1974) was that two crucial steps in the history of work—the extension of the division of labour at the subproduct level and the concentration of production in factories—were instituted by capitalists in order to enhance their control. Subsequent papers (Marglin 1979, 1984) have been variations on the theme of control.[3]

3. The Division of Labour and the Rise of the Factory

Let me now briefly recapitulate the role of the division of labour in the perspective of control. My "enemy" is evidently Adam Smith, for whom the efficiency of a highly developed division of labour was the starting-point of economic analysis. Indeed, Smith is commonly given credit for "discovering" the division of labour. There is some justice in this, for certainly nobody before Smith (and, with the exception of Durkheim, nobody since) has made the division of labour so central to his argument. But the credit should be for emphasis, not discovery. The Greeks anticipated Smith in all important respects, down to the size of the market as the main factor limiting the division of labour (Xenophon). Plato went one better than Smith. In the *Republic,* the putative efficiency of the *economic* division of labour is the basis of the argument for a *political* division of labour. The chief drawback of democracy is precisely that everybody does everything, a defect which Plato's own blueprint of a specialized political caste was supposed to remedy.

Neither Smith nor the Greeks distinguished between the division of labour at the product level and the division of labour at the subproduct level, the division of labour *between* workshops and the division of labour *within* the workshop. Both were seen as reflecting only efficiency considerations, the second being simply an extension of the first as the size of the market becomes large enough to warrant further specialization.

Karl Marx perceived an important difference once the division of labour ruled within the workshop as well as without: the division of labour at the subproduct level, the technical or detailed division of labour in Marx's terminology, makes the worker dependent on the capitalist. By contrast, the division of labour at the product level, the social division of labour, in no way presupposes the capitalist as integrator of the production process.

In the main, however, Marx followed Smith in invoking efficiency to explain the extension of the division of labour from the social to the technical level. The increased dependence of the workman on the boss was simply the unfortunate by-product. In this respect I differ from Marx; I argue that what Marx understood to be a by-product was in fact intentional.

The problem of the capitalist, as seen in my perspective, is to maintain a position for himself in the production process. Sometimes an adequate position is made possible by high capital requirements and indivisibilities, which put the activity beyond the reach of the individual workman or even of an association of workmen. Coal-mines and shipyards and even Arkwright's spinning mill come to mind as examples. But these are, I believe, the exceptions rather than the rule.

In the general case indivisibilities and associated capital requirements are not sufficient to maintain a position for the capitalist in the production process. Here, I have argued (Marglin 1974), the capitalist maintains his role by specializing workers to particular tasks, reserving to himself a critical task, frequently the task of integrating the separate operations into a marketable product. This allows him to stand between the workers and the product market, obliging the workers to sell their labour power rather than the product of their labour. Robert Cookson, a British woollen manufacturer in the period of the industrial revolution, succinctly put the essential point to a parliamentary committee: "Suppose a man goes into a room and is confined in a room where there are twelve, thirteen, or fourteen looms, how is that man to be proficient in any part of the business [other] than that?" (*Report from the Select Committee to Consider the State of Woollen Manufacture in England,* British Parliamentary Papers (1806), I, p. 74. Quoted in Morris 1972.) Lest the committee harbour any doubts about his meaning, Cookson answered his own question: "People trained up in a manufactory are never likely to set up for themselves."

Thus, division of labour at the subproduct level, or more accurately, specialization at the subproduct level, became an instrument of capitalist control. Even if less efficient than alternative forms of work organization in which the worker exercised more control, a highly developed division of labour would enhance the capitalist's control over the production process and increase his profits.

Specialization ensured the dependence of the worker on the capitalist, but it did not get him to work. The problem of discipline was of course not a new one. Xenophon in the fourth century BC, Columella in the first century AD, Walter of Henley and other medieval writers, addressed the problem of worker discipline, anticipating such thoroughly modern ideas as incentive systems (Columella) and even time and motion studies (Walter). But at the time of the industrial revolution the legal freedom of the workers compounded the problem of discipline. The worker laboured primarily under economic rather than political compulsion, and the market was not much help.

Capitalists consistently complained about the perversity of the labour market. Higher wages, instead of coaxing out more effort, served only to reduce the worker's dependence, to the point that one eighteenth-century observer noted "the sentiment universal" among cotton manufacturers "that their best friend is high provisions" (Arthur Young 1770). A little later, the same observer put the point in somewhat stronger terms: "every one but an idiot knows that the lower classes must be kept poor, or they will never be industrious" (quoted in Thompson 1963: 358).

The putting-out system made matters worse: in his own cottage the worker had control of raw materials and set the pace of his work. His control over raw materials led to endless squabbles over product quality as well as over embezzlement and fraud. (The worker was in a position to substitute inferior goods; give short weight; put "wastes" to his own, rather than the boss's profit.) Control over the pace of work increased the possibilities for perverse—from the boss's point of view—responses to the incentive of higher wages.

No wonder that capitalists sought ways of limiting workers' control: organizational forms in which the boss, not the worker, fixed the hours and intensity of work, and where the worker would labour under the eye of a boss so that the fringe benefits (the worker's view of fraud and embezzlement) that accrued from control of raw materials would be harder to come by. The end result of this search was the factory.

This is not to suggest that efficiency considerations (in the sense of note 1) played no role in the rise of the factory. Indeed, in some industries, such as cotton textiles, efficiency considerations may have been very important. The transition from cottage to factory in cotton appears to have been predicated on the greater efficiency of the water-mill and steam-engine and the associated technical compulsion to centralization. Boilers could not be practically adapted to the dispersed production of the putting-out system.

But two aspects of the transition from cottage to factory make it difficult to accept the proposition that efficiency considerations were generally decisive. On the one hand, the transition from cottage to factory also took place without the appreciable change in technology that accompanied the shift in cotton spinning and weaving. Woollen textiles are a case in point: the first woollen mills did not make use of water- or steam-based technologies, but utilized the same hand-powered technologies that workers had in their own homes. On the other hand, where workers were sufficiently powerful and motivated to resist factory organization, as in the case of the Coventry silk ribbon weavers, they were able to adapt steam-powered technologies to their own purposes. In Coventry, weavers "rented" capital from capitalists: the capitalist's steam-engine powered a shaft that ran through the lofts of a row of attached houses, the lofts being the workshops in which the weavers' looms were located (Prest 1960).

The existence of industries like woollens in which factories arose without any technological innovation argues against the *necessity* of a technological basis for the factory. The existence of non-factory forms of organization around a new technology like steam, as deployed by the Coventry ribbon weavers, argues against the *sufficiency* of a technological explanation.

4. The Evolution of Production Relations

The subproduct division of labour and the factory were of course neither the beginning nor the end of capitalist innovation in the organization of work. Capitalists established their dominance over production only gradually; even in the late nineteenth century, workers—at least some of them—exercised substantial control over important aspects of work which would today, in the United States at least, be regarded as "management prerogatives": for example, hiring and firing of assistants, setting work rules, and distributing the workers' share of the pie (Montgomery 1979, Buttrick 1952).

The basis of this control was twofold. First, the working class maintained a cohesion reflected in strikes and other forms of mutual support. Second, knowledge and skills were carefully cultivated and protected from outsiders—particularly from the boss and his agents. "The boss's brains," according to a popular aphorism of a hundred years ago, "are under the worker's cap." In the words of Frederick Winslow Taylor, the father of scientific management,

> foremen and superintendents know better than anyone else, that their own knowledge and personal skill fall far short of the combined knowledge and

dexterity of all the workmen under them. The most experienced managers therefore frankly place before their workmen the problem of doing the work in the best and most economical way (1967: 32).

To consolidate and extend their dominance over production, capitalists had a double task, first to break the solidarity of the workers and, second, to restructure production so as to reduce to a minimum the role of worker's knowledge and skills. The destruction of solidarity focused on transforming the orientation of the trade-union movement to "business unionism," with a narrow focus on the dollar and an almost total abdication from issues of control. The role of confrontations, of which the Pullman and Homestead strikes are representative US examples, was central to this process. These were setbacks from which the labour movement took decades to recover.

In the restructuring of work key steps were the development of what Richard Edwards (1979) has labelled *technical* and *bureaucratic* control, symbolized by the assembly line and the rule book. Both were attempts to depersonalize authority relations, to legitimize capitalist control by appealing to the shared cultural value of the superiority of impersonal to personal relations (Banuri 1990, Chapter 3). The intention of both technical and bureaucratic control was to create and foster the impression of a transcendent authority—the assembly line or the rule book—to which all, boss and worker alike, are subject. What the capitalist forgets to mention is that somebody makes the rules, just as somebody sets the speed of the line.

The capitalist project of reorganizing work was epitomized by scientific management, or "Taylorism" as it is sometimes called in honour of its principal founding father, whose description of the traditional, "pre-scientific," state of affairs was earlier quoted at length. Contrasting his proposal with traditional systems of organizing production, Taylor (1967) had this to say:

> Under scientific management . . . the managers assume . . . the burden of gathering together all of the traditional knowledge which in the past has been possessed by the workmen and then of classifying, tabulating, and reducing this knowledge to rules, laws, and formulae (p. 36). These replace the judgment of the individual workman (p. 37). Thus all of the planning which under the old system was done by the workman, as a result of his personal experience, must of necessity under the new system be done by management in accordance with the law of the science (p. 38).

Scientific management has been the subject of considerable controversy. Even the degree to which it has succeeded in eliminating the worker as a thinking participant in the production process is controversial. My own view is that friend and foe alike have misread Taylor's project as accomplished fact.[4] There is however no gainsaying the considerable success achieved by capital in carrying through the larger project of which scientific management was a part, that of

both reorganizing the workplace and channelling the expression of worker opposition into "bread and butter" issues of pay and employment security.

It has been emphasized that these changes could not be brought about by
unilateral fiat on the part of capital. They were rather the outcome of struggle, in
which both resistance and accommodation played important parts. But notwithstanding protracted and sometimes heroic resistance, the fact is that accommodation predominated.

There are many reasons for this. Capitalists wielded disproportionate power,
politically as well as economically. Capitalism also delivered the goods, to use
Herbert Marcuse's (1966) apt phrase; the restructuring both of work and of the
field of resistance took place during a period of rapid growth of real wages. This
is well known and needs no elaboration.

What is less well understood is the cultural dimension of class struggle. Indeed, a premise of this chapter is that classes do not act in history until they are
armed by culture, as culture normally finds expression in setting the terms of
class conflict. Resistance to oppression, like oppression itself, is invariably the
union of class interest with cultural justification. The accommodation of the
working class to capitalist domination can only be comprehended when we
understand the limits of the cultural basis for working-class resistance.

My thesis is that the capitalist class held the high ground not only economically and politically, but culturally as well. For, on the one hand, work was never
embedded in the life of the Western community and the Western cosmic order,
as it is in holistic societies. (Lutheran Protestantism and the communities coming
under its sway present an exception that tests this rule.) Neither was the worker
empowered by culture to defend the union of conceptualization and execution
which underpins control by the individual worker. So the worker was unable to
find the holistic meaning immanent in embedded work and he was discouraged
by cultural values which he shared with the capitalist from defending the conditions of individualistic meaning.

. . .

6. Knowledge Systems: Techne and Episteme

The disembeddedness of work means that a defense against the capitalist project
of assuming control of process and product could not be based on the cultural
significance of the worker's activity, on its *holistic* meaning.

But what if cloth-making or gun-making or wheel-making had the personal
significance for the weaver or the gunsmith or the wheelwright that teaching and
research have for the university professor? What if the same possibilities for
investing work with *individualistic* meaning were perceived in the first set of
occupations as in the second? Is it not plausible that the prerequisites of meaningful work would have been defended more passionately? The premise of the

argument that will be made in this section is that workers' accommodation to the capitalist project of controlling work was facilitated by the shared cultural assumptions of workers and capitalists which devalued the worker's efforts. Specifically, it will be argued, first, that a basis of workers' control of the production process was a system of knowledge that intimately linked conception and execution; and, second, that this system of knowledge was implicitly regarded—by workers and capitalists alike—as inferior to the knowledge system which capitalists used to restructure production so as to separate conception from execution, the better to bring execution under their control.

Scientific management provides a useful and important text for examining this argument, and the cultural values at issue are once again deeply rooted in Western culture. But before we attempt to read the text or explore its roots, we require much more clarity concerning what is meant by the notion of a *system* of knowledge. "Knowledge system" has by now come to have a fairly wide currency, frequently being associated with French structuralists and post-structuralists of the ilk of Claude Levi-Strauss and Michel Foucault. But the concept is used too idiosyncratically to have a standard meaning to which one can refer.

Knowledge system here is used to characterize different ways of knowing in terms of four characteristics: epistemology, transmission, innovation, and power. *Epistemology* is the first issue: how do we know what we know? Every system of knowledge has its own theory of knowledge, that is, its own theory of what counts as knowledge. *Transmission* is closely related to epistemology. How do we go about distributing and receiving knowledge? *Innovation* refers to the process of change: how does the content of what we (collectively) know get modified over time? Finally, *power:* what are the political relationships between members of a community who make use, in greater or lesser measure, of the same system of knowledge? And how does a particular knowledge community relate to other knowledge communities?

The point of the term *system* is twofold. Its first purpose is to suggest that epistemology, transmission, innovation, and power are not attributes of knowledge in general but characteristics of particular ways of knowing. There is no single epistemology, but specific epistemologies which belong to distinct ways of knowing. Equally there are distinctive ways of transmitting and modifying knowledge over time. And different ways of knowing imply different power relationships among the people who share knowledge and between "insiders" and "outsiders."

The *links* among these several characteristics are a second systematic aspect of knowledge. How we know and how we learn and teach, how we innovate and how we relate to power—these characteristics of knowledge mutually interact, as well as interacting with the basic constructions that underlie each particular way of knowing.

All this may become clearer if we concretise the discussion in terms of distinct knowledge systems which I shall call *techne* and *episteme*. It should be explained that the Greek terms are intended to evoke rather than to define; *techne* and *episteme* will be defined, not by (approximate) English equivalents of the Greek, but by a series of oppositions.

On the one hand, *episteme* is knowledge based on *logical deduction from self-evident first principles.* The best model is perhaps Euclidean geometry, though Euclid's axioms have turned out with the passage of time to be less self-evident than had once been supposed—we now have a variety of geometries each with its own axiomatic basis. "Logical deduction" implies proceeding by small steps with nothing left out, nothing left to chance or to the imagination. Besides the mathematical theorem, the computer program comes to mind as a model of epistemic knowledge.

Epistemic knowledge is *analytic.* It decomposes, breaks down, a body of knowledge into its components. It is thus directly and immediately reproducible. It is fully *articulate,* and within *episteme* it may be said that what cannot be articulated does not even count as knowledge.

Episteme lays claims to *universality,* to being applicable at all times and places to all questions. Indeed adherents of *episteme* do not in general see it as one system of knowledge among many, but as knowledge pure and simple.

Epistemic knowledge is purely *cerebral.* Mind is separate from body, and *episteme* pertains to the mind alone. The statement "I feel there is something wrong with what you are saying," which is to say "I sense something is wrong, but I cannot articulate what or why," has no place within *episteme.*

Even when pressed into action, *episteme* is *theoretical.* Once the tentative and provisional nature of any axiomatic scheme is recognized, epistemic statements are necessarily hypotheses. Indeed, without entering into the nuances of the debate between Karl Popper (1968) and his critics (Kuhn 1970; Lakatos 1970; Putnam 1974) it can be said that *episteme* is geared one way or another to *verification.* Its very procedure, the insistence on small steps that follow immediately and directly upon one another, precludes discovery and creativity. To discover or to create through *episteme* would be like the proverbial monkey typing Shakespeare: he might some day do it, but we would be hard pressed to find the wheat among the chaff.

Finally, *episteme* is *impersonal* knowledge. Like the Christian God (Romans 2: II), *episteme* is impartial; it is in principle accessible to all on equal terms. It is thus not only theoretical knowledge, it is theoretical knowledge of theoretical equals. By contrast, like the Christian faith, *episteme* not only distinguishes those within from those outside the knowledge community; as Christianity denies the possibility of salvation to unbelievers, *episteme disenfranchises* those outside. From the universalistic claim of *episteme* it is an easy and direct step to the view that those lacking in *episteme* are lacking in knowledge itself. Table 3.1 opposes these attributes of *episteme* to corresponding attributes of *techne.*

In contrast with the basis of *episteme* in logical deduction from self-evident axioms, the bases of *techne* are as varied as the *authority* of recognized masters

Table 3.1

Corresponding Attributes of *Episteme* and *Techne*

Episteme	*Techne*
Logical deduction/Self-evident axioms	Intuition/Authority
Analytic	Indecomposable
Articulate	Implicit
Universal	Contextual
Cerebral	Tactile/Emotional
Theoretical	Practical
Verification	Discovery/Creativity
Impersonal	Personal
Egalitarian internally/Hierarchical externally	Hierarchical internally/Pluralistic externally

to one's own *intuition.* Opposed to the small steps of *episteme* are both received doctrine and the imaginative leaps which all at once enable one to fit the jigsaw puzzle together. It is in either case a knowledge of the whole, difficult to break down into parts. In contrast with the analytic nature of *episteme, techne* is *indecomposable.*

Possessors of *techne* often find it impossible to articulate their knowledge. They are generally aware that they possess special knowledge, but their knowledge is *implicit* rather than explicit. It is revealed in production of cloth or creation of a painting or performance of a ritual, not in manuals for weavers, artists, or priests.

Technic knowledge makes no claims to universality. It is specialized in nature and closely allied to time and place. It always exists for a particular purpose at hand; *techne* is *contextual.*

Techne belies the mind/body dualism which is basic to *episteme.* Under *techne* one knows with and through one's hands and eyes and heart as well as with one's head. *Techne* is knowledge which gives due weight to what Martha Nussbaum and Amartya Sen (1989: 316) have called the "cognitive role of the emotions" as well as to the knowledge of touch. Feeling, in both senses of the term, is central to *techne; techne* is at once both *tactile* and *emotional.*

Techne is intensely *practical,* to the point that, as has been suggested, it reveals itself only through practice. This is not to deny the existence of an underlying theory, but the theory is implicit rather than explicit, not necessarily available, perhaps not even usually available, to practitioners.

Technic knowledge is geared to *creation* and *discovery* rather than to verification. Even a mathematical theorem is largely the product of *techne,* although the proof must, by the very requirements of the knowledge system on which mathematics is based, be cast in terms of *episteme.*

Finally, where *episteme* is impersonal, *techne* is not and cannot be. It normally exists in networks of relationships and cannot be transmitted or even maintained apart from these relationships. The normal avenues of transmission— parent-child, master-apprentice, *guru-shisha*—are intensely *personal*. . . .

These are not normally relationships among equals. There is a hierarchy blending age, power, and knowledge. But it should be observed that the hierarchy is typically linear rather than pyramidal, as wide at the top as at the base. Thus those at the bottom have a reasonable expectation (though no guarantee) of moving up to the top with the passage of time. It is the hierarchy of the guild, where every apprentice can expect to be a master, not that of the factory, where few workers can become foremen, let alone executives.[5]

If *techne* is internally hierarchical, it is more open externally. Laying no claim to universality, recognizing limits of time, place, and purpose, *techne* does not inherently subordinate those outside a particular community of knowledge to those inside the community. *Techne* may not be inherently egalitarian in terms of its external relations, but it is at least *pluralistic*.

In terms of the four characteristics that have been proposed to distinguish knowledge systems, the differences between *episteme* and *techne* are striking. *Episteme* recognizes as knowledge only that which is derived by the rules of logic from axioms acceptable as self-evident first principles. *Techne* by contrast recognizes a variety of avenues to knowledge, from authority to immediate experience: the test of knowledge is practical efficacy.

The transmission mechanisms are as different as the epistemologies. Epistemic knowledge in principle is accessible through pure ratiocination, but in practice, *episteme* is generally acquired through formal schooling. Indeed knowledge in the West has more and more come to be equated with what is taught in the schools, and the schools in general are dedicated to *episteme,*[6] so much so that a young friend suggested opposing book knowledge and street knowledge in place of the opposition between *episteme* and *techne*. The canonical way of transmitting *techne* is, as has been indicated, through a personal nexus epitomized by the master-apprentice relationship. The master's example more than any precept instructs the apprentice, who absorbs almost unconsciously what he is taught. Almost anybody can acquire the rudiments of a craft in this way, but quality is a matter of intuition, of a heightened sense of touch and feel developed through years of practice.

Epistemic innovation leads a double life. The formal model allows one only to replace an erroneous logical derivation with a correct one or to change the assumptions. One can supplement existing axioms, or, more rarely, replace existing axioms by new ones, as Newton did for his predecessors and Einstein did for Newton. With new axioms one can proceed to new theorems by old methods: the new theorems are simply logical entailments of the new assumptions. In practice, as has been noted, a considerable admixture of *techne* is involved even in epistemic innovation: the innovator has to know where he is going and the map is provided by his intuition rather than his logic. Technic innovation is largely a matter of trial and error. This is not to say it is haphazard, but the underlying structure of technic innovation, like the *techne* it modifies, is often hidden from the innovator himself.

If knowledge is a text, the canonical form of epistemic innovation is *criticism.* Innovation takes the form of a direct assault, a challenge to logic or to first principles themselves. The canonical form of technic innovation, by contrast, is *commentary,* emendation and explanation of the text. The authority of the fathers is not challenged but reinterpreted. For this reason, epistemic innovation can flourish only in a community of equals, where respect for personal authority is relatively attenuated. The attacks of Peter Abelard on the doctrinal authority of popes and saints presupposed that in the West even religious knowledge had, by the year AD 1100, come to be regarded as epistemic in nature.

Episteme and *techne* reverse internal and external power relations. As has been noted, *episteme* assumes a community of equals, whose superior knowledge makes them collectively and individually superior to those outside. *Techne,* by contrast, presupposes a hierarchy of knowledge and a corresponding hierarchy of power within the knowledge community. But the community as a whole can relate in different ways to other communities. According to context, it can be more knowledgeable, and hence wield greater power, or less knowledgeable and correspondingly weaker.

It will be recognized that *episteme* and *techne* are ideal types. *Episteme* comes close to what many mean by science, and "science" is indeed one of the words used to translate the Greek. ("Knowledge" is another translation, which suggests that the claims of *episteme* to universality are long-standing.) *Techne* is more difficult to pin down. As the root indicates, it contains elements of "technique"; "art," one translation of *techne,* conveys some of its flavour. But contemporary scholarship glosses both *episteme* and *techne* as "science," a translation perhaps more congenial to my purposes in its emphasis on the common field of these terms (see Nussbaum 1986: 444). In any case an opposition between "science" and "art" would unduly and prematurely constrain the meaning of these terms, and the very openness of the Greek terms (to those of us who would claim to be largely innocent of classical Greek) has much to commend it at this stage of our proceedings.

. . .

7. Techne and Episteme in Production:
The Wheelwright's Shop

Though practical knowledge invariably combines the two systems, workers' knowledge has traditionally been organized much more in terms of *techne* than in terms of *episteme.* The extent to which *techne* predominates is well illustrated by George Sturt's account of wheelwrights and their work in a small town in Victorian England. Sturt's account was first published in 1923 and has been reprinted ten times since, its enduring popularity a tribute to Sturt's ability to evoke the quality of work and life in a place and time both nearby and far away.

Sturt was a disciple of Ruskin, under whose influence "I felt that man's only decent occupation was in handicraft" (Sturt 1923: 12). Unfortunately, although the son and grandson of master wheelwrights, Sturt had not learned the wheelwright's trade as a young man, a lack he was to regret after his father's terminal illness obliged him in 1884 to abandon the village schoolhouse, where he had been a teacher, for the wheelwright's shop, where for the next third of a century he was to be the proprietor.

Even allowing for Sturt's Ruskinian predilections, his description of the shop is arresting:

> Reasoned science for us did not exist . . . eye and hand were left to their own cleverness . . . A good wheelwright knew by art but not by reasoning the proportion to keep between spokes and felloes; and so too a good smith knew how tight a two-and-a-half inch tyre should be made for a five foot wheel and how tight for a four-foot, and so on. He felt it in his bones. It was a perception with him. But there was no science in it; no reasoning. Every detail stood by itself, and had to be learnt by trial and error or by tradition.
> . . . it was years before I understood why a cart wheel needed a certain convexity . . . none of [the men], any more than myself could have explained why it had to be so (pp. 19–20).

Equally arresting is the power that knowledge gave the worker:

> . . . I have known old-fashioned workmen refuse to use likely-looking timber because they held it to be unfit for the job.
> And they knew. The skilled workman was the final judge. Under the plane (it is little used now) or under the axe (it is all but obsolete) timber disclosed qualities hardly to be found otherwise. My own eyes know because my own hands have felt, but I cannot teach an outsider, the difference between ash that is "tough as whipcord," and ash that is "frow as a carrot," or "doaty," or "biscuity." In oak, in beech, these differences are equally plain, yet only to those who have been initiated by practical work (p. 24).

All the elements of *techne* are present. The emphasis on touch and feel, trial and error, and tradition: "My own eyes know because my own hands have felt. . . . " The knowledge that cannot be articulated: "but I cannot teach an outsider. . . . "

Tradition and rule of thumb come before understanding. Sturt indeed spends an entire chapter (ch. 18) explaining "dish," the convexity necessary for a proper wheel to which the extensive quotation above alludes. Sturt emphasizes that wheelwrights—that he himself—was putting dish into wheels long before he understood why. For the men, that their fathers had built wheels this way was reason enough. Only "intellectuals" like himself felt it necessary to epistemise the lore of wheel and wagon construction. As Sturt wrote in another context, "No rule of or scale of foreway was known in my shop, but wheelwrights of great experience could get the right effect by exercising their judgment on it" (p. 137).

Sturt's summary deserves to be quoted at length:

> The nature of this knowledge should be noted. It was set out in no book. It was not scientific. I never met a man who professed other than an empirical acquaintance with the waggon builder's lore . . .
>
> In a farm yard, in tap room, at market, the details were discussed over and over again; they were gathered together for remembrance in village workshop . . . the whole body of knowledge was a mystery, a piece of folk knowledge, residing in the folk collectively, but never wholly in any individual (pp. 73–4).

Sturt must have been aware of the irony. Having lived far enough into the twentieth century to see a world which had no further use for the wheelwright's *techne,* Sturt sought to preserve this *techne* by recasting it as *episteme:* one almost feels capable of crafting an entire wagon after reading *The Wheelwright's Shop,* but undoubtedly this is the spell of Sturt's *techne*—as author rather than wheelwright.

The automobile must bear final responsibility for the demise of the wheelwright's craft, but even before the automobile, innovations in the technology of wheel manufacture had combined with the extension of the market wrought by the railway to change the business environment in which Sturt and others like him operated. Moreover, the production relations of Sturt's shop had a dynamic of their own, which nicely illustrates the power relations that inhere in *techne.*

Long before the advent of the automobile, Sturt began a saga of innovation, one that started from disillusionment. Within a few years of taking over from his father, Sturt abandoned Ruskin:

> I realized how impossible it would be to carry out any of the Ruskinian notions, any of the fantastic dreams of profit sharing, with which I started. The men in the shop, eaten up with petty jealousies, would not have made any ideals work at all (p. 200).

Sturt did not spare himself. He, as well as the men, was to blame: "under my ignorant management, the men had grown not so much lazy as leisurely" (p. 200).

Sturt evidently felt himself caught between the proverbial rock and the equally proverbial hard place:

> To discharge the men was not to be thought of. How could I ever find fault with those who had taught me what little I knew of the trade and who could but be only too well aware of how little that was? Moreover they were my friends. Business was troublesome even on the best of terms, but I could not have found the heart to go on with it at all at the cost of the friction which must have come if I had begun trying to "speed up" my friends and instructors. Meanwhile, none the less, the trade these friends of mine depended on for a living was slipping away, partly by their own fault (p. 200).

"What," Sturt asks rhetorically, "was to be done?" His solution was less original than the anguish it caused him:

> Eventually—probably in 1889—I set up machinery: a gas engine, with saws, lathe, drill, and grindstone. And this device, if it saved the situation, was (as was long afterwards plain) the beginning of the end of the old style of business . . .
>
> . . . there in my old-fashioned shop the new machinery had almost forced its way in—the thin end on the wedge of scientific engineering . . . "The men," though still my friends, as I fancied, became machine "hands." Unintentionally, I had made them servants waiting on gas combustion . . . they were under the power of molecular forces. But to this day the few survivors of them do not know it. They think "Unrest" most wicked (pp. 200–1).

Some will read the conclusion to Sturt's tale as simple sentimentality. One cannot have gas-driven machinery without the new production relations it entails. But a close reading suggests a different interpretation.

Consider the nature of authority in a shop like Sturt's. Formally the boss's power rests in ownership. But substantively ownership is an insufficient basis. To command effectively requires legitimacy, and to achieve legitimacy requires that the boss be a superior wheelwright. A legitimate ruler commands by example as well as by fiat. He sets the pace because he knows by experience what constitutes a fair day's work and he can, if need be, do that much and more.

George Sturt's father commanded by example. So did his grandfather. As superiors in *techne,* both held the respect as well as the affection of the men. But lacking the apprenticeship necessary for the development of superior skill, Sturt could only, as he says, lay claim to their friendship—not to their respect. Unable to exercise power in the traditional "mechanical" mode based on a superior command of *techne,* Sturt, in this reading, turns to a new "organic" mode; a new technology makes the men dependent on him in a new way in which their traditional knowledge plays a much diminished role. With gas-driven machinery comes a new system of knowledge, "scientific engineering," in which Sturt is on a more than even footing.

It is not machinery which gave rise to a new system of production relations, but the need for a new system of production relations which led to the introduction of particular kinds of machinery. Had Sturt been able to command in the way of his forefathers, gas-driven machinery need not have transformed production relations any more than the steam-powered looms transformed the production relations of Coventry ribbon weavers (Prest 1960, summarized above in Section 3).

8. Scientific Management

Sturt's problem was fundamentally the same as Frederick Taylor's. In the words of the father of scientific management, "The shop was really run by the workmen, and not by the bosses. The workmen together had carefully planned just how fast each job should be done, and they had set a pace for each machine throughout the shop" (Taylor 1967: 48–9).

Appointed a gang boss in the Midvale Steel Company, Taylor set about challenging worker control. Lacking Sturt's fastidiousness—his father and grandfather had not run the shop before him—Taylor was initially determined not to let any bonds of affection (which in Taylor's case were unlikely in any case to have been reciprocal—see Kakar 1970) stand in his way.

The story of scientific management begins with his essentially pyrrhic victory in those early Midvale efforts. Despite considerable success, he regarded these efforts as a failure—for the same reason that made George Sturt hesitate to intervene at all. As Taylor later told the story (Taylor 1967: 52–3), it was an-guish at the "bitter relations" caused by these first attempts to take control of production which spurred him on to more fundamental efforts at reorganizing work. It is these later efforts that he labelled "scientific management" and which others have called simply "Taylorism."

Evidently there was not only a residue of bitter relations, but continuing resistance to Taylor's efforts to speed up work. The immediate problem was "the ignorance of the management as to what really constitutes a proper day's work for a workman" (p. 53).[7] But underlying the problem of a fair day's work was a more basic problem of knowledge. The narrative continues. "He [Taylor] fully realized that, although he was foreman of the shop, the combined knowledge and skill of the workmen who were under him was certainly ten times as great as his own" (p. 53).

In our terminology, the underlying problem, as perceived by Taylor, was a knowledge system based on *techne*. Within it, he could never hope for a decisive victory; as long as his project took the form of a simple appropriation of the worker's *techne*, success would be at best partial. His vision of total dominance required a thoroughgoing reorganization of production itself. Only a recapitulation of workers' knowledge in the form of an *episteme* to which management alone had access would provide a firm basis for managerial control. Only such a recapit-ulation would allow management to escape the constraints of subordinating pro-duction to the worker's *techne*, within which the best the manager can do is

> frankly to place before the workmen the problem of doing the work in the best and most economical way . . . inducing each workman to use his best endeav-our, his hardest work, all his traditional knowledge, his skill, his ingenuity, and his good will—in a word, his "initiative," so as to yield the largest possible return to his employers (p. 32).

Taylor knew *techne* all right—he has articulated it in this passage as nearly as one can—and he knew it for the obstacle it was to managerial control. To remove this obstacle, not only must managers get hold of the knowledge of workers, they must change its form. Thus scientific management is not simply appropriation, it is also transformation. Reread the passage from *The Principles of Scientific Management* which was used in Section 4 to describe the basic idea of Taylorism:

> Under scientific management, the managers assume . . . the burden of gathering together all of the traditional knowledge which in the past has been possessed by the workmen and then of classifying, tabulating, and reducing this knowledge to rules, laws, and formulae (p. 36). These replace the judgment of the individual workman (p. 37). Thus all of the planning which under the old system was done by the workman, as a result of his personal experience, must of necessity under the new system be done by management in accordance with the laws of the science (p. 38).

Taylor was sanguine about the consequences of separating execution from control. As was indicated in note 4, he was never the lackey of capital which critics on the left have consistently portrayed him: his suspicions and resentments of capitalists ran as deep as his reservations about workers (Kakar 1970). Rather, he saw scientific management as a third way, a way of making "the interests of the workmen and the management . . . the same, instead of antagonistic" (pp. 52–3). According to Taylor, and there is every reason to believe he was being sincere,

> Scientific management . . . has for its very foundation the firm conviction that the true interests of employees and employers are one and the same; that prosperity for the employer cannot exist through a long term of years unless it is accompanied by prosperity for the employee, and *vice versa;* and that it is possible to give the worker what he wants—high wages—and the employer what he wants—a low labour cost—for his manufactures (p. 10).

Taylor paid less attention to the non-material interests of the worker and dealt with these interests in a contradictory fashion. He first suggested that scientific management would actually increase workers' on-the-job satisfaction; but he immediately fell back on the argument that the omelette of progress required a few broken eggs. On the one hand (pp. 120–1),

> All of us are grown-up children and it is equally true that the average workman will work with the greatest satisfaction, both to himself and to his employer, when he is given each day a definite task which he is to perform in a given time, and which constitutes a proper day's work for a good workman. This furnishes the workman with a clear-cut standard, by which he can throughout the day measure his own progress, and the accomplishment of which affords him the greatest satisfaction.

On the other hand (p. 125),

> Now when through all of this teaching and this minute instruction the work is apparently made so smooth and easy for the workman, the first impression is

that this all makes him a mere automaton, a wooden man. As the workmen frequently say when they first come under the system, "Why, I am not allowed to think or move without someone interfering or doing it for me!" The same criticism and objection, however, can be raised against all other modern subdivision of labour.

Taylor's guinea-pigs were less enthusiastic about separating conception and execution. Charles Shartle, a subordinate, later reminisced

> . . . he [Taylor] would always say that he had others to think, and we are supposed to do the work. I remember he said to me, many times, I have you for your strength and mechanical ability, and we have other men paid for thinking, and I think he used to try to carry this out pretty well. But I would never admit to him that I was not allowed to think. We used to have some pretty hot arguments just over this point. (Charles Shartle, *Recollections,* Taylor Collection, Stevens Institute of Technology, Hoboken, New Jersey. Quoted in Kakar 1970: 98–9.)

In the end, Taylor never achieved more than the partial success he enjoyed when working within the framework of *techne*. Running a factory on *episteme* alone was a fantasy. Like one of Oliver Sacks's more extremely afflicted patients, a factory run on pure *episteme* might be grotesque or comical, but it could never function with any semblance of normality.[8]

9. Numerical Control

But such is the power of ideas that the project of epistemizing production has never been abandoned. David Noble's book, *Forces of Production* (1984), is a superbly instructive chronicle of scientific management reincarnated in the automation of machine-tool manufacture. Noble's story describes how a particular strategy of automation, numerical control (or N/C) came to dominate in the United States. The other side of Noble's tale is why the alternative, record playback (or R/P) was put aside.

Recast in our terminology, the choice was between a technology based on *episteme* and one based on *techne*. Whereas N/C, the epistemic technology, attempted to bypass the skilled machinist altogether, R/P built directly on the skilled machinist's *techne*. N/C envisioned a direct transition from the blueprint of a part into a series of instructions expressed in mathematical form with the help of a computer, which, once encoded on a magnetic tape or punched paper, were supposed to activate the machine tool to perform an appropriate series of operations. By contrast, R/P prepared the tape by recording the motions of a skilled machinist. Noble describes the difference between the two technologies thus:

> Whereas with the motional approach, the skills and tacit knowledge of the machinist were automatically recorded as he interpreted the blueprint and put the machine through its paces manually, without ever having to be formally or

explicitly articulated, with N/C, all interpretation was performed by a "part programmer," at his office desk, who was required to spell out precisely in mathematical and algorithmic terms what had heretofore been largely sight, sound, and feel (p. 84).

The merits of N/C in terms of efficiency were in Noble's view dubious, to say the least, though their economic defects were hidden for a long time by the generosity of the United States Air Force in supporting the research and development of N/C technologies. Rather, the appeal of N/C was the fantasy of a production process so thoroughly epistemized that workers, at least skilled workers, would no longer be necessary. His imagination stirred by a demonstration at the Massachusetts Institute of Technology (a prime contractor in the early development of N/C), one early enthusiast wrote to the MIT project leader in early 1952 that N/C signals "our emancipation from human workers" (Noble 1984: 235).

Shortly thereafter, in 1954, the trade magazine *American Machinist* observed more soberly: "Numerical control is not a strictly metalworking technique, it is a philosophy of control" (quoted in Noble 1984: 237–8). In 1976, with two decades of hindsight, *Iron Age* reached a similar conclusion: "The fundamental advantage of numerical control [is that] it brings production control to the Engineering Department" (p. 238).

This was still part fantasy. The reality, in Noble's view, was that N/C was a costly and cumbersome technology which had little built-in flexibility to cope with the variety of conditions under which production actually takes place. "Different materials, temperatures, irregularities in the workpiece, tool-wear, machine malfunction—all of them would affect reproduction accuracy and their final quality" (Noble 1984: 151). And require, willy-nilly, the intervention of the machinist's *techne*. Indeed, although, in the words of a production supervisor, "The whole purpose of N/C is to remove the operator from the process" (p. 242), operators had to learn to read the tapes in order to make adjustments for changes in operating conditions. "N/Cs are supposed to be like magic," observed one operator, "but all you can do automatically is produce scrap."[9]

Of course R/P technologies were not immune to these problems. The difference between R/P and N/C lay in how the control tapes were prepared rather than in how these tapes were operated.[10] For the most part the architects of R/P as well as of N/C technologies had imagined that the system would function with minimal operator intervention, and what little was required could be handled by unskilled workers (Noble 1984: 151). In short, the designers of R/P also saw little need to incorporate provision for the operator to "override" the program when conditions warranted.

There was however an essential philosophical difference between these two approaches: the N/C system, based on pure *episteme*, presupposed the redundancy of the machinist and his *techne;* the R/P system by contrast built on that *techne*. Practically, under an R/P technology the skilled machinist would still be available on the shop-floor when his *techne* was required. The goal of N/C technology was to eliminate the skilled machinist altogether.

It is unfortunate that Noble could not include more comparative material in his study; the experience of other countries, to judge from the tantalizing hints Noble drops along the way, has been different in ways of direct relevance to our primary concern. In particular, Japan provides a revealing contrast with the American predilection towards complex N/C systems, and the corresponding rejection of simpler R/P systems (see Noble 1984: 169n. and 182n.). In a comparative study of the Japanese and American firm, Masahiko Aoki (1988) remarks specifically on this difference; for Aoki it reflects a Japanese attitude towards workers' knowledge fundamentally different from the attitudes that characterize the West.

This brings us to one of the basic questions of this essay: how does the nature and role of knowledge in the production process figure in the odd mixture of resistance and accommodation with which workers have received technical changes that have undermined their autonomy? Resistance is perhaps the easier part of the story. Workers are able to resist successfully because their *techne* is essential to the production process. Noble's operator spoke volumes when he observed that "all you can do automatically [read *"epistemically"*] is produce scrap." The point is that *episteme* can never be a self-sufficient system for organizing thought, much less action.[11] As Pirsig remarked of "classical" knowledge in *Zen and the Art of Motorcycle Maintenance,* "the motorcycle, so described, is almost impossible to understand unless you already know how one works. The immediate surface expressions that are essential for primary understanding are gone. Only the underlying form is left" (1976: 71). Practical managers, however disposed they might be to *episteme* and the control it promises, come eventually to learn its limits. One executive had this to say in 1957 to a meeting of the Electronics Industry Association:

> In my opinion there is too much talk about giant brains, computer-controlled factories, and the abolition of the factory worker . . . N/C will never be able to do away with factory workers . . . experience leads me to believe that the engineer is incapable of doing an efficient job without the know-how of the factory worker (quoted in Noble 1984: 236).

An article in *Fortune* put it this way: "Factory operations may seem orderly enough until you try to describe them in computer programs, then they begin to look quite irregular" (quoted in Noble 1984: 344).

The limitations of *episteme* are a running theme of Noble's account of the introduction of N/C technologies. On the shop-floor, the focal point was control over machine speeds. On the one hand, machine speed was, as it were, the cutting edge of managerial control. On the other hand, the variations of conditions made it necessary for managers to permit workers to use their judgment in deciding when to override the computer program. But the capacity to override was at the same time the capacity to "pace" and maintain "stints"—the very heart of the traditional system that management had been struggling against since well before Taylor's time. As Noble put it, "Management attempts to control the freedom of the work force invariably run up against the contradiction that the freedom is necessary for quality production" (p. 277).

Accommodation is more difficult to explain. Since time out of mind workers have been concerned with the effects of technical change, beginning with the most obvious question of the effects on employment. But in the end, resistance on the shop-floor is limited to the kind of guerrilla struggle that uses overrides to pace production or in the kind of rearguard action that defends job classifications against "deskilling."

It is easy to understand why individual workers have not played an active role in influencing the course of innovation. Isolated from the design process by the very organization of work under capitalism and by their own limitations in the *episteme* of production, workers are necessarily on the receiving end.

But the same arguments cannot apply to the trade unions. All the same, trade union intervention in the process of technical change has, in the United States at least, long been marked by reticence, hesitation, and timidity—when it occurs at all.

The trade union imagination is limited to protecting the jobs and incomes of the existing labour force, a strategy successfully pursued for many years by John L. Lewis of the United Mine Workers. Unions no more than individual workers have sought a role in shaping the content of technical change.

Noble's account of the unions' role in the automation of machine-tool production fits this general picture. Even when their assistance was actively sought by the developers of "Specialmatic," a rarity as a technology more conducive to worker control, the labour unions showed little interest and less enthusiasm. According to Noble, "labour unions in the metalworking industries never championed the Specialmatic, or any other potentially labour-oriented technological advance for that matter, leaving such decisions to management alone" (1984: 95–6). In short, the trade union attitude was that of Harry Bridges, the militant leader of the International Longshoremen, who "concluded that the fate of technology was irresistible and that [labour] would have to 'adjust' to survive" (quoted in Noble 1984: 259).

This fatalism, of course, has many roots. It has already been observed that the emergence of "business unionism" in America was itself the outcome of a protracted struggle. But the abdication of trade unions with respect to questions of technology, more precisely the *content* of technology, cannot in my judgment be understood without reference to the cultural values attached to *episteme*. In the West *episteme* is held at the very least to be a superior form of knowledge, if not the *only* form of knowledge. Moreover this value is widely held. It may serve the interests of capital in legitimizing scientific management (or indeed any enterprise that can lay claim to being "scientific"), but it derives its legitimacy from the circumstance that workers as well as capitalists, craftsmen as well as school-men, believe in the superiority of *episteme* over *techne*. This shared belief, in my view, is a key ingredient in the accommodation of workers and their leaders to the project of capitalist domination of production. If you believe that *episteme* subsumes *techne*, it is hard to make a determined defence of your *techne*.

. . .

14. Conclusion

This essay has put forward the argument that in the West workers have largely accommodated themselves to the capitalist project of dominating the workplace because Western culture provides neither compelling reasons nor compelling means for workers to resist this project. In contrast to Hindu culture, workers who are heirs to the Greek and Judaeo-Christian traditions find both that their work stands outside the cosmic order and that the system of knowledge in which their work is organized is held to be an inferior system, if indeed it counts as knowledge at all. Lacking both cultural reason and cultural means to defend himself, the worker has been, to paraphrase Thomas Jefferson, easy prey for the designs of capitalist ambition.

It seems to me this argument has profound implications for the project of building a decent society. Socialists in particular have consistently stressed the importance of work organization in their project, and it is, in my opinion, right to do so. With less consistency, socialists have neglected the role of culture in shaping both the possibilities for, and the constraints on, work organization.

We in the West probably do not have the option of embedding work in our cosmology. We perhaps have more control over our theory of knowledge. We must at least hope so, for, if not, the socialist project is probably doomed. As Robert Pirsig put it (1974: 94),

> [T]o tear down a factory or to revolt against a government or to avoid repair of a motorcycle because it is a system is to attack effects rather than causes; and as long as the attack is upon effects only, no change is possible. The true system, the real system, is our present construction of systematic thought itself, rationality itself, and if a factory is torn down but the rationality which pro-duced it is left standing, then that rationality will simply produce another factory. If a revolution destroys a systematic government, but the systematic patterns of thought that produced that government are left intact, then those patterns will repeat themselves in the succeeding government.

The same socialist project which has exalted workplace democracy as the foundation of a decent society denies this foundation by making participation conditional on accepting the dominant knowledge system: workers are free to participate on condition that they accept the knowledge system of the party cadres and the engineers. But that is an option open only to a minority. As there is room for only so many cadres and engineers, most must remain workers, consigned to inferior status by virtue of the inferiority of their knowledge.

The point of my argument is not to glorify but to rediscover and to legitimize *techne;* to argue for a balance and even for a tension between *techne* and *episteme.* I have neither the intention nor the need to denigrate *episteme* in order to attack the hierarchical ordering in which *episteme* is placed above *techne;* my purpose is to argue against an imbalance that puts the very project of erecting a decent society at risk.

Outside the West, conditions are at once more problematic and more promising. To take India as a concrete example, the problems of poverty and internal conflict are intertwined with the problems posed by the encounter, cultural as well as economic, with the West. The economic consequences of that encounter are ambiguous. Whether the British deindustrialized India or laid the basis for its industrialization (or perhaps did some of each) is still debated by scholars and the issue will perhaps never be settled.

But the cultural consequences seem to me to be much more clear-cut. If India is to build a society on the foundations of democratic and participatory work organization, it will do better to follow the impulse of Mohandas Gandhi and his kind to look to India's own tradition than to follow the impulse of the ilk of Rajiv Gandhi to look to the West.

Notes

1. "Efficiency" is the economists' preferred term for describing the virtue of the market. An efficient set of economic arrangements is one that precludes the provision of more of one good except at the sacrifice of some other good. "Goods," it should be noted, has an elastic meaning: a good can be defined as narrowly as a specific commodity like bread or ice-cream or it can be stretched to mean the well-being of individuals. In its second meaning, an efficient set of arrangements is one which precludes increasing the well-being of one individual except at the expense of another.

The advantage of the more technical terminology of "efficiency" over a more informal notion like "the size of the economic pie" is that it permits comparison of situations where tastes differ: "size of the pie" becomes ambiguous when some people like blackberry pie while others like apple pie. But taste differences are not matters of great moment for present purposes, and we lose correspondingly little if we take the informal route of identifying efficiency with pie size.

Observe that the economist's definition of efficiency is somewhat at odds with conventional usage. A businessman thinks he is increasing efficiency if he is successful in imposing a speed-up. But the economist will object that the higher output is at the expense of greater effort. It is not necessarily more efficient in the sense of providing more of one good without sacrificing something elsewhere.

2. "Pyramids, Empire State Building—these things just don't happen. There's hard work behind it. I would like to see a building, say the Empire State, I would like to see on one side of it a foot-wide strip from top to bottom with the name of every bricklayer, the name of every electrician, with all the names. So when a guy walked by, he could take his

son and say, 'See, that's me on the forty-fifth floor. I put the steel beam in.' Picasso can point to a painting. What can I point to? A writer can point to a book. Everybody should have something to point to" (p. xxxii).

3. Observe that control is not being opposed to profit. Contrary to "invisible hand" arguments, in which profitability is a function of efficiency alone, profitability is here held to depend jointly on control and efficiency. Efficiency at best creates a *potential* profit; without control the capitalist cannot realize that profit. Thus organizational forms which enhance capitalist control may increase profits and find favour with capitalists even if they affect productivity and efficiency adversely. Conversely, more efficient ways of organizing production which reduce capitalist control may end up reducing profits and being rejected by capitalists.

This is not to say that businessmen actually do maximize profits. This is a controversial point on which it is unnecessary for present purposes to take a view one way or another. To assume that capitalists are motivated solely by profits may be an overly narrow, economistic perspective, but there is no need for present purposes to assume that control is an end in itself which is sought independently of its contribution to profits. In the present circumstances Occam's Razor suggests that control be regarded simply as a means to profit. *Entia non sunt multiplicanda praeter necessitatem.* (But see Albert Hirschman 1984.)

4. Taylor himself was far from the lackey of capital he is portrayed by critics on the left (for instance, Braverman 1974). Over time he became as suspicious of capital as he was of labour. Of course, capitalists made use of Taylor. But then so did Lenin, whose encomiums for scientific management were already prefigured in Marx's characterization of "socialized man, the associated producers, rationally regulating their interchange with Nature, bringing it under their collective control ... and achieving this with the least expenditure of energy ..." (Marx 1894: 800). Sudhir Kakar (1970) has written a rewarding psychobiography of Taylor, including an account of the experiences which soured Taylor on captains of industry.

5. It can also be a hierarchy of sex, in which case the linearity notion obviously does not apply. But traditional societies typically allocate separate *technai* to men and women, so that in so far as power relationships between sexes are related to knowledge they reflect rules of power *between* rather than *within* knowledge systems. Carol Gilligan's well-known work, *In A Different View* (1982), can be interpreted as a defense of (feminine) *techne* against (masculine) *episteme.*

6. There are exceptions; the law and business faculties of my own university have since their inception given pride of place to the "case method" of instruction, which attempts to condense the *techne* of the law office and the executive suite into a form accessible to students, and to allow learning to take place in a simulated environment in which mistakes are not too costly. But even these exceptions are coming increasingly under fire from the epistemic academic establishment.

7. Taylor had amplified this observation in testifying before a governmental commission, "When I got to be a foreman of the shop and had finally won out and we had an agreement among the men that there would be so much work done—not a full day's work, but a pretty good day's work—we all came to an understanding, and had no further fighting. Then I tried to analyze it, and said: The main trouble with this thing is that you have been quarrelling because there have been no proper standards for a day's work. You do not know what a proper day's work is. Those fellows know the times more than you do, but personally, we do not know anything about what a day's work is. We make a bluff at it and the other side makes a guess at it and then we fight. The great thing is that we do not know what is a proper day's work." (Testimony before the Industrial Relations Commission, cited in Copley 1923.)

8. Whyte 1961, ch. 10, and Burawoy 1979 provide excellent accounts of scientific management in operation in the same plant at an interval of 30 years. (The account in Whyte was contributed by Donald Roy. See Roy 1952*a*, 1952*b* for a more detailed discussion of the dynamics of boss-worker relations in the plant during the 1940s.)

9. And worse. One machine operator reported on the potentially fatal consequences of a programming error: "He tabbed it wrong one time and we were in a hole; I had a two-inch drill and I was seven inches in the hole. The machine took off and it threw that drill fifty feet down the shop. It weighted two pounds and it just missed me; it went over the helper's head and took his hat off. So after that I said, 'I'm going to know this thing, because this might kill me' "(p. 246).

10. But see Noble (1984: 164) for the view that R/P systems inherently gave the operator control over production speeds.

11. Even at the level of pure thought. Gödel, at least as he is translated for the non-specialist (see, for example, Kline 1980: 260–4), is supposed to have demonstrated the impossibility of a consistent and complete theory on *any* set of axioms: either there will be inconsistencies (theorems which will be at once "true" and "false") or there will be incompleteness (theorems whose truth status cannot be determined). With this unpromising beginning, it is hard to see how one would even be tempted to rely on pure *episteme*.

References

Aoki, Masahiko (1988) *Information, Incentives and Bargaining in the Japanese Economy,* Cambridge: Cambridge University Press.

Apffel Marglin, Frédérique (1985) [catalogued under Marglin, Frédérique Apffel] *Wives of the God King: The Rituals of the Devadasis of Puri,* New Delhi and Oxford: Oxford University Press.

Aristotle (1934) *Nichomachean Ethics,* trans H. Rackham, Cambridge, Mass.: Harvard University Press.

—— (1944) *Politics,* trans. H. Rackham, Cambridge, Mass.: Harvard University Press.

Banuri, Tariq, ed. (1990) *Economic Liberalization: No Panacea,* Oxford: Clarendon Press.

Braverman, Harry (1974) *Labor and Monopoly Capital: The Degradation of Work in the Twentieth Century,* New York: Monthly Review Press.

Bruner, Jerome (1962) *On Knowing: Essays for the Left Hand,* Cambridge, Mass.: Harvard University Press, 1979.

Buchler, Alfred, Fischer, Eberhard, and Nabholz, Marie-Louise (1980) *Indian Tie-Dyed Fabrics,* Ahmedabad: Calico Museum of Textiles.

Burawoy, Michael (1979) *Manufacturing Consent,* Chicago: the University of Chicago Press.

Buttrick, John (1952) "The Inside Contract System," *Journal of Economic History,* 12: 205–21.

Cobden-Ramsay, L.E.B. (1982) *Feudatory States of Orissa,* Calcutta: Firma KLM (first published 1910).

Copley, Frank B. (1923) *Frederick W. Taylor, Father of Scientific Management,* vol. i, New York: Harper & Row.

Detienne, Marcel, and Vernant, Jean-Pierre (1974) *Les Ruses de l'Intelligence: la Mètis des Grecs,* Paris: Flammarion.

Dumont, Louis (1977) *From Mandeville to Marx: The Genesis and Triumph of Economic Ideology,* Chicago: Chicago University Press.

Edgerton, Franklin (1933) "Jñāna and Vijñāna," Otto Stein and Wilhelm Gampert (eds.), *Festschrift Moriz Winternitz,* Leipzig: Harrassowitz.

———— (1944) *The Bhagavad Gita,* Cambridge, Mass.: Harvard University Press.

Edwards, Richard (1979) *Contested Terrain: The Transformation of the Workplace in the Twentieth Century,* New York: Basic Books.

Ellsberg, Daniel (1961) "Risk, Ambiguity, and the Savage Axioms," *Quarterly Journal of Economics,* 75: 643–69.

Floris, Peter (1934) *Voyage of Floris to the East Indies,* ed. W.H. Moreland, London: The Hakluyt Society.

Freud, Sigmund (1961) *Civilization and its Discontents,* ed. J. Strachey, New York: W.W. Norton (first published 1930).

Friedman, Milton (1953) "The Methodology of Positive Economics," in *Essays in Positive Economics,* Chicago: University of Chicago Press.

Gilligan, Carol (1982) *In a Different Voice: Psychological Theory and Women's Development,* Cambridge, Mass.: Harvard University Press.

Hacking, Ian (1975) *The Emergence of Probability: A Philosophical Study of Early Ideas About Probability, Induction and Statistical Inference,* Cambridge: Cambridge University Press.

Hesiod (1914) "Works and Days," in *The Homeric Hymns and Homerica,* trans. Hugh Evelyn-White, Cambridge, Mass.: Harvard University Press.

Hirschman, Albert (1984) "Against Parsimony," *Economics and Philosophy,* 7: 7–21.

Kakar, Sudhir (1970) *Frederick Taylor: A Study in Personality and Innovation,* Cambridge, Mass.: MIT Press.

Kline, Morris (1980) *Mathematics: The Loss of Certainty,* New York: Oxford University Press.

Klosko, George (1986) *The Development of Plato's Political Theory,* New York and London: Methuen.

Knight, Frank (1921) *Risk, Uncertainty and Profit,* Boston and New York: Houghton Mifflin Company.

Kuhn, Thomas (1970) *The Structure of Scientific Revolutions,* International Encyclopedia of Unified Science, vol. ii, no. 2, Chicago: University of Chicago Press, 2nd edn. (first published 1962).

Lakatos, Imre (1970) "Falsification and the Methodology of Scientific Research Programmes," in Imre Lakatos and Alan Musgrave (eds.), *Criticism and the Growth of Knowledge,* Cambridge: Cambridge University Press.

Langland, William (1959) *Piers the Ploughman,* ed. J.F. Goodridge, Hammondsworth: Penguin.

Lifton, Robert Jay (1983) *The Broken Connection: On Death and the Continuity of Life,* New York: Basic Books.

Lyons, John (1969) *Structural Semantics: An Analysis of Part of the Vocabulary of Plato,* Oxford: Basil Blackwell.

Marcuse, Herbert (1966) *One Dimensional Man: Studies in the Ideology of Advanced Industrial Society,* Boston: Beacon Press.

Marglin, Stephen (1974) "What Do Bosses Do? The Origins and Functions of Hierarchy in Capitalist Production," Part I, *Review of Radical Political Economics,* 60: 60–112, repr. in A. Gorz (ed.) *The Division of Labour,* Sussex: Harvester, 1976.

———— (1979) "Catching Flies with Honey: An Inquiry into Management Initiatives to Humanize Work," *Economic Analysis and Workers' Management,* 12: 473–87.

———— (1984) "Knowledge and Power," in Frank Stephen (ed.), *Firms, Organization and Labour,* London: Macmillan.

———— (1987) "Investment and Accumulation," in John Eatwell, Murray Milgate, and Peter Newman (eds.) *The New Palgrave,* London: Macmillan.

———— and Bhaduri, Amit (1990) "Profit Squeeze and Keynesian Theory," in Stephen

Marglin and Juliet Schor (eds.), *The Golden Age of Capitalism,* Oxford: Clarendon Press.

Marx, Karl (1959) *Capital,* vol. iii, Moscow: Foreign Languages Publishing House (first published 1894).

—— and Engels, F. (1947) *German Ideology,* ed. R. Pascal, New York: International (first published 1846).

Mohanty, Bijoy Chandra, and Krishna, Kalyan (1974) *Ikat Fabrics of Orissa and Andhra Pradesh,* Ahmedabad: Calico Museum of Textiles.

Montgomery, David (1979) *Workers' Control in America,* Cambridge: Cambridge University Press.

Morris, Frederic (1972) "From Cottage to Factory," (unpublished senior honours thesis) Harvard College.

Noble, David F. (1984) *Forces of Production: A Social History of Automation,* New York: Oxford University Press.

Nussbaum, Martha (1986) *The Fragility of Goodness: Luck and Ethics in Greek Tragedy and Philosophy,* Cambridge: Cambridge University Press.

—— and Sen, Amartya (1989) "Internal Criticism and Indian Rationalist Traditions," in Michael Krausz (ed.), *Relativism: Interpretation and Confrontation,* Notre Dame: Notre Dame University Press.

Pirsig, Robert (1976) *Zen and the Art of Motorcycle Maintenance: An Inquiry into Values,* London: Transworld.

Plato (1925) "Gorgias" in *Lysis, Symposium, and Gorgias,* trans. W.R.M. Lamb, Cambridge, Mass.: Harvard University Press.

—— (1925) "Philebus" in *Statesman, Philebus, and Ion,* trans. Harold N. Fowler and W.R.M. Lamb, Cambridge, Mass.: Harvard University Press.

—— (1941) *The Republic of Plato,* trans. F. Cornford, New York and London: Oxford University Press.

Polanyi, Karl (1944) *The Great Transformation,* New York: Rinehart.

Polanyi, Michael (1958) *Personal Knowledge: Towards a Post-Critical Philosophy,* Chicago: University of Chicago Press.

Popper, Karl (1968) *The Logic of Scientific Discovery,* New York: Harper & Row.

Prest, John (1960) *The Industrial Revolution in Coventry,* Oxford: Oxford University Press.

Putnam, Hilary (1974) "The Corroboration of Scientific Theories," *The Philosophy of Karl Popper,* ed. K. Schilpp, La Salle, Ill.: Open Court.

Ricardo, David (1951) *On the Principles of Political Economy and Taxation,* ed. P. Sraffa with the collaboration of M.H. Dobb, Cambridge: Cambridge University Press (first published 1817, 3rd edn. 1821).

Roy, Donald (1952*a*) "Quota Restriction and Goldbricking in a Machine Shop," *American Journal of Sociology,* 57: 427–42.

—— (1952*b*) "Restrictions of Output in a Piecework Machine Shop," (Ph.D. dissertation) University of Chicago.

Sacks, Oliver (1985) *The Man Who Mistook His Wife for a Hat: And Other Clinical Tales,* New York: Summit Books.

Smith, Adam (1937) *The Wealth of Nations,* ed. E. Canaan, New York: Random House (first published 1776).

Staal, J.F. (1965) "Euclid and Panini," *Philosophy East and West,* 15: 99–115.

Strauss, Leo (1970) *Xenophon's Socratic Discourse: An Interpretation of the Oeconomicus,* (trans. of the *Oeconomicus* by Carnes Lord), Ithaca: Cornell University Press.

Sturt, George (1923) *The Wheelwright's Shop,* Cambridge: Cambridge University Press.

Tawney, R.H. (1938) *Religion and the Rise of Capitalism: A Historical Study,* Harmondsworth: Penguin (first published 1926).

Taylor, Frederick (1967) *The Principles of Scientific Management,* New York: Norton (first published 1911).

Terkel, Studs (1972) *Working,* New York: Random House.

Thompson, E.P. (1963) *The Making of the English Working Class,* New York: Vintage Books.

Vernant, Jean-Pierre (1982) *Mythe et Pensée chez les Grecs: Études de Psychologie Historique,* vol. ii, Paris: François Maspero (first published 1965).

Vidal-Naquet, Pierre (1983) *Le Chasseur Noir: Formes de Pensée et Formes de Societé dans le Monde Grec,* Paris: La Découverte/Maspero.

Weber, Max (1930) *The Protestant Ethic and the Spirit of Capitalism,* trans. Talcott Parsons, New York: Scribner's and London: George Allen and Unwin (first published 1904–5).

Whyte, William F. (1955) *Money and Motivation: An Analysis of Incentives in Industry,* New York: Harper & Row.

Young, Arthur (1770) *A Six Months' Tour Through the North of England,* London: W. Strahan.

Yule, Henry and A.C. Burnell (1903) *Hobson-Jobson: A Glossary of Colloquial Anglo-Indian Words and Phrases, and of Kindred Terms, Etymological, Historical, Geographical and Discursive,* 2nd edn., ed. William Crooke, London: John Murray (first published 1886).

II

Class

4

An Approach to Class Analysis

Howard J. Sherman

This essay begins with a discussion of individualism, which is opposed to a class analysis. It then presents a definition of class. A class is not defined by more or fewer of certain characteristics, but by its relation to another class in the production process. The essay also shows how class is conceptualized in a historical setting. There is no eternal elite and no eternal under-class, but rather a class relationship specific to one mode of production—though there may also be non-class societies.

Individualism

With respect to the relationship of the individual and society, there have been two extreme and incorrect viewpoints in the history of social analysis. The dominant view in the United States has been what is commonly called individualism, the concept that all social-economic explanation must begin with individual behavior—and individual behavior is assumed to result from individual psychology. On the other side of the spectrum are those who sometimes seem to treat institutions and classes as existing above individuals and who seldom even find time to discuss individual motivations or behavior. This approach might be labeled extreme collectivism. Both of these viewpoints have had great impact on social scientists as well as upon large numbers of people, translating into political behavior. Most of this article will present class analysis as an alternative to both of these extreme perspectives.

Neoclassical economics is based on the assumed psychology of individuals. It assumes that the individual consumer maximizes his or her utility, beginning from the assumption of individual preferences. In that sense, individualism forms one of the three pillars of neoclassical economics—the others being psychological reductionism and an ahistorical equilibrium approach. Some examples may make clearer the consequences of individualist assumptions.

Example: Robinson Crusoe

Robinson Crusoe was a fictional character who spent much of his life ship-wrecked on an island. Soon after the novel appeared, many neoclassical economists used Crusoe as the perfect example of how an individual allocates his time and material resources so as to maximize his utility. Stephen Marglin comments that "the basic idea of mainstream economics that the world can be modelled as a group of Robinson Crusoes who live each on his own island maximizing utility and meeting to trade with each other is not only a simplification but a fundamental distortion of reality" (1989, p. 7). Such a picture, in which individuals with sets of given preferences meet to trade in the market on an equal basis ignores the differences of power among groups, such as workers and capitalists. Marglin spells out in great detail how this approach distorts relationships in the labor market, as if an individual worker met a giant corporation on an equal basis.

Example: Individualism and Whom to Blame

Like all others using the individualist approach, many conservative neoclassical economists tend to blame the victim for all economic problems. For example, a large literature on "search theory" asserts that workers in recessions are unhappy with their low pay, so they voluntarily prefer to search for a new job. Robert Lucas takes the individual preference approach even farther, saying: "To explain why people allocate time to . . . unemployment we need to know why they prefer it to all other activities" (Lucas, 1986, p. 38). So unemployment is voluntary and is explained by the preferences of the unemployed.

In neoclassical theory, the individual worker chooses how much education to get (balancing it against leisure time). So lack of training and lack of education are due to the preferences of the individual. In neoclassical theory, the individual worker competes in the labor market against all other workers. That competition results in each worker being paid according to the marginal product produced by that worker. Thus, if there is perfect competition in the labor market, a worker who receives less than the average wage must be producing a product less valuable than the average worker (whether due to lack of training or biological inheritance or any other reason). It follows that the working poor (who work full-time, but still get low wages) and all those with lower than average wages (such as women and African Americans), are poorer than others because they are less productive. If the individual is as productive as other individuals, then competition assures equal wages. (The conclusion need not be attacked here because it will be shown that the entire approach is unrealistic in the extreme.)

Example: Individualism and Consumer Demand

The use of individual preferences as ultimate building blocks by pure neoclassical economics has had a profound effect on theories of aggregate consumer demand. When John Maynard Keynes (1936) pioneered this field, he talked about psychology, but also considered the objective facts of income distribution. Modern Marxists and Post-Keynesians have put forth theories of aggregate demand based on class or the functional distribution of income among consumers (see Sherman 1991). These theories form one basis for demands for redistribution of income in capitalism, or for revolutionary changes to produce a new income structure. But neoclassical economics rules all such theories out of order by examining only the individual preferences which are said to form the microfoundations of aggregate theories. Thus, the dominant neoclassical consumption theories, the Permanent Income Theory and the Life Cycle Hypothesis, are purely individualist and therefore ignore institutions and class relations—making these theories quite inadequate (see Green 1984).

What is lacking in the neoclassical theories is any attempt to understand what determines individual consumer preferences and changes in those preferences. Since individual preferences are taken as given, they are never explained. Because neoclassical economics has no explanation of individual preferences, it has been said that there are no macro-foundations of neoclassical micro-economics (see Hodgson 1986).

Example: Individualism and the Environment

One interesting example of a critique of neoclassical individualism is presented by Peter Soderbaum (1990). He argues that the usual neoclassical approach to environmental problems limits itself to the purely individual economic costs when doing cost-benefit studies of environmental impacts of new projects. He contends that this is totally inadequate because environmental problems require an interdisciplinary approach to the entire environment, not just to costs clearly allocated to individuals. Such a report should not merely emphasize economic factors such as dollar cost (which can be apportioned to individuals), but must also consider biological impact on nature as well as biological impact on human beings, impact on and through political and social institutions, and so forth.

Definition of Class

There are two excellent discussions of the problems of defining class by modern Marxists; one is by Erik Olin Wright (1985) and the other is by Stephen Resnick and Richard Wolff (1987). This analysis draws on their insights, though it does not follow either one on some issues.

Definitions and concepts of class have important political implications. For example, if there are only two classes in capitalism, and if capitalists are always dominant over workers in politics, then the only way to make basic changes in class relations is by a revolution. If after a socialist revolution, only the working class remains and it runs the government, then there must be perfect democracy by definition. Soviet Marxism tended toward these conclusions in its popular propaganda.

Of course, one can formulate any definition, so long as it is constant during a discussion. Moreover, somewhat different definitions of class will be useful to tackle different problems. In an abstract model of exploitation, two classes are sufficient to clarify the main issues. Marx used such a model in volume 1 of *Capital*, but he was perfectly clear that this was a simplification of reality: "the actual composition of society ... by no means consists of only two classes, workers and industrial capitalists" (Marx 1968, p. 493).

Modern Marxists use a multi-class model when they ask concrete political or historical questions. In fact, neoclassical economists also use an abstract two-factor model of "labor" and "capital" to explain the simplest case of distribution of income. There is nothing wrong with such simplification unless it is used to draw policy conclusions, for which a more realistic model is necessary.

In discussing any real historical case, such as the origins and development of the French Revolution, one must use a definition capable of grasping the very complex multi-class conflicts that shaped this event. The same multi-class analysis will be necessary in an examination of a budget battle in the U.S. Congress. In terms of the political understanding and tactics of the Left in modern capitalist countries, a two-class concept of reality is a disaster. There is no homogeneous working-class majority, so class coalitions are necessary tactics—and understanding must include "the middle class" as discussed below.

Marxist class analysis, if used properly, can be a very helpful tool in democratic politics. It forces political analysts to go beyond personalities and ask what class interests are involved in each issue. In the modern Marxian view, this requires a very complex analysis of the many classes and class strata. Marxian analysis exposes the fact that political democracy under capitalism is limited by the awesome power of money and wealth, which makes the playing field very unfair and uneven.

Because it is based on a class analysis, Marxist research leads to the conclusion that there will be a very limited political democracy unless democracy is extended to the economy. Economic democracy—the control of the economy by the people through democratic processes in national, state, local, and enterprise elections—is the only firm foundation for a vibrant political democracy.

Three Levels of Class Conflict

Most modern Marxists have distinguished three levels of class conflict, each of which must be considered in reaching a proper understanding. The three levels are the purely economic level, the political level, and the ideological level (each discussed below). Because of these different levels of class conflict, class is a concept that unites Marxian economics, sociology, anthropology, political science, and history (see discussion of this point in John Elliot 1979; also Ralph

Miliband 1991). Because class is a central Marxian concept, it is the reason that Marxist scholars frequently stray into various related disciplines. In fact, they should stray as often as possible; since there is only one society with many inter-related aspects, most real-world problems are multi-disciplinary.

At the economic level, a class is defined by its relation to other classes and the means of production. To be more specific, the question must be asked as to who controls the means of production and who works with the means of production. The question must also be asked whether one class (or classes) may exploit others, while one class (or classes) is exploited. Marxists answer that in the process of production in every class-divided social formation there is a class (or classes) that exploits producers and there is a class (or classes) that is exploited. Wolff and Resnick state carefully that "classes are . . . defined as groups of persons who share the common . . . position of performing surplus labor [such as workers] or of appropriating it from the performers [such as capitalists] or of obtaining . . . shares of surplus from the appropriators [such as financiers]" (Wolff and Resnick 1986, p. 98). St. Croix comments that: "Class . . . is . . . the way in which *exploitation* is embodied in a social structure. By *exploitation* I mean the appropriation of part of the labour of others" (St. Croix 1981, p. 51).

The Marxist concept of exploitation is at the heart of Marxist class analysis. By definition, exploitation occurs when one class appropriates without payment the surplus labor of another class.

Most modern Marxists divide the working day—whether in slavery, feudalism, or capitalism—into the necessary labor time and surplus labor time. Necessary labor time is that working time that goes to feed, clothe, and shelter the worker, while the surplus labor time is that time during which products are produced beyond the necessary amount. Even under slavery, the slave is given food, clothing, and shelter, but Marxists point out that the slave also works beyond the amount needed to produce the daily necessities, providing surplus labor to the slave-owner. Similarly, under capitalism the worker not only does necessary labor for his or her own necessities, but continues to work much longer providing surplus labor to the capitalist. Thus it is the role of each in the production process as exploiter or exploited that defines the capitalist class and the working class.

Slave economies and capitalist economies are similar in the fact of exploitation, but what distinguishes these two types of class economies? Marxists stress that the differences between different class societies are based on the form of exploitation or appropriation of surplus labor. Marx wrote:

> The essential difference between the various economic forms of society, between, for instance, a society based on slave labor, and one based on wage labor, lies only in the mode in which this surplus labor is in each case extracted from the actual producer, the laborer (Marx 1867, 1965, p. 217).

Thus the mode of extraction of surplus labor (the form of exploitation) by one class of another is for Marxists the determining feature of the entire mode of production. For example, in production under slavery, the slave can be bought and sold like any other tool of production; but workers under capitalism may voluntarily change jobs and make a new contract, so they can be fired, but not sold to another capitalist.

Since class relations are the key defining feature of each mode of production, it is easy to see why modern Marxists treat class relations of exploitation as the entry point to the social sciences, the place where one should start in doing social science research. An intensive empirical study by Miliband found that "class conflict remained the most important, indeed the absolutely central, fact in the life of advanced capitalist societies" (Miliband 1991, p. v).

Similarly, in reference to a debate led by Robert Brenner on the transition from feudalism to capitalism, R.H. Hilton states, "For Brenner and for many Marxist historians, the issue of class exploitation and class struggle is fundamental for understanding essential aspects of the medieval economy" (R.H. Hilton, in Ashton and Philpin 1985, p. 5). Brenner was arguing against historians who gave priority to many other factors, such as trade or demographic trends.

The relation of classes to the means of production is not simply a question of ownership (or the laws in which ownership is embodied). Some Marxists have used property ownership as the main criterion for class, but the real issues are the power to exploit (rather than just ownership) and the control of the means of production (not just the legal rights of ownership). The laws defining Roman slavery are preceded by the conquest and enslavement of peoples, so the exploitation of slaves rests on these social-economic bases.

Under capitalism, we usually speak of ownership of capital as a defining characteristic of capitalists, but it is the control which is important, not the legal ownership. More generally, it is not the laws of ownership, but the power to make decisions in the enterprise that is crucial. Thus a manager without ownership may nevertheless have control of the means of production and, consequently, the power over workers that goes with it. Moreover, the manager may be able to determine his or her own salary, which will then incorporate much profit or surplus labor into it. In this respect, corporate capitalism does differ from individual capitalism (where there is only one owner or a few partners).

Perhaps the best example of how legal forms may not reflect power was the former Soviet Union. All of the means of production in the Soviet Union were owned by the state for many decades. Since it was argued that the working class (or the whole people) controlled the state, this fact was used as an excuse for saying that there were no classes and no exploitation in the Soviet Union. On the contrary, a small elite class ruled the USSR politically, which meant control of the state, which in turn meant control of the means of production. The Soviet ruling class used that control to set its own salaries, so the salaries of the Soviet ruling class did contain surplus labor extracted from the Soviet worker. In this sense, the former Soviet ruling class had much in common with the U.S. ruling class.

A second level of class conflict is within the state. Modern Marxists recognize that the relationship between the political and the economic is a close one—and has been closer in some social formations, such as the Soviet Union, than in others. As a result some Marxists in the last few decades have argued that political domination should be part of the definition of class. They think of the term "ruling class," and wish to integrate this concept with that of the exploiting class—or may even argue that domination is a more important concept than exploitation. While accepting the fact that political domination is important and directly affects the economy, it would give rise to much confusion to include political domination within the definition of class. One can argue that something is important without muddying the analysis by including it in every definition.

Class consciousness may be defined as the ideological view of the majority of a class, including its self-identification and understanding of itself. Modern Marxists consider consciousness and ideology to be a vital part of the social process. If one class has an objective conflict with another, but no one in either class has any knowledge or belief in that conflict, then for all practical purposes the conflict does not exist. Only if a class has conscious knowledge of itself does that consciousness affect history. In that sense, class consciousness is a decisive issue. But the fact that it is so important does not mean that one should muddy the waters of the definition by adding the ideological factor into the definition itself. It is clearer in an analysis to define class objectively, then ask the question as to what ideology the class holds.

In a similar fashion, many Marxists in recent decades have talked about including nationality, race, or gender in the definition of class because these distinctions have proven to be so important for our understanding. Indeed, Marxist feminists have shown how to use both class and gender as powerful tools of analysis; while Marxists concerned with racial problems have shown how an understanding of the relation of class to race is an equally powerful tool of analysis. Again, the analysis will be clearer if race, gender, and nationality are handled as concepts separate from class, even though the relationship is extremely close in many cases. The importance of the issue should not be confused with its definition.

Marxists have always traced the effects of class on politics, consciousness, race, gender, and nationality. Modern Marxists have now begun to trace the opposite effects of each of these upon class and upon each other.

Erik Olin Wright has set out the structural properties of the modern Marxist concept of class. First, it is relational, relating each class to all others and to the means of production. It must be stressed that the Marxian concept of class is not based on incremental, gradational, or quantitative measures, such as income—but rather on the qualitative differences in relations among groups. Second, it is an antagonistic relation although there may be harmony at times, there may be compromises, and all the classes are interdependent in one social formation at a given time. They are antagonistic in the sense that "the welfare of the exploiting class depends upon the work of the exploited class" (Wright 1985, p. 75). Notice that this distinguishes exploitation from oppression; the relationship of oppression may also exist, but it is not a defining characteristic of class. Third, the relationship is based on the process of exploitation. For example, there is a causal relation between the riches of the feudal lords and the poverty of the feudal serfs (though exploitation does not always result in poverty). Fourth, the exploitation is based on the relationship of groups in production, not on ideology, legal ideas, or power. Such a definition is a powerful tool because it can be used to define modes of production and to understand the change from one mode of production to another.

What Is the Middle Class?

Any class analysis of the United States must confront the concept of the middle class because most U.S. citizens think of themselves as middle class—when they think of class at all. Barbara Ehrenreich poses the issues: "Karl Marx predicted that capitalist society would eventually be torn apart by the conflict between a greedy bourgeoisie and a vast rebellious proletariat. He did not foresee the emergence within capitalism of a vast middle class that would mediate between the extremes and create a stable social order. But with the middle class in apparent decline and with the extremes diverging further from each other, it would be easy to conclude that the Marxist vision at last fits America's future." (Ehrenreich [1991, p. 203] from a set of very amusing and provocative essays. For the objective data on the "decline of the middle class" in recent decades, see the exceptionally thorough study by Winnick [1989].)

One hundred years ago, most of the United States was composed of small farmers and small business people. Today those two categories are tiny remnants. There is, however, a new set of groups that could be described as middle-class, including managers and professionals. There is a widespread debate among modern Marxists over exactly how to categorize these new groups. One could argue that they are all workers, albeit white-collar, higher-income, salaried workers. Or one could characterize them by their degree of dominance and power, or by how close they are ideologically to capitalists or to workers.

Erik Wright suggests that these groups are in a somewhat contradictory class position. On the one hand, they are not ordinary workers in that they have more power, prestige, and income; they tend to identify ideologically with the capitalist class; and they are often in positions of power or control over other workers. On the other hand, they are still paid employees and may have far lower incomes than their capitalist employers. Managers dominate workers and can tell workers what to do, yet they must also do as they are told.

Professionals do not own the means of production, must sell their labor-power for a salary, and must take orders on the job; yet they also have a wide degree of independence and control over their immediate environment. Wright argues that experts are like ordinary workers in that they do not own the means of production, but they "have interests opposed to workers because of their effective control of organization and skill assets" (Wright 1985, p. 87). In assuming that experts have power because of their "skill assets," Wright is asserting that the sale of skills may put one in a position to exploit others. When it is stated so strongly, this notion—that exploitation of others may occur through exchange of skills in the market—is contrary to the Marxian view that exploitation results from control over the production process. The view that exploitation can be explained by individual exchange is contrary to the relational methodological approach.

Taken to a lesser extreme, however, Wright's point that people are sometimes placed in contradictory positions between capitalists and workers has a large measure of common sense to it. It is not important whether these groups are described as strata of the working class or described as middle classes or described as being in contradictory positions. Behind these verbal differences is an important issue that may be stated as follows: For tactical political purposes as well as scholarly understanding, we need to recognize that some of these groups will gravitate in some situations toward a pro-capitalist consciousness (based on some pro-capitalist interests) and in other situations toward working-class consciousness (based on some pro-working-class interests). Beyond this major analytic principle, a factual picture of how these middle groups, as well as capitalists and workers, are actually related in the United States is given in Appendix A to this chapter. (For still more detailed discussion, see Wright 1985).

Relational Approach to Class Conflicts

The relational method emphasizes the need to look at human beings not as isolated individuals, but as part of groups that are related to one another and sometimes in conflict. Modern Marxists do not argue that conflict must always exist in society. But modern Marxists do insist that the questions should always be asked: Are the class relations of this society antagonistic ones? Are there other conflicts as well?

Modern Marxists have explored not only class conflicts, but conflicts between big business and small business, racial conflicts, gender conflicts, nationality conflicts, and environmental conflicts—as well as the relationships among all of these in a given society. The modern Marxist approach—which asks relational questions, and specifically questions about antagonistic relations—provides a useful approach for examining each of these conflicts.

There is nothing in modern Marxism that says that class conflict is the only conflict or even that it is always the most important. Class relations and class conflict are considered the best beginning point to understand the structure of

any class-divided society. Without understanding the social and economic processes of a society, one cannot understand race, gender, or nationality within it.
Having found and examined class conflicts, however, critical Marxism insists
that one must then study separately racial, gender, and nationality conflicts. Of
course, one must examine how each of these conflicts is affected by class conflict—but one must also examine how class conflict is affected by race, gender,
and nationality conflicts. As one example of class and economic processes affecting class, at the time of the 1992 Los Angeles riots (which were perceived by
many solely in racial terms) 43 percent of all African-American youth, ages
sixteen to nineteen, were unemployed, which surely explained much of the rage
and frustration. As one example of race affecting class, the riots in Los Angeles
led to an outcry for more help to the inner cities, which may benefit all poor
people, and not just African-American poor.

Here, discussion begins with the three main levels of class conflict: the economic, the social and political, and the ideological. Modern Marxists argue that
it is wrong to speak as if one only had to pay attention to the economic level of
class conflict. On the contrary, modern Marxists insist on a careful investigation
of all three levels.

Class Conflict in the Economy

The U.S. class structure—described in Appendix A to this chapter—reveals a
small class of capitalists in conflict in different ways and to different degrees
with professionals and managers as well as with the large class of workers (plus
the unemployed, small farmers, and so forth). Modern Marxists see a whole
spectrum of classes, though there may be polarization on some issues in some
periods. One critic of Marxism claims that the greatest "distortion of the facts is
seen in Marx's polarization theory. It may even be true that the number of
classes has become smaller, but modern society has certainly not been reduced to
two classes" (Dupre 1966, p. 211).

No modern Marxist claims there are only two classes in modern capitalism;
there are many classes and strata. There has been polarization, however, in two
significant ways. In 1840, the small farmers and small businessmen and independent professionals constituted perhaps 90 percent of the populace. Today, those
groups are only 7 or 8 percent, while over 80 percent of Americans are in the
working class, including both poor and well-paid, both low-status and presti-
gious, both manual and mental workers. Because of this objective polarization,
the main political issues—such as unemployment benefits or capital gains
taxes—are also polarized around a capitalist's position versus a worker's position. Issues involving farmers or small business exist, but are more peripheral,
and may be seen as one of many secondary conflicts in society.

Within the productive process, there are several varieties of class conflict. The
conclusion of modern Marxist economic theory is that capitalists exploit workers

by extracting profits from the values created by the workers' toil. Workers resist this exploitation by individual slowdowns, by tossing monkey wrenches into the productive process in many ways, and by organized activity such as collective bargaining and strikes. In many industries the collective arm of the workers, their union, meets head on against the collective arm of capital, whether a single monopolistic giant or a trade association. The strength on either side—modified by supply and demand conditions—determines the split between wages and profits. Obviously, these class conflicts are neither random nor accidental; they are internal to the normal working of the productive process.

These class conflicts are partly reflected in and partly intensified by workers' alienation. Workers are alienated from their product by capitalists who own it and sell it at a profit, thus exploiting the workers. Workers are alienated from their work because each worker does only a tiny, routinized, part of the whole job. Subjectively, workers are alienated, not only from capitalists, but from each other as the result of competition against each other in the labor market.

A large number of radicals of the 1960s (such as Eric Fromm), basing themselves on the young Marx's *Economic and Political Manuscripts of 1844,* stressed subjective alienation as the main basis of class struggle, replacing the objective alienation of product and jobs caused by capitalist exploitation. The mass of poor and often unemployed workers, particularly minorities and women, tend to be most conscious of objective economic alienation through exploitation and unemployment. The better paid and more fully employed workers, particularly professional workers, are more aware of subjective alienation caused by competitive pressures and dictatorial authorities over them. Critical Marxists stress that both subjective and objective types of alienation are present, to a varying degree, in all jobs under capitalism. They result from the class conflicts within capitalist relations of production.

Social-Political Class Conflicts

Class conflict at the productive level is often mirrored in and modified by class conflict within all social and political institutions. For example, when Californians debated a proposition to permanently cut the progressive state income tax, it was attacked by the AFL-CIO and other working-class and middle-class organizations, but was supported by the California Manufacturers' Association, Builders' Association, Farm Bureau Association, Real Estate Association, and Chamber of Commerce. Obviously, neither the defense nor the attack was random; each represented class interests.

This second level of class conflict includes political struggle for control of the government. These issues are discussed in great detail in Sherman (1987, Chapter 7), where there is an extensive review of the literature, and also thoroughly surveyed in Sawyer (1989, Chapter 10). Here, there is only space for a brief summary and comment on a few recent controversies. Neoclassical economics says little on the state, but usually assumes that issues are decided on a rational basis by voters. At the other extreme, Stalinist Marxism contended that in capitalism there are only two classes locked in combat (thus precluding any real democracy), while in socialism there is only one class and it governs (so socialism is democratic by definition in this view).

Modern Marxism considers that, under capitalism, capitalist, working-class, and other class interests and views clash within the media of propaganda, within the churches, within the educational system, within the legal system and the courts, and within the legislative and executive branches of government. In all of these institutions, capitalist interests tend to be dominant, though there is varying pressure from and expression of working-class interests as well as interests of other classes—with differing degrees of success by the non-dominant classes.

Some modern Marxists emphasize that there are innumerable ways in which the economic power of big business is translated into political power, such as control of the media, churches, universities, candidates, and political parties through the direct use of wealth—this has been called the instrumentalist position. Other modern Marxists have emphasized that the structure of capitalism forces all politicians to follow the interests of capital, regardless of ideology— this has been called the structuralist position. For example, when Chrysler Corporation was on the verge of bankruptcy in the late 1970s, labor supported a government bail-out for Chrysler Corporation to protect jobs. Probably, capitalism influences social and political institutions through both the instrumentalist and structuralist ways.

It is certainly true that *under some circumstances and to some extent,* universal suffrage can express working-class views as against those of the propertied class. To put it another way, however, if there is no formal democracy with universal suffrage, then working-class views will not be represented; this was the case in Hitler's Germany. Thus, universal suffrage combined with formal democracy is one necessary condition for a wide degree of political democracy; other necessary conditions are a high degree of equality in income, and public or cooperative ownership of most productive property. With universal suffrage accompanied by a continued concentration of wealth and power in a few capitalist hands, there can be only a very limited amount of democratic control by the masses of workers.

Under either capitalism or socialism, one cannot say that democracy "exists" or "does not exist"; it exists *to some degree.* Where there is formal democracy, but capitalist ownership, the degree of democracy for most people is very low; there are "democratic" struggles among factions of the capitalist class, with only a small amount of "outside" pressure exerted by farmers and industrial and professional workers. On the other hand, where there is government ownership but no formal democracy, and the universal vote is only allowed for the purpose of endorsing a single party, the degree of democracy for most people is minute. This was the case in the Soviet Union before Gorbachev, though some pressure was always exerted by the non-ruling groups in various ways. A high degree of democracy requires both a formal democratic process and public or cooperative control of much industry to ensure a high degree of equality of economic power.

In the 1970s and 1980s, there was a confusing controversy among modern Marxists over just how autonomous the capitalist state is from the capitalist class. Theda Skocpol vigorously attacks the economic reductionist position that views the state as a mere reflection of "socioeconomic forces and conflicts" (1979, p. 25). Her work shows in detail how control of state power is used in revolutionary periods to help shape events—as the relational view has always emphasized.

Skocpol also has contributed to the discussion of how major reforms are made if capitalists control the state. She shows how the extensive New Deal reforms were not given away freely by farsighted capitalists (though there were a few such), but were conceded in response to working-class pressure (Skocpol 1980). She thus stresses the importance of organized movements on the political-economic matrix. Her work on revolution also illustrates the fact—emphasized by many Marxist historians—that the relationship of the state to the economic system is very different in different societies; so no single description of this relationship holds true in all cases, an important point in refuting economic reductionism.

The later works of G. William Domhoff similarly stress that "Marxian analysis of the state in democratic societies . . . creates a tendency to downplay the importance of representative democracy. For many Marxists, representative democracy is an illusion that grows out of the same type of mystification that is created by the market place" (Domhoff 1990, p. 8). Like Skocpol, Domhoff criticizes the economic reductionism of the old Stalinist Marxism, but states a position compatible with most of modern Marxism. The view of most modern Marxists is that popular illusions about democracy exist, but the illusions are based on the exaggeration of an important aspect of reality. In other words, democratic representation is vital, but is very much affected by the economic power of the capitalist class.

The conflict between the economic power of the capitalist class and the formal right to vote of the other classes is expressed somewhat differently by Samuel Bowles and Herbert Gintis: "Liberal democratic capitalism is a system of contradictory rules, empowering the many through . . . citizen rights—and empowering the few through property rights" (Bowles and Gintis 1990, p. 39). They define "citizen rights" to be the formal freedoms fought for by the working class, women, and minorities, while they define "property rights" to be the legal representation of the actual economic power used by the capitalist class. They show that the history of capitalist democracies is the history of conflict between citizen rights and property rights. The result has been formal equality, as in the Civil Rights acts, but actual continuing inequality for workers, women, and minorities.

Bowles and Gintis stress the clash between "two fundamental historical tend-

encies. The first is the expansionary logic of personal rights, progressively bringing ever wider spheres of society . . . under at least the formal . . . rubric of
liberal democracy. The second tendency concerns the expansionary logic of
capitalist production, according to which the capitalist firm's ongoing search for
profits progressively encroaches upon all spheres of social activity" (Bowles and
Gintis 1986, p. 29). On the one hand, working-class parties extended the suffrage
to all U.S. white males regardless of property in the early nineteenth century, the
women's movement extended suffrage to women in the early twentieth century,
and the African-American civil rights movement extended effective suffrage to
minorities in the late twentieth century. On the other hand, corporations grow
larger and larger, with more power over government, as shown in the counter-
revolution of the Reagan years, which rolled back many previous reforms.

Like Domhoff, Bowles and Gintis attack "Marxists" for paying too little
attention to democratic rights, concentrating only on class exploitation. They call
on all of the Left to push for the extension of citizen's rights from the political
sphere to the economy, a call for economic democracy. They make the point that
capitalists exert undemocratic (unelected) power and that all economic authority
should be democratically elected.

An interesting review by Jeff Goodwin (1990) points out the obvious facts
relevant to our methodological discussion. First, Bowles and Gintis are actually
attacking the economic reductionism of the old Soviet Marxism. All modern
Marxists, however, would agree with their attack on Soviet Marxism—so they
are speaking the prose of modern Marxism whether they care to use that terminology or not. There are, of course, many differences among modern Marxists
about (a) the tactics needed to achieve political and economic democracy, and
(b) the detailed characteristics of a future political and economic democracy.

Second, the actual political program of Bowles and Gintis is no different than
that of other modern Marxists, namely democratic socialism, which they call
"economic democracy." Goodwin points out that economic democracy is "something qualitatively different from socialism . . . only . . . if one accepts the curious notion that [socialism] . . . is inherently undemocratic" (1990, p. 138).
Goodwin says quietly: "Isn't the extension of democratic rights to the economy
precisely what socialism is all about?" (1990, p. 143). Of course, in the United
States, where socialism is a bad word (and even liberalism is sometimes a dangerous word), it should be emphasized that the rhetoric of economic democracy
proposed by Bowles and Gintis is excellent for Left movements!

Finally, Goodwin says that it is true that the fight for economic democracy
takes the form of a conflict between liberal democracy and capitalism. It is also
the case, however, that this fight is "grounded in the contradiction between the
material interests of workers and capital . . ." (Goodwin 1990, p. 142). Thus, the
political struggle remains one level of class conflict. The fact that politics is an
arena of class conflict does not mean that it is not also an arena of racial and
gender conflict. Goodwin stresses, as do Bowles and Gintis and anyone else who

may be called a modern Marxist, the crucial importance of racial and gender conflicts in our society. The civil rights movement, including all minority organizations and minority theorists, has shown with great clarity that racial conflicts shape and are shaped by politics and class conflict (see, e.g., Thomas Baron [1985] as well as the extensive discussion of the literature in Sherman [1987]). The women's movement, including organizations and theorists, has shown with equal clarity that gender conflicts shape and are shaped by politics and class conflict (see, e.g., Nancy Hartsock [1985] as well as the extensive discussion of the literature in Sherman [1987]). These contributions by women and by African-Americans and other minorities have been incorporated into the heart of modern Marxism.

Ideological Class Conflicts

The third level of class conflict is the reflection of class conflicts in clashing ideologies. The previous section discussed conflicts in social and political institutions, but here the conflict is in the related ideas. Of course, in reality it is hard to separate the Catholic Church as an institution from Catholic theology, or to separate the institution of slavery from the ideology of racism, or to separate the Democratic Party from its ideology. Yet it is very useful to separate each of these for analysis. One question that may then be asked is: How closely is each institution related to the ideas circulating in it, and exactly what are those relationships?

There are very real conflicts between ideologies. Examples include the arguments between those for and those against taxation of capital gains, between feminists and sexists, and between the defenders of ecology and the growth-at-any-cost school. Moreover, each of these ideologies develops with more and more sophistication and elegance (at least in academia; politicians, such as Ronald Reagan, may state the arguments very crudely). The path of development of each opposing idea is partly determined by the battle with its opposite. Yet these internal developments of ideologies are not independent of class relations but are both highly influenced by changing class relations and highly influential on the course of class relations. Thus the fact that the prevention of pollution could cause loss of profits for powerful capitalists has a great deal to do with the promotion of conflicting ideologies on pollution. On the other side, the surge of interest in ecological protection was related to the involvement of intellectuals in the civil rights and anti-war movements of the 1960s.

It should be noted that no class in history has ever had a simple, narrow, materialistic ideology that values things simply for its own class interest. On the contrary, the majority of each class usually believes that its desires represent the good of the whole of society. Thus, the bourgeoisie did not lead the French Revolution on the basis of what was good narrowly defined for its own interests, but as a crusade for liberty, equality, and fraternity (or the brotherhood of all men)—while the bourgeoisie in the American Revolution fought for life, liberty, and the pursuit of happiness.

Marxists argue that the ideas of the ruling class are the dominant ideology because (1) they control economic power, (2) they control the flow of information, and (3) most people assume that what is always will be (except under enormous pressure). But Marxists also note that the ruling ideology is subject to attacks from other classes depending on the degree of social disequilibrium. Callinicos (1991) contends that rulers do not always succeed in convincing most people that their ideology is correct, but they are usually successful in convincing most people that it is impossible to change the present situation—and Callinicos presents survey data supporting this view for the United States (1988, pp. 137–47). One reflection of the belief that nothing can be changed might be the fact that the U.S. electorate certainly does not vote in favor of alternatives to capitalism, but about half the electorate does not vote at all—and a belief that nothing can be changed by their vote is one of the reasons for not voting.

Questions, Not Answers

No one has discovered any eternal laws that apply to classes or to class conflict in every society. On the contrary, class relationships are strikingly different in different social formations. Therefore, there are no easy and general answers concerning class. Modern Marxism does suggest what questions to ask—and that is saying a lot in the social sciences where the hardest problem is often to figure out what are the most important questions to ask.

The Marxist approach instructs us to begin with questions about group relations, while its historical perspective tells us that these relations are specific to each mode of production. Therefore, in each social investigation, modern Marxists begin by asking: What are the class relations, if any? Are the relationships all of conflict, or all of harmony, or do the relationships involve both harmony and conflict in varying degrees? If there is class conflict, what are the forms it assumes? Are there economic, political, and ideological class conflicts? Are there conflicts within classes? Are there racial, gender, and/or nationality conflicts? Are there conflicts between developers and the ecology movement? How are the non-class conflicts related to class conflicts in the society?

Conclusions

The analysis of class, rather than individual psychology, is the entry point to all social, political, and economic analysis. Once the class relations of a society are understood, one can then proceed within that framework to explore race, gender, environment, and all other problems. Class relations are the logical starting point from a Marxist view; but it is meaningless to ask what is the most important relation, except at a given political moment.

Appendix A: Class Structure of the United States

Wright (1985) presents an enormous amount of useful empirical data on class, which is the basis for this section (but also see the interesting collection of criticisms of Wright in Wright, ed., 1989). He finds that in attitudes and income, most white-collar workers are actually quite similar to blue-collar workers; or at least they are far more so than the current myths would indicate. He finds no evidence of much distinction between manual and non-manual workers. Nor does he find any evidence to indicate that productive versus non-productive is a useful empirical division for workers (he generally defines non-productive workers to be in retail sales, finance, insurance, and government—a controversial definition).

Among other general findings is the interesting point that workers' attitudes are shaped far more by their previous work experiences than by their present work experience. Thus, all workers have the common experiences of being forced to sell their labor-power to live, being subordinate at the work place, and having no control over the use of the surplus. But previous experiences may differ in many ways, for example, by race and gender. Thus, a woman who has been previously limited to housework will have a somewhat different attitude than a woman who has worked at paid labor all her life. Wright also points out that present experiences may influence people in conflicting ways; for example, professionals are exploited, but they also have pleasant work experiences and may not feel subordinated to bosses. Finally, workers may be pulled in different directions by (a) having two different levels of jobs, (b) living with someone with a different level job or even of a different class, and (c) going through rapid changes (for example, from student to assistant professor to tenured professor).

Capitalist countries have different degrees of inequality. Sweden had only a three to one difference between the 95th percentile and the 5th percentile of income receivers. In the United States the difference is thirteen to one, one of the more unequal among capitalist distributions of income.

Wright (1985, pp. 194–96) finds that the "bourgeoisie," living primarily on property income, are 2 percent of the economically active population (all data here are rounded). The "petty bourgeoisie," that is, people who are self-employed but have no employees, are 7 percent. Small business, that is employers of only a few people, constitute 6 percent. Managers are 12 percent. Supervisors are 17 percent. Experts and technical workers are 16 percent. Finally, wage workers, including manual and non-manual as well as productive and non-productive, are 40 percent.

Wright (1985, pp. 192–201) finds that women are a majority of the working class, that is, 61 percent of unskilled workers and 53 percent of all workers. Yet women are only 30 percent of small employers, 32 percent of managers, and 26 percent of skilled workers. In the active economic population, 57 percent of white women are workers (skilled and unskilled), 78 percent of black women are workers, 69 percent of black males are workers, but only 27 percent of white males are workers in this definition. On the other hand, among the active economic population only 10 percent of white women are managers, only 8 percent of black men are managers, only 6 percent of black women are managers, but 17 percent of white males are managers and supervisors. Finally, of all unskilled workers, two-thirds are women and/or blacks.

It should be remembered that not all employment is in the private sector. In the United States, 18 percent of all ordinary workers and 30 percent of all experts are hired by federal, state, and local governments. Thus a very significant portion of the labor force is employed in the public sector.

In terms of income in the United States in 1980, Wright (1985, p. 235) finds that it rises by class as follows: unskilled workers had $11,161 mean income, skilled had $16,034, supervisors had $23,057, small employers had $24,828, managers had $28,665, and the bourgeoisie had $52,621. Note that income derives from one's class position; BUT class is not defined by income. It is especially important to find that ordinary workers reported unearned (or property) income of only $363, but managers reported unearned income of $1,646 annually. Thus, the average worker has very little stake in the present system, but the average manager owns enough income-producing property to have a significant stake in the capitalist system—and of course top managers of large firms have a large amount of unearned income.

Appendix B: Class Structure of the Former Soviet Union

During the Cold War, just as non-Marxist U.S. sociologists found no antagonistic classes in the United States, official Soviet Marxist sociology found no antagonistic classes in the Soviet Union. Official Soviet Marxists claimed that there were no exploiting classes in the Soviet Union. They claimed that there were only workers, divided into non-antagonistic strata; there were manual workers, intellect workers, and farm workers, none of whom exploited one another. It is true that if class is defined by whether or not a particular group owns the means of production, then there were no classes in the former Soviet Union. Aside from the collective farms, all means of production were owned by the Soviet government (the detailed information and references for this whole section may be found in Zimbalist, Sherman, and Brown 1988).

Obviously, a small group of people held political power in the former Soviet Union, while most people had little or no political power. But that fact by itself is of little help in analyzing Soviet class structure since it was equally true of many very different times and different countries, for example, Hitler's Germany. Classes are not defined by political power, though one can analyze which class holds the ruling power.

Let us examine the facts. All factual statements here refer to the former Soviet Union in the period 1928 to 1988, that is, the period of extremely centralized ownership and planning. In the pre-reform period, it was a fact that (a) the means of production were owned by the Soviet government, and (b) the Soviet government was controlled by a relatively small group. It follows that, given the former Soviet system, those who exercised political power automatically exercised economic power as well.

In the former Soviet system, wages and salaries were set by political decree, not by the market. Therefore, those with political and economic power set their own wages and salaries—or had some impact on setting those salaries. In official Soviet theory, all wages and salaries were paid according to the labor that was done, so there was no exploitation. But it would be naive to think that the people at the top set their own salaries so as to just equal their labor expenditure.

It was also the case—even according to official Soviet analysis—that the average Soviet worker had extracted from his or her labor expended a certain amount of surplus labor, that is, labor expended above the necessary labor going to produce their own individual consumption of goods and services. This does not prove exploitation; it must be true of any modern economy. The surplus labor, extracted from the Soviet working class, was—in the official view—supposed to go to (a) the creation of new means of production to expand the economy, and (b) collective consumption by the whole population, such as parks.

Whether or not there was exploitation depends on the answer to two questions. First, was there also a third part of the surplus labor of workers going to pay the salaries (and fringe benefits) of top Soviet officials beyond the remuneration due to the labor of those officials? Second, did the ruling class of the former Soviet Union control expenditures on new investment and collective consumption for its own purposes, or did the average Soviet worker have an equal say concerning that expenditure?

It has been noted that the people at the top of pre-reform Soviet society set their own salaries. These salaries had three components. First, the official salary itself was several times higher than the average wage. Second, there were many important fringe benefits, including chauffeurs and automobiles, specialized health treatment, special luxury stores, and summer homes in the countryside. Third, there were large additional secret sums of money. In the Gorbachev period, however, enough of the secret data was leaked to prove that the top Soviet leaders did receive the surplus labor of others as part of their own remuneration. Since they received surplus labor, their own remuneration was far above what their own labor produced. That surplus labor was extracted through the exploitation of the Soviet working class.

But the total amount of surplus labor transferred directly from Soviet workers to the Soviet ruling class was very small by U.S. standards. The main issue of income distribution in the former Soviet Union was the use of the huge surplus labor product that went to investment, collective consumption, and military spending. As noted earlier, there was nothing wrong or exploitative per se in such uses of the surplus product. If workers agreed that some of their surplus labor should go to build a swimming pool for everyone in their enterprise to use, that was obviously not exploitation. If all Soviet workers agreed that 10 percent of GNP—coming from their surplus labor—should be invested in new plant and equipment, that was not exploitation.

The problem in the former Soviet Union was that workers did not make these decisions. Self-selected leaders decided on the entire allocation of the surplus labor. Suppose a small, dictatorial group decided that a large amount of workers' surplus labor should be used to build nuclear bombs rather than hospitals. Is that exploitation?

It could be argued that extraction of surplus for purposes dictated exclusively by the ruling class is exploitation just as much as the extraction of surplus labor directly into the pockets of the ruling class. Both forms of surplus labor extraction depended on ruling class control of the Soviet political process and political control of the means of production.

There were four main hierarchies in the former Soviet Union: the Communist Party, the government apparatus, the economic pyramid, and the military. Within the Communist Party, the top functionaries (such as in the Politburo) had enormous power and were appointed rather than elected—though there were "elections" after the real decision was made. There was also a political pyramid composed of powerful officials in the government, such as the Council of Ministers and their deputies. The economic pyramid was ruled by a small group of economic planners at the top (responsible to the government and party leaders) plus some powerful directors of sectors and very large enterprises. The military was completely hierarchical, with the top generals also being party leaders in most cases. In each of the four hierarchies, orders flowed downward, while some information flowed upward. At the top were fifty to a hundred people who controlled all four hierarchies and frequently transferred from one to the other. These people received high salaries, huge fringe benefits, and probably enormous secret income. Thus, their income levels approximated those of the top U.S. capitalists, relatively speaking.

Below the very top Soviet group, there were another 100,000 to 200,000 Soviet officials who had high salaries and huge fringe benefits (with perhaps some illegal income). The total income, however, of each of these high Soviet officials was still far below that of most U.S. capitalists, in both absolute and relative terms. One U.S. study finds that the Soviet "elite" made up only 0.2 percent of all gainfully employed Soviet citizens, or only 220,000 people (Bergson 1984, p. 1085). The "elite" were defined in this study as those who received at least 3.1 times the average wage or at least 5.7 times the minimum wage. These 220,000 included most enterprise directors, party officials, government officials, top military officers, and some professionals.

Since the total number of the Soviet rich was perhaps one-tenth of the U.S. number, and since their average income was much lower than the U.S.

capitalist's average income, the total amount of surplus labor going into individual pockets was much lower in the Soviet Union than in the United States. The reason is that exploitation for individual wealth is more difficult in an economy where it appears to flow directly from raw political power rather than from the private investment of funds. In both systems the reality was ruling-class control of the means of production.

On the other hand, the top members of the Soviet ruling class probably had far more power over social decision making (on jobs, investment, and allocation of goods and services) than does the U.S. capitalist class. This is because, in their normal role, the Soviet leaders directly controlled all of the levers of political and economic decision making—and economic decisions were highly centralized. Taken together, U.S. capitalists do control jobs, investment, and the allocation of resources in the private sector, but the decisions are more decentralized (though a fairly small number of capitalists control the thousand largest corporations that own a majority of the U.S. assets). U.S. capitalist control of political decisions, such as military spending, is more indirect and is limited in certain ways.

U.S. ruling-class members are more secure in their power than the former Soviet ruling class was, both for themselves and for their children. If a U.S. capitalist loses or gives up an executive job, he or she retains wealth and status. In the Soviet Union, on the other hand, power and wealth adhered to a particular official position. If you lost the position, you lost all your power. If your power was lost, your income disappeared.

The children of the top twenty thousand Soviet leaders did not hold the same jobs and were not usually at the same rank as their parents (see Nove 1975, pp. 615–38). If one goes much lower, however, to examine the top 10 percent of all Soviet income receivers, one does find that their children were also usually somewhere in that category. Thus, it can be concluded that the very top leadership was not hereditary, but that the bulk of the officials, managers, and highly-placed professionals did give their children enough moral and monetary support—and good connections—that those children also usually landed good jobs.

The former Soviet working class presented a wide spectrum of income and status differences, from high-paid artistic and sports stars to very low-paid menial workers. Thus, in 1981 the top 10 percent of Soviet wage and salary workers earned three times what the bottom 10 percent earned (Bergson 1984, p. 1063). By comparison, in the United States in 1975 the top 10 percent of wage and salary workers earned four times what the bottom 10 percent earned. So there appeared to be somewhat less inequality within the Soviet working class than within the U.S. working class, but the main differences in income inequality between the two countries came in the much greater wealth of the U.S. elite. One overall estimate, with considerable guess work and limited data, found that a standard measure of inequality (the Gini coefficient) for the pre-tax income of all households in the United States was .376 in 1972 (Bergson 1984, p. 1070). The same measure of inequality for the pre-tax income of all urban households in the USSR was only .288 in 1972–74, reflecting significantly less inequality (see Zimbalist and Sherman 1984, p. 288, for details).

References

Ashton, T.H., and C.H.E. Philpin, eds. 1985. *The Brenner Debate: Class Structure and Economic Development in Pre-Industrial Europe.* New York: Cambridge University Press.
Baron, Harold. 1985. "Racism Transformed: The Implications of the 1960s," *Review of Radical Political Economics*, vol. 17 (Fall), pp. 10–33.
Bergson, Abram. 1984. "Income Inequality under Soviet Socialism." *Journal of Economic Literature,* vol. 22 (September), pp. 1052–99.
Bowles, Samuel, and Herbert Gintis. 1986. *Democracy and Capitalism.* New York: Basic Books.
Bowles, Samuel, and Herbert Gintis. 1990. "Rethinking Marxism and Liberalism from a Radical Democratic Perspective." *Rethinking Marxism*, vol. 3 (Fall–Winter), nos. 3–4, pp. 37–45.
Callinicos, Alex. 1991. *The Revenge of History.* Cambridge, UK: Polity Press.
Domhoff, G. William. 1990. *The Power Elite and the State.* New York: Aldine de Gruyter.
Dupre, Louis. 1966. *The Philosophical Foundations of Marxism.* New York: Harcourt, Brace, and World.
Ehrenreich, Barbara. 1991. *The Worst Years of Our Lives.* New York: Harper-Collins.
Elliot, John. 1979. "Social and Institutional Dimensions of Marx's Theory of Capitalism." *Review of Social Economy*, vol. 37, no. 3 (December), pp. 261–74.
Goodwin, Jeff. 1990. "The Limits of 'Radical Democracy.' " *Socialist Review*, vol. 90, no. 2, pp. 131–44.
Green, Francis. 1984. "A Critique of the Neo-Fisherian Consumption Function." *Review of Radical Political Economics*, vol. 16, nos. 2 and 3, pp. 95–114.
Hartsock, Nancy. 1985. *Money, Sex, and Power: Toward a Feminist Historical Materialism.* Boston: Northeastern University Press.
Hodgson, Geoff. 1986. "Behind Methodological Individualism." *Cambridge Journal of Economics*, vol. 10 (September), pp. 211–24.
Keynes, John Maynard. 1936. *The General Theory of Money, Interest, and Employment.* New York: Harcourt-Brace.
Lucas, Robert. 1986. "Models of Business Cycles." Paper prepared in mimeo for the Yrjo Jansson Lectures, Helsinki, Finland (March).
Marglin, Steven. 1989. "Understanding Capitalism: Control versus Efficiency." In *Power and Economic Institutions*, ed. Bo Gustafsson, pp. 85–99. Brookfield, Vt.: Edward Elgar.
Marx, Karl. 1867. *Capital,* I. London: Allen & Unwin, printed 1965.
Marx, Karl. 1968. *Theories of Surplus Value.* Moscow: Progress Publishers.
Miliband, Ralph. 1991. *Divided Societies: Class Struggle in Contemporary Capitalism.* New York: Oxford University Press.
Nove, Alec. 1975. "Is There a Ruling Class in the USSR?" *Soviet Studies*, vol. 27 (October), pp. 615–38.
Resnick, Stephen, and Richard Wolff. 1987. *Knowledge and Class.* Chicago: University of Chicago Press.
St. Croix, G.E.M. de. 1981. *The Class Struggle in the Ancient Greek World.* London:

Routledge.
Sawyer, Malcolm. 1989. *The Challenge of Radical Political Economy.* Savage, Md.: Barnes and Noble.
Sherman, Howard. 1987. *Foundations of Radical Political Economy.* Armonk, N.Y.: M.E. Sharpe.
Skocpol, Theda. 1979. *States and Social Revolutions.* New York: Cambridge University Press.
Skocpol, Theda. 1980. "Political Responses to Capitalist Crisis: NeoMarxist Theories of the State and the Case of the New Deal." *Politics and Society,* vol. 10, no. 2, pp. 23–46.
Soderbaum, Peter. 1990. "Neoclassical and Institutional Approaches to Environmental Economics." *JEI,* vol. 24 (June), pp. 481–91.
Winnick, Andrew. 1989. *Toward Two Societies: The Changing Distribution of Income and Wealth in the United States since 1960.* New York: Praeger.
Wolff, Richard, and Stephen Resnick. 1986. "Power, Property and Class." *Socialist Review,* vol. 16, no. 2 (March/April), pp. 97–124.
Wright, Erik Olin. 1985. *Classes.* New York: Verso.
Zimbalist, Andrew, and Howard Sherman. 1984. *Comparing Economic Systems: A Political-Economic Approach,* 1st ed. San Diego: Harcourt Brace Jovanovich.
Zimbalist, Andrew, Howard Sherman, and Stuart Brown. 1988. *Comparing Economic Systems: A Political-Economic Approach,* 2nd ed. San Diego: Harcourt Brace Jovanovich.

5

Power, Property, and Class

Richard Wolff and Stephen Resnick

Among Marxists and non-Marxists alike, the term "class" appears often within their analyses of society. By itself or with adjectives such as "working," "ruling," "under-," or "capitalist," the term is clearly central to most Marxist and not a few non-Marxist arguments about social structure and social change. Yet reviewing those arguments yields a curious problem. The meanings assigned to the term are definitely not the same. Moreover, debates over many topics other than class per se can be seen to stem largely from disagreements—infrequently acknowledged as such—over what class is.

We share with many a central focus upon class as an indispensable concept for analyzing society. Thus the multiplicity of concepts of class inside and outside the Marxist tradition poses problems. Are there some concepts of class that prevail over others within Marxist literature? Are there criteria for preferring theoretically one against another of such concepts? We think that these questions demand answers. Otherwise, class analyses will continue to display inconsistent and often confused usages of one of their most central terms.

We intend to show that there are some basically different concepts of class at play in Marxist writings. We believe that a writer's choice, whether conscious or not, of one such concept rather than another will lead him or her to correspondingly different theoretical and political conclusions. In other words, it matters which concept of class is used to make sense of social structures and strategies for social change. We will cite examples where largely unexamined commitments to particular concepts of class have played major roles in shaping key theoretical and political struggles waged by and also within the Marxist tradition. We intend an intervention in that tradition which will clarify its usages of class and also re-establish the importance of one particular conception: the surplus labor theory of class.

Originally published in *Socialist Review,* vol. 16, no. 2, March/April 1986, pp. 97–124. Reprinted with permission.

An analyst can group persons within a community or society according to any one of a literally infinite number of possible characteristics. A group, or "class" in this abstract sense, could be conceptualized as all persons sharing a common muscular build, bone structure, vocal tone, athletic prowess, skill at various functions, degree of religious or secular education, level of prestige or wealth, or any other possible characteristic. Grouping people in such ways has been a hallmark of most sorts of social analysis including those called "class" analyses. Often other terms for similar kinds of grouping—strata, elites, fractions, sections—are woven into analyses also utilizing class.

Class in particular has long been a term narrowed by actual usage to designate a few specific kinds of groupings.[1] Especially since the eighteenth century, there have been three rather distinct groupings meant by the term class. Class is sometimes used to designate groups of persons in society according to the property they do or do not own. Varying qualities and/or quantities of property are used to categorize persons into classes. A second and different usage holds class to mean a group of persons who share the fact that they either do or do not wield power or authority in society.[2] Different kinds and amounts of social authority are here understood to define class boundaries. Thirdly, there is a notion of class as concerning the production, appropriation, and distribution of surplus labor (defined and discussed below). Classes are then defined as groups of persons who share the common social position of performing surplus labor or of appropriating it from the performers or of obtaining distributed shares of surplus from the appropriators.[3]

A fourth kind of approach amounts to composite conceptualizations of class: various mixtures of the basic three notions. These involve defining class in terms of power *and* property or surplus labor production *and* property or all three together. For example, one such composite approach conceives of the capitalist class structure as "a system rooted in a dichotomy between possessing masters and subject dispossessed."[4] Writings in the Marxist tradition often signal composite conceptualizations by defining classes as persons who share common positions in or connections to the "relations of production" or "mode of production." Upon inspection, classes defined in terms of relations of production usually turn out to be composites whose authors variously emphasize the power, property, or surplus-labor components of such relations of production (classes).

In singular or composite definitions, the three distinct concepts of class—qua property, power, and/or surplus labor—prevail both within and without the Marxian tradition. However, they are irreducibly different and not to be conflated. Persons with property may or may not also wield power and vice versa. To own property in a particular society need not empower the owner to employ another human being or to participate in state decisions; that would depend, for example, on ideological and political conditions in that society. To be propertyless need not require a person to sell labor power; that would depend, for example, on whether propertyless persons had socially recognized access to income from other sources. To wield state powers of all sorts need not require ownership of property; that would depend on the social rules whereby power is granted to individuals. In sum, the ownership of property (whether in means of production or more generally) is neither a necessary nor a sufficient condition for the wielding of power and vice versa.

Class analyses using one definition will yield different results from analyses using another. No little political importance attaches to this conundrum. Moreover, as we shall show, class designations according to surplus labor production/distribution will not necessarily correspond to the class designations drawn according to either the property or the power concepts. Usages of class that do not recognize and address these differences invite all manner of misunderstandings.

In our view, distributions of property and power have long been social conditions used to define class. Radicals and conservatives among the ancient Greeks classified persons according to the property they owned and attributed great analytical significance to such classes. Conceptualizations of class in terms of property ownership have recurred periodically ever since. Similarly, concepts of class defined by the qualities and quantities of power wielded by social groupings are endemic through the literature for centuries. However, the concept of class as surplus labor has a special relation to Marx.

Marx conceived of class in a unique manner as the production and distribution of surplus labor. Of course, Marx was aware of and deeply impressed with the early class-analytical literature. His work is filled with allusions to classes in terms of property and power. However, he was also sharply critical of his predecessor class analysts' concepts on the grounds that they had missed something crucial to the success of their—and his—goals for a more just and free society. They had underestimated or missed altogether the economic process of surplus labor production and distribution. By missed, Marx meant that their analyses of contemporary society overlooked the structural position of the surplus labor process. Thus, in his view, their projections of strategies for social change inadequately addressed the changes in the surplus labor process needed to sustain the anticipated socialist or communist society.

Marx's goal was never to deny or displace the importance of property and power in the structure of contemporary society or in the plans for the sort of socialist society he longed for. Rather, he sought to add something to the understanding of his fellow revolutionists and radicals, namely a worked-through grasp of the surplus labor process and the ways in which it both supported and depended upon the processes of property and power (among the other social processes that concerned him).[5]

A few examples may clarify the important implications of these different concepts of class. Consider the debates over the class structure of the Soviet Union. On one side the argument is advanced that it represents a classless society because private property was abolished there. Defenders of this view operate with a property concept of class. Opponents often do likewise with the more subtle argument that what was abolished was merely de jure private property while de facto it still persists in the USSR and hence so do classes. Similarly, social-democrats around the world frequently equate socialism, or the transition from capitalism to socialism with the socialization of property in the means of production; again concepts of class qua patterns of property ownership figure significantly.

More prevalent in recent debates over the Soviet Union's class structure has been argumentation deploying power rather than property concepts of class. Such formulations often attack the property theorists of class by claims that notwithstanding the socialization of private property, a ruling class still exists in the USSR. These are then demonstrated by reference to patterns of power and authority there. The term class is ascribed to groupings found to possess and wield more or fewer quanta of power regardless of who owns or is separated from property.

The debates over the USSR's class structure teach that not only are different concepts of class at play (with an array of variations, of course) but also that the same argument often contains confused and confusing mixtures of these concepts. Further, the debates' focus on property and power leads those on all sides to play down or ignore what we understand as class: the processes of producing, appropriating, and distributing surplus labor in the USSR. Our interest here is not to deny the importance of property and power to any assessment of the USSR, but rather to correct a defect typical of most assessments, namely their neglect of the surplus labor type of class analytics. Which alternative conceptualization of class is used affects an individual's political practices in regard to the USSR: a potent political issue since 1917.

As a second example, consider the attraction of Marxists to the social analysis of what are usually called the "middle classes" in capitalist societies. Do they really exist between the two main classes? Are they friends or foes of the working class or might they go either way depending upon circumstances? How do we properly allocate those who do not fall neatly into either main class into the various possible categorizations of middle class? To answer such questions, Marxists and others have deployed class analytics which again demonstrate their prevalent commitment to discussions limited to matters of property and power.

In general, most Marxist treatments start from a dissatisfaction with the typical dichotomous class model ascribed to Marxism. They decry efforts to collapse a complex class structure into a bipolar confrontation. Often taking a cue from Marx's distinction between bourgeoisie and petite bourgeoisie, notably a quantitative distinction, they seek to show how gradations beyond a mere two can admit of middle classes. Does the notion of a petite bourgeoisie refer to the smallness of the quantity of means of production owned? Are middle classes then persons situated somewhere between propertylessness and some large quantum of means of production whose owner is considered to be a bourgeois? Much debate based on such conceptions of middle classes has drawn sharply opposed conclusions regarding whether and how working classes can approach such middle classes in terms of class-struggle alliances.

On the other hand, class-as-power theorists frequently oppose the property theorists; they rather favor investigating the power/authority nexus. Can we locate persons who are neither pure order-givers nor pure order-takers, neither ruling nor ruled classes? Are there such middle classes who take as well as give orders, and if so, who exactly are they and how do they figure into class struggles? From these theoretical roots has sprouted an ingenious sequence of analyses of complex, non-dichotomous class structures. Not a few theorists combine, sometimes explicitly, both property and power to generate matrices of multiple and complex classes. Again, different proposals for political actions and alliances flow from power than from property analyses of middle classes.

While we share the desire to move beyond the sterility of simple two-class models of social structure, we regret that there has been relatively little theoretical movement beyond the old concepts of class as property and/or power. Our goal is to elaborate Marx's beginnings in constructing class groupings in terms of how persons perform, appropriate, or receive distributed shares of surplus labor. Thus, if performers and appropriators of surplus labor comprise two classes of society, then another sort of class is defined in terms of the recipients of distributed shares of the appropriated surplus labor. "Middle" is then certainly not an appropriate adjective since it precisely suggests a class location in the space between two others, a location that makes much less sense in our approach.[6]

The Problem of Reductionism

The discussion of class is beset not only by different and often clashing definitions of class. There is also a major problem of how to theorize the relationship between class and non-class aspects of society. Some authors reduce their particular definition of class to an effect of other, more fundamental aspects of society. Others, equally reductionist, reverse the argument and make their notion of class into the key cause while the rest of society is reduced to its effect. Much of the Marxist tradition has been understood to argue reductively that class structure ("the base") determines social structure ("the superstructure") and class struggle determines historical change. Indeed, many debates in and over the Marxist tradition have turned precisely over whether the economy determines the society (economic determinism or reductionism) or whether the economy is itself determined by/reduced to the effect of other social aspects (e.g., the political, the cultural, or the natural).

We find this reductionism to be problematic because of its a priori presumption that some causes must outweigh others in determining an effect. Reductionism has, in our view, contributed to disastrous theoretical and political consequences as changes in one social factor—the presumed "most effective cause"—have been expected to usher in all manner of necessary effects which never materialized.

In any case, whether reductionism is acceptable or not, it is certainly not the only way to theorize the relationship between class and non-class aspects of society. It can be replaced analytically by a non-reductionist perspective. Class, however defined, can be understood as the effect of many different social aspects with none of them playing the role of "most fundamental" determinant. Similarly, class can also be understood as itself a cause affecting all the other aspects of society. The stress here is upon class as one among many causes of social structure and history; it need not be seen reductively as *the* cause. Social aspects, then, may all be approached as necessarily both causes and effects at the same time.[7]

Our point here is to emphasize that discussions of class can and do vary in two major ways. They display different definitions of class. They also differ on whether to link class and non-class aspects of society reductively or not, in a relation of determinism or overdetermination. Our critique of the prevalent Marxist and non-Marxist treatments of class takes them to task on both counts: (1) for their definitions of class as power and/or property concepts, and (2) for their reductionism. Our alternative below reflects this critique.

A non- or anti-reductionist approach to class eschews in principle the analytical search for last, final, or ultimate causes or determinants. Hence it can never find class or any other social aspect to be such a cause. Instead, the goal is to explore the complex way in which a chosen set of social aspects interrelate as simultaneous causes and effects. Marxists can then choose, for diverse reasons, to explore sets that include class without this implying any reductionist conception of class either as *the* determinant cause or as the effect of something else designated as such a determinant cause. Notwithstanding pronouncements in favor of complex conceptions of causality, reductionist celebrations of "key explanatory variables" dominate discussions of class. Thus, a property theorist of class will likely make power and surplus labor mere effects of property distributions. A power theorist will reply that property distributions and the structure of surplus labor production are necessary consequences of particular power relations. Finally, the class-as-surplus-labor theorist can insist that allocations of power and property follow from individuals' different relationships to the production and appropriation of surplus labor. These three groups are thus locked into a debate over whether class, as each defines it, is key cause or mere effect.

There are also more subtle kinds of reductionism found particularly in Marxist discussions of class. They occur in conceptualizations of class as a composite entity composed of economic, political, and cultural constituents. Indeed, such composite conceptualizations often emerge as critical reactions against unidimensional concepts of class as either power, property, or surplus labor groupings. The reductionism surfaces in arguments among proponents of such composite theories over which aspect of class is "the most fundamental" in determining that a class exists (rather than merely a group of persons).

One example of this is the influential formulation of the distinction between class "in itself" and class "for itself." The former is thought to be structurally defined in terms of power, property, surplus labor, etc. The latter is defined as the former plus an element of self-consciousness: class for itself as an ideological (cultural) as well as economic and political entity. Classes, in effect, are defined to exist at two levels, one more complete than the other. Proponents of such formulations have often been reductionist in them, striving to make consciousness the key determinant of class in the second and fuller sense.[8]

The Prevalent Forms of Class Analysis

Our brief overview of the most prevalent forms of class analysis requires several preliminary observations. First, writers and texts are rarely pure exponents of one conception of class. They typically exhibit more than one. Thus, when we cite an author to exemplify one conception, we do not mean to imply that he or she never formulated another view of class. Secondly, this is far from a complete or exhaustive literature review; we range broadly across the literature to cull typical examples of the most prevalent formulations. Finally, our survey divides these formulations into three types: conceptions of class as property, as power, and as a complex composite entity of several different elements. We begin with illustrations of the property approach.

A well known and influential recent study of the links between Marxist and feminist analyses asserts that "a Marxist definition of class rests on relationship to ownership of the means of production."[9] Indeed, innumerable Marxist texts for a hundred years contain virtual identifications of class structure with property distribution. In a famous article Paul Sweezy posed the following basic question: "What is it that determines how many classes there are and where the dividing lines are drawn?" He responded directly and precisely: "Generally speaking, the answer is obvious (and is borne out by all empirical investigations): the property system plays this key role."[10] Thinkers as diverse as Oskar Lange, Ralf Dahrendorf, C. Wright Mills, Anthony Giddens, Robert Lekachman, and E.G. Pashunakis made clear statements defining class quite strictly and narrowly in terms of property ownership.[11]

One of the most thorough and theoretically self-conscious explorations of a property concept of class occurs in the recent work of Paul Hirst and Barry Hindess. In several books, they develop, correct, and elaborate "concepts of possession and separation from the means of production . . . central to the analysis of economic classes."[12] The property theory of class also appears in some variant forms. One of the most widespread shifts the definition of class away from ownership or separation from the means of production to more general differentiations either between wealth and poverty ("rich" and "poor" classes) or between high and low incomes (non-wage vs. wage earners). In particular, the latter criterion of class—as a matter of one's position in the hierarchy of income levels—is very widely used in both Marxist and non-Marxist discussions. Expressions such as "the class of poor people" or "middle class" or "wage-earning class" or "the rich" denote a theory allocating individuals to classes according to either the size or type of their current income/asset positions.[13] In any case, whether "property" referred to means of production, wealth in stocks of commodities, or levels of income flows, most interpreters have attributed such property theories of class to Marx. He was understood to conceive such classes as prone to struggles for redistributions of property and/or income. These struggles functioned as the "motor" of social change historically. As we shall argue, ours is a very different interpretation of Marx on class.

Instead of defining class in terms of property, it may be conceived as a matter of wielding power over persons, controlling other people's behavior. Groups of persons are then treated as classes to the extent that they share a common status as either wielders of power or subject to the power of others. The social distribution of authority defines class positions. The adjectives that usually signal the presence of power theories of class are "ruling" vs. "ruled" or "dominant" vs. "dominated." Class struggles then become struggles over power, especially though not exclusively state power. The powerless classes struggle to acquire power while their adversaries struggle to retain or expand their power.

Non-Marxists have long been particularly interested in affirming pointedly political concepts of class which they often distance sharply from property concepts which they ascribe to Marx and Marxists. A canon of such interpretation is, for example, Gaetano Mosca's view of class analysis as a specifically political science focused on the issue of who rules whom.[14] C. Wright Mills oriented many in the United States with a class analysis summarized in his famous term and 1956 book title, *The Power Elite*. Ralf Dahrendorf offers a particularly clear formulation which directly confronts alternative notions of class:

> But Marx believed that authority and power are factors which can be traced back to a man's share in effective private property [ownership]. In reality, the opposite is the case. Power and authority are irreducible factors from which the social relations associated with legal private property as well as those associated with communal property can be derived.[15]

Here Dahrendorf moves from a rejection of the property notion of class to a general theory of classes as constituted in and through power struggles per se. Whenever people associate into groups to contend against other groups over any particular objective(s), these groups are classes. "If, in a given society, there are fifty associations, we should expect to find a hundred classes, or conflict groups in the sense of the present study."[16] Dahrendorf reduces property distribution to an effect of power and authority relations.

Many Marxist theorists have recently moved toward a kind of political conception of class not far removed from Dahrendorf's approach. One stimulus has been a feeling that particularly in Western capitalist nations, a broadly comfortable "middle income class" has made issues of income and wealth less urgent and less central than issues of inequitable power distributions. Thus activist and analytical focus shifted from struggles over property to struggles over power and its social distribution. Property seems to have given way to power—in the home, at the workplace, in the state—as the cutting edge of social struggles animating socialists and thus Marxist theorists.

Another motivation toward a power theory of class among Marxists has come from their conclusion that classlessness and its rewards did not appear in societies that nationalized or socialized ownership in the means of production. Rather intolerable power distributions—if not property distributions—were seen to remain in such societies. This interpretation connects to the critique of capitalist society which attacks its property allocation but even more its unjust distributions of power and authority. Marx's writings are then probed for analyses of classes as groups which either possess or are separated from power over the social behavior of others (or Marx is faulted, as in Dahrendorf, for insufficient attention to power). In any case, analytical focus shifts toward comprehending social dynamics increasingly in terms of power centers, more or less understood as ruling classes, counterposed to relatively powerless and dominated classes.

Groups of distinctly powerless persons move to the center of Marxist analyses. General concepts such as oppression, which function in terms of powerful/powerless dichotomies, or more specific concepts such as patriarchy, which build upon a gender distribution of social power, then prevail in Marxist discussions.

Ernesto Laclau endorses "the Marxist conception of classes according to which they constitute themselves through the act of struggle itself."[17] Struggle between social groups implies dispute over objectives; one group contests with another to attain their different objectives in some specific social context. Struggle is first of all a matter of power. Which struggling group of persons wins its objectives depends on their relative power positions in that society at that time. To define classes in terms of actual social struggles amounts to a form of the power conception of class.

This is significantly different from the non-Marxist power theorists such as Dahrendorf. Where the latter make the structural allocation of power the definition of class, Marxists such as Laclau argue that classes do not pre-exist actual struggles over social issues. Classes are rather the social entities constituted by and in the process of actual struggles; they are "effects of struggles." Bob Jessop and Adam Przeworski work with similar formulations: "class struggle is first of all a struggle about the formation of class forces before it is a struggle between class forces."[18] Jessop arrived at such a formulation by rejecting what he saw as the unacceptable Marxist tendency to reduce complex social power struggles to mere effects of class understood in property or surplus labor terms. Marxists, he reasons, need to overcome their denigration of power and produce social analyses that integrate class and non-class relationships. In seeking to right the analytical balance which he thinks is tipped too far toward property concepts, Jessop stresses power.[19]

Not surprisingly, the theoretical pendulum that swings from property to power concepts of class soon provokes the reverse movement. Alex Callinicos criticizes the theoretical move toward a focus on power as a departure from Marxism which he sees as properly oriented elsewhere, chiefly on property (the social distribution of means of production) and also on surplus labor production.[20] His reaction against analyses of class qua power/domination/subordination propels him to reaffirm a concept of class as primarily property and secondarily surplus labor production. Another sort of pendulum swing runs from the non-Marxists A.A. Berle, Jr. and Gardiner Means to the Marxists Paul A. Baran and Paul M. Sweezy. The former saw modern capitalists as defined no longer by property but rather by power: business-owners replaced by non-owning corporate executives.[21] The latter reacted by declaring that "far from being a separate class, they [corporate managers] constitute in reality the leading echelon of the property-owning class"; for them property and power are indissolubly linked in the definition of class.[22]

Besides the theorizations of class that define the term quite straightforwardly in terms either of property or power, there are what might best be described as complex, multi-dimensional conceptions of class. These conceptions insist that class cannot be defined simply as either a property, a power, or even a surplus labor matter. Rather, class is celebrated as a specific but complex social phenomenon with several component elements: class becomes a composite term to denote part or even all of "the social relations of production."[23] Composite conceptions of class are sometimes attributed to Marx and sometimes offered instead as improvements on a narrow, uni-dimensional concept attributed to him.

Many who prefer composite concepts of class not only criticize the narrow conceptions as inadequate, they also differ among themselves about which among the component elements of class are the most important. They disagree about which component to emphasize as the key element of class. Interestingly, most of such writers favor either power or property as the chief components of class. Then there are some who emphasize still other components of their composite concepts of class as the most important.

For example, Nicos Poulantzas has made major contributions to Marxian class analytics, summarized in the rich and condensed "Introduction" to his *Classes in Contemporary Capitalism*.[24] Poulantzas there advances arguments involving several definitions of class. His is certainly a composite conceptualization. He gives a special place and emphasis to ownership of the means of production. He also writes of "the decisive role of the division between manual labour and mental labour in the determination of social classes." And he devotes much attention to relations of "domination/subordination" in constituting classes as well. Despite the coexistence in his work of such different conceptualizations, it displays a clear movement toward power becoming the dominant component of class.

Poulantzas' work represents a move away from property and narrowly economic concepts of class toward power concepts. In his distinction between class places (given by the social structure) and class positions (given by conjunctural struggles in a society), what is most striking is the centrality of the concept of domination/subordination to both place and position. Classes in his sense of class places exist at three social levels: the economic, political, and ideological. At each level, Poulantzas juxtaposes a dominant and a dominated group, i.e., classes. At the economic level, the dominant are exploiters while the dominated are exploited; this is his acknowledgment of the economic (surplus labor) aspect of class. At the other levels he cites domination and subordination—in terms of political control and ideological influence—as the contrasts defining class places. Actually classes then would appear to be defined by reference necessarily to all three levels.

Now what all levels have in common is precisely not property dimensions nor dimensions in terms of the production or distribution of surplus labor. They all share the dichotomy of domination/subordination, a concept of power among persons. Poulantzas' prevalent notion of class places thus centers on powerful/powerless differentiations. In this sense, his is a power theory of class. When he turns to an analysis of class positions—the actual sides taken in what he calls "conjunctural struggles"—he emphasizes that persons in one class place can and do often take positions in social struggles that do not "correspond to its interests." The key point here is Poulantzas' evident determination to call the sides taken in social conflicts—power struggles—class positions, i.e., classes in the sense developed further by Laclau, Jessop, and Przeworski. Poulantzas' theory of class places and class positions raises concepts of power above those of property or surplus labor as most central and basic to class analysis.[25]

Another Marxist approach to class as a complex composite is typified by E.P. Thompson's *The Making of the English Working Class*. This work inspires and serves as a model for many Marxists precisely because it succeeds in presenting the interplay among economic, political, and cultural processes which combined to create (or "overdetermine") the English working class. Thompson's work involves his strong desire to escape the simple, economistic definitions of class which, in his view, mar the Marxist tradition. Thus, his emphasis shifts rather to the consciousness component of his complex notion of class: "Class is defined by men as they live their own history, and, in the end, this is its only definition."[26] The shift of emphasis in Thompson's composite view of class becomes a reductionism: class is only finally historically real and effective when its key constituent element, class consciousness, has been fashioned. Of all the components of class, consciousness is the most important, at least from the standpoint of concrete historical class relations.

Another composite conceptualization of class is carefully crafted to include property, power, and surplus labor appropriation and yet also to reduce the composite to its political component: power. "Class relations are forms of domination involving the expropriation of surplus labor time through the operation of property relations in the means of production."[27] In this statement, the essential social force has become interpersonal relations of domination; these are understood to shape social structure and change. A critique of economic determinism propels its proponents to a political (power or domination relations) determinism instead. For Bowles and Gintis, class is certainly a composite relation of production involving power, ideology, and economics in the narrow sense of surplus labor appropriation. However, they proceed to reduce the extraction of surplus labor itself to an effect of power. They reason that after the economic process of buying labor power is completed, the capitalist still must exert effective power in order to obtain surplus labor. For them, power is the essence of class, its determining component.[28]

One kind of composite conceptualization of class that has drawn increasing attention recently focuses upon the division of labor between mental and manual exertion. Such theorizations typically see in modern science and technology a major component of class definitions and distinctions. The French upheavals of 1968 spawned a host of reformulations of class in terms that combined older criteria (property, power, etc.) with a special emphasis upon science and technology in shaping what were understood as class divisions between manual and mental labor.[29] Interestingly, dissident theorists in Eastern Europe seem also to attach importance and even an ultimately determinant role to mental/manual labor divisions as the key components of classes. In Rudolf Bahro's view,

> If the classes bound up with private property are destroyed or rendered impotent, the earlier element of the division of mental and manual labour emerges once again as an autonomous factor of class formation.[30]

As noted, among the theories of class as a composite entity many include surplus labor production as one component. Some even make the extraction of surplus labor the most important and determining of the several elements that define class. An exemplary formulation is the following:

> Marx's emphasis on consciousness and community clearly suggests, therefore, a complex rather than unidimensional theory of class. Class is never a single homogeneous structure, but rather a cluster of groups. . . . Thus the ruling class is never a simple homogeneous whole, but consists of contradictory elements—the representatives of heavy industry and light industry, finance capitalists—although the whole, the unity of the various competing elements, is held together by one overriding interest, the exploitation of labor power.[31]

What is striking about the theorizations of class as a composite entity is the prevalent tendency to establish a most important or ultimately determinant element within class. Class is many things of which one is the dominant element. It is usually property or power, which is not surprising given the widespread conceptualizations of class as uni-dimensionally property or power. In general then, the prevalent theories of class either define it narrowly as a matter of property or power distribution or more broadly as a composite of several elements within which power or property are the ultimate determinants. There are relatively few exceptions to this prevalence in either Marxist or non-Marxist literature (although, as noted, many Marxists include and some emphasize surplus labor appropriation in their conceptualization of class).

An Alternative and Non-Reductionist Concept of Class

An alternative concept of class, derived from Marx, may be distinguished along two dimensions. We understand class to be defined narrowly in terms of the specific processes of producing and distributing surplus labor. Secondly, we understand class to be neither reduced to an effect of any non-class aspect of society, nor are any non-class aspects reducible to the mere effects of class defined in surplus labor terms.

Since our reading of Marx and the specific concept of class we find there has been presented exhaustively elsewhere, only a brief summary is appropriate here.[32] We use the word class to mean a very particular economic process: the production of surplus labor. In all human societies, some people directly produce goods and services. Part of what they produce they also consume: we follow Marx in labeling this consumed portion the fruit of the *necessary labor* of the direct producers. However, these direct producers also perform labor beyond this necessary amount: the surplus labor. The process of performing or producing this surplus labor is what we mean by class: the class process.

What is necessary labor in any society at any particular time depends on the entirety of that society's history to that time. It is a quantity complexly determined and in no way reducible to any physical or subsistence minimum. Moreover, the existence of a surplus labor production process raises immediately the questions of how much surplus labor is performed, who appropriates its fruits, and how they are further distributed throughout the society. The production and appropriation of surplus labor are two sides of the class process. A human being can function on one or the other or both sides; he or she may produce or appropriate surplus labor or do both. The class process defines, thus, two different class positions: performer and appropriator of surplus labor.

This leaves the question of the distribution of surplus labor's fruits from its appropriators to other persons. This is itself a distinct social process: the distribution of already appropriated surplus labor (or its fruits). Although different from the production/appropriation of surplus labor, it is closely related.

We may say that there are two kinds of class processes. The first or what we term the fundamental class process is the production/appropriation of surplus labor. It defines two fundamental classes: producers and appropriators. The second, which we call the subsumed class process, refers to the distribution of surplus labor from its appropriators to others. It defines two subsumed classes: distributors and recipients of surplus labor. Any individual may occupy all, none, or any combination of these class positions. Class analysis is precisely the effort to think about society by focusing upon which people occupy which class positions and with what social effects.

The appropriators distribute the surplus labor (or its fruits) to persons who perform other (non-class) social processes without which the production/appropriation of surplus labor would be jeopardized or not occur at all. That is, for direct producers to perform surplus labor, a great many other processes must be in place. Cultural, political, natural, and economic processes of all sorts literally create the conditions for, i.e., bring into existence, the fundamental class process. However, for many of these conditions to occur requires human labor, and this human labor needs to be sustained. It is sustained precisely by means of distributions to it of surplus labor appropriated from the direct producers.

Subsumed classes are those people who did not produce or appropriate surplus labor, but rather live by providing the conditions of existence for the production/appropriation of surplus labor. Fundamental and subsumed class processes thus require each other if each is to continue to exist, if the social class structure which they comprise is to be reproduced. We find useful Marx's shorthand differentiation between laborers performing surplus labor in the capitalist fundamental class process (producing surplus value) and laborers providing conditions of existence for the fundamental class process: "productive" vs. "unproductive."[33]

Fundamental and subsumed class processes are distinct; they relate differently to the society within which they occur. A person occupying a subsumed class position is dependent upon different social forces and individuals as compared to someone occupying a fundamental class position. Class analysis aims to understand precisely what difference it makes whether and how a person participates in different class processes. This is, we believe, the contribution offered by Marxist theory to social revolutionary movements. Its point is that surplus labor production, appropriation, and distribution exist and that the class processes affect people in specific, different ways which must be understood and integrated into revolutionary strategies if they are to succeed in constructing a just society.

This kind of theory of class does not reduce all the myriad non-class aspects of social life to mere effects of some ultimately determinant set of class processes. Nor do we reduce class processes to being mere effects of non-class processes such as interpersonal power/authority relations or consciousness, etc. The logic used in linking class and non-class aspects of social life is not determinist or reductionist; rather it is overdeterminist in the sense developed below.

Overdetermination denotes a complex general approach to causation as a seamless web of cause and effect tying together all aspects of any society. Its predecessor term was the "dialectics" so much discussed and debated in the pre–World War II Marxist tradition. That tradition has since been enriched and transformed significantly by the particular contributions of Georg Lukács and Louis Althusser, who adapted Sigmund Freud's term "overdetermination" to characterize a strictly non-reductionist (or anti-essentialist) notion of social causality.[34] Indeed, overdetermination expands the idea of causality into the more encompassing notion of constitutivity: each aspect of society exists—is constituted—as the effect of all the others.

Given the commitment to overdetermination, our alternative class theory neither requires nor permits an assertion that class is the central moving force of social history. Rather, class exists as the effect of all the non-class aspects of the social totality and at the same time its existence has constitutive effects on all of those non-class aspects. Thus, power, property, technology, and consciousness are all social processes irreducibly different from one another and from the class process. Our analytical goal is always to produce the complex, mutually constitutive relations between these class and non-class processes.

We are not arguing that the surplus labor definition of class is somehow right while alternative definitions are wrong. Our preference for the surplus labor definition reflects our appreciation of Marx's unique contribution in discovering a distinctive social process: class qua surplus labor production.

Capitalists and productive laborers are understood as the two fundamental classes of the distinctively capitalist fundamental class process. They are the appropriators and producers of surplus labor respectively. In order for this capitalist form of surplus labor production to exist, all manner of non-class processes must be in place. They comprise the conditions of existence of the capitalist fundamental class process. It is constituted as their effect.

Some of these conditions of existence will not be in place unless resources are made available to sustain them. To accomplish this, the capitalists must distribute portions of their appropriated surplus value to individuals who perform those non-class processes without which surplus value production could not occur. For example, corporate personnel managers perform specific political processes of governing the group behavior of productive laborers such as designing and enforcing work discipline. Owners of property perform a specific non-class political process of providing capitalists with access to such privately owned property. Bankers provide an economic process of extending credit to capitalists. This discipline, property, and credit are only three conditions of existence of the production/appropriation of surplus value. To secure them, the appropriators of the surplus distribute portions of it to these managers (salaries), owners (dividends), and bankers (interest): the latter thereby enter into the subsumed class process as recipients of surplus.

Finally, consider religious institutions which perform various rituals and instruct the faithful in moral living. If and when such religious activities are conditions of existence of capitalist surplus labor production/appropriation, in the sense of shaping the willingness of productive laborers to produce surplus for others, the institutions may obtain contributions from capitalists out of their surpluses. By virtue of performing certain religious (non-class) processes, they can and do enter into the subsumed class process.

Our alternative theory of class specifically links the fundamental and subsumed class processes to a host of non-class processes. The linkage between political, cultural, and economic (including class) processes is one of over-determination: each distinct process exists as the combined effect of all the others. No reductionism is possible here, no ranking of the relative effectivity of one vs. another process. The point is to affirm and integrate class processes into the conception of the social totality to be changed; it is not to deny, denigrate, or subordinate the social effectivity of non-class processes. To collapse class into processes of power or property or consciousness would then precisely lose the specific difference and unique contribution of this theory and of Marx's original insight.

Implications of Different Class Theories

If we can gain agreement that the process of power, property, surplus labor production and distribution, consciousness and so on are different, then certain conclusions may reasonably be drawn. Calling them all "class" conflates and confuses what would better be kept clearly distinct. More important, a change in any one of these processes leaves open the question of just how that change will impact upon the other processes. For example, a change in power processes, say toward more democratic control over the state, may or may not alter the funda-mental and subsumed class processes from a capitalist to a communist form. A change in laborers' consciousness can affect processes of property in different ways depending on all the other processes comprising the full social context of the change in consciousness. A transition from private to socialized property in the means of production—a change in the process of property—may or may not change the class processes from capitalist to communist; that depends on all the other processes in the society at the time of such transition.

The crucial point here is that no invariant relation exists between class and non-class processes. The relations between any two social processes (e.g., class and consciousness or property and power or power and class) vary according to the ever-changing configurations of all the other social processes that mediate such relations. We may not deduce change in one social process as some in-variantly necessary consequence of a change in another.

The examples of the Soviet Union and France can underscore the significance of both the specificity of our definition of class and its anti-reductionism. A revolution can basically alter property ownership after 1917 in the USSR. An electoral victory for François Mitterrand can similarly alter French ownership of banks and large corporate enterprises in the 1980s. In each case, our theoretical framework asks about the impact of the change in property upon class, i.e., the production, appropriation, and distribution of surplus labor. How was the capital-ist form of the class processes changed? Was it abolished? Given the changes in class that did result from the change in property, how secure is the change in property itself?

These questions would less likely arise for theorists who hold a change in property distribution *to be* a change in class, who conflate class and property. They might well equate the USSR with classlessness because it socialized the means of production. They might also think that any further discussion of classes in the USSR would be unnecessary, absurd, or indicative of hostile intent. Theorizing similarly, social-democrats in France might judge socialism in France to be definitively launched by the property nationalizations there. In both cases, and despite oppositions between social-democrats and defenders of Soviet socialism, the analyses make changes in property more or less tantamount to socialist class transformation. By contrast, we would have to ask: under what conditions will nationalization or socialization lead toward rather than away from a strengthened capitalist class structure? Such a question is as urgent for us as it is remote for property theorists of class.

The French example is especially instructive here. The Mitterrand government's actions have transformed France's class structure according to some conceptions of class. Its additional distributions to certain social-welfare recipients of state subsidies plus the provision of a legally mandated fifth week of paid vacation for employees moved significantly toward less inequality of income. If class is defined in terms of income distribution, such alterations of income distribution amount to a significant move toward class change and hence socialism. Where property rather than income distribution defines class, Mitterrand's nationalizations of banks and the large industrial groups are widely seen as changing France's class structure.

French Socialists and Communists could and did eventually dissolve their governing alliance in a dispute frequently debated in terms of class qua property or income distribution. Defenders of Mitterrand argued that the property nationalizations proved the socialist content of government policy notwithstanding the income effects of closing large steel and other French factories thought to be inefficient. Some Communist critics of Mitterrand countered that the factory shutdowns and indeed the general policy of switching government support to high-tech investments had income effects amounting to an "abandonment" of socialist goals and commitments. Increasingly, Communists attack Mitterrand as not really socialist, as carrying out a capitalist restructuring program strengthening France's unequal income distribution, i.e., its capitalist class structure. Mitterrand's defenders reply that their high-tech investment program and industrial streamlining pave the way for higher, more secure incomes for workers and thus the promised transition toward socialism which, they insist, cannot be won other than by a successful restructuring of industry first.

By the same token, changes in power relations, say toward democratic control of state policies, pose the question of the impact these changes may have upon class processes. We can entertain no presumption that any simple cause and effect relation leads from a particular political change to a particular class change. We must ask how the social context of the political change mediates its effects upon class to understand what the class changes are or might be. Such a question is urgent for us, while it makes little sense to power theorists of class. For them, the democratization of power (the demise of the ruler's authority) is or leads necessarily to the end of the ruling/ruled "class structure."

Again, contemporary France offers useful examples. Both defenders and critics of Mitterrand sometimes appeal to power considerations to substantiate their arguments about class and socialism. Defenders point with pride to the government's commitments to "autogestion" (worker self-management programs), to specific achievements in integrating women into government employment and abolishing capital punishment, and to the simple fact of a government run by socialists. These factors, they claim, warrant the label socialist because they are transformations of France's class structure. Detractors insist that Mitterrand has betrayed socialism precisely because autogestion remains an abstract ideal and not an effective worker-power program being implemented anywhere and because power relations generally in France seem unchanged. These critics argue that a socialist government which does not radically alter power relations (i.e., class relations) is therefore not socialist.

Our argument with these debates in France is not that they do not concern social issues of vital importance; they do. However, they literally ignore the issue of class as the production and distribution of surplus labor. They make judgments about socialism in France and the role of the Mitterrand government without substantive interest in class as we understand it and hence without attention to the impact of the Mitterrand policies upon production and distribution of surplus in France. Socialist and Communist parties make political decisions which do impact France and beyond in momentous ways *usually without sustained discussion and inquiry into the issue of surplus production and distribution.*

In our judgment, this makes it likely that French socialism of the Mitterrand government variety will founder for the sorts of reasons Marx suggested long ago. Many of its plans to change France will fail because it fails to consider and directly address the production and distribution of surplus. Further, the changes which the French socialists can make in France will, we believe, be very vulnerable to reversal in large measure because they were not secured by accompanying and mutually supportive transformations of surplus production and distribution. In sum, the lack of awareness about the multiplicity and complexity of class definitions has had and will have major negative implications for modern socialism.

To approach the issue from another vantage point we may ask: is a change from capitalist to communist class processes possible without certain changes in the configuration of non-class processes within a society? Our answer must be "no." For example, it may be that specific changes in social processes concerned with gender relationships would provide conditions for a change in the class processes of Western capitalist societies today. A change in popular consciousness about what "male" and "female" means (i.e., a change in certain cultural processes) alongside a change in the authority distribution process within families (a change in political or power processes) might combine with a change as women sell more of their labor power as a commodity (a change in the economic process of exchange) to jeopardize capitalist class processes. With other changes in still other social processes—which our class analysis seeks to identify—such altered gender relationships might provide the conditions of existence for a revolutionary change to a new social system including a different class structure.

It follows that practical work must aid those particular changes in social processes which the proposed class theory connects, as conditions of existence, to the desired revolutionary social change. In turn, the practical work changes the theory in terms of how it understands the complex linkages between class and non-class social processes. Theoretical and practical work depend upon and shape one another, subject to the mediations exercised upon both by all the other processes comprising the social context of Marxism.

The implications of Marxist theory as here understood are particularly important for practical politics by the current movements for basic change to a more just society. As in Marx's time, the theory aims to add two basic ideas to the thinking of those movements: (a) class is a distinct process of surplus labor production/distribution which is different from the important processes of power, property, consciousness, etc., and (b) the analytical method of linking distinct processes together into a social totality is overdetermination rather than reductionism. We believe that these ideas form a basis for unity within current movements and thereby enhance their chances for success.

Unity around these two ideas would not preclude significant differences among Marxists over which particular social processes occupy their analytical and practical energies. The differences would then concern matters of focus. Some would continue the Marxist focus upon class, upon the forms and interactions of the fundamental and subsumed class processes within a society. They would presumably be animated by the feeling that these were the urgent insights that needed to be contributed to revolutionary movements. Others within such a unity would analyze the society via different foci. Processes of power or property or consciousness, etc., would be their concern; insights about those processes would be their contribution. However, the unity of all would consist in the common recognition of the existence of fundamental and subsumed class processes and the common commitment to non-reductionist ways of thinking.

Of course, the differences will occasion debate and disagreements. Different foci will influence social analyses and the practical and theoretical conclusions reached. This will pose thorny problems in terms of strategic and tactical decisions. However, these are useful as well as unavoidable disagreements. They involve disputes over how to see and affect the non-reductionist linkages between class and non-class processes. They are all disputes over these particular issues. They are all conditioned by commitments to basic social changes, although the changes sought will also reflect the different foci.

The unity underpinning the differences and debates will take several forms. First, we might finally set aside our sterile disputations over which aspects of society (power, property, class, etc.) are "the most important" or involve "the most fundamental contradiction." Which social struggle is "ultimately determinant" on historical change will cease to engage debate. Our commitments to different foci will be understood as results of our unique overdeterminations as individuals and not as signs that we do or do not grasp the essential determinants of history. We will all be aiming to understand the complex linkages among class and non-class processes in the societies we want to change.

Secondly, whatever the term "class" comes to mean, we will be unified by having learned Marx's lessons about the production, appropriation and distribution of surplus labor. We will integrate his insights into all the others born of peoples' struggles for social and personal justice. Our movements will understand and include the class processes in their strategies for change and proposals for the future. Thirdly, unifying commitments to class as surplus labor and to overdetermination would sharply and clearly differentiate Marxist from bourgeois theories which rarely share either of those commitments and never share both.

Notes

1. Cf. Stanislaw Ossowski, *Class Structure in the Social Consciousness* (London: Routledge & Kegan Paul, 1963), pp. 121ff.

2. Strictly speaking, property is itself a particular kind of power, namely the power to exclude others from access to an object (or, as in slavery, to another person). However, since the tradition has separated property from other kinds of power, we will continue that practice. Hence, our references to power refer here to all kinds other than those involved in property, e.g., the power to design and enforce all sorts of interpersonal behavior rules within families, the power to design and enforce laws and regulations governing all sorts of interpersonal behavior within communities and nations, etc. The powers to control another person's political, legal, sexual, recreational, and travel activities are among the sorts of power other than property.

3. See Resnick and Wolff, "Classes in Marxian Theory," *Review of Radical Political Economics,* vol. 13, no. 4 (Winter 1982), pp. 1–18.

4. Maurice Dobb, *Political Economy and Capitalism* (New York: International, n.d.,), p. 58. In a later formulation, Dobb wrote of capitalism as a system comprising "an employing master class and a subject wage-earning class" in *Studies in the Development of Capitalism* (New York: International, 1947), p. 253. In both works Dobb also added the appropriation of surplus to power and property in his composite conceptualization of what constituted a capitalist class. Indeed, he also once wrote of "the common interest which constitutes a certain social grouping a class." Ibid., p. 14.

5. This sentence requires a brief comment on the puzzling and often cited end of *Capital,* Volume 3. There Marx has a chapter entitled "Classes" which runs a page and a half followed by Engels' remark: "At this point the manuscript breaks off." Many commentators have inferred that Marx thus never worked out a complex class theory. We disagree: all of *Capital* is an elaboration of his notion of class as the production, appropriation, and distribution of surplus labor. He probably intended that last chapter to be an explicit summary of the preceding class analytics.

6. See the distinction between "fundamental" and "subsumed" classes in Resnick and Wolff, "Classes in Marxian Theory."

7. Such anti-reductionist notions of causality inform the passage from determinism to "overdeterminism" in the works of Louis Althusser and in our own different development of the notion of overdetermination: see Althusser's "Overdetermination and Contradiction," in his *For Mars,* trans. Ben Brewster (New York: Vintage Books, 1970), pp. 87–128, and our "Marxist Epistemology: The Critique of Economic Determinism," *Social Text,* vol. 6 (1982), pp. 31–72.

8. The best modern example is Edward P. Thompson's *The Making of the English Working Class* which opens with a preface insisting that class only finally "happens" when persons in certain "productive relations" acquire a certain consciousness (New York: Vintage Books, 1963), p. 9. Nicos Poulantzas and Erik Olin Wright share this notion: see Wright's *Class Crisis and the State* (London: New Left Books, 1979), pp. 33ff. In contrast, G.A. Cohen directly rebuts Thompson with a pure power theory: class exists whether or not consciousness of class does; it is only a matter of a person's "effective power over persons and productive forces." *Karl Marx's Theory of History: A Defense* (Princeton, N.J.: University Press, 1978), p. 63.

9. Michèle Barrett, *Women's Oppression Today: Problems in Marxist Feminist Analysis* (London: New Left Books, 1980), p. 131. Compare how the Marxist historian Jurgen Kuczynski defines the "modern working class" as different from other classes: "It is a question of property." *The Rise of the Working Class,* trans. C.T.A. Ray (New York: McGraw-Hill, 1967), p. 10.

10. See "The American Ruling Class" in his *The Present as History* (New York: Monthly Review, 1953), p. 124.

11. Lange, *Political Economy,* vol. 1, trans. A.H. Walker (New York: Macmillan, 1963), p. 16; Dahrendorf, *Class and Class Conflict in an Industrial Society* (London: Routledge & Kegan Paul, 1959), p. 137; Mills, *The Marxists* (New York: Dell Publishing, 1962), pp. 106ff.; Giddens, *The Class Structure of Advanced Societies* (New York: Harper & Row, 1975), pp. 107ff.; Lekachman, *A History of Economic Ideas* (New York: McGraw-Hill, 1969), p. 224; and Pashukanis, *General Theory of Law and Marxism* (London: Ink Links, 1978), pp. 176ff. Stalin's 1936 report to the Seventh Congress of Soviets on the draft constitution affirmed that the USSR had "no longer any exploiting classes" because it had eradicated private ownership in the means of production. *Leninism* (London: Lawrence & Wishart, 1940), pp. 561–567.

12. Anthony Cutler, Barry Hindess, Paul Hirst, and Athar Hussain, *Marx's Capital and Capitalism Today: Volume I* (London and Boston: Routledge & Kegan Paul, 1977), p. 243. In Hirst's formulation "the private possession of the means of production" implies "the consequent division of society into classes." *On Law and Ideology* (London: Macmillan, 1979), p. 96. See also Hindess and Hirst, *Mode of Production and Social Formation* (London: Macmillan, 1977) and their first book, *Pre-capitalist Modes of Production* (London and Boston: Routledge & Kegan Paul, 1975). Their approach has also been influential in its systematic and strict anti-reductionism.

13. Consider, as one example, a major publication in the early years of the USSR: "The Soviet Power openly proclaims its class character. It makes no attempt to conceal that it is a class power . . . the dictatorship of the poor." Nicolai Bukharin and E. Preobrazhensky, *The ABC of Communism,* ed. E.H. Carr (Baltimore: Penguin, 1969), p. 220. Similarly Samir Amin today analyzes the capitalist center of the world economy as polarized into basic classes, bourgeoisie and proletariat, with the latter defined as "made up of wage-earning employees of capitalist enterprises." *Unequal Development: An Essay on the Social Formations of Peripheral Capitalism,* trans. Brian Pearce (New York and London: Monthly Review, 1976), p. 293. One's class position is here determined by the kind of income flow one gets.

14. See his *The Ruling Class,* trans. Hannah D. Kahn (New York: McGraw-Hill, 1939), especially pp. 50ff.

15. Ralf Dahrendorf, *Class and Class Conflict in an Industrial Society,* p. 137.

16. Ibid., p. 213.

17. See his *Politics and Ideology in Marxist Theory* (London: New Left Books, 1977), p. 106.

18. The quotation is from Jessop, "The Political Indeterminacy of Democracy," in Alan Hunt, ed., *Marxism and Democracy* (London: Lawrence & Wishart, 1980), p. 63; see also Przeworski's "Proletariat into a Class," *Politics and Society,* vol. 7, no. 4 (1977), pp. 343–401.

19. Cf. Jessop, "Political Indeterminacy," p. 76.

20. *Is There a Future for Marxism?* (Atlantic Highlands, N.J.: Humanities Press, 1982), pp. 98–111 and 148–163. In his view, the events of May 1968 in France placed power relations and ideology (knowledge, discourse, universities, culture, etc.) at the center of theoretical critiques of capitalism.

21. See their *The Modern Corporation and Private Property* (New York: Commerce Clearing House, 1932).

22. *Monopoly Capital* (New York: Monthly Review Press, 1966), chapter 2 and especially pp. 19–35.

23. Max Weber is one source for composite notions of class and strata: see the bewildering variety of formulations scattered throughout his *Economy and Society: An Outline of Interpretive Sociology.* Demonstrating Weber's influence among Marxists, Guglielmo Carchedi defines a person's class position in terms of the following list of component elements: does he/she own means of production; does he/she exploit or suffer exploitation; does he/she oppress or suffer oppression; does he/she "perform the function of global capital or of the collective laborer." See his *On the Economic Identification of Social Classes* (London and Boston: Routledge & Kegan Paul, 1977), pp. 162–167; much the same listing procedure is followed in Manuel Castells, *The Economic Crisis and American Society* (Princeton, N.J.: Princeton University Press, 1980), pp. 141–142.

24. Trans. David Fernbach (London: New Left Books, 1978), pp. 13–55 and especially pp. 14–24.

25. Poulantzas' last book presents his most explicit formulation of a power concept of class: *State, Power, Socialism* (London: New Left Books, 1978), pp. 43ff. However, Poulantzas often insisted that class be defined in terms of surplus labor production: a point made in his support for a narrow conception of the working class as just productive and not also unproductive laborers. See his paper, "The New Petty Bourgeoisie," in Alan Hunt, ed., *Class and Class Structure* (London: Lawrence & Wishart, 1977), pp. 113–124. While Poulantzas evidently operated with a complex and composite conceptualization of class, power prevails over his other definitions of class. A similar approach also characterizes Erik Olin Wright's work on classes. See *Class Crisis and the State.*

26. *The Making of the English Working Class,* p. 11.

27. Samuel Bowles and Herbert Gintis, "On the Class-Exploitation-Domination Reduction," *Politics and Society,* vol. 2, no. 3 (1982), p. 23. That domination/subordination relations are the "primary" or ultimately determinant aspects of social life is reaffirmed throughout the article.

28. See their "Structure and Practice in the Labor Theory of Value," *Review of Radical Political Economics,* vol. 12, no. 4 (Winter 1981), pp. 1–26.

29. For example, Serge Mallet, *La Nouvelle Classe Ouvrière* (Paris: Éditions du Seuil, 1969).

30. See *The Alternative in Eastern Europe,* trans. David Fernbach (London: New Left Books, 1978), p. 77. On page 140 he also writes: "The law of the division of labour lies therefore at the root of class divisions."

31. Alan Swingewood, *Marx and Modern Sociology* (London: Macmillan, 1975), p. 118. Also see Roman Rosdolsky's *The Making of Marx's Capital,* trans. Pete Burgess (London: Pluto Press, 1977), pp. 31–35.

32. See our "Classes in Marxian Theory" and chapter 3 of our book, *Knowledge and Class* (Chicago: University of Chicago Press, 1987). These references list and discuss those of Marx's texts that occasioned and support our interpretations.

33. Marx's point was to underscore their different places in the class structure; it was not a judgment of their relative importance in securing the reproduction of the class structure. Both productive and unproductive workers, Marx insisted, were crucial to that reproduction.

34. This argument is developed fully in our "Marxist Epistemology" and in chapters 1 and 2 of our book, *Knowledge and Class.*

III

Discrimination

6

The Unhappy Marriage of Marxism and Feminism

Towards a More Progressive Union

Heidi I. Hartmann

This paper argues that the relation between marxism and feminism has, in all the forms it has so far taken, been an unequal one. While both marxist method and feminist analysis are necessary to an understanding of capitalist societies, and of the position of women within them, in fact feminism has consistently been subordinated. The paper presents a challenge to both marxist and radical feminist work on the "woman question," and argues that what it is necessary to analyze is the combination of patriarchy and capitalism. It is a paper which, we hope, should stimulate considerable debate.

The "marriage" of marxism and feminism has been like the marriage of husband and wife depicted in English common law: Marxism and feminism are one, and that one is marxism.[1] Recent attempts to integrate marxism and feminism are unsatisfactory to us as feminists because they subsume the feminist struggle into the "larger" struggle against capital. To continue our simile further, either we need a healthier marriage or we need a divorce.

The inequalities in this marriage, like most social phenomena, are no accident. Many marxists typically argue that feminism is at best less important than class conflict and at worst divisive of the working class. This political stance produces an analysis that absorbs feminism into the class struggle. Moreover, the analytic power of marxism with respect to capital has obscured its limitations with respect to sexism. We will argue here that while marxist analysis provides essential insight into the laws of historical development, and those of capital in particular, the categories of marxism are sex-blind. Only a specifically feminist

Reprinted with permission from *Capital and Class,* Summer 1979, pp. 1–33.

analysis reveals the systemic character of relations between men and women. Yet feminist analysis by itself is inadequate because it has been blind to history and insufficiently materialist. Both marxist analysis, particularly its historical and materialist method, and feminist analysis, especially the identification of patriarchy as a social and historical structure, must be drawn upon if we are to understand the development of western capitalist societies and the predicament of women within them. In this essay we suggest a new direction for marxist feminist analysis.

Part I of our discussion examines several marxist approaches to the "woman question." We then turn, in Part II, to the work of radical feminists. After noting the limitations of radical feminist definitions of patriarchy, we offer our own. In Part III we try to use the strengths of both marxism and feminism to make suggestions both about the development of capitalist societies and about the present situation of women. We attempt to use marxist methodology to analyze feminist objectives, correcting the imbalance in recent socialist feminist work, and suggesting a more complete analysis of our present socioeconomic formation. We argue that a materialist analysis demonstrates that patriarchy is not simply a psychic, but also a social and economic structure. We suggest that our society can best be understood once it is recognized that it is organized both in capitalist and in patriarchal ways. While pointing out tensions between patriarchal and capitalist interests, we argue that the accumulation of capital both accommodates itself to patriarchal social structure and helps to perpetuate it. We suggest in this context that sexist ideology has assumed a peculiarly capitalist form in the present, illustrating one way that patriarchal relations tend to bolster capitalism. We argue, in short, that a partnership of patriarchy and capitalism has evolved.

In the concluding section, Part IV, we argue that the *political* relations of marxism and feminism account for the dominance of marxism over feminism in the left's understanding of the "woman question." A more progressive union of marxism and feminism, then, requires not only improved intellectual understanding of relations of class and sex, but also that alliance replace dominance and subordination in left politics.

I. Marxism and the Woman Question

The "woman question" has never been the "feminist question." The feminist question is directed at the causes of sexual inequality between women and men, of male dominance over women. Most marxist analyses of women's position take as their question the relationship of women to the economic system, rather than that of women to men, apparently assuming the latter will be explained in their discussion of the former. Marxist analysis of the woman question has taken three main forms. All see women's oppression in our connection (or lack of it) to production. Defining women as part of the working class, these analyses consistently subsume women's relation to men under workers' relation to capital. First, early marxists, including Marx, Engels, Kautsky, and Lenin, saw capitalism drawing all women into the wage labor force, and saw this process destroying the sexual division of labor. Second, contemporary marxists have incorporated women into an analysis of "everyday life" in capitalism. In this view, all aspects of our lives are seen to reproduce the capitalist system and we are all workers in that system. And third, marxist feminists have focused on housework and its relation to capital, some arguing that housework produces surplus value and that houseworkers work directly for capitalists. These three approaches are examined in turn.

Engels, in *Origins of the Family, Private Property and the State,* recognized the inferior position of women and attributed it to the institution of private property.[2] In bourgeois families, Engels argued, women had to serve their masters, be monogamous, and produce heirs to inherit property. Among proletarians, Engels argued, women were not oppressed, because there was no private property to be passed on. Engels argued further that as the extension of wage labor destroyed the small-holding peasantry, and women and children were incorporated into the wage labor force along with men, the authority of the male head of household was undermined, and patriarchal relations were destroyed.[3]

For Engels then, women's participation in the labor force was the key to their emancipation. Capitalism would abolish sex differences and treat all workers equally. Women would become economically independent of men and would participate on an equal footing with men in bringing about the proletarian revolution. After the revolution, when all people would be workers and private property abolished, women would be emancipated from capital as well as from men. Marxists were aware of the hardships women's labor participation meant for women and families, which resulted in women having two jobs, housework and wage work. Nevertheless, their emphasis was less on the continued subordination of women in the home than on the progressive character of capitalism's "erosion" of patriarchal relations. Under socialism housework too would be collectivized and women relieved of their double burden.

The political implications of this first marxist approach are clear. Women's liberation requires first, that women become wage workers like men, and second, that they join with men in the revolutionary struggle against capitalism. Capital and private property, the early marxists argued, are the cause of women's particular oppression just as capital is the cause of the exploitation of workers in general.

Though aware of the deplorable situation of women in their time the early marxists failed to focus on the *differences* between men's and women's experiences under capitalism. They did not focus on the feminist questions—how and why women are oppressed as women. They did not, therefore, recognize the vested interest men had in women's continued subordination. As we argue in Part III below, men benefitted from not having to do housework, from having their wives and daughters serve them and from having the better places in the labor market. Patriarchal relations, far from being atavistic leftovers, being rapidly outmoded by capitalism, as the early marxists suggested, have survived and thrived alongside it. And since capital and private property do not cause the oppression of women as *women*, their end alone will not result in the end of women's oppression.

Perhaps the most popular of the recent articles exemplifying the second marxist approach, the everyday life school, is the series by Eli Zaretsky in *Socialist Revolution*.[4] Zaretsky agrees with feminist analysis when he argues that sexism is not a new phenomenon produced by capitalism, but he stresses that the particular form sexism takes now has been shaped by capital. He focuses on the differential experiences of men and women under capitalism. Writing a century after Engels, once capitalism had matured, Zaretsky points out that capitalism has not incorporated all women into the labor force on equal terms with men. Rather capital has created a separation between the home, family, and personal life on the one hand and the workplace on the other.[5]

Sexism has become more virulent under capitalism, according to Zaretsky, because of this separation between wage work and home work. Women's increased oppression is caused by their exclusion from wage work. Zaretsky argues that while men are oppressed by having to do wage work, women are oppressed by not being allowed to do wage work. Women's exclusion from the wage labor force has been caused primarily by capitalism, because capitalism both creates wage work outside the home and requires women to work in the home in order to reproduce wage workers for the capitalist system. Women reproduce the labor force, provide psychological nurturance for workers, and provide an island of intimacy in a sea of alienation. In Zaretsky's view women are laboring for capital and not for men; it is only the separation of home from workplace, and the privatization of housework brought about by capitalism that creates the *appearance* that women are working for men privately in the home. The difference between the *appearance*, that women work for men, and the *reality*, that women work for capital, has caused a misdirection of the energies of the women's movement. Women should recognize that women, too, are part of the working class, even though they work at home.

In Zaretsky's view,

> the housewife emerged, alongside the proletarian [as] the two characteristic laborers of developed capitalist society,[6]

and the segmentation of their lives oppresses both the husband-proletarian and the wife-housekeeper. Only a reconceptualization of "production" which includes women's work in the home and all other socially necessary activities will allow socialists to struggle to establish a society in which this destructive separation is overcome. According to Zaretsky, men and women together (or separately) should fight to reunite the divided spheres of their lives, to create a humane socialism that meets all our private as well as public needs. Recognizing capitalism as the root of their problem, men and women will fight capital and not each other. Since capitalism causes the separation of our private and public lives, the end of capitalism will end that separation, reunite our lives, and end the oppression of both men and women.

Zaretsky's analysis owes much to the feminist movement, but he ultimately argues for a redirection of that movement. Zaretsky has accepted the feminist argument that sexism predates capitalism; he has accepted much of the marxist feminist argument that housework is crucial to the reproduction of capital; he recognizes that housework is hard work and does not belittle it; and he uses the concepts of male supremacy and sexism. But his analysis ultimately rests on the notion of separation, on the concept of *division*, as the crux of the problem, a division attributable to capitalism. Like the "complementary spheres" argument of the early twentieth century, which held that women's and men's spheres were complementary, separate but equally important, Zaretsky largely denies the existence and importance of *inequality* between men and women. His focus is on the relationship of women, the family, and the private sphere to capitalism. Moreover, even if capitalism created the private sphere, as Zaretsky argues, why did it happen that *women* work there, and *men* in the labor force? Surely this cannot be explained without reference to patriarchy, the systemic dominance of men over women. From our point of view, the problem in the family, the labor market, economy, and society is not simply a division of labor between men and women, but a division that places men in a superior, and women in a subordinate, position.

Just as Engels sees private property as the capitalist contribution to women's oppression, so Zaretsky sees privacy. Because women are laboring privately at home they are oppressed. Zaretsky and Engels romanticize the preindustrial family and community—where men, women, adults, children worked together in family-centered enterprise and all participated in community life. Zaretsky's humane socialism will reunite the family and recreate that "happy workshop."

While we argue that socialism *is* in the interest of both men and women, it is not at all clear that we are all fighting for the same kind of "humane socialism," or that we have the same conception of the struggle required to get there, much less that capital alone is responsible for our current oppression. While Zaretsky thinks women's work *appears* to be for men but in reality is for capital, we think women's work in the family *really is* for men—though it clearly reproduces capitalism as well. Reconceptualizing "production" may help us to think about the kind of society we want to create, but between now and its creation, the struggle between men and women will have to continue along with the struggle against capital.

Marxist feminists who have looked at housework have also subsumed the feminist struggle into the struggle against capital. Mariarosa Dalla Costa's theoretical analysis of housework is essentially an argument about the relation of housework to capital and the place of housework in capitalist society and not about the relations of men and women as exemplified in housework.[7] Neverthe-less, Dalla Costa's political position, that women should demand wages for housework, has vastly increased consciousness of the importance of housework among women in the women's movement. The demand was and still is debated in women's groups all over the United States.[8] By making the claim that women at home not only provide essential services for capital by reproducing the labor force, but also create surplus value through that work,[9] Dalla Costa also vastly increased the left's consciousness of the importance of housework, and provoked a long debate on the relation of housework to capital.[10]

Dalla Costa uses the feminist understanding of housework as real work to claim legitimacy for it under capitalism by arguing that it should be waged work. Women should demand wages for housework rather than allow themselves to be forced into the traditional labor force, where, doing a "double day," women would still provide housework services to capital for free as well as wage labor. Dalla Costa suggests that women who received wages for housework would be able to organize their housework collectively, providing community child care, meal preparation, and the like. Demanding wages and having wages would raise their consciousness of the importance of their work; they would see its *social* significance, as well as its private necessity, a necessary first step toward more comprehensive social change.

Dalla Costa argues that what is socially important about housework is its necessity to capital. In this lies the strategic importance of women. By demand-ing wages for housework and by refusing to participate in the labor market women can lead the struggle against capital. Women's community organizations can be subversive to capital and lay the basis not only for resistance to the encroachment of capital but also for the formation of a new society.

Dalla Costa recognizes that men will resist the liberation of women (that will occur as women organize in their communities) and that women will have to struggle against them, but this struggle is an auxiliary one that must be waged to bring about the ultimate goal of socialism. For Dalla Costa, women's struggles are revolutionary not because they are feminist, but because they are anti-capitalist. Dalla Costa finds a place in the revolution for women's struggle by making women producers of surplus value, and as a consequence part of the working class. This legitimates women's political activity.[11]

The women's movement has never doubted the importance of women's strug-gle because for feminists the *object* is the liberation of women, which can only be brought about by women's struggles. Dalla Costa's contribution to increasing our understanding of the social nature of housework has been an incalculable advance. But like the other marxist approaches reviewed here her approach focuses on capital—not on relations between men and women. The fact that men and women have differences of interest, goals, and strategies is obscured by her very powerful analysis of how the capitalist system keeps us all down, and the important and perhaps strategic role of women's work in this system. The rhetoric of feminism is present in Dalla Costa's writing (the oppression of women, struggle with men) but the focus of feminism is not. If it were, Dalla Costa might argue, for example, that the importance of housework as a social relation lies in its crucial role in perpetuating male supremacy. That women do housework, performing labor for men, is crucial to the maintenance of patriarchy.

Engels, Zaretsky, and Dalla Costa all fail to analyze the labor process within the family sufficiently. Who benefits from women's labor? Surely capitalists, but also surely men, who as husbands and fathers receive personalized services at home. The content and extent of the services may vary by class or ethnic or racial group, but the fact of their receipt does not. Men have a higher standard of living than women in terms of luxury consumption, leisure time, and personalized services.[12] A materialist approach ought not to ignore this crucial point.[13] It follows that men have a material interest in women's continued oppression. In the long run this may be "false consciousness," since the majority of men could benefit from the abolition of hierarchy within the patriarchy. But in the short run this amounts to control over other people's labor, control which men are unwilling to relinquish voluntarily.

While the approach of the early marxists ignored housework and stressed women's labor force participation, the two more recent approaches emphasize housework to such an extent they ignore women's current role in the labor market. Nevertheless, all three attempt to include women in the category working class and to understand women's oppression as another aspect of class oppression. In doing so all give short shrift to the object of feminist analysis, the relations between women and men. While our "problems" have been elegantly analyzed, they have been misunderstood. The focus of marxist analysis has been class relations; the object of marxist analysis has been understanding the laws of motion of capitalist society. While we believe marxist methodology *can* be used to formulate feminist strategy, these marxist feminist approaches discussed above clearly do not do so; their marxism clearly dominates their feminism.

As we have already suggested, this is due in part to the analytic power of marxism itself. Marxism is a theory of the development of class society, of the accumulation process in capitalist societies, of the reproduction of class dominance, and of the development of contradictions and class struggle. Capitalist societies are driven by the demands of the accumulation process, most succinctly summarized by the fact that production is oriented to exchange, not use. In a capitalist system production is important only insofar as it contributes to the making of profits, and the use value of products is only an incidental consideration. Profits derive from the capitalists' ability to exploit labor power, to pay laborers less than the value of what they produce. The accumulation of profits systematically transforms social structure as it transforms the relations of production. The reserve army of labor, the poverty of great numbers of people and the near-poverty of still more, these human reproaches to capital are by-products of the accumulation process itself. From the capitalist's point of view, the reproduction of the working class may "safely be left to itself."[14] At the same time, capital creates an ideology, which grows up alongside of it, of individualism, competitiveness, domination, and in our time, consumption of a particular kind. Whatever one's theory of the genesis of ideology one must recognize these as the dominant values of capitalist societies.

Marxism enables us to understand many things about capitalist societies: the structure of production, the generation of a particular occupational structure, and the nature of the dominant ideology. Marx's theory of the development of capitalism is a theory of the development of "empty places." Marx predicted, for example, the growth of the proletariat and the demise of the petit bourgeoisie. More precisely and in more detail, Braverman among others has explained the creation of the "places" clerical worker and service worker in advanced capitalist societies.[15] Just as capital creates these places indifferent to the individuals who fill them, the categories of marxist analysis, "class," "reserve army of labor," "wage-laborer," do not explain why particular people fill particular places. They give no clues about why *women* are subordinate to *men* inside and outside the family and why it is not the other way around. *Marxist categories, like capital itself, are sex-blind.* The categories of marxism cannot tell us who will fill the "empty places." Marxist analysis of the woman question has suffered from this basic problem.

Towards More Useful Marxist Feminism

Marxism is also a *method* of social analysis, historical dialectical materialism. By putting this method to the service of feminist questions, Juliet Mitchell and Shulamith Firestone suggest new directions for marxist feminism. Mitchell says, we think correctly, that

> It is not "our relationship" to socialism that should *ever* be the question—it is the use of scientific socialism [what we call marxist method] as a method of analyzing the specific nature of our oppression and hence our revolutionary role. Such a method, I believe, needs to understand radical feminism, quite as much as previously developed socialist theories.[16]

As Engels wrote:

> According to the materialistic conception, the determining factor in history is, in the final instance, the production and reproduction of immediate life. This, again, is of a twofold character: on the one side, the production of the means of existence, of food, clothing, and shelter and the tools necessary for that production; on the other side, the production of human beings themselves, the propagation of the species. The social organization under which the people of a particular historical epoch live is determined by both kinds of production. . . .[17]

This is the kind of analysis Mitchell has attempted. In her first essay, "Women: The Longest Revolution," Mitchell examines both market work and the work of reproduction, sexuality, and child-rearing.[18]

Mitchell does not entirely succeed, perhaps because not all of women's work counts as production for her. Only market work is identified as production; the other spheres (loosely aggregated as the family) in which women work are identified as ideological. Patriarchy, which largely organizes reproduction, sexuality, and child-rearing, has no material base for Mitchell. *Women's Estate,* Mitchell's expansion of this essay, focuses much more on developing the analysis of women's market work than it does on developing the analysis of women's work within the family. The book is much more concerned with women's relation to, and work for, capital than with women's relation to, and work for, men; more influenced by marxism than by radical feminism. In a later work, *Psychoanalysis and Feminism,* Mitchell explores an important area for studying the relations between women and men, namely the formation of different, gender-based personalities by women and men.[19] Patriarchy operates, Mitchell seems to be saying, primarily in the psychological realm, where female and male children learn to be women and men. Here Mitchell focuses on the spheres she initially slighted, reproduction, sexuality, and child-rearing, but by placing them in the ideological realm, she continues the fundamental weakness of her earlier analysis. She clearly presents patriarchy as the fundamental ideological structure, just as capital is the fundamental economic structure:

> To put the matter schematically . . . we are . . . dealing with two autonomous areas: the economic mode of capitalism and the ideological mode of patriarchy.[20]

Although Mitchell discusses their interpenetration, her failure to give patriarchy a material base in the relation between women's and men's labor power, and her similar failure to note the material aspects of the process of personality formation and gender creation, limits the usefulness of her analysis.

Shulamith Firestone bridges marxism and feminism by bringing materialist analysis to bear on patriarchy.[21] Her use of materialist analysis is not as ambivalent as Mitchell's. The dialectic of sex, she says, is the fundamental historical dialectic, and the material base of patriarchy is the work women do reproducing the species. The importance of Firestone's work in using marxism to analyze women's position, in asserting the existence of a material base to patriarchy, cannot be overestimated. But it suffers from an overemphasis on biology and reproduction. What we need to understand is how sex (a biological fact) becomes gender (a social phenomenon). It is necessary to place all of women's work in its social and historical context, not to focus only on reproduction. Although Firestone's work offers a new and feminist use of marxist methodology, her insistence on the primacy of men's dominance over women as the cornerstone on which all other oppression (class, age, race) rests, suggests that her book is more properly grouped with the radical feminists than with the marxist feminists. Her work remains the most complete statement of the radical feminist position.

Firestone's book has been all too happily dismissed by marxists. Zaretsky, for example, calls it a "plea for subjectivity." Yet what was so exciting to women about Firestone's book was her analysis of men's power over women, and her very healthy anger about this situation. Her chapter on love was central to our understanding of this, and still is. It is not just about "masculinist ideology," which marxists can deal with (just a question of attitudes), but an exposition of the subjective consequences of men's power over women, of what it feels like to live in a patriarchy. "The personal is political" is not, as Zaretsky would have it, a plea for subjectivity, for feeling better: it is a demand to recognize men's power and women's subordination as a social and political reality.

II. Radical Feminism and Patriarchy

The great thrust of radical feminist writing has been directed to the documentation of the slogan "the personal is political." Women's discontent, they argued, is not the neurotic lament of the maladjusted, but a response to a social structure in which women are systematically dominated, exploited, and oppressed. Women's inferior position in the labor market, the male-centered emotional structure of middle-class marriage, the use of women in advertising, the so-called understanding of women's psyche as neurotic—popularized by academic and clinical psychology—aspect after aspect of women's lives in advanced capitalist society was researched and analyzed. The radical feminist literature is enormous and defies easy summary. At the same time, its focus on psychology is consistent. The New York Radical Feminists' organizing document was "The Politics of the Ego." "The personal is political" means, for radical feminists, that the original and basic class division is between the sexes, and that the motive force in history is the striving of men for power and domination over women, the dialectic of sex.[22]

Accordingly, Firestone rewrote Freud to understand the development of boys and girls into men and women in terms of power.[23] Her characterizations of what are "male" and "female" character traits are typical of radical feminist writing. The male seeks power and domination; he is egocentric and individualistic, competitive and pragmatic; the "technological mode," according to Firestone, is male. The female is nurturant, artistic, and philosophical; the "aesthetic mode" is female.

No doubt the idea that the "aesthetic mode" is female would have come as quite a shock to the ancient Greeks. Here lies the error of radical feminist analysis: the "dialectic of sex" as radical feminists present it projects "male" and "female" characteristics as they appear in the present back into all of history. Radical feminist analysis has greatest strength in its insights into the present. Its greatest weakness is a focus on the psychological which blinds it to history.

The reason for this lies not only in radical feminist method, but also in the nature of patriarchy itself, for patriarchy is a strikingly resilient form of social organization. Radical feminists use "patriarchy" to refer to a social system characterized by male domination over women. Kate Millet's definition is classic:

> our society . . . is a patriarchy. The fact is evident at once if one recalls that the military, industry, technology, universities, science, political offices, finances—in short, every avenue of power within the society, including the coercive force of the police, is entirely in male hands.[24]

This radical feminist definition of patriarchy applies to most societies we know of and cannot distinguish among them. The use of history by radical feminists is typically limited to providing examples of the existence of patriarchy in all times and places.[25] For both marxist and mainstream social scientists before the women's movement, patriarchy referred to a system of relations between men, which formed the political and economic outlines of feudal and some pre-feudal societies, in which hierarchy followed ascribed characteristics. Capitalist societies are understood as meritocratic, bureaucratic, and impersonal by bourgeois social scientists; marxists see capitalist societies as systems of class domination.[26] For both kinds of social scientists neither the historical patriarchal societies nor today's western capitalist societies are understood as systems of relations between men that enable them to dominate women.

Towards a Definition of Patriarchy

We can usefully define patriarchy as a set of social relations between men, which have a material base, and which, though hierarchical, establish or create interdependence and solidarity among men that enable them to dominate women. Though patriarchy is hierarchical and men of different classes, races, or ethnic groups have different places in the patriarchy, they also are united in their shared relationship of dominance over their women; they are dependent on each other to maintain that domination. Hierarchies "work" at least in part because they create vested interests in the status quo. Those at the higher levels can "buy off" those at the lower levels by offering them power over those still lower. In the hierarchy of patriarchy, all men, whatever their rank in the patriarchy, are bought off by being able to control at least some women. There is some evidence to suggest that when patriarchy was first institutionalized in state societies, the ascending rulers literally made men the heads of their families (enforcing their control over their wives and children) in exchange for the men's ceding some of their tribal resources to the new rulers.[27] Men are dependent on one another (despite their hierarchical ordering) to maintain their control over women.

The material base upon which patriarchy rests lies most fundamentally in men's control over women's labor power. Men maintain this control by excluding women from access to some essential productive resources (in capitalist societies, for example, jobs that pay living wages) and by restricting women's sexuality.[28] Monogamous heterosexual marriage is one relatively recent and efficient form that seems to allow men to control both these areas. Controlling women's access to resources and their sexuality, in turn, allows men to control women's labor power, both for the purpose of serving men in many personal and sexual ways and for the purpose of rearing children. The services women render men, and which exonerate men from having to perform many unpleasant tasks (like cleaning toilets) occur outside as well as inside the family setting. Examples outside the family include the harassment of women workers and students by male bosses and professors as well as the common use of secretaries to run personal errands, make coffee, and provide "sexy" surroundings. Rearing children (whether or not the children's labor power is of immediate benefit to their fathers) is nevertheless a crucial task in perpetuating patriarchy as a system. Just as class society must be reproduced by schools, workplaces, consumption norms, etc., so must patriarchal social relations. In our society children are generally reared by women at home, women socially defined and recognized as inferior to men, while men appear in the domestic picture only rarely. Children raised in this way generally learn their places in the gender hierarchy well. Central to this process, however, are the areas outside the home where patriarchal behaviors are taught and the inferior position of women enforced and reinforced: churches, schools, sports, clubs, unions, armies, factories, offices, health centers, the media, etc.

The material base of patriarchy, then, does not rest solely on child-rearing in the family, but on all the social structures that enable men to control women's labor. The aspects of social structures that perpetuate patriarchy are theoretically identifiable, hence separable from their other aspects. Gayle Rubin has increased our ability to identify the patriarchal elements of these social structures enormously by identifying "sex/gender systems":

> a "sex/gender system" is the set of arrangements by which a society transforms biological sexuality into products of human activity, and in which these transformed sexual needs are satisfied.[29]

We are born female and male, biological sexes, but we are created woman and man, socially recognized genders. *How* we are so created is that second aspect of the *mode* of production of which Engels spoke, "the production of human beings themselves, the propagation of the species."

How people propagate the species is socially determined. For example, if people are biologically sexually polymorphous, reproduction would be accidental. The strict division of labor by sex, a social invention common to all known societies, creates two very separate genders and a need for men and women to get together for economic reasons. It thus helps direct their sexual needs toward heterosexual fulfillment. Although it is theoretically possible that a sexual division of labor should not imply inequality between the sexes, in most known societies, the socially acceptable division of labor by sex is one which accords lower status to women's work. The sexual division of labor is also the underpinning of sexual subcultures in which men and women experience life differently; it is the material base of male power which is exercised (in our society) not just in not doing housework and in securing superior employment, but psychologically as well.

How people meet their sexual needs, how they reproduce, how they inculcate social norms in new generations, how they learn gender, how it feels to be a man or a woman—all occur in the realm Rubin labels the sex/gender system. Rubin emphasizes the influence of kinship (which tells you with whom you can satisfy sexual needs) and the development of gender-specific personalities via child-rearing and the "oedipal machine." In addition, however, we can use the concept of the sex/gender system to examine all other social institutions for the roles they play in defining and reinforcing gender hierarchies. Rubin notes that theoretically a sex/gender system could be female dominant, male dominant, or egalitarian, but declines to label various known sex/gender systems or to periodize history accordingly. We choose to label our present sex/gender system patriarchy, because it appropriately captures the notions of hierarchy and male dominance which we see as central to the present system.

Economic production (what marxists are used to referring to as *the* mode of production) and the production of people in the sex/gender sphere both determine "the social organization under which the people of a particular historical epoch and a particular country live," according to Engels. The whole of society, then, can only be understood by looking at both these types of production and reproduction, people and things.[30] There is no such thing as "pure capitalism," nor does "pure patriarchy" exist, for they must of necessity coexist. What exists is patriarchal capitalism, or patriarchal feudalism, or egalitarian hunting/gathering societies, or matriarchal horticultural societies, or patriarchal horticultural societies, and so on. There appears to be no *necessary* connection between *changes* in the one aspect of production and changes in the other. A society could undergo transition from capitalism to socialism, for example, and remain patriarchal.[31] Common sense, history, and our experience tell us, however, that these two aspects of production are so closely intertwined that change in one ordinarily creates movement, tension, or contradiction in the other.

Racial hierarchies can also be understood in this context. Further elaboration may be possible along the lines of defining "color/race systems," arenas of social life that take biological color and turn it into a social category, race. Racial hierarchies, like gender hierarchies, are aspects of our social organization, of how people are produced and reproduced. They are not fundamentally ideological; they constitute that second aspect of our mode of production, the production and reproduction of people. It might be most accurate then to refer to our societies not as, for example, simply "capitalist," but as "patriarchal capitalist white supremacist." In Part III below, we illustrate one case of capitalism adapting to and making use of racial orders and several examples of the interrelations between capitalism and patriarchy.

Capitalist development creates the places for a hierarchy of workers, but traditional marxist categories cannot tell us who will fill which places. Gender and racial hierarchies determine who fills the empty places. *Patriarchy is not simply hierarchical organization,* but hierarchy in which *particular* people fill *particular* places. It is in studying patriarchy that we learn why it is women who are dominated and how. While we believe that most known societies have been patriarchal, we do not view patriarchy as a universal, unchanging phenomenon. Rather patriarchy, the set of interrelations among men that allows men to dominate women, has changed in form and intensity over time. It is crucial that the relation of men's interdependence to their ability to dominate women be examined in historical societies. It is crucial that the hierarchy among men, and their differential access to patriarchal benefits, be examined. Surely, class, race, nationality, and even marital status and sexual orientation, as well as the obvious age, come into play here. And women of different class, race, national, marital status, or sexual orientation groups are subjected to different degrees of patriarchal power. Women may themselves exercise class, race, or national power, or even patriarchal power (through their family connections) over men lower in the patriarchal hierarchy than their own male kin.

To recapitulate, we define patriarchy as a set of social relations which has a material base and in which there are hierarchical relations between men and solidarity among them which enable them in turn to dominate women. The material base of patriarchy is men's control over women's labor power. That control is maintained by denying women access to necessary economically productive resources and by restricting women's sexuality. Men exercise their control in receiving personal service work from women, in not having to do housework or rear children, in having access to women's bodies for sex, and in feeling powerful and being powerful. The crucial elements of patriarchy as we *currently* experience them are: heterosexual marriage (and consequent homophobia), female child-rearing and housework, women's economic dependence on men (enforced by arrangements in the labor market), the state, and numerous institutions based on social relations among men—clubs, sports, unions, professions, universities, churches, corporations, and armies. All of these elements need to be examined if we are to understand patriarchal capitalism.

Both hierarchy and interdependence among men and the subordination of women are *integral* to the functioning of our society; that is, these relationships are *systemic*. We leave aside the question of the creation of these relations and ask, can we recognize patriarchal relations in capitalist societies? Within capitalist societies we must discover those same bonds between men which both bourgeois and marxist social scientists claim no longer exist, or are, at the most, unimportant leftovers. Can we understand how these relations among men are perpetuated in capitalist societies? Can we identify ways in which patriarchy has shaped the course of capitalist development?

III. The Partnership of Patriarchy and Capital

How are we to recognize patriarchal social relations in capitalist societies? It appears as if each woman is oppressed by her own man alone; her oppression seems a private affair. Relationships among men and among families seem equally fragmented. It is hard to recognize relationships among men, and between men and women, as systematically patriarchal. We argue, however, that patriarchy as a system of relations between men and women exists in capitalism, and that in capitalist societies a healthy and strong partnership exists between patriarchy and capital. Yet if one begins with the concept of patriarchy and an understanding of the capitalist mode of production, one recognizes immediately that the partnership of patriarchy and capital was not inevitable; men and capitalists often have conflicting interests, particularly over the use of women's labor power. Here is one way in which this conflict might manifest itself: the vast majority of men might want their women at home to personally service them. A smaller number of men, who are capitalists, might want most women (not their own) to work in the wage labor market. In examining the tensions of this conflict over women's labor power historically, we will be able to identify the material base of patriarchal relations in capitalist societies, as well as the basis for the partnership between capital and patriarchy.

Industrialization and the Development of Family Wages

Marxists made quite logical inferences from a selection of the social phenomena they witnessed in the nineteenth century. But they ultimately underestimated the strength of the pre-existing patriarchal social forces with which fledgling capital had to contend and the need for capital to adjust to these forces. The industrial revolution was drawing all people into the labor force, including women and children; in fact the first factories used child and female labor almost exclusively.[32] That women and children could earn wages separately from men both undermined authority relations (as discussed in Part I above) and kept wages low for everyone. Kautsky, writing in 1892, described the process this way:

> [Then with] the wife and young children of the working-man . . . able to take care of themselves, the wages of the male worker can safely be reduced to the level of his own personal needs without the risk of stopping the fresh supply of labor power.
> The labor of women and children, moreover, affords the additional advantage that these are less capable of resistance than men [sic]; and their introduc-

tion into the ranks of the workers increases tremendously the quantity of labor that is offered for sale in the market.

Accordingly, the labor of women and children . . . also diminishes [the] capacity [of the male worker] for resistance in that it overstocks the market; owing to both these circumstances it lowers the wages of the working-man.[33]

The terrible effects on working class family life of the low wages and of the forced participation of all family members in the labor force were recognized by marxists. Kautsky wrote:

The capitalist system of production does not in most cases destroy the single household of the working-man, but robs it of all but its unpleasant features. The activity of woman today in industrial pursuits . . . means an increase of her former burden by a new one. *But one cannot serve two masters.* The household of the working-man suffers whenever his wife must help to earn the daily bread.[34]

Working men as well as Kautsky recognized the disadvantages of female wage labor. Not only were women "cheap competition" but working women were their very wives, who could not "serve two masters" well.

Male workers resisted the wholesale entrance of women and children into the labor force, and sought to exclude them from union membership and the labor force as well. In 1846 the *Ten-Hours' Advocate* stated:

It is needless for us to say, that all attempts to improve the morals and physical condition of female factory workers will be abortive, unless their hours are materially reduced. Indeed we may go so far as to say, that married females would be much better occupied in performing the domestic duties of the household, than following the never-tiring motion of machinery. We therefore hope the day is not distant, when the husband will be able to provide for his wife and family, without sending the former to endure the drudgery of a cotton mill.[35]

In the United States in 1854 the National Typographical Union resolved not to "encourage by its act the employment of female compositors." Male unionists did not want to afford union protection to women workers; they tried to exclude them instead. In 1879 Adolph Strasser, president of the Cigarmakers International Union, said: "We cannot drive the females out of the trade, but we can restrict their daily quota of labor through factory laws."[36]

While the problem of cheap competition could have been solved by organizing the wage-earning women and youths, the problem of disrupted family life could not be. Men reserved union protection for men and argued for protective labor laws for women and children.[37] Protective labor laws, while they may have ameliorated some of the worst abuses of female and child labor, also limited the participation of adult women in many "male" jobs.[38] Men sought to keep high wage jobs for themselves and to raise male wages generally. They argued for wages sufficient for their wage labor alone to support their families. This "family wage" system gradually came to be the norm for stable working class families at the end of the nineteenth century and the beginning of the twentieth.[39] Several observers have declared the non-wage working wife to be part of the standard of living of male workers.[40] Instead of fighting for equal wages for men and women, male workers sought the "family wage," wanting to retain their wives' services at home. In the absence of patriarchy a unified working class might have confronted capitalism, but patriarchal social relations divided the working class, allowing one part (men) to be bought off at the expense of the other (women). Both the hierarchy between men and the solidarity among them were crucial in this process of resolution. "Family wages" may be understood as a resolution of the conflict over women's labor power which was occurring between patriarchal and capitalist interests at that time.

Family wages for most adult men imply men's acceptance, and collusion in, lower wages for others, young people, women and socially defined inferior men as well (Irish, blacks, etc., the lowest groups in the patriarchal hierarchy who are denied many of the patriarchal benefits). Lower wages for women and children and inferior men are enforced by job segregation in the labor market, in turn maintained by unions and management as well as by auxiliary institutions like schools, training programs, and even families. Job segregation by sex, by ensuring that women have the lower paid jobs, both assures women's economic dependence on men and reinforces notions of appropriate spheres for women and men. For most men, then, the development of family wages secured the material base of male domination in two ways. First women earn lower wages than men. The lower pay women receive in the labor market perpetuates men's material advantage over women and encourages women to choose wifery as a career. Second, then, women do housework, childcare, and perform other services at home which benefit men directly.[41] Women's home responsibilities in turn reinforce their inferior labor market position.[42]

The resolution that developed in the early twentieth century can be seen to benefit capitalist interests as well as patriarchal interests. Capitalists, it is often argued, recognized that in the extreme conditions which prevailed in the early nineteenth century industrialization, working class families could not adequately reproduce themselves. They realized that housewives produced and maintained healthier workers than wage-working wives and that educated children became better workers than non-educated ones. The bargain, paying family wages to men and keeping women home, suited the capitalists at the time as well as the male workers. Although the terms of the bargain have altered over time, it is still true that the family and women's work in the family serve capital by providing a labor force and serve men as the space in which they exercise their privilege. Women, working to serve men and their families, also serve capital as consumers.[43] The family is also the place where dominance and submission are learned, as Firestone, the Frankfurt School, and many others have explained.[44] Obedient children become obedient workers; girls and boys each learn their proper roles.

While the family wage shows that capitalism adjusts to patriarchy, the changing status of children shows that patriarchy adjusts to capital. Children, like women, came to be excluded from wage labor. As children's ability to earn money declined, their legal relationship to their parents changed. At the beginning of the industrial era in the United States, fulfilling children's need for their fathers was thought to be crucial, even primary, to their happy development; fathers had legal priority in cases of contested custody. Carol Brown has shown that as children's ability to contribute to the economic well-being of the family declined, mothers came increasingly to be viewed as crucial to the happy development of their children, and gained legal priority in cases of contested custody.[45] Here patriarchy adapted to the changing economic role of children: when children were productive, men claimed them; as children became unproductive, they were given to women.

The Partnership in the Twentieth Century

The prediction of nineteenth century marxists that patriarchy would wither away in the face of capitalism's need to proletarianize everyone has not come true. Not only did they underestimate the strength and flexibility of patriarchy, they also overestimated the strength of capital. They envisioned the new social force of capitalism, which had torn feudal relations apart, as virtually all powerful. Contemporary observers are in a better position to see the difference between the tendencies of "pure" capitalism and those of "actual" capitalism as it confronts historical forces in everyday practice. Discussions of the "partnership" between capital and racial orders and of labor market segmentation provide additional examples of how "pure" capitalist forces meet up with historical reality. Great flexibility has been displayed by capitalism in this process.

Marxists who have studied South Africa argue that although racial orders may not allow the equal proletarianization of everyone, this does not mean that racial barriers prevent capital accumulation.[46] In the abstract, analysts could argue about which arrangements would allow capitalists to extract "the most" surplus value. Yet in a particular historical situation, capitalists must be concerned with social control, the resistance of groups of workers, and the intervention of the state. The state might intervene in order to reproduce the society as a whole; it might be necessary to police some capitalists, to overcome the worst tendencies of capital. Taking these factors into account, capital*ists* maximize greatest *practicable* profits. If for purposes of social control, capitalists organize work in a particular way, nothing about capital itself determines who (that is, which individuals with which ascriptive characteristics) shall occupy the higher, and who the lower rungs of the wage labor force. It helps, of course, that capitalists themselves are likely to be of the dominant social group and hence racist (and sexist). Capitalism inherits the ascribed characteristics of the dominant groups as well as of the subordinate ones.

Recent arguments about the tendency of monopoly capital to create labor market segmentation are consistent with this understanding.[47] Where capitalists purposely segment the labor force, using ascriptive characteristics to divide the working class, this clearly derives from the need for social control rather than accumulation imperatives in the narrow sense.[48] And over time, not all such divisive attempts are either successful (in dividing) or profitable. The ability of capital to shape the workforce depends both on the particular imperatives of accumulation in a narrow sense (for example, is production organized in a way that requires communication among a large number of workers? If so, they had better all speak English)[49] and on social forces within a society which may encourage/force capital to adapt (the maintenance of separate wash-room facilities in South Africa for whites and blacks can only be understood as an economic cost to capitalists, but one less than the social cost of trying to force South African whites to wash up with blacks).

If the first element of our argument about the course of capitalist development is that capital is not all-powerful, the second is that capital is tremendously flexible. Capital accumulation encounters pre-existing social forms, and both destroys them and adapts to them. The "adaptation" of capital can be seen as a reflection of the *strength* of these pre-existing forms to persevere in new environments. Yet even as they persevere, they are not unchanged. The ideology with which race and sex are understood today, for example, is strongly shaped by the reinforcement of racial and sexual divisions in the accumulation process.

The Family and the Family Wage Today

We argued above, that, with respect to capitalism and patriarchy, the adaptation, or mutual accommodation, took the form of the development of the family wage in the early twentieth century. The family wage cemented the partnership between patriarchy and capital. Despite women's increased labor force participation, particularly rapid since World War II, the family wage is still, we argue, the cornerstone of the present sexual division of labor—in which women are primarily responsible for housework and men primarily for wage work. Women's lower wages in the labor market (combined with the need for children to be reared by someone) assure the continued existence of the family as a necessary income-pooling unit. The family, supported by the family wage, thus allows the control of women's labor by men both within and without the family.

Though women's increased wage work may cause stress for the family (similar to the stress Kautsky and Engels noted in the nineteenth century), it would be wrong to think that as a consequence, the concepts and the realities of the family and of the sexual division of labor will soon disappear. The sexual division of labor reappears in the labor market, where women work at women's jobs, often the very jobs they used to do only at home—food preparation and service, cleaning of all kinds, caring for people, and so on. As these jobs are low-status and low-paying patriarchal relations remain intact, though their material base shifts somewhat from the family to the wage differential. Carol Brown, for example, has argued that we are moving from "family-based" to "industrially based" patriarchy within capitalism.[50]

Industrially based patriarchal relations are enforced in a variety of ways. Union contracts which specify lower wages, lesser benefits, and fewer advancement opportunities for women are not just atavistic hangovers—a case of sexist attitudes or male supremacist ideology—they maintain the material base of the patriarchal system. While some would go so far as to argue that patriarchy is already absent from the family (see, for example, Stewart Ewen, *Captains of Consciousness*),[51] we would not. Although the terms of the compromise between capital and patriarchy are changing as additional tasks formerly located in the family are capitalized, and the location of the deployment of women's labor power shifts,[52] it is nevertheless true, as we have argued above, that the wage differential caused by the extreme job segregation in the labor market reinforces the family, and, with it, the domestic division of labor, by encouraging women to marry. The "ideal" of the family wage—that a man can earn enough to support an entire family—may be giving way to a new ideal that both men and women contribute through wage earning to the cash income of the family. The wage differential, then, will become increasingly necessary in perpetuating patriarchy, the male control of women's labor power. The wage differential will aid in *defining* women's work as secondary to men's at the same time as it necessitates women's actual continued economic dependence on men. The sexual division of labor in the labor market and elsewhere should be understood as a manifestation of patriarchy which serves to perpetuate it.

Many people have argued that though the partnership between capital and patriarchy exists now, it may *in the long run* prove intolerable to capitalism; capital may eventually destroy both familial relations and patriarchy. The logic of the argument is that capitalist social relations (of which the family is not an example) tend to become universalized, that as women are increasingly able to earn money they will increasingly refuse to submit to subordination in the family, and that since the family is oppressive particularly to women and children, it will collapse as soon as people can support themselves outside it.

We do not think that the patriarchal relations embodied in the family can be destroyed so easily by capital, and we see little evidence that the family system is presently disintegrating. Although the increasing labor force participation of women has made divorce more feasible, the incentives to divorce are not overwhelming for women. Women's wages allow very few women to support themselves and their children independently and adequately. The evidence for the decay of the traditional family is weak at best. The divorce rate has not so much increased, as it has evened out among classes; moreover, the remarriage rate is also very high. Up until the 1970 census, the first-marriage rate was continuing its historic decline. Since 1970 people seem to have been delaying marriage and childbearing, but most recently, the birth rate has begun to increase again. It is true that larger proportions of the population are now living outside traditional families. Young people, especially, are leaving their parents' homes and establishing their own households before they marry and start traditional families. Older people, especially women, are finding themselves alone in their own households after their children are grown and they experience separation or death of a spouse. Nevertheless, trends indicate that the new generations of young people will form nuclear families at some time in their adult lives in higher proportions than ever before. The cohorts, or groups of people, born since 1930 have much higher rates of eventual marriage and child-rearing than previous cohorts. The duration of marriage and child-rearing may be shortening, but its incidence is still spreading.[53]

The argument that capital "destroys" the family also overlooks the social forces which make family life appealing. Despite critiques of nuclear families as psychologically destructive, in a competitive society the family still meets real needs for many people. This is true not only of long-term monogamy, but even more so for raising children. Single parents bear both financial and psychic burdens. For working class women, in particular, these burdens make the "independence" of labor force participation illusory. Single parent families have recently been seen by policy analysts as transitional family formations which become two-parent families upon remarriage.[54]

It could be that the effects of women's increasing labor force participation are found in a declining sexual division of labor within the family, rather than in more frequent divorce, but evidence for this is also lacking. Statistics on who does housework, even in families with wage earning wives, show little change in recent years; women still do most of it.[55] The "double day" is a reality for wage-working women. This is hardly surprising since the sexual division of labor outside the family, in the labor market, keeps women financially dependent on men—even when they earn a wage themselves. The future of patriarchy does not, however, rest solely on the future of familial relations. For patriarchy, like capital, can be surprisingly flexible and adaptable.

Whether or not the patriarchal division of labor, inside the family and elsewhere, is "ultimately" intolerable to capital, it is shaping capitalism now. As we illustrate below, patriarchy both legitimates capitalist control and delegitimates certain forms of struggle against capital.

Ideology in the Twentieth Century

Patriarchy, by establishing and legitimating hierarchy among men (by allowing men of all groups to control at least some women), reinforces capitalist control, and capitalist values shape the definition of patriarchal good.

The psychological phenomena Firestone identifies are particular examples of what happens in relationships of dependence and domination. They follow from the realities of men's social power—which women are denied—but they are shaped by the fact that they happen in the context of a capitalist society.[56] If we examine the characteristic of men as radical feminists describe them—competitive, rationalistic, dominating—they are much like our description of the dominant values of capitalist society.

This "coincidence" may be explained in two ways. In the first instance, men, as wage laborers, are absorbed in capitalist social relations at work, driven into the competition these relations prescribe, and absorb the corresponding values.[57] The radical feminist description of men was not altogether out of line for capitalist societies. Second, even when men and women do not actually behave in the way sexual norms prescribe, men *claim for themselves* those characteristics which are valued in the dominant ideology. So, for example, the authors of *Crestwood Heights* found that while the men, who were professionals, spent their days manipulating subordinates (often using techniques that appeal to fundamentally irrational motives to elicit the preferred behavior), men and women characterized men as "rational and pragmatic." And while the women devoted great energies to studying scientific methods of child-rearing and child development, men and women in Crestwood Heights characterized women as "irrational and emotional."[58]

This helps to account not only for "male" and "female" characteristics in capitalist societies, but for the particular form sexist ideology takes in capitalist societies. Just as women's work serves the dual purpose of perpetuating male domination and capitalist production, so sexist ideology serves the dual purpose of glorifying male characteristics/capitalist values, and denigrating female characteristics/social need. If women were degraded or powerless in other societies, the reasons (rationalizations) men had for this were different. Only in a capitalist society does it make sense to look down on women as emotional or irrational. As epithets, they would not have made sense in the renaissance. Only in a capitalist society does it make sense to look down on women as "dependent." "Dependent" as an epithet would not make sense in feudal societies. Since the division of labor ensures that women as wives and mothers in the family are largely concerned with the production of use values, the denigration of these activities obscures capital's inability to meet socially determined needs at the same time that it degrades women in the eyes of men, providing a rationale for male dominance. An example of this may be seen in the peculiar ambivalence of television commercials. On one hand, they address themselves to the real obstacles to providing for socially determined needs: detergents that destroy clothes and irritate skin, shoddily made goods of all sorts. On the other hand, concern with these problems must be denigrated; this is accomplished by mocking women, the workers who must deal with these problems.

A parallel argument demonstrating the partnership of patriarchy and capitalism may be made about the sexual division of labor in the work force. The sexual division of labor places women in low-paying jobs, and in tasks thought to be appropriate to women's role. Women are teachers, welfare workers, and the great majority of workers in the health fields. The nurturant roles that women play in these jobs are of low status in part because men denigrate women's work. They are also of low status because capitalism emphasizes personal independence and the ability of private enterprise to meet social needs, emphases contradicted by the need for collectively provided social services. As long as the social importance of nurturant tasks can be denigrated because women perform them, the confrontation of capital's priority on exchange value by a demand for use values can be avoided. In this way, it is not feminism, but sexism that divides and debilitates the working class.

IV. Towards a More Progressive Union

Many problems remain for us to explore. Patriarchy as we have used it here remains more a descriptive term than an analytical one. If we think marxism alone inadequate, and radical feminism itself insufficient, then we need to develop new categories. What makes our task a difficult one is that the same features, such as the division of labor, often reinforce both patriarchy and capitalism, and in a thoroughly patriarchal capitalist society, it is hard to isolate the mechanisms of patriarchy. Nevertheless, this is what we must do. We have pointed to some starting places: looking at who benefits from women's labor power, uncovering the material base of patriarchy, investigating the mechanisms of hierarchy and solidarity among men. The questions we must ask are endless.

Can we speak of the laws of motion of a patriarchal system? How does patriarchy generate feminist struggle? What kinds of sexual politics and struggle between the sexes can we see in societies other than advanced capitalist ones? What are the contradictions of the patriarchal system and what is their relation to the contradictions of capitalism? We know that patriarchal relations give rise to the feminist movement, and that capital generates class struggle—but how has the relation of feminism to class struggle been played out in historical contexts? In this section we attempt to provide an answer to this last question.

Historically and in the present, the relation of feminism and class struggle has been either that of fully separate paths ("bourgeois" feminism on one hand, class struggle on the other), or, within the left, the dominance of feminism by marxism. With respect to the latter, this has been a consequence both of the analytic power of marxism, and of the power of men within the left. These have produced both open struggles on the left, and a contradictory position for marxist feminists.

Most feminists who also see themselves as radicals (anti-system, anti-capitalist, anti-imperialist, socialist, communist, marxist, whatever) agree that the radical wing of the women's movement has lost momentum while the "bourgeois" sector seems to have seized the time and forged ahead. Our movement is no longer in that exciting, energetic period when no matter what we did, it worked—to raise consciousness, to bring more women (more even than could be easily incorporated) into the movement, to increase the visibility of women's issues in the society, often in ways fundamentally challenging to both the capitalist and patriarchal relations in society. Now we sense parts of the movement are being coopted and "feminism" is being used against women—for example, in court cases when judges argue that women coming out of long-term marriages in which they were housewives don't need alimony because we all know women are liberated now. The failure to date to secure the passage of the Equal Rights Amendment indicates the presence of legitimate fears among many women that "feminism" will continue to be used against women, and it indicates a real need for us to reassess our movement, to analyze why it has been coopted in this way. It is logical for us to turn to marxism for help in that reassessment because it is a developed theory of social change. Marxist theory is well developed compared to feminist theory, and in our attempt to use it, we have sometimes been sidetracked from feminist objectives.

The left has always been ambivalent about the women's movement, often viewing it as dangerous to the cause of socialist revolution. When left women espouse feminism, it may be personally threatening to left men. And of course many left organizations benefit from the labor of women. Therefore, many left analyses (both in progressive and traditional forms) are self-serving, both theoretically and politically. They seek to influence women to abandon their attempt to develop an independent understanding of women's situation and to adopt their understanding of the situation. As for our response to this pressure, it is natural that, as we ourselves have turned to marxist analysis, we would try to join the "fraternity" using this paradigm, and we may end up trying to justify our struggle to the fraternity rather than trying to analyze the situation of women to improve our political practice. Finally, many marxists are satisfied with the traditional marxist analysis of the woman question. They see class as the correct framework with which to understand women's position. Women should be understood as part of the working class; the working class's struggle against capitalism should take precedence over any conflict between men and women. Sex conflict must not be allowed to interfere with class solidarity.

As the economic situation in the United States has worsened in the last few years, traditional marxist analysis has reasserted itself. In the sixties the civil rights movement, the student free speech movement, the antiwar movement, the women's movement, the environmental movement, and the increased militancy of professional and white collar groups all raised new questions for marxists. But now the return of obvious economic problems such as inflation and unemployment has eclipsed the importance of these demands and returned the left to the "fundamentals"—working class (narrowly defined) politics. The growing marxist-leninist pre-party sects are committed anti-feminists, in both doctrine and practice. And there are signs that the presence of feminist issues in the academic left is declining as well. Day care is disappearing from left conferences. As marxism or political economy become intellectually acceptable, the old boys' network of liberal academia is replicated in a sidekick young boys' network of marxists and radicals, nonetheless male in membership and outlook despite its youth and radicalism.

The pressures on radical women to abandon this silly stuff and become "serious" revolutionaries have increased. Our work seems like a waste of time compared to "inflation" and "unemployment." It is symptomatic of male dominance that our unemployment was never considered a crisis. In the last major economic crisis, the 1930s, the vast unemployment was partially dealt with by excluding women from all kinds of jobs—one wage job per family, and that job was the man's. Capitalism and patriarchy recovered strengthened from the crisis. Just as economic crises serve a restorative function for capitalism by correcting imbalances, so they might serve patriarchy. The thirties put women back in their place.

The struggle against capital and patriarchy cannot be successful if the study and practice of the issues of feminism are given up. A struggle aimed only at capitalist relations of oppression will fail, since their underlying supports in patriarchal relations of oppression will be overlooked. And the analysis of patriarchy is essential to a definition of the kind of socialism that would destroy patriarchy, the only kind of socialism useful to women. While men and women share a need to overthrow capitalism they retain interests particular to their gender group. It is not clear—from our sketch, from history, or from male socialists—that the "socialism" being struggled for is the same for both men and women. For a "humane socialism" would require not only consensus on what the new society should look like and what a healthy person should look like, but more concretely, it would require that men relinquish their privilege.

As women we must not allow ourselves to be talked out of the urgency and importance of our tasks, as we have so many times in the past. We must fight the attempted coercion, both subtle and not so subtle, to abandon feminist objectives.

This suggests two strategic considerations. First, a struggle to establish socialism must be a struggle in which groups with different interests form an alliance. Women should not trust men to "liberate" them "after the revolution," in part because there is no reason to think they would know how; in part because there is no necessity for them to do so; in fact their immediate self-interest lies in our continued oppression. Instead we must have our own organizations and our own power base. Second, we think the sexual division of labor within capitalism has given women a practice in which we have learned to understand what human interdependence and needs are. We agree with Lise Vogel that while men have long struggled *against* capital, women know what to struggle *for*.[59] As a general rule, men's position in patriarchy and capitalism prevents them from recognizing both human needs for nurturance, sharing, and growth, and the potential for meeting those needs in a non-hierarchical, non-patriarchal society. But even if we raise their consciousness, men might assess the potential gains against the potential losses and choose the status quo. Men have more to lose than their chains.

As feminist socialists, we must organize a practice which addresses both the struggle against patriarchy and the struggle against capitalism. We must insist that the society we want to create is a society in which recognition of interdependence is liberation rather than shame, nurturance is a universal, not an oppressive practice, and in which women do not continue to support the false as well as the concrete freedoms of men.

Notes

. . .

1. Often paraphrased as "the husband and wife are one and that one is the husband," English law held that "by marriage, the husband and wife are one person in law: that is, the very being or legal existence of the woman is suspended during the marriage, or at least is incorporated and consolidated into that of the husband," I. Blackstone, *Commentaries,* 1765, pp. 442–445, cited in Kenneth M. Davidson, Ruth B. Ginsburg, and Herma H. Kay, *Sex Based Discrimination* (St. Paul, Minn.: West Publishing Co., 1974), p. 117.

2. Friedrich Engels, *The Origin of the Family, Private Property and the State,* edited, with an introduction by Eleanor Burke Leacock (New York: International Publishers, 1972).

3. Friedrich Engels, *The Condition of the Working Class in England* (Stanford, Calif.: Stanford University Press, 1958). See especially pp. 162–166 and p. 296.

4. Eli Zaretsky, "Capitalism, the Family, and Personal Life," *Socialist Revolution,* Part I in no. 13–14 (January–April 1973), pp. 66–125, and Part II in no. 15 (May–June 1973), pp. 19–70. Also Zaretsky, "Socialist Politics and the Family," *Socialist Revolution* (now *Socialist Review*), no. 19 (January–March 1974), pp. 83–98, and *Capitalism, the Family and Personal Life* (New York: Harper & Row, 1976). Insofar as they claim their analyses are relevant to women, Bruce Brown's *Marx, Freud, and the Critique of Everyday Life* (New York: Monthly Review Press, 1973) and Henri Lefebvre's *Everyday Life in the Modern World* (New York: Harper & Row, 1971) may be grouped with Zaretsky.

5. In this Zaretsky is following Margaret Benston ("The Political Economy of Women's Liberation," *Monthly Review,* vol. 21, no. 4 [September 1969], pp. 13–27), who made the cornerstone of her analysis that women have a different relation to capitalism than men. She argued that women at home produce use values, and that men in the labor market produce exchange values. She labeled women's work precapitalist (and found in women's common work the basis for their political unity). Zaretsky builds on this essential difference in men's and women's work, but labels them both capitalist.

6. Zaretsky, "Personal Life," Part I, p. 114.

7. Mariarosa Dalla Costa, "Women and the Subversion of the Community," in *The Power of Women and the Subversion of the Community* by Mariarosa Dalla Costa and Selma James (Bristol, England: Falling Wall Press, 1973; second edition) pamphlet, 78 pp.

8. It is interesting to note that in the original article (cited in n. 7 above) Dalla Costa suggests that wages for housework would only further institutionalize women's housewife role (pp. 32, 34) but in a note (n. 16, pp. 52–53) she explains the demand's popularity and its use as a consciousness raising tool. Since then she has actively supported the demand. See Dalla Costa, "A General Strike," in *All Work and No Pay: Women, Housework, and the Wages Due,* ed. Wendy Edmond and Suzie Fleming (Bristol, England: Falling Wall Press, 1975).

9. The text of the article reads: "We have to make clear that, within the wage, domestic work produces not merely use values, but is essential to the production of surplus value" (p. 31). Note 12 reads: "What we mean precisely is that housework as work is *productive* in the marxian sense, that is, producing surplus value" (p. 52, original emphasis). To our knowledge this claim has never been made more rigorously by the wages for housework group. Nevertheless marxists have responded to the claim copiously.

10. The literature of the debate includes Lise Vogel, "The Earthly Family," *Radical America,* Vol. 7, no. 4–5 (July–October 1973), pp. 9–50; Ira Gerstein, "Domestic Work and Capitalism," *Radical America,* Vol. 7, no. 4–5 (July–October 1973), pp. 101–128; John Harrison, "Political Economy of Housework," *Bulletin of the Conference of Socialist Economists,* Vol. 3, no. 1 (1973); Wally Seccombe, "The Housewife and Her Labour under Capitalism," *New Left Review,* no. 83 (January–February 1974), pp. 3–24; Margaret Coulson, Branka Magas, and Hilary Wainwright, "The Housewife and Her Labour under Capitalism: A Critique," *New Left Review,* no. 89 (January–February 1975), pp. 59–71; Jean Gardiner, "Women's Domestic Labour," *New Left Review,* no. 89 (January–February 1975), pp. 47–58; Ian Gough and John Harrison, "Unproductive Labour and Housework Again," *Bulletin of the Conference of Socialist Economists,* Vol. 4, no. 1 (1975); Jean Gardiner, Susan Himmelweit and Maureen Mackintosh, "Women's Domestic Labour," *Bulletin of the Conference of Socialist Economists,* Vol. 4, no. 2 (1975); Wally Seccombe, "Domestic Labour: Reply to Critics," *New Left Review,* no. 94 (November–December 1975), pp. 85–96; Terry Fee, "Domestic Labor: An Analysis of Housework and its Relation to the Production Process," *Review of Radical Political Economics,* Vol. 8, no. 1 (Spring 1976), pp. 1–8; Susan Himmelweit and Simon Mohun, "Domestic Labour and Capital," *Cambridge Journal of Economics,* Vol. 1, no. 1 (March 1977), pp. 15–31.

11. In the U.S., the most often-heard political criticism of the wages for housework group has been its opportunism.

12. Laura Oren documents this for the working class in "The Welfare of Women in Laboring Families: England, 1860–1950," *Feminist Studies,* Vol. 1, no. 3–4 (Winter–Spring 1973), pp. 107–25.

13. The late Stephen Hymer pointed out to us a basic weakness in Engels' analysis in *Origins,* a weakness that occurs because Engels fails to analyze the labor process within the family. Engels argues that men enforced monogamy because they wanted to leave their property to their own children. Hymer argued that far from being a "gift," among the petit bourgeoisie, possible inheritance is used as a club to get children to work for their fathers. One must look at the labor process and who benefits from the labor of which others.

14. This is a paraphrase. Karl Marx wrote: "The maintenance and reproduction of the working class is, and must ever be, a necessary condition to the reproduction of capital. But the capitalist may safely leave its fulfillment to the labourer's instincts of self-preservation and propagation." (*Capital* [New York: International Publishers, 1967], Vol. 1, p. 572.)

15. Harry Braverman, *Labor and Monopoly Capital* (New York: Monthly Review Press, 1975).

16. Juliet Mitchell, *Women's Estate* (New York: Vintage Books, 1973), p. 92.

17. Engels, *Origins,* "Preface to the First Edition," pp. 71–72. The continuation of this quotation reads, ". . . by the stage of development of labor on the one hand and of the family on the other." It is interesting that, by implication, labor is excluded from occurring within the family; this is precisely the blind spot we want to overcome in this essay.

18. Juliet Mitchell, "Women: The Longest Revolution," *New Left Review,* no. 40 (November–December 1966), pp. 11–37, also reprinted by the New England Free Press.

19. Juliet Mitchell, *Psychoanalysis and Feminism* (New York: Pantheon Books, 1974).

20. Mitchell, *Psychoanalysis,* p. 412.

21. Shulamith Firestone, *The Dialectic of Sex* (New York: Bantam Books, 1971).

22. "Politics of Ego: A Manifesto for New York Radical Feminists," can be found in *Rebirth of Feminism,* ed. Judith Hole and Ellen Levine (New York: Quadrangle Books, 1971), pp. 440–443. "Radical feminists" are those feminists who argue that the most fundamental dynamic of history is men's striving to dominate women. "Radical" in this context does *not* mean anti-capitalist, socialist, countercultural, etc., but has the specific meaning of this particular set of feminist beliefs or group of feminists. Additional writings of radical feminists, of whom the New York Radical Feminists were probably the most influential, can be found in *Radical Feminism,* ed. Ann Koedt (New York: Quadrangle Press, 1972).

23. Focusing on power was an important step forward in the feminist critique of Freud. Firestone argues, for example, that if little girls "envied" penises it was because they recognized that little boys grew up to be members of a powerful class and little girls grew up to be dominated by them. Powerlessness, not neurosis, was the heart of women's situation. More recently, feminists have criticized Firestone for rejecting the usefulness of the concept of the unconscious. In seeking to explain the strength and continuation of male dominance, recent feminist writing has emphasized the fundamental nature of gender-based personality differences, their origins in the unconscious, and the consequent difficulty of their eradication. See Dorothy Dinnerstein, *The Mermaid and the Minotaur* (New York: Harper Colophon Books, 1977), Nancy Chodorow, *The Reproduction of Mothering* (Berkeley: University of California Press, 1978), and Jane Flax, "The Conflict Between Nurturance and Autonomy in Mother-Daughter Relationships and Within Feminism," *Feminist Studies,* Vol. 4, no. 2 (June 1978), pp. 141–189.

24. Kate Millett, *Sexual Politics* (New York: Avon Books, 1971), p. 25.

25. One example of this type of radical feminist history is Susan Brownmiller's *Against Our Will: Men, Women, and Rape* (New York: Simon & Schuster, 1975).

26. For the bourgeois social science view of patriarchy, see, for example, Weber's distinction between traditional and legal authority, *Max Weber: The Theories of Social and Economic Organization,* ed. Talcott Parsons (New York: The Free Press, 1964), pp. 328–357. These views are also discussed in Elizabeth Fee, "The Sexual Politics of Victorian Social Anthropology," *Feminist Studies,* Vol. 1, nos. 3–4 (Winter–Spring 1973), pp. 23–29, and in Robert A. Nisbet, *The Sociological Tradition* (New York: Basic Books, 1966), especially Chapter 3, "Community."

27. See Viana Muller, "The Formation of the State and the Oppression of Women: Some Theoretical Considerations and a Case Study in England and Wales," *Review of Radical Political Economics,* Vol. 9, no. 3 (Fall 1977), pp. 7–21.

28. The particular ways in which men control women's access to important economic resources and restrict their sexuality vary enormously, both from society to society, from sub-group to sub-group, and across time. The examples we use to illustrate patriarchy in this section, however, are drawn primarily from the experience of whites in western capitalist countries. The diversity is shown in *Towards an Anthropology of Women,* ed. Rayna Rapp Reiter (New York: Monthly Review Press, 1975), *Woman, Culture and Society,* ed. Michelle Rosaldo and Louise Lamphere (Stanford, California: Stanford University Press, 1974), and *Females, Males, Families: A Biosocial Approach,* by Lila Leibowitz (North Scituate, Massachusetts: Duxbury Press, 1978). The control of women's sexuality is tightly linked to the place of children. An understanding of the demand (by men and capitalists) for children is crucial to understanding changes in women's subordination.

Where children are needed for their present or future labor power, women's sexuality will tend to be directed towards reproduction and child-rearing. When children are seen as superfluous, women's sexuality for other than reproductive purposes is encouraged, but men will attempt to direct it toward satisfying male needs. The Cosmo girl is a good example of a woman "liberated" from child-rearing only to find herself turning all her energies towards attracting and satisfying men. Capitalists can also use female sexuality to their own ends, as the success of Cosmo in advertising consumer products shows.

29. Gayle Rubin, "The Traffic in Women," in *Anthropology of Women,* ed. Reiter, p. 159.

30. Himmelweit and Mohun point out that both aspects of production (people and things) are logically necessary to describe a mode of production because by definition a mode of production must be capable of reproducing itself. Either aspect alone is not self-sufficient. To put it simply the production of things requires people, and the production of people requires things. Marx, though recognizing capitalism's need for people, did not concern himself with how they were produced or what the connections between the two aspects of production were. See Himmelweit and Mohun, "Domestic Labour and Capital" (note 10 above).

31. For an excellent discussion of one such transition to socialism, see Batya Weinbaum, "Women in Transition to Socialism: Perspectives on the Chinese Case," *Review of Radical Political Economics,* Vol. 8, no. 1 (Spring 1976), pp. 34–58.

32. It is important to remember that in the pre-industrial period, women contributed a large share to their families' subsistence—either by participating in a family craft or by agricultural activities. The initiation of wage work for women both allowed and required this contribution to take place independently from the men in the family. The new departure, then, was not that women earned income, but that they did so beyond their husbands' or fathers' control. Alice Clark, *The Working Life of Women in the Seventeenth Century* (New York: Kelly, 1969) and Ivy Pinchbeck, *Women Workers in the Industrial Revolution, 1750–1850* (New York: Kelly, 1969) describe women's pre-industrial economic roles and the changes that occurred as capitalism progressed. It seems to be the case that Marx, Engels, and Kautsky were not fully aware of women's economic role before capitalism.

33. Karl Kautsky, *The Class Struggle* (New York: Norton, 1971), pp. 25–26.

34. We might add, "outside the household," Kautsky, *Class Struggle,* p. 26, our emphasis.

35. Cited in Neil Smelser, *Social Change and the Industrial Revolution* (Chicago: University of Chicago Press, 1959), p. 301.

36. These examples are from Heidi I. Hartmann, "Capitalism, Patriarchy, and Job Segregation by Sex," *Signs: Journal of Women in Culture and Society,* Vol. 1, no. 3, pt. 2 (Spring 1976), pp. 162–163.

37. Just as the factory laws were enacted for the benefit of all capitalists against the protest of some, so too, protective legislation for women and children may have been enacted by the state with a view toward the reproduction of the working class. Only a completely instrumentalist view of the state would deny that the factory laws and protective legislation legitimate the state by providing concessions and are responses to the demands of the working class itself.

38. For a more complete discussion of protective labor legislation and women, see Ann C. Hill, "Protective Labor Legislation for Women: Its Origin and Effect," mimeographed (New Haven, Conn.: Yale Law School, 1970) parts of which have been published in Barbara A. Babcock, Ann E. Freedman, Eleanor H. Norton, and Susan C. Ross, *Sex Discrimination and the Law: Cases and Remedies* (Boston: Little, Brown & Co., 1975), an excellent law text. Also see Hartmann, "Job Segregation by Sex," pp. 164–166.

39. A reading of Alice Clark, *The Working Life of Women,* and Ivy Pinchbeck, *Women Workers,* suggests that the expropriation of production from the home was followed by a social adjustment process creating the social norm of the family wage. Heidi Hartmann, in *Capitalism and Women's Work in the Home, 1900–1930* (Unpublished

Ph.D. dissertation, Yale University, 1974; forthcoming Temple University Press, 1980) argues, based on qualitative data, that this process occurred in the U.S. in the early 20th century. One should be able to test this hypothesis quantitatively by examining family budget studies for different years and noting the trend of the proportion of the family income for different income groups, provided by the husband. However, this data is not available in comparable form for our period. The "family wage" resolution has probably been undermined in the post World War II period. Carolyn Shaw Bell, in "Working Women's Contributions to Family Income," *Eastern Economic Journal,* Vol. 1, no. 3 (July 1974), pp. 185–201, presents current data and argues that it is now incorrect to assume that the man is the primary earner in the family. Yet whatever the *actual* situation today or earlier in the century, we would argue that the social norm *was* and *is* that men should earn enough to support their families. To say it has been the norm is not to say that it has been universally achieved. In fact, it is precisely the failure to achieve the norm that is noteworthy. Hence the observation that in the absence of sufficiently high wages, "normative" family patterns disappear, as for example, among immigrants in the nineteenth century and third world Americans today. Oscar Handlin, *Boston's Immigrants* (New York: Atheneum, 1968) discusses mid-nineteenth century Boston, where Irish women were employed in textiles; women constituted more than half of all wage laborers and often supported unemployed husbands. The debate about family structure among Black Americans today still rages; see Carol B. Stack, *All Our Kin: Strategies for Survival in a Black Community* (New York: Harper & Row, 1974), esp. Chap. 1. We would also argue (see below) that for most families the norm is upheld by the relative places men and women hold in the labor market.

40. Hartmann, *Women's Work,* argues that the non-working wife was generally regarded as part of the male standard of living in the early twentieth century (see p. 136, n. 6) and Gerstein, "Domestic Work," suggests that the norm of the working wife enters into the determination of the value of male labor power (see p. 121).

41. The importance of the fact that women perform labor services for men in the home cannot be overemphasized. As Pat Mainardi said in "The Politics of Housework," "[t]he measure of your oppression is his resistance" (in *Sisterhood is Powerful,* ed. Robin Morgan [New York: Vintage Books, 1970], p. 451). Her article, perhaps as important for us as Firestone on love, is an analysis of power relations between women and men as exemplified by housework.

42. Libby Zimmerman has explored the relation of membership in the primary and secondary labor markets to family patterns in New England. See her *Women in the Economy: A Case Study of Lynn, Massachusetts, 1760–1974* (Unpublished Ph.D. dissertation, Heller School, Brandeis, 1977). Batya Weinbaum is currently exploring the relationship between family roles and places in the labor market. See her "Redefining the Question of Revolution," *Review of Radical Political Economics,* Vol. 9, no. 3 (Fall 1977), pp. 54, 78, and *The Curious Courtship of Women's Liberation and Socialism* (Boston: South End Press, 1978). Additional studies of the interaction of capitalism and patriarchy can be found in Zillah Eisenstein, ed., *Capitalist Patriarchy and the Case for Socialist Feminist Revolution* (New York: Monthly Review Press, 1978).

43. See Batya Weinbaum and Amy Bridges, "The Other Side of the Paycheck: Monopoly Capital and the Structure of Consumption," *Monthly Review,* Vol. 28, no. 3 (July–August 1976), pp. 88–103, for a discussion of women's consumption work.

44. For the view of the Frankfurt School, see Max Horkheimer, "Authority and the Family," in *Critical Theory* (New York: Herder & Herder, 1971) and Frankfurt Institute of Social Research, "The Family," in *Aspects of Sociology* (Boston: Beacon, 1972).

45. Carol Brown, "Patriarchal Capitalism and the Female-Headed Family," *Social Scientist* (India), no. 40–41 (November–December 1975), pp. 28–39.

46. For more on racial orders, see Stanley Greenberg, "Business Enterprise in a Racial Order," *Politics and Society,* Vol. 6, no. 2 (1976), pp. 213–240, and Michael Burroway, *The Color of Class in the Copper Mines: From African Advancement to Zambianization* (Manchester, England: Manchester University Press, Zambia Papers No. 7, 1972).

47. See Michael Reich, David Gordon, and Richard Edwards, "A Theory of Labor Market Segmentation," *American Economic Review,* Vol. 63, no. 2 (May 1973), pp. 359–365, and the book they edited, *Labor Market Segmentation* (Lexington, Mass.: D.C. Heath, 1975) for a discussion of labor market segmentation.

48. See David M. Gordon, "Capitalist Efficiency and Socialist Efficiency," *Monthly Review,* Vol. 28, no. 3 (July–August 1976), pp. 19–39, for a discussion of qualitative efficiency (social control needs) and quantitative efficiency (accumulation needs).

49. For example, Milwaukee manufacturers organized workers in production first according to ethnic groups, but later taught all workers to speak English, as technology and appropriate social control needs changed. See Gerd Korman, *Industrialization, Immigrants, and Americanizers, the View from Milwaukee, 1866–1921* (Madison: The State Historical Society of Wisconsin, 1967).

50. Carol Brown, "Patriarchal Capitalism."

51. (New York: Random House 1976.)

52. Jean Gardiner, in "Women's Domestic Labour" (see n. 10), clarifies the causes for the shift in location of women's labor, from capital's point of view. She examines what capital needs (in terms of the level of real wages, the supply of labor, and the size of markets) at various stages of growth and of the business cycle. She argues that in times of boom or rapid growth it is likely that socializing housework (or more accurately capitalizing it) would be the dominant tendency, and that in times of recession, housework will be maintained in its traditional form. In attempting to assess the likely direction of the British economy, however, Gardiner does not assess the economic needs of patriarchy. We argue in this essay that unless one takes patriarchy as well as capital into account one cannot adequately assess the likely direction of the economic system.

53. For the proportion of people in nuclear families, see Peter Uhlenberg, "Cohort Variations in Family Life Cycle Experiences of U.S. Females," *Journal of Marriage and the Family,* Vol. 36, no. 5 (May 1974), pp. 284–292. For remarriage rates see Paul C. Glick and Arthur J. Norton, "Perspectives on the Recent Upturn in Divorce and Remarriage," *Demography,* Vol. 10 (1974), pp. 301–314. For divorce and income levels see Arthur J. Norton and Paul C. Glick, "Marital Instability: Past, Present, and Future," *Journal of Social Issues,* Vol. 32, no. 1 (1976), pp. 5–20. Also see Mary Jo Bane, *Here to Stay: American Families in the Twentieth Century* (New York: Basic Books, 1976).

54. Heather L. Ross and Isabel B. Sawhill, *Time of Transition: The Growth of Families Headed by Women* (Washington, D.C.: The Urban Institute, 1975).

55. See Kathryn E. Walker and Margaret E. Woods, *Time Use: A Measure of Household Production of Family Goods and Services* (Washington, D.C.: American Home Economics Association, 1976).

56. Richard Sennett's and Johnathan Cobb's *The Hidden Injuries of Class* (New York: Random House, 1973) examines similar kinds of psychological phenomena within hierarchical relationships between men at work.

57. This should provide some clues to class differences in sexism, which we cannot explore here.

58. See John R. Seeley, et al., *Crestwood Heights* (Toronto: University of Toronto

Press, 1956), pp. 382–394. While men's place may be characterized as "in production" this does not mean that women's place is simply "not in production"—her tasks, too, are shaped by capital. Her non-wage work is the resolution, on a day-to-day basis, of production for exchange with socially determined need, the provision of use values in a capitalist society (this is the context of consumption). See Weinbaum and Bridges, "The Other Side of the Paycheck," for a more complete discussion of this argument. The fact that women provide "merely" use values in a society dominated by exchange values can be used to denigrate women.

59. Lise Vogel, "The Earthly Family" (see n. 10).

7

Racial Inequality

Michael Reich

Racial inequality in the United States has persisted since the slaves won emancipation in 1865. The patterns of inequality continue not only in the South, with its state-sanctioned and enforced history of discrimination and segregation, but also in the North, where racial-based government policies have exerted less impact on the operation of markets. The persistence of racial inequality thus cannot be explained simply as the results of past and present coercion exercised through the channels of the state. It appears that the market economy has also worked in a manner that is consistent with continuing racial inequality.

The persistence of racial inequality is particularly striking in view of the major changes that have taken place in the economic and political position of blacks in the United States in the post–World War II era. Since 1945 most racial barriers to equal political and civil rights have been torn down and, at the Federal level at least, government activity has shifted from promoting discrimination to combating it. There also have been some improvements at the state and local levels. The oppressive sharecropping system of the agrarian South that reproduced black poverty and racial inequality for so many decades has diminished to a fraction of its former size and importance. A majority of blacks in the United States now reside in metropolitan areas, many of them in the North, and work for a wage or salary for private industry or government. A small but significant number of these blacks have professional and managerial jobs, but the majority of them are employed in low-level clerical, blue collar, or service positions, and some survive through welfare, unemployment compensation, and other transfer payments.

In the post–World War II era the intersectoral shift of the economy from agriculture to industry and services reduced the number of blacks in agrarian

---

Reprinted with permission from *Racial Inequality*, Princeton, N.J.: Princeton University Press, 1981.

classes and expanded their number in an urban working class with a large secondary labor force component and a small professional-managerial stratum. This structural change and the equalizing governmental activities together account for most, if not all, of the aggregate improvement in the relative position of blacks that has taken place since 1945. But this structural change has not reduced levels of racial inequality in private industry or in metropolitan areas. The incorporation of blacks into the metropolitan economies has occurred with the reproduction of entrenched patterns of racial inequality. However, government employment has provided greater opportunities for black advancement.

Before we can understand how to combat the forces that have reproduced racial inequality in the urban setting, we must understand what these forces are. The best-known economic explanations of racial inequality have been developed in the discrimination models of neoclassical economists. But these neoclassical attempts have not proven successful. They are either logically incomplete or inconsistent, or they require strong empirical assumptions that are extremely implausible. This conclusion holds whether the main discriminating agent is the individual capitalist, the white worker, or whites acting collectively as a conspiracy. One way or another, in a neoclassical world, competition among economic agents should be expected to break down structures of racial discrimination.

These failings of the neoclassical economic discrimination theories reflect more general failings of neoclassical economic theory. This theory has a general, market-determined income distribution analysis that contains very few specific conclusions regarding the observed patterns of income inequality in every capitalist economy. One of its few results predicts that non-productivity-related differences in economic returns to productive factors will be competed away by the operation of the market.

Neoclassical theorists rarely analyze conflict among individuals and groups who are engaged in collective action, largely because the logical structure of neoclassical analysis turns attention away from the existence of such activity. Although imperfect product markets have been analyzed empirically and, with less success, theoretically by neoclassical writers, the study of collective action within firms, in the labor market, and in the determinants of government activity remains underdeveloped. Neoclassical economics thus focuses unduly on individualistic behavior in explaining income distribution.

Once we jettison the view that individuals are only self-interest-maximizing individuals who rarely engage in coalitions, and begin to examine the social relations in firms and political and governmental units in a manner that places conflict, power, and collective activity at the center of our vision, an alternative political-economic analysis can easily be conceptualized. This alternative approach takes the analyses of class conflict and of markets as the starting points of its understanding of political and economic processes. It views the determination of income distribution as resulting both from market processes and processes of power and conflict between workers and capitalists. The workplace is now understood to be a contested terrain, where capitalists organize work and workers with the objective of extracting the most work for the least amount of pay, while workers resist these efforts, both individually and collectively. Profitability therefore depends on limiting worker collective action. The organization of jobs, including bureaucratic structures that exploit the existence of racial and other divisions among workers, becomes a key variable. Government activity is now seen as determined by economic and political power. This activity is organized through political parties and a variety of formal and informal pressure groups.

The class conflict theory indicates the outlines of a formal analysis that suggests why racial inequality is reproduced over time in a capitalist economy. The result holds both for competitive and monopsonistic labor markets and does not depend on employers' conscious intentions. The class conflict theory thus challenges the neoclassical theories of racial discrimination. It offers an explanation of why the market by itself does not eliminate racial inequality and suggests, in contrast to neoclassical theories, that most white workers do not benefit from racial inequality while capitalists do.

An econometric investigation of who benefits from racism permits a uniform test of the neoclassical and class conflict theories. The evidence presented here contradicts the neoclassical theories and supports the class conflict analysis. Racial inequality disproportionately benefits rich whites, in the sense that their share of the white income distribution increases. This pattern holds both for the entire nation and for the non-South, in 1960 and 1970. This econometric evidence thus suggests that racism is best understood in the class conflict perspective that is presented here.

Historical investigation yields the same conclusions. The divisive effects of racism on coalition formation are apparent both in the agrarian history of the postbellum South and in the industrial history of both the South and the North. Historical examples indicate that the capacity of farmers and workers to organize interracial coalitions depends upon macroeconomic conditions affecting the unemployment rate, upon the role of the state, and upon differences in the economic positions of blacks and whites.

In recent decades blacks have been incorporated into industry in large numbers, and since the 1930s the industrial union movement has attempted, with some success, to counter racial inequality. Since the late 1940s, however, organized labor in the private sector has stagnated; this stagnation constitutes both cause and consequence of the stagnation of the position of blacks in industry. The inability of the labor movement to organize unions or to extend welfare-state programs to workers in the low-wage competitive periphery, or secondary segment of the labor market, has hurt both black and white workers. Perhaps not coincidentally, unionism has developed most during the postwar period among public employees. Many of these unions include high and growing proportions of black members.

The class conflict theory proposes two testable mechanisms that link racial inequality with income inequality among whites: the effects on unionism and the effects on inequality in public services. Econometric tests indicate that these mechanisms do operate. In 1960 unionism was inhibited and schooling inequality among whites was exacerbated by racial inequality. These mechanisms became the focus of considerable public policy efforts during the 1960s, and their strength apparently diminished by the end of the decade. However, the distribution of benefits from racism remained unchanged during the 1960s. In 1970 white workers' wages, the extent of unionism, and profit rates of manufacturing industries were each significantly influenced by racial inequality. Wages and unionism were lower and profits were higher where racial inequality was greater. Given the limitations of available data and the resulting considerable gap between the conceptual definitions of variables and their empirical counterparts, the econometric evidence proves remarkably unambiguous in supporting the contentions that are suggested by the theoretical and historical inquiry.

The econometric investigations . . . do not directly reveal the extent to which the processes that currently produce racial inequality are located within firms or outside the workplace, in schooling, housing, and other community settings. This somewhat different question has been the focus of considerable research efforts made by others, and the results suggest that the processes are located in both workplace and the community. However, the interpretation of the evidence . . . , I have argued, does not depend on identification of the actual processes that produce racial inequality. The divisive effects of racial inequality on coalition formation are the same whatever those associated processes are.

The theoretical, historical, and econometric investigations . . . notably all point in the same direction. The combination of these separate inquiries therefore reinforces the main conclusions of each. Despite the claims of neoclassical economists, income distribution is determined by the conflictual exercise of power between workers and capitalists, and racism benefits capitalists while hurting most white workers.

Implications for Economic Theory and Public Policy

[Our] findings . . . contain important implications for economic theory and important suggestions for blacks and whites who are concerned with formulating strategies to combat racial inequality.

The results . . . suggest that economic analysis is better served by a class conflict and power analysis than by the individualistic and market-oriented emphasis of neoclassical economics. This does not imply throwing out all aspects of market analysis. Markets do function in a capitalist economy, and no economic analysis of capitalism can be complete without a discussion of these market forces. But equally important, no analysis of a capitalist economy can be complete without a discussion of class conflict and power forces. Although only a limited quantity of the evidence . . . pertains directly to the determinants of government policy, the results also suggest the importance of class power in the political process.

The two analytical foci of market and power forces can and must be united to form a complete and coherent political-economic analysis. This unity, however, cannot be created successfully by simply labeling market phenomena as the economic realm, and class conflict and power as the political or governmental realm. Class conflict occurs within firms, and government policy frames worker-capitalist relations at both the microeconomic and macroeconomic levels. Therefore, political variables enter fundamentally into what is usually specified as the realm of economic analysis. Similarly, economic power is used to influence government policy within the constraint that governments functioning in capitalist economies must maintain profitable conditions for private investment. Consequently, economic variables enter into the conventional realm of political analysis. Thus, both market and class forces must be incorporated into the economic and the political analysis.

. . . I have suggested some ways that market and power variables can be integrated into a unified theory. These suggestions only begin the needed discussion, however, since there are many additional aspects of markets and power factors to consider.

The theoretical, econometric, and historical findings . . . contain important strategic implications for the continuing struggle against racial inequality in the United States. The finding that racism works against most whites' economic interests suggests that most whites need not be hostile to campaigns against racism. On the contrary, it should be possible to mobilize a coalition against racism that encompasses broad segments of the American population. To succeed, however, such efforts must indicate to whites that the achievement of racial economic equality need not occur at their cost.

At the present time, white racism in the United States remains deeply rooted. Most whites are either unaware of the unequal distribution of benefits that arise from racial inequality or feel unable to respond collectively with other whites and blacks in a manner that would benefit both. The perception that fighting racism means sacrifice is understandable, if not inevitable. So too are individualistic reactions to the economic and psychological insecurities of life in a capitalist society.

While racism continues to divide workers, it is not created solely or even primarily today by conscious efforts of capitalists to trick their workers. The racism of whites is being reinforced today by the insecurities created by the decline of the American economy, by the decline of individual autonomy in craft and professional occupations, by the strains that affect family structure, and by the increase of individualism in our culture. In this context, racist appeals and responses can and do appear attractive to broad segments of the white population. Racism provides a vulnerable scapegoat group upon whom the frustrations of life in a capitalist society can be directed.

The struggle for racial equality thus must stress the collective situation of most workers and the efficacy of solidarity and collective action. The economic pie that gets divided between black and white workers does not have a fixed size. Both blacks and whites can make and share a larger pie by appropriating a share of what capitalists now receive, and they can increase the total economic pie by pressuring government to institute economic policies that stress full employment and social welfare programs. Such objectives may seem distant. But they can be achieved through broad economic and political reforms.

Given the likely continuing difficulties facing the American economy, the presence or absence of antiracism as a popular theme will be crucial not only for the immediate economic interests of blacks and whites, and not just for the realization of reformist programs, but also for the entire social and cultural character of coming decades. There are signs that the social meanness that has already appeared against blacks and other racial minorities can easily spill over into broader currents of American life.

Yet the range of possible responses remains quite broad. The recent experience of the various northern European nations with immigrant workers of dark complexion reveals the range of possible outcomes. Among these countries Sweden and Holland contain the most established labor movements and exhibit the most egalitarian income distributions. Sweden and Holland have pioneered in extending political and economic rights to immigrant workers and in actively opposing racial intolerance and discrimination. France and West Germany, by contrast, have weaker labor movements and greater degrees of income inequality. They have done little to incorporate foreign workers into their mainstream; in France, particularly, overt racial violence has erupted repeatedly.[1]

Within the United States, we have, at one extreme, the important example of the antiracist struggles conducted by the Left and the labor movement in the 1930s, and the associated progressive victories of that era. At perhaps the other extreme, we have the racist violence surrounding school busing controversies in cities such as Boston, and the associated conservative turn of the 1970s. This range of experiences suggests that until the Left and the labor movement become capable once again of creating a popular collective vision, culture, program, and movement, the reproduction of racism will be one of the consequences.

Note

1. See Stephen Castles and Godula Kosack, *Immigrant Workers and Class Structure in Western Europe* (New York: Oxford University Press, 1973).

IV

Macroeconomic Instability

8

Marxian and Post Keynesian Developments in the Sphere of Money, Credit and Finance

Building Alternative Perspectives in Monetary Macroeconomics

Robert Pollin

Introduction

Is the financial structure—the market interactions between borrowers and lenders and the balance sheets of nonfinancial firms, intermediaries and households that reflect these interactions—a significant determinant of the pace and direction of a capitalist economy's aggregate activity? For the past 150 years, the basic fault lines in monetary macroeconomics have been established according to how various schools respond to this question of whether financial structure matters in determining macroeconomic outcomes.

Contemporary research from both the Post Keynesian and Marxist traditions have answered in the affirmative, advancing several fundamental arguments as to why financial structure matters. The most important of these include the following:

- The supply of money, and more importantly credit, is generated endogenously through financial market activity. This correspondingly means that credit avail-

This paper was presented at the conference "Comparisons of Post Keynesian, Classical and Marxian Economic Theories," Department of Economics, University of Utah, January 8–9, 1993. I benefitted greatly from the discussion of the paper at the conference, and especially from the comments of Duncan Foley, the paper's discussant.

Source: Reprinted with permission from Mark A. Glick (editor), *Competition, Technology and Money*. Hants, England: Edward Elgar, 1994. The version here also includes additional material provided by the author.

ability is, to a significant degree, independent of the supply of savings and
central bank activity.

- Financial factors—such as existing balance sheets of nonfinancial firms and
  the effects of uncertainty on financial market practices—play a major role in
  establishing the pace and direction of real investment.
- Financial fragility, as measured by an increase in debt obligations relative to
  the ability to service these commitments, emerges through endogenous market practices, including the forces on the real side of the economy that generate a tendency toward downward profitability as the accumulation process
  proceeds. The emergence of financial fragility creates the preconditions for
  financial crises and contributes to aggregate instability.
- The financial market is an important site of inter and intra-class conflict,
  especially as manifested through the policies of central banks and other important governmental institutions.

The aim of this paper is to follow some of the main strands of thought through
which Marxian and Post Keynesian analysts have reached these conclusions. In
following these analytic trails, we will observe basic differences in the two
approaches. The most important is the far greater weight Post Keynesians give to
psychological factors, and Marxists to material forces, in determining the sources
of financial dislocations and macroeconomic instability. Another key difference
is that Marxists place considerable importance, even in the analysis of financial
issues, on the role of class and power. Post Keynesian financial analysis has
never seriously embraced this concern.

While pointing out these differences, I will also argue a point already suggested in this introduction: that the areas of common ground between these two
schools are quite large, especially when compared with the fundamental differences each has with most mainstream approaches. I will attempt to show how
both can be fruitfully deployed in understanding some of the central events in the
area of monetary macroeconomics in recent years.

In section 2, I explore the roots of the contemporary Post Keynesian and
Marxian schools. This will lead, in section 3, to a discussion of the contributions
of Keynes and Marx themselves in this sphere of analysis. The work of both
figures is open to a wide range of interpretation and one of the major projects of
the contemporary Post Keynesian and Marxian thinkers has been the reinterpretations they have provided of the classical canon. Section 4 surveys the range of
contemporary empirical phenomena that orthodox theory has proven incapable
of explaining adequately. A major inspiration for the development of heterodox
theory has been to provide systematic answers to what appear as anomalous or
random occurrences from an orthodox framework. Section 5, the heart of the
paper, then considers the developments in the two contemporary schools. This
will also enable us to sort out both the commonalities and differences between
them. Following this, we will be in a position, in section 6, to consider how

useful these two approaches are in shedding light on two of the most important recent phenomena in the realm of monetary macroeconomics, the third world debt crisis and the merger and acquisition wave in the U.S.

This paper is a survey and therefore applies broad brush strokes to a range of topics. Even still, it is not possible to consider several important issues, including theories of the determination of interest rates and a range of policy-related questions.[1] However, perhaps the discussion of the selected topics may also shed some indirect light on the neglected questions.

Finally, by way of introduction, I must issue a *caveat emptor*. While this is a survey, it does not pretend to be balanced. The issues and authors considered here reflect my own interests and judgments as to the relative merits of various positions. I also cite my own work extensively. Delusions of grandeur aside, the explanation is that this is where more extensive discussions can be found for many of the arguments that are only fleetingly sketched here.

Conflicting Approaches to Monetary Macroeconomics

Throughout most of the history of economics, mainstream analysis has embraced the view that financial structure does not matter in any fundamental way. This includes the initial developments of the quantity theory by Hume and Ricardo, continuing with the arguments of the Currency School in the 1840s, and on to the modern monetarist and New Classical schools. The common thread running through these approaches is the view that money—and financial markets more broadly—are "neutral" at least in the long run, in the sense that long-term relative prices, incomes and outputs do not depend on the quantity of money. At the same time, in this view, the general level of prices is determined exclusively by the quantity of money, so that *changes* in the price level—inflations and deflations—are entirely the result of changes in the quantity of money. But changes in the quantity of money—and here is the final key idea—are themselves not determined by financial market forces, but by forces *exogenous* to the financial market. These include the discovery and subsequent circulation of new sources of the precious metals serving as commodity money; the import of new supplies of commodity money; or, under a credit money system, the creation of new money by the government.[2]

The modern formulation of this perspective, led by Prof. Milton Friedman, has of course been extremely influential. But monetarists and New Classicals are not the only postwar school which cast aside financial market considerations in their theoretical models. Mainstream Keynesians, prior to some recent developments in the area of asymmetric information and credit rationing, followed the IS-LM framework initiated by Hicks in accepting that financial institutions and market forces could be adequately characterized within a model which focused only on money supply and demand rather than a broader array of institutional variables. The Keynesians' primary dispute with monetarists here was over the degree of interest-elasticity of the money demand function, and this only weakly established any independent influence for private market forces in determining aggregate activity. Beyond this, orthodox Keynesians accepted Modigliani and Miller's conclusion that financial structures were "irrelevant" for the valuation of non-financial firms, and, by implication, for broader macroeconomic outcomes as well.[3]

The opposing position, that the financial system is an important independent variable for aggregate outcomes, was first articulated by Thomas Tooke and other members of the Banking School, in their debate with the Currency School over the 1844 Banking Act in Britain. Tooke developed what we may call a "credit theory of money."

Tooke advanced two primary arguments that carry relevance today: first, there is a fundamental identity between different financial instruments, so that theory needs to focus on the array of instruments rather than on any single one; and second, the creation of credit by intermediaries takes place only because the non-bank public demands its creation. Thus, from Tooke, we begin to develop a theoretical framework in which, contrary to modern orthodoxy, broad credit conditions rather than narrow monetary aggregates are the focus of concern; and that demand forces, relative to supply, are given at least as important, if not a more prominent a role in determining financial market behavior.[4]

Keynes, Marx and the "Credit Theory of Money"

The ideas of both Keynes and Marx on financial questions have been subject to widely varying interpretations. At least in part, this is due to the different views they themselves expressed under varying circumstances and while operating at different levels of abstraction. It is also due to ambiguities or changes in their thinking. But the argument developed by contemporary Post Keynesians and Marxists would regard the overall thrust of their work squarely within the credit-ist tradition established by Tooke.

Keynes.[5] Keynes, of course, was primarily a monetary specialist prior to writing the *General Theory* (*GT*). However, his work was largely within the framework of analysis defined by the quantity theory. But even prior to the *GT*, and in particular in the *Treatise on Money,* Keynes expressed dissatisfaction with the facile assumptions underlying the quantity theory—that the notion of long-run money neutrality was necessarily consistent with all short-run periods of transition from one price level to another.

Keynes sought in the *Treatise* to specify the channels through which changes in the quantity of money are transmitted via the financial structure to changes in the price level; and, in particular, what the short-period mechanism is through which these changes can occur without fundamentally affecting real variables. His argument was that changes in money lead to increased business financing, which in turn increases demand. But the new output associated with the growth of demand is not yet in place, and therefore the excessive demand raises prices. While this argument does not contain Keynes' more developed thoughts on the nature of investment, it nevertheless offers a deep institutional analysis of financial markets consistent with his later ideas on the independence of finance from saving.

In the *General Theory* itself, Keynes put aside the institutional analysis of the *Treatise,* focusing instead on the broader theoretical issue of determining effective demand. Nevertheless, financial markets and practices still play a fundamental role in the *GT.* The central argument of the *GT* is that capitalist economies are unstable because investment spending is liable to fluctuation. Investment spending fluctuates because investment decisions are necessarily based on uncertain estimates of future profitability. This is where financial markets become crucial to his argument.

Keynes explains that financial markets are organized because investors want to maximize the liquidity of their assets, thereby reducing the uncertainty associated with investment decisions. But by doing so, financial markets also contribute to encouraging speculation and an informational climate dominated by short-term concerns of "liquid" investors. This only contributes to the uncertainty surrounding investment decisions, heightening the volatility of investment and aggregate demand.

Considering Keynes through both the *Treatise* and the *GT,* we can discern two reasons why financial markets matter for macroeconomic outcomes: because money and credit are generated through complex institutional processes, not through simple mechanisms via the central bank and private saving; and because the financial market deepens the degree of uncertainty and instability necessarily associated with private investment decisions.

Marx. Marxian economics had until recently almost completely overlooked monetary and financial phenomena. As against this prior neglect, Marxian economists more recently have been drawing out the central role Marx himself assigned to money and finance.[6] The first point one obtains from this literature is the indisputable one that Marx himself actually focused extensively on financial questions in all his major writings on economics. More controversial, of course, is the relative weight Marx assigned to these issues. From the perspective of macro analysis, recent interpretations have argued that these financial factors are of substantial importance—and perhaps of even equal weight relative to contradictions in the real economy—in understanding the sources and dimensions of macroeconomic instability.

For our purposes, Marx's most important insights on money and finance emerge in Volume III of *Capital* and *Theories of Surplus Value,* when he is discussing economic crisis. Here, Marx operates at a relatively low level of abstraction, reaching the point where the Tookian understanding of financial institutions and markets becomes important.[7] From this discussion we see why the role of finance is an integral part of Marx's understanding of macroeconomic instability.

In Marx's analysis, credit is integral to the development of the circuits of industrial production and exchange. The existence of credit stimulates industrial and commercial activities by underwriting them, thus allowing them to advance more rapidly than they would otherwise. As the credit structure expands in tandem with the production process, it develops a degree of relative autonomy from production and commodity exchanges. This means that the financial structure develops its own forms and rhythms of operation; techniques of credit extension and the extent of financial leveraging burgeon. Marx recognized that a sophisticated financial system can create self-generated dislocations and crises. However, these crises will affect the spheres of industry and commerce "only indirectly" as long as these latter spheres are functioning soundly, i.e. "as long as the reproduction process is continuous and therefore the return flow" of revenue is assured (1967 III: 483).

To explain aggregate instability, we must return to the fundamental notion in Marxian crisis theory, which is a falling average rate of profit. For Marx, the tendency towards a falling average profit rate emerges from contradictions on the real side of the accumulation process. Nevertheless, there are two reasons why money and finance play a central role within this crisis framework. First, the flexibility of a developed financial system allows the real sector to "seek to break through its own barriers and to produce over and above its own limits," (1968, III: 122). In addition, this stretching of financial resources creates the conditions in which a downturn in real sector profitability will produce a general crisis of the system. Without the financial fragility which accompanies the profitability downturn, it would be far easier for the system to live with a lower profit rate, along a relatively stable growth path. Thus, without incorporating the financial sphere into the analysis, it is unclear, as Crotty has argued, "why a fall in the rate of profit should lead to crisis at all; a lower but positive rate of growth is a more logical outcome of a decline in the profit rate taking only production relations into consideration," (1985: 48).

The Failures of Orthodoxy

Of course, contemporary developments in Post Keynesian and Marxian monetary macroeconomics have not emerged in a vacuum. They rather result from two interrelated sources: the failure of mainstream theory to offer a coherent explanation of the phenomena they purport to explain, and thereby to provide effective guidance on policy issues; and the rise of financial instability in the First and Third Worlds, which have produced tremendous human costs.

The failures of mainstream theory are pervasive. Thus, orthodox monetary policy is predicated on the central bank's ability to define, measure and control the growth of "money." But contrary to the most basic tenets of orthodox theory, Friedman and Kuttner have recently shown (1992) that, for the U.S. economy over the past 30 years, there is no consistent relationship between money and credit aggregates, and contemporaneous or subsequent movements of nominal incomes, prices, or interest rates.

In fact, this breakdown of orthodox theoretical and policy models is one consequence of a broader phenomenon: the emergence of frequent and increasingly severe financial dislocations over the past 25 years. Such dislocations had not occurred for roughly the first 20 years of the post World War II period, even though they were, as Kindleberger (1977) has put it, "a hardy perennial" of the previous history of capitalism. Indeed, in the 1960s high noon of macroeconomic fine-tuning, such phenomena were considered relics of a bygone era.

But since the mid-1960s, we have seen the process of financial innovation gather relentless momentum, circumventing, and then rendering ineffectual, the system of financial regulation created during the Depression. The monetary decontrol legislation of 1980 and 1982 merely formalized the by-then effective collapse of the financial regulatory structure. In addition, since the 1966 credit crunch, financial crises have recurred regularly—in 1970 (Penn Central), 1974 (Franklin National), 1980 (silver market), 1982 (Latin American debt), 1984 (Continental Illinois), 1987 (stock market), and 1989 (stock market, junk bonds). The unexpectedly long recession and sluggish recovery of the early 1990s was also largely due to the excessive levels of private indebtedness incurred in the 1980s.[8]

How do orthodox economists explain these phenomena? The short answer is that they have no systematic explanation. They rather produce detailed analyses of particular circumstances—focusing on shocks, policy failures, or the incompetence or venality of important personalities—to explain each episode of financial crisis, and even broad patterns of financial change. Such explanations are fully consistent with mainstream theory's overarching vision that the macroeconomy is a system which tends towards a stable equilibrium.

Of course, shocks, human error and other distortions all play a role in any given situation. But the project of heterodox economists has been to move beyond that, to explore the systemic forces at work generating problems that appear to be conducive to generalization. How well have they fared? What are the differences between Marxians and Post Keynesians on these issues? We have now set the context in which we can ask these questions in a fruitful way.

Post Keynesian and Marxian Contributions

A. Post Keynesians

Drawing on their radical rereading of Keynes, the Post Keynesians have made important contributions in three areas of monetary macroeconomics: developing the concept of a flexible financial structure through theories of endogenous money and the independence of finance from saving; incorporating financial elements and uncertainty into the theory of investment; and developing a theory of systemic instability. Let us consider these in turn.

Flexible Finance. Post Keynesians have advanced the Tookian argument that demand-side pressures emerging endogenously within financial markets are the basic determinant both of fluctuations in money supply growth and, more broadly, of credit availability. As such, Post Keynesian theory has again centered monetary theory on the behavior of private financial institutions as well as central banks; and also on how demand forces from non-intermediaries shape the behavior of the intermediaries and central bank.

As this Post Keynesian literature has developed, what has also become clear is that two distinct theories of money supply endogeneity have emerged within this tradition. The two approaches diverge in explaining the process whereby banks and other intermediaries obtain the needed additional reserves once they have extended credit and created new deposits in the process.

One perspective argues that when banks and other intermediaries hold insufficient reserves, central banks must necessarily accommodate their needs. To act otherwise would threaten the viability of the financial structure, and hence the overall economy. Central banks can choose the means through which they will accommodate: either by increasing the availability of non-borrowed reserves through expansionary open market operations, or by forcing the banks to obtain borrowed reserves through the discount window. This decision will affect the *cost* to the banks of obtaining their needed reserves. But because central banks are obligated to accommodate the demand for reserves at the discount window, no effective *quantity* constraint exists on banks' reserve needs. We may therefore term this approach a theory of **accommodative** money supply endogeneity.

According to the perspective I find more persuasive (Pollin 1991, 1995), central bank efforts to control the growth of non-borrowed reserves through open market restrictiveness exert significant quantity constraints on reserve availability. Discount window borrowing, in this view, is not a perfect substitute for open market operations. But what this view also stresses is that, when central banks do choose to restrict the growth of non-borrowed reserves, then additional reserves, though not necessarily a fully adequate supply, are generated within the financial structure itself—through innovative liability management practices such as borrowing in the federal funds, Eurodollar and certificate of deposit markets. We may thus refer to this second Post Keynesian approach as a theory of **structural endogeneity.** [9]

One of the strengths of the structural endogeneity view is that it extends logically to the issue of whether, and to what extent, credit supply can be generated independent of new saving flows. If the financial system is capable of generating cash reserves without having to rely on infusions of new central bank funds, it follows that the system would be similarly capable of generating cash reserves independently of new saving flows.

A vigorous debate on this question among Post Keynesians began with a provocative article by Asimakopulos (1983), and there are undoubtedly numerous interpretations of the outcome of the debate. My own view (Pollin and

Justice 1993) is that this debate confirmed what Keynes called his "most fundamental" conclusion in the field of money and finance: that "the investment market" can never be congested by the supply of saving, but only through a shortage of cash supplied by the financial system. More specifically, the ability of the financial structure to generate new cash reserves, without generating concomitant increases in saving, will depend on: central bank policy; the liquidity preferences of banks and the non-bank public; and the innovative capacity of the financial structure, i.e. its ability to raise velocity without generating equivalent increases in interest rates.

Uncertainty and Investment. The first key Post Keynesian contribution toward establishing the linkages between finance, uncertainty and investment relies on explaining the concepts, presented initially in both Keynes and Kalecki, of lender's and borrower's risk. Minksy's use of these concepts, in constructing what he calls "a financial theory of investment" and an "investment theory of instability" have been highly influential.[10]

Investment is financed either through drawing down existing assets, from current retained earnings, or through external finance. When it is externally financed, this brings new considerations into the investment project—those of borrower's and lender's risk. Minsky argues that borrower's risk arises to the extent that purchasers of capital assets must debt finance their investment projects and hence increase their exposure to default risk. To compensate for their increased risk, borrowers lower the price at which they are willing to purchase the asset. But how much will the demand price of assets decline? According to Minsky, this cannot be measured objectively, but rather depends on borrower leveraging, how external financing influences borrower assessment of project risk and return, and the borrowing terms offered. The demand price for capital assets will thus fall when asset purchases are debt financed, but by an analytically indeterminate amount.

Lender's risk arises because lenders will insist on being compensated for excessive risk and moral hazard. Lender's risk therefore exerts upward pressure on the supply price of investment goods. Bankers (or other lenders) extract compensation for their lender's risk by imposing harsher terms on borrowers— higher loan rates, shorter terms to maturity, collateral, and restrictions on dividend payouts. The costs extracted for lender's risk vary directly with the leveraging of the investing firm. While lender's risk appears on signed contracts, the amount of lender's risk that will be required on any investment project is, like borrower's risk, analytically indeterminate.

Minsky argues that, "the pace of investment will vary as borrower's and lender's risk vary," (1986: 193). But how much will they vary? This question returns us to the other central element in establishing the finance/investment link: the meaning and significance of uncertainty. In a recent paper which both surveys and deepens the Post Keynesian theory of investment uncertainty, Crotty (1993) argues as follows.

For decentralized agent choice to generate stable macro equilibria, agents must be assumed to have correct expectations about a future equilibrium. This is an untenable assumption for what Shackle calls "crucial" decisions, which are unique, non-repeatable and reversible only at substantial cost. In other words, there is simply no way for investors to acquire correct information about a future that their own investment, and that of other market participants, will itself create.

For Crotty, agents are willing to make investment decisions only because they believe in conventional forecasts. But this also means that when events contradict agents' prior conventional judgments, such as when government policy interventions are incapable of delivering the anticipated degree of stability, investors' confidence will suffer a double-pronged disillusion: they will lose confidence both in what to expect and in their ability to recreate a new set of conventional judgments. The loss of confidence is then transmitted to the investment market by increasing the premia associated with borrower's and lender's risk.

The Thrust Towards Fragility. These arguments about finance and investment uncertainty then become the foundation for Minsky's theory that there is an inherent tendency for capitalist financial structures to move from states of robustness to fragility over time. Systemic fragility results from the shift in expectations that occurs over the course of a business cycle, and the way this shift is transmitted through the financial system.

At the trough of a business cycle, realized profits and profit expectations are both low. At the same time, the financial structure is robust, in the sense that the general level of leveraging is low. This is because the just completed downturn will have brought a significant proportion of highly leveraged firms to bankruptcy. As the economy moves up from the trough, profits begin to rise. But expectations are still low due to memories of the trough, and lender's and borrower's risk premia are correspondingly high. Financing patterns thus remain relatively cautious. However, as the upturn continues and realized profits exceed expectations, expectations shift upwards. Animal spirits are now ignited, and firms become more willing to borrow in the pursuit of profit opportunities. In these circumstances, even more cautious firms feel pressure to either pursue all apparent profit opportunities or forfeit them to competitors.

As full employment is reached and sustained, "euphoric expectations" take hold. The growth rate of debt exceeds that of profits, since—for a given distribution of income between wages and profits—profit opportunities are constrained by the growth of productivity, while the extension of credit is not so constrained. In addition, banks and other lending institutions generally accommodate—and even aggressively promote—the growing demand for credit, regardless of the posture assumed by the central bank. The lenders' expectations may have shifted upwards as well. But more importantly, they do not generally refuse loan requests by large-scale solvent customers.

This is the central argument by which Minsky and much subsequent Post

Keynesian literature concludes that a period of full employment is not a natural equilibrium point for a capitalist economy. It rather is a transitory moment in a cycle, one which leads to overheating and increasing financial fragility.

B. Marxians

Many authors within the Marxian tradition have embraced and deepened the Post Keynesian literature in monetary macroeconomics, particularly in the areas of investment uncertainty and the flexibility of the financial structure.[11] The question we consider now is what are the specifically Marxian contributions to the heterodox literature on monetary macroeconomics? By posing the question in this way, we also suggest an angle through which the Marxian framework may be used to identify the weaknesses within the Post Keynesian approach and to build constructively from such critiques.

Keynes ended the *General Theory* with the observation that "the outstanding faults of the economic society in which we live are its failure to provide for full employment and its arbitrary and inequitable distribution of wealth and income," (1936: 372). However, Post Keynesians, much like Keynes himself, have never seriously addressed the implications of the existence of differential wealth and power in capitalist economies. This issue, of course, has been central within the Marxian literature.

One recent line of research that incorporates class and power considerations within financial analysis is the development of a "contested exchange" model of monetary policy. This work has been developed most fully by Gerald Epstein and various associates (see Epstein 1993 for a clear presentation of this approach and further references). Epstein's most recent contribution acknowledges the significance of the Post Keynesian position on money endogeneity, but then argues that the crucial missing feature of the Post Keynesian endogeneity argument is the role of political forces in the formulation of central bank policy.

The contested exchange model is based on two principles. First, it views the state, and therefore the central bank, as a terrain of both class and intra-class struggle. It also argues that policy is constrained by structural factors, including the structure of capital and labor markets and the position of the domestic economy in the world economy.

Considering large OECD economies, Epstein finds that the configuration of political forces is an important determinant of both central bank reaction functions and the impact of central bank policy on the macroeconomy. One of Epstein's major specific findings is that central banks which are integrated in the political process are more exposed to pressures from coalitions of labor and non-financial industry, and therefore more inclined towards expansionary policies. Countries that pursue expansionary policies, in turn, are associated with higher rates of capital utilization and lower interest rates. Epstein interprets these findings as supporting a case for integrated central banks.

This approach makes a useful contribution towards injecting a class perspective to the realm of monetary analysis. One can fruitfully extend the model to other areas as well, such as International Monetary Fund policies with respect to the Third World debt crisis (to which we return below). However, the limitation of the approach is that, unlike the work of Marx himself, it does not integrate the role of financial forces into a more extensive model of investment and instability comparable to the Post Keynesian framework.

This lacuna in the contested exchange central banking model parallels the neglect of financial forces—either as causal or propagating mechanism—in much of the Marxian research to date on macroeconomic instability. Most work has instead focused on the various factors within the real economy which produce declining profitability and productivity—e.g. wage squeeze; rising costs and/or declining efficiency of social structures of accumulation; disproportionalities or deficient aggregate demand; and declining "capital productivity" or organic composition of capital.[12]

Despite their neglect of finance, these models still serve a useful purpose even within a framework of monetary analysis because they demonstrate the centrality of *non-financial* determinants of systemic instability to an extent that Post Keynesians never attempt. Working from a far richer understanding of the production and distribution mechanisms, the task of Marxian analysis in the realm of money and finance therefore becomes readily distinguishable from the Post Keynesian agenda. Its purpose is to build the appropriate links between the real and financial spheres, recognizing them as complex interdependent systems.

Some work of this nature has been accomplished in recent years, both at the theoretical and empirical levels. Foley (1986), for example, has developed a model derived from the circuits of capital in Volume II of *Capital.* He shows the source of capitalist crisis as being systematic changes in the underlying parameters of the accumulation process. The crisis begins with symptoms of overrapid expansion of the economy: rising money prices of commodities, shortages of certain commodities and certain types of labor power, and high interest rates. These lead to a decline in profitability. The economy then reaches a turning point at which aggregate demand and output turn down sharply and the demand for labor power falls.

Within this framework, Foley shows that the provision of financial assets is itself an important phase in the circuit of capital which also operates independently of the central bank's influence. For example, firms take on a level of indebtedness on the assumption that commodities can be sold at a given mark-up. When that mark-up cannot be sustained, the firms' profit rate falls. At this point, the firms' debt burdens become unexpectedly severe and financial commitments more difficult to sustain. As firms are unable to meet financial commitments, the financial system becomes destabilized and new capital outlays will also decline. This creates the preconditions for a financial crisis as well as a deepening real-sector downturn. Thus, from Foley's model, we see first, how crises can begin in the sphere of production and exchange but then be transmitted into the financial sphere. We also see how the persistence of crises depends strongly on the persistence of financial imbalances that have grown during periods of accumulation. Foley concludes that "without feedback through financial variables to capital outlays there is no reason why the system could not adapt smoothly and gradually to a lower markup without a crisis," (p. 54).[13]

At an empirical level, I (1986) have traced through the relationship between declining profitability and rising leverage of U.S. non-financial corporations from the mid-1960s to 1980. Declining profitability in this period led to a corresponding decrease in corporate internal funds. Corporations were thus faced with the options of either reducing investment spending to a level commensurate with the decline in internal funds, reducing dividend payouts, or increasing borrowing to sustain spending and dividend payouts at a level greater than that of profitability. I found a close correlation between the rise of leverage and the decline in internal funds, suggesting that while corporations did reduce investment spending as profitability declined, their reductions were not as great as the decline in profitability. And because they were unwilling to cut back sharply on dividend payouts, they were forced to raise their level of borrowing. Such increases in borrowing then contributed to financial instability because the firms' subsequent investments did not generate sufficient increases in profits to finance the higher levels of leverage.[14]

The most basic point of this and related research within the Marxian tradition has been to show that material forces associated with a decline in profitability are themselves capable of generating financial dislocations in a system where the financing of investment activity depends significantly on external sources of funds. This view is in sharp contrast with that of Post Keynesians, who rely on psychological factors—uncertainty and associated shifts in expectations—in deriving the links between accumulation, finance and instability.

From a Marxian perspective, one could argue that both approaches capture important features of reality but that the impact of material forces should be regarded as more fundamental. Consider the case in which profitability could be sustained as accumulation proceeded. Financial crises could still result through psychological factors, as transmitted through a flexible financial structure. However, the Marxian models suggest that these financial crises would tend to be relatively brief and shallow as long as profitability were high enough to both meet financial commitments and sustain investment spending.

Can They Explain the Real World?

How well do the two schools of thought actually perform by this standard? Holding them up to this test is an important exercise both in its own right and because it should help clarify some major concerns of this essay: How compatible are the two approaches? What are the intersections between them? How important are their relative strengths and weaknesses when it comes to applying them to understanding and changing the world?

We cannot hope to take a serious stab at these questions in a brief space. Nevertheless, by way of conclusion, let us briefly consider how useful both approaches are at illuminating two of the most important recent phenomena within the realm of monetary macroeconomics: the Third World debt crisis and the merger, acquisition and buyout wave in the U.S.

Third World Debt. The debt crisis had three interlocking causes: the exhaustion of the import substitution model of accumulation in Latin America; the globalization of financial markets; and the way various social forces in Latin America and internationally responded to these conditions.[15]

By the early 1970s, the fact that import-substitution policies had created heavy balance of payments deficits in the major Latin economies meant that the material foundations for growth had reached a crisis. Concurrently, the globalization of financial markets had created vast new opportunities for moving credit readily into Latin America when conditions seemed favorable. But why, given the demise of import substitution policies, did conditions seem so favorable? This was largely a psychological phenomenon: then Citicorp Chair Walter Wriston had apparently persuaded his colleagues and competitors, contrary to all historical evidence, that sovereign countries do not default on debts.

An enormous burst of international lending flowed into Latin America in the 1970s, as international banks became zealous loan merchants and the Latin countries equally ardent recipients of funds. The funds were channeled in several directions, varying by country according to the configuration of class power in each country, and especially due to the specific character of the elite groups in power. A substantial portion, if not the majority, of these funds were channeled to wasteful projects and capital flight. It is thus not surprising that, over time, borrower countries' debt burdens outstripped their capacity to service the debt. Financial fragility deepened. A systemic shock then occurred when, in the depths of the 1982 recession, Mexico announced its intention of defaulting on its obligations. At that point, international financial institutions shut off further voluntary lending to the region. This converted much of the region, including Argentina and Brazil as well as Mexico—the three largest Latin economies—into what Minsky calls Ponzi units: entities which must increase involuntary borrowing just to meet interest payments.

The preconditions for a debt deflation and depression were therefore in place. But here is where the recent Latin experience diverges so sharply from that of the advanced capitalist economies. The policy tools for preventing such an incipient financial crisis from culminating in a debt deflation and depression were well known in 1982. They consist of a combination of deficit spending and lender of last resort operations of the central bank. Such policies have been used regularly and, when deemed necessary, intensively in the advanced economies to prevent debt deflations and depressions. However, an explicit decision was made not to use these tools in Latin America to prevent a depression. Quite the contrary: macroeconomic policy, especially in the hands of the International Monetary Fund, was instead employed to impose severe government budget cuts and labor market austerity. That is, it accelerated the contractionary spiral. Thus, the 1980s Latin American depression was the first to occur since the toolbox for depression prevention was well known and available for use. It was therefore a political decision—one that is best illuminated through Marxian notions of class and power—to forsake these tools and allow the crisis to proceed in its downward path.[16]

In short, both Marxian and Post Keynesian elements have been prominent in the debt crisis. The combination of both Marxian and Post Keynesian thinking thus yields an understanding of the debt crisis that an exclusive focus on either approach could not.

Mergers and Acquisitions. In this case, unlike the debt crisis, very little work has as yet emerged from either an explicit Post Keynesian or Marxian framework. It therefore allows us to conjecture as to how these approaches would guide researchers in constructive directions.

From the Post Keynesian viewpoint, one might start with the observation of a persistent trend towards financial fragility in U.S. financial markets since the 1960s. One might then argue that because a financially fragile economy is susceptible to rapid and unforeseeable reversals in business conditions, the time horizons of investors have shortened. Investors have thus become increasingly resistant to the idea of undertaking long-term projects like building new physical plant. This would explain why the types of investments that are sought increasingly are short-term commitments in the financial sphere and in speculation. Thus, according to this Post Keynesian line of thinking, the trend towards fragility would feed upon itself and becomes ever more entrenched in the contemporary U.S. economy. At the same time, the shortening of time horizons and corresponding decline in real investment would suggest that productivity growth would also decline as the trend towards fragility persists.

A plausible Marxian framework would differ from the Post Keynesian one in several basic respects. To begin with, it would not seek to explain the rise of speculative finance as independent of the problems with the real side of the accumulation process. One approach at least would rather proceed as follows.[17] The merger and buyout binge would be seen as a symptom of a deeper problem, the decline in "capital productivity," which produced a decline in the real profitability for fixed investment. As a result of the declining returns from real investment, stock market values fell. This meant that the potential returns from investing in the transfer of assets came to exceed the returns from investing in new fixed investment. In addition, the declining rate of profit also meant that capital needed to formulate a strategy for attacking the relative strength of the working class. The merger and buyout binge was quite successful at that (what Schleifer and Summers, 1989, have called a redistribution from stakeholders to shareholders). It created new wealth for capital without providing new output and jobs; and more specifically, it enabled the new owners of assets to break both explicit and implicit contracts with workers and communities.

Thus, from a Marxian perspective, the rise of speculative finance in this case would not be due simply to the build-up of financial instability itself, but rather to the interaction between financial and non-financial forces in confronting the long-term structural problems of the economy. Nevertheless, there would be important commonalities between a Post Keynesian and Marxian approach. Most important, both explanations would hinge on the idea of a flexible supplier of credit—personified here by Michael Milken rather than Walter Wriston—ready and able to provide the needed funds, regardless of either the Federal Reserve's policy posture or the prior supply of savings.

In short, the weight of evidence here tips the scales in favor of the Marxian over the Post Keynesian approach. However, this victory is not decisive, especially when we recognize that the ideas of flexible finance have really been an outgrowth of Post Keynesianism which the Marxists have wisely chosen to appropriate.

The more general point is that both the Post Keynesian and Marxian literature have advanced to the point where the various elements of each can now be profitably combined in both theoretical and empirical work as well as in the formulation of progressive policy alternatives. Borrowing David Gordon's (1993) term, a new "left structuralist" monetary macroeconomics needs to emerge, combining elements of flexible finance, investment uncertainty, and systemic forces generating interactive profit and financial cycles. Class and power factors will intersect with each of these other variables. The challenge in making such an approach coherent and persuasive is considerable. And yet, the need for pursuing this task could not be more apparent.

Notes

1. A policy-oriented project informed by the theoretical perspectives explored here is Dymski, Epstein and Pollin eds. (1993).

2. A major impetus in the development of the quantity theory was to counter John Law's mercantilist argument that a country's wealth would rise with its ability to export goods and import gold. The counterargument developed by quantity theorists, led by David Hume, was that such an "export-led growth strategy" would only generate an increase in the price level of the metal importing country, and thus make its exports less competitive in subsequent periods (see Rist's 1940 discussion of this). Interest on this question in Europe was of course greatly heightened by conjectures over the impact of the vast precious metal imports from the Americas. Indeed, in a famous passage in his *Treatise on Money* (1976), Keynes surmised that the profit inflation engendered by the flow of precious metals from the Americas during the 16th and 17th centuries "may fairly be considered the fountain and origin of British foreign investment," (p. 156).

3. Recently, some important steps towards a financial market approach to monetary macroeconomics have been made by mainstream economists such as Benjamin Friedman,

Alan Blinder, Joseph Stiglitz, and Ben Bernanke. Building from the theory of imperfect information in financial markets, they have embraced the argument that the availability of credit and the quality of balance sheets are important determinants of the rate of investment. Moreover, they accept the view that the money supply is not a key variable in determining the price level and output. They recognize that, through increasing velocity, the financial system is sufficiently flexible to generate as much credit as might be needed to finance any given level of activity. Though operating from a different analytic framework, this mainstream approach has much in common with the work in the late 1950s and early 1960s of Gurley and Shaw and Tobin. Fazzari (1992) provides an interesting discussion arguing that there is much in common in the New and contemporary Post Keynesian perspectives. Delli Gatti and Gallegati (1992) and these authors with Gardini (1993) develop formal models incorporating elements of both New and Post Keynesian thinking. Dymski (1993), however, argues that the distinctions are significant between New Keynesian notions of asymmetric information and credit rationing and Post Keynesian ideas about uncertainty and systemic instability. This is one question deserving further exploration which, due to space considerations, will have to be bypassed here.

4. An excellent study of the development of Tooke's monetary framework is Arnon (1991).

5. Davidson (1972) and Minsky (1975) were two pioneering reinterpretations of Keynes incorporating what we would now call Post Keynesian perspectives on money and finance.

6. Thus, for example, the survey articles on Marxian crisis theory by Wright (1977) and Shaikh (1978) present no discussion of the role of finance in crises. Similarly, Howard and King's two volume *History of Marxian Economics* (1989, 1991) offers only scattered discussions of the role of money and finance in Marx generally, and nothing on this aspect in crisis theory. Among the initial contemporary Marxian authors who explored this dimension of Marx's work were Sweezy and Magdoff (1972, 1977, 1981), De Brunhoff (1976), Mandel (1978), Aglietta (1979), Itoh (1980) and Crotty (1985).

7. The links between Tooke and Marx are explored in Arnon (1984 and 1993).

8. Wolfson (1986) chronicles all but the most recent episodes. Pollin (1992) discusses the impact of high debt levels on the recession of the early 1990s.

9. Desai (1987, 1989) provides a clear exposition of some general tenets of an endogeneity perspective relative to the exogeneity framework of analysis. Leading proponents of the Post Keynesian accommodative view have included Nicholas Kaldor (1970, 1985), Sidney Weintraub (1978) and Basil Moore (1988), whose major book, *Horizontalists and Verticalists,* among many other writings on the subject, provides the most thoroughgoing presentation of this approach. Major recent contributors to the structuralist view include Hyman Minsky (1982, 1986), Stephen Rousseaus (1985, 1986), James Earley (1983), and Earley and Evans (1982). Wray (1990) provides an excellent overview of the development of the endogenous money theory and contemporary debates on the topic, as well as advancing original ideas in several important areas, especially the link between endogenous money and liquidity preference theory. Palley (1992a, 1992b) develops useful models which incorporate some features of both perspectives. Duncan Foley has suggested that it is more appropriate to refer to the "relative autonomy" of financial institutions in the liquidity creation process rather than the "endogeneity" of money and credit. His concern is that the term "endogeneity" suggests that the creation of liquidity through the financial structure is unconstrained. His terminological point may be appropriate. However, substantively, as the discussion here shows, there is no sense in the structuralist Post Keynesian framework in which reserve creation is unconstrained. The accommodative approach argues that reserve creation is unconstrained in quantity terms, but not price terms.

10. Minsky's ideas are most fully presented in (1986). Dymski and Pollin (1992) is a survey of Minsky's theoretical perspective, from which the present discussion borrows.

11. A sampling of these would include Crotty (1993), Grabel (1992), Wolfson (1986), and Franke and Semmler (1989).

12. The literature here is considerable. For a sampling of various perspectives with additional references, see Union for Radical Political Economics (1986) and Cherry et al. eds. (1987). Though the perspective is more limited, Marglin and Schor eds. (1990) is also a stimulating collection. Two innovative empirical studies on profitability decline are Michl (1988) and Weisskopf (1988).

13. In a parallel contribution, Shaikh (1989) has developed a model similar to Foley's but differs in that it assumes no change in interest rates over the course of the cycle. Shaikh thus shows that even with constant interest rates, an increase in the quantity of debt alone during the rising phase of a cycle becomes unsustainable when the rate of profit falls. See also Dumeneil and Levy (1989) for another related effort, which is also notable in that it seeks to link the features of its model with historical developments in advanced capitalist economies.

14. Two empirical studies which consider the interrelationships between real and financial crises in the context of advanced economies other than the U.S., and Britain in particular, are Coakley and Harris (1983) and Harris, Coakley, Croasdale and Evans (1988).

15. The arguments presented here are developed in Pollin and Alarcon (1988). Felix (1993) is an outstanding effort to explain the debt crisis by synthesizing Post Keynesian monetary macroeconomics with some elements of elementary ethics.

16. Pollin and Dymski (1993) discusses this issue in the broader context of the declining effectiveness of the Keynesian interventionist toolkit.

17. These ideas, though still preliminary, are sketched more fully in Pollin (1990 and 1992). Crotty and Goldstein (1993) is an excellent critical survey of the literature on the market for corporate control.

References

Aglietta, Michel (1979), *A Theory of Capitalist Regulation: The U.S. Experience,* London: New Left Books.

Arnon, Arie (1984), "Marx's theory of money: the formative years," *History of Political Economy* 4(16): 555–74.

———— (1991), *Thomas Tooke: Pioneer of Monetary Theory,* Ann Arbor: University of Michigan Press.

———— (1993), "Marx, Minsky, and Monetary Economics," in Dymski, Gary and Robert Pollin (eds.), *New Perspectives in Monetary Macroeconomics: Explorations in the Tradition of Hyman P. Minsky,* Ann Arbor: University of Michigan Press.

Asimakopulos, A. (1983), "Kalecki and Keynes on finance, investment, and saving," *Cambridge Journal of Economics,* Vol. 7, 221–33.

Cherry, Robert, Christine D'Onofrio, Cigdem Kurdas, Thomas Michl, Fred Moseley, and Michele I. Naples (eds.) (1987), *The Imperiled Economy, Book I: Macroeconomics from a Left Perspective,* New York: Union for Radical Political Economics.

Coakley, Jerry and Laurence Harris (1983), *The City of Capital: London's Role as a Financial Centre,* London: Basil Blackwell.

Crotty, James (1985), "The centrality of money, credit and financial intermediation in Marx's crisis theory: An interpretation of Marx's methodology," in Resnick, Stephen and Richard Wolff (eds.), *Rethinking Marxism: Essays for Harry Magdoff and Paul Sweezy,* New York: Autonomedia.

——— (1993) "Are Keynesian uncertainty and macrotheory compatible? Conventional decision making, institutional structures and conditional stability in Keynesian macromodels," in Dymski, Gary and Robert Pollin (eds.), *New Perspectives in Monetary Macroeconomics: Explorations in the Tradition of Hyman P. Minsky*, Ann Arbor: University of Michigan Press.

——— and Donald Goldstein (1993) "Do U.S. financial markets allocate credit efficiently? The case of corporate restructuring in the U.S." in Dymski, Gary, Gerald Epstein and Robert Pollin (eds.) *Transforming the U.S. Financial System: An Equitable and Efficient Structure for the 21st Century*, Armonk, NY: M.E. Sharpe.

Davidson, Paul (1972), *Money and the Real World*, New York: Macmillan.

De Brunhoff (1976), *Marx on Money*, New York: Urizen Books.

Desai, Megnad (1987), "Endogenous and exogenous money," in Eatwell, John, Murray Milgate and Peter Neuman (eds.), *The New Palgrave: A Dictionary of Economics*, New York: The Stockton Press.

——— (1989), "The scourge of the monetarists: Kaldor on monetarism and on money," *Cambridge Journal of Economics*, 1989, 171–82.

Delli Gatti, Domenico and Mauro Gallegati (1992), "Imperfect information, corporate finance, debt commitments, and business fluctuations," in Fazzari, Steven and Dimitri Papadimitriou (eds.), *Financial Conditions and Macroeconomic Performance: Essays in Honor of Hyman P. Minsky*, Armonk, NY: M.E. Sharpe.

——— and Laura Gardini (1993), "Complex dynamics in a simple macroeconomic model with financing constraints," in Dymski, Gary and Robert Pollin (eds.), *New Perspectives in Monetary Macroeconomics: Explorations in the Tradition of Hyman P. Minsky*, Ann Arbor: University of Michigan Press.

Dumenil, Gerard and Dominique Levy (1989), "The real and financial determinants of stability: the law of the tendency toward increasing instability," in Semmler, Willi (ed.), *Financial Dynamics and Business Cycles*, Armonk, NY: M.E. Sharpe.

Dymski, Gary (1993), "Asymmetric information, uncertainty, and financial structure: 'new' versus 'post' Keynesian microfoundations," in Dymski, Gary and Robert Pollin (eds.), *New Perspectives in Monetary Macroeconomics: Explorations in the Tradition of Hyman P. Minsky*, Ann Arbor: University of Michigan Press.

———, Gerald Epstein and Robert Pollin eds., (1993), *Transforming the U.S. Financial System: An Equitable and Efficient Structure for the 21st Century*, Armonk, NY: M.E. Sharpe.

——— and Robert Pollin (1992), "Hyman Minsky as hedgehog: the power of the Wall Street paradigm," in Fazzari, Steven and Dimitri Papadimitriou (eds.), *Financial Conditions and Macroeconomic Performance: Essays in Honor of Hyman P. Minsky*, Armonk, NY: M.E. Sharpe.

Earley, James S. (1983), "The relations between saving and the supply of loan funds," in *Essays on the 'Credit Approach' to Macro-Finance*, Working Paper #1, Department of Economics, University of California, Riverside.

——— and Gary Evans (1982) "The problem is bank liability management," *Challenge*, January/February: 54–6.

Epstein, Gerald (1993), "A political economy model of comparative central banking," in Dymski, Gary and Robert Pollin (eds.), *New Perspectives in Monetary Macroeconomics: Explorations in the Tradition of Hyman P. Minsky*, Ann Arbor: University of Michigan Press.

Fazzari, Steven (1992), "Keynesian theories of investment and finance: neo, post and new," in Fazzari, Steven and Dimitri Papadimitriou (eds.), *Financial Conditions and Macroeconomic Performance: Essays in Honor of Hyman P. Minsky*, Armonk, NY: M.E. Sharpe.

Felix, David (1993), "Debt crisis adjustment in Latin America: have the hardships been necessary?" in Dymski, Gary and Robert Pollin (eds.), *New Perspectives in Monetary Macroeconomics: Explorations in the Tradition of Hyman P. Minsky,* Ann Arbor: University of Michigan Press.

Foley, Duncan (1986), *Money, Accumulation and Crisis,* New York: Harwood Academic Publishers.

Franke, Reiner and Willi Semmler (1989), "Debt-financing of firms, stability, and cycles in a dynamical macroeconomic growth model," in Semmler, Willi (ed.), *Financial Dynamics and Business Cycles,* Armonk, NY: M.E. Sharpe.

Friedman, Benjamin and Kenneth Kuttner (1992), "Money, income, prices and interest rates," *American Economic Review* 3(82) June: 472–92.

Gordon, David (1993), "Growth, distribution, and rules of the game: left structuralist macro foundations for a democratic economic policy," forthcoming in Epstein, Gerald and Herbert Gintis, *Investment, Saving, and Finance: A Progressive Strategy for Renewed Economic Growth,* forthcoming.

Grabel, Ilene (1992), "Fast money, 'noisy' growth: a noise-led theory of development," typescript, Graduate School of International Studies, University of Denver.

Harris, Laurence, Jerry Coakley, Martin Croasdale and Trevor Evans eds. (1988), *New Perspectives on the Financial System,* London: Croom Helm.

Howard, M. C. and J. E. King (1989, 1991), *A History of Marxian Economics, Volumes I and II.* Princeton, NJ: Princeton University Press.

Itoh, Makoto (1980), *Value and Crisis,* New York: Monthly Review Press.

Kaldor, Nicholas (1970), "The new monetarism," *Lloyds Bank Review,* July, 1–18.

———— (1985), "How monetarism failed," *Challenge,* 28(2): 4–13.

Keynes, J. M. (1936), *The General Theory of Employment, Interest and Money,* New York: Harcourt Brace.

———— (1976 [1930]), *A Treatise on Money,* New York: AMS Press.

Kindleberger, Charles (1977), *Manias, Crashes and Panics,* New York: Basic Books.

Mandel, Ernest (1978), *Late Capitalism,* London: Verso.

Marglin, Stephen and Juliet Schor, eds. (1990), *The Golden Age of Capitalism: Reinterpreting the Postwar Experience,* New York: Oxford University Press.

Marx, Karl (1967), *Capital, Volume III,* New York: International Publishers.

———— (1968), *Theories of Surplus Value, Part II.* Moscow: Progress Publishers.

Michl, Thomas R. (1988), "The two-stage decline in U.S. nonfinancial corporate profitability, 1948–86." *Review of Radical Political Economics* 20(4): 1–22.

Minsky, Hyman P. (1975), *John Maynard Keynes,* New York: Columbia University Press.

———— (1982), "Central Banking and Money Market Changes," in *Can "It" Happen Again?* Armonk, N.Y.: M.E. Sharpe, pp. 162–78.

———— (1986), *Stabilizing an Unstable Economy,* New Haven: Yale University Press.

Moore, Basil (1988), *Horizontalists and Verticalists: The Macroeconomics of Credit Money,* New York: Cambridge University Press.

Palley, Thomas (1992a), "Beyond endogenous money; toward endogenous finance," unpublished mss., Department of Economics, New School for Social Research.

———— (1992b), "Competing views of the money supply process: theories and evidence," unpublished mss., Department of Economics, New School for Social Research.

Pollin, Robert (1986), "Alternative perspectives on the rise of corporate debt dependency: the U.S. postwar experience," *Review of Radical Political Economics* 1&2(18): 205–35.

———— (1990), "The market for corporate control: sickness, symptom, or cure?" manuscript, Department of Economics, University of California-Riverside.

———— (1991), "Two theories of money supply endogeneity," *Journal of Post Keynesian Economics,* 13(3) Spring, 366–96.

―――― (1992), "Destabilizing finance worsened this recession," *Challenge*, March/April: 17–24.

―――― (1995), "Money supply endogeneity: what are the questions and why do they matter?" in Nell, Edward and Ghislain Deleplace (eds.), *Money in Motion: The Circulation and Post Keynesian Approaches*, New York: Macmillan.

―――― and Diana Alarcon (1988), "Debt crisis, accumulation crisis and economic restructuring in Latin America," *International Review of Applied Economics*, June: 127–54.

―――― and Gary Dymski (1993), "The costs and benefits of financial instability: big government capitalism and the Minsky paradox," in Dymski, Gary and Robert Pollin (eds.), *New Perspectives in Monetary Macroeconomics: Explorations in the Tradition of Hyman P. Minsky*, Ann Arbor: University of Michigan Press.

―――― and Craig Justice (1993), "Saving, finance and interest rates: an empirical consideration of some basic Keynesian propositions," in Dymski, Gary and Robert Pollin (eds.), *New Perspectives in Monetary Macroeconomics: Explorations in the Tradition of Hyman P. Minsky*, Ann Arbor: University of Michigan Press.

Rist, Charles (1940), *History of Monetary and Credit Theory from John Law to the Present Day*, New York: Macmillan.

Rousseaus, Stephen (1985), "Financial Innovation and Control of the Money Supply," in Marc Jarsulic (ed.), *Money and Macro Policy*, Boston: Kluwer-Nijhoff.

―――― (1986), *Post Keynesian Monetary Theory*, Armonk, NY: M.E. Sharpe.

Schleifer, Andre and Lawrence Summers (1989), "Breach of trust in hostile takeovers," in Auerbach, A. (ed.), *Takeovers: Causes and Consequences*, Chicago, University of Chicago Press.

Shaikh, Anwar (1978), "An introduction to the history of crisis theories," in Union for Radical Political Economics, *U.S. Capitalism in Crisis*, New York: URPE.

―――― (1989), "Accumulation, finance and effective demand in Marx, Keynes and Kalecki," in Semmler, Willi (ed.), *Financial Dynamics and Business Cycles*, Armonk, NY: M.E. Sharpe.

Sweezy, Paul and Harry Magdoff (1972), *The Dynamics of U.S. Capitalism*, New York: Monthly Review Press.

―――― (1977), *The End of Prosperity*, New York: Monthly Review Press.

―――― (1981), *The Deepening Crisis of U.S. Capitalism*, New York: Monthly Review Press.

Union for Radical Political Economics (1986), *Empirical Work in Marxian Crisis Theory*, a special double issue of *The Review of Radical Political Economics* 1&2(18).

Weintraub, Sidney (1978), *Keynes, Keynesians, and Monetarists*, Philadelphia: University of Pennsylvania Press.

Weisskopf, Thomas E. (1988), "An analysis of profitability change in eight capitalist countries," *Review of Radical Political Economics* 20(2&3): 68–79.

Wolfson, Martin (1986), *Financial Crises*, Armonk, NY: M.E. Sharpe.

Wray, L. Randall (1990), *Money and Credit in Capitalist Economies: The Endogenous Money Approach*, Brookfield, VT: Edward Elgar.

Wright, Eric Olin (1977), "Alternative perspectives in Marxist theory of accumulation and crisis," in Schwartz, Jesse (ed.), *The Subtle Anatomy of Capitalism*, Santa Monica, CA: Goodyear Publishing Co.

9

Power, Accumulation, and Crisis

The Rise and Demise of the Postwar Social Structure of Accumulation

David M. Gordon, Thomas E. Weisskopf, and Samuel Bowles

Introduction

Crisis may occur in capitalist economies because the capitalist class is "too strong" or because it is "too weak."[1]

When the capitalist class is "too strong" it shifts the income distribution in its favor, reducing the ratio of working class consumption to national income and rendering the economy prone to crises of underconsumption or—in more contemporary Keynesian terms—a failure of aggregate demand. When the capitalist class is "too weak," the working class or other claimants on income reduce the rate of exploitation, squeezing the profit rate and reducing the level of investment (perhaps by inducing investors to seek greener pastures elsewhere).

Karl Marx referred to the first as a crisis in the realization of surplus value and the second as a crisis in the production of surplus value. They may also be characterized (respectively) as "demand-side" and "supply-side" crises. The result in each case is ultimately the same—a decline in the rate of profit, a reduction in the level of investment, a stalled accumulation process, and a stagnation or decline in the rate of growth of both demand and output. Thus what begins as a crisis in surplus-value production, for example, sooner or later turns into a crisis in surplus-value realization.

The authors' names are ordered randomly. Reprinted with permission from *The Imperiled Economy, Book I: Macroeconomics from a Left Perspective* (New York: Union for Radical Political Economics, 1987), pp. 43–57.

Some United States historians have argued that the Great Depression of the 1930s was a demand-side crisis, brought about in part by the political and economic defeats of the working class in the post–World War I era. The most recent crisis of the United States economy, in contrast, appears to have originated as a supply-side crisis brought about by the erosion of the hegemony of the United States capitalist class in the world economic system and by effective challenges to capitalist prerogatives mounted by workers and citizens during the 1960s and early 1970s. Once and only after these mounting barriers to surplus-value production had initially reduced corporate profitability, both stagnating investment and political efforts to roll back these challenges resulted in demand-side problems as well, further reinforcing the dynamic of crisis (Bowles, Gordon and Weisskopf 1983, 1986).

We elaborate this Marxian "supply-side" interpretation in this essay, arguing that the stagflation of the last nearly two decades in the United States can best be viewed as a general crisis of the legitimacy and stability of the postwar capitalist system, one which challenged not only the wealth of capital but its power as well. We build upon two complementary perspectives to elaborate this argument.

The first pursues the general approach to economic crisis which we call "challenges to capitalist control" (Weisskopf, Bowles and Gordon 1985). The second erects a bridge between this general approach and more concrete analysis of specific crises: We argue that understanding capitalist crisis requires building on general institutional concepts such as class and the capitalist mode of production to construct more historically specific institutional concepts encompassed by the concept of a "social structure of accumulation" (SSA).[2] Combining these two perspectives, we believe, provides the most promising foundation for understanding the recent crisis of the United States economy.

We develop our argument here in four principal sections. We first elaborate the two cornerstones of our interpretation and use them for an analysis of the rise and demise of the postwar capitalist system in the United States. We then apply this analysis to a review of the contradictions of conservative economics in the 1980s. We further compare this kind of interpretation with alternative macroeconomic perspectives. We close with a brief review of the political implications of this analysis.

Challenges to Capitalist Control of the Social Structure of Accumulation

Our analysis builds on an intrinsic proposition of the Marxian approach to macroeconomic dynamics. The pace of the economy is driven by the rate of capital accumulation while capital accumulation in turn is fundamentally conditioned by the level and stability of capitalist profitability. As profits go, in short, so goes the economy. In order to analyze crisis, therefore, it is essential first to determine the sources of declining profitability and then from there to trace through the connections from profitability to accumulation to economic growth.

Figure 9.1. **The Rate of Profit and the Rate of Accumulation**

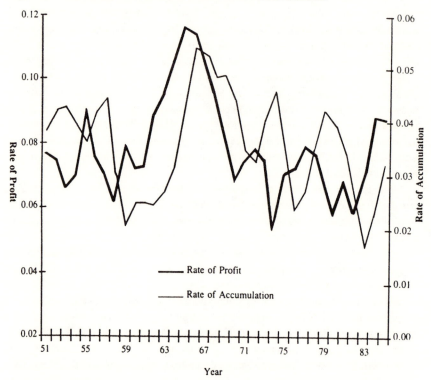

Figure 9.1 expresses part of this connection, graphing the time pattern of the relationship between the rate of corporate profit and the rate of net capital accumulation from 1951 to 1985.[3] Profitability fell first after the mid-1960s and accumulation soon followed, at a lag of roughly two years. While no graph can ever establish causal linkages, the relationship depicted in Figure 9.1 is certainly consistent with general Marxian expectations.

Power and Profits

We turn then to the corporate rate of profit as a fundamental underlying determinant of accumulation and growth. Profits are not a payment to a scarce productive input.[4] Nor can the capitalist class as a whole make profits from its dealings with itself, for as Marx stressed in the early chapters of *Capital* (1967), the buying and selling of commodities is a zero-sum game for the buyers and sellers as a group: the gains of those who buy cheap and sell dear are necessarily offset by the losses of those who sell cheap and buy dear.

Profits are made possible, rather, by the power of the capitalist class over other economic actors which it confronts. Capitalists can indeed make profits through their economic relations with economic actors outside the capitalist class. When workers sell their labor power cheap and buy their wage goods dear, for example, a profit may be made. The capitalist class of a given economy may make profits, similarly, through its exchange with other buyers and sellers outside that economy, given favorable prices of exports and imports.

While some of the relationships between a national capitalist class and other economic actors are market exchanges, many are not. First of all, the worker who sells labor power cheap and buys wage goods dear will not contribute to profits unless the worker's employer also succeeds in getting the worker to work hard and well enough to produce a net output greater than the wage. And while the extraction of labor from the worker is influenced by wages, prices, and other market phenomena, it is proximately effected through an authority relationship at the workplace itself. Second, and similarly, while the international terms of trade depend on import and export prices, the determination of these prices involves the exercise of diplomatic, military and other pressures quite different in character from marketplace exchange.

A third relationship affecting the profit rate—that between the capitalist class and the state—also reflects the exercise of power: The alignment of forces in the formation of state policy may affect the after-tax profit rate directly through the effective tax rate on profits, and it may affect the profit rate as well through state policies affecting the supply of labor, the rate of capacity utilization, the direction of technical change, and many aspects of capital's relations with workers and with foreign buyers and sellers.

It may be illuminating, then, to consider profits as the spoils of a three-front war fought by capital in its dealings with workers, foreign buyers and sellers, and the state (or indirectly with the citizenry). Capital's ability to fight effectively on these three fronts will further be affected by the intensity of inter-capitalist competition, determining how tightly and cohesively its troops are organized for battle. The military analogies are deliberate; they are intended to stress the essentially political nature of the profit rate and the strategic nature of the social interactions involved in its determination.

The fundamentally political character of the determination of profits does not imply, however, that we cannot analyze the impact of this kind of political struggle with some precision. It is possible to identify quite clearly the channels through which the condition of this three-front war is likely to have direct impact on an aggregate measure of corporate profitability.

These channels can be highlighted with a relatively simple model of a capitalist economy in an open world system (Bowles, Gordon and Weisskopf 1986:137–139 and Appendix A). In such a model, it can be shown that the economy-wide average net after-tax profit rate of capitalists depends on six specific factors:

1. The *real wage rate,* or the cost of hiring an hour of labor power as a productive input: the lower the real wage, the higher the rate of profit.

2. The *intensity of labor,* or the amount of labor services extracted from an hour of labor power purchased for production: the higher the intensity of labor, the higher the profitability.

3. The *terms of trade,* or the relative cost (in domestic products) of acquiring foreign-produced inputs for production: the more favorable the terms of trade, the lower will be the costs of acquiring foreign-produced inputs and the higher will be the rate of profit.

4. The *input-output coefficients of production,* or the amount of output which can be produced with one unit of any given factor input: the larger the amount of output which can be produced with given inputs, the higher will be the rate of profit.

5. The *rate of capacity utilization,* or the ratio of productive capital used in production to the stock of capital actually owned: the higher the utilization rate, the less waste of owned capital will take place and the higher will be the rate of profit.

6. The *profit tax rate,* or the percentage of before-tax profits which are taxed by the government: the higher this tax rate, the lower will be profitability.

It is reasonably obvious, given our introductory remarks, that at least the first three factors and the last in this list clearly and directly reflect power relationships. The greater the power of capital over labor, other things being equal, the lower will be the real wage rate and/or the higher will be the intensity of labor. The more dominating domestic capital is in its relationships with foreign buyers and sellers, similarly, the more favorable will be the terms of trade. And the more effectively capital wages battle with citizens through the state, finally, the lower will be the corporate tax rate.

It takes only a little more investigation to ascertain the power relationships which might affect the other items in the list. Power relationships between capital and the citizenry, mediated by the state, may profoundly affect the kinds of subsidies and R&D which influence the direction of technical change and therefore the input-output coefficients. State relations will also directly determine the corporate-profit tax rate. And it may be the case, as we have argued for the specific case of the United States after World War II, that power relations between capital and labor are likely to affect the level of utilization in the aggregate economy.

The intensity of inter-capitalist rivalry, influenced by the relative power of capitalist firms, is also likely to affect several of the profit-rate determinants: for example, moderated competition will make it easier for firms to pass on rising costs through higher prices, thus lowering real wages, while the global market power of United States firms will help sustain relatively favorable terms of trade.

If one could adequately chart the course of the power relationships affecting these variables, in short, one could make considerable progress toward understanding the sources of movements in the rate of profit and the pace of capital accumulation. Where to turn in that mapping exercise?[5]

Social Structures of Accumulation

We believe that the perspective afforded by the concept of a social structure of accumulation (SSA) provides an invaluable guide for this kind of analytic project.

The SSA model begins with the basic Marxian proposition outlined above: Profitability conditions the pace of accumulation which in turn substantially regulates the rate of economic growth.

But the accumulation of capital through capitalist production cannot be analyzed as if it takes place either in a vacuum or in chaos. Capitalists cannot and will not invest in production unless they are able to make reasonably determinate calculations about their expected rate of return. And the socioeconomic environment external to the individual firm will profoundly affect those expectations. *Without a stable and favorable external environment,* capitalist investment in production will not proceed.

The specific set of institutions which make up this external environment has been called the "social structure of accumulation." Its specific elements include the institutions whose structure and stability are necessary for capital accumulation to take place, such as the state of labor-management relations and the stability of the financial system. It is at least theoretically plausible that such an SSA will alternatively stimulate and constrain the pace of capital accumulation. If the constituent institutions of the social structure of accumulation are favorable to capital and working smoothly without challenge, capitalists are likely to feel enthusiastic and secure about the prospects for investing in the expansion of productive capacity. But if the social structure of accumulation begins to become shaky, if class conflict or past capital accumulation have pressed the institutions to their limits and they begin to lose their legitimacy, capitalists will be more disposed to put their money to other uses—consumption, financial investments, or assets abroad.

It is not simply a problem, moreover, of achieving a sufficiently high and stable rate of profit. For the profit rate can be *too* high. If wage income is relativeiy low and capitalists do not spend enough out of their relatively high profits on investment, there may not be enough effective demand to absorb the products of capitalist production. If inventories of unsold goods then pile up, capitalists will eventually cut back on production unless the state can continuously make up the difference.

The functions of the constituent institutions of a given social structure of accumulation, in short, are both daunting and fundamental. Their health and vitality substantially determine *both* whether or not capitalists expect the profit rate to settle stably at a sufficiently attractive level to justify investment over alternative uses *and* whether or not the right balance is achieved between profitability and effective demand.

There is good reason, moreover, for believing that capitalism has experienced successive *stages* in its institutional capacity to achieve these daunting tasks.[6]

The history of at least the United States economy over the past 150 years suggests a clear historical rhythm of alternating expansion and contraction over roughly 50-year swings. In each of the two previous instances of crisis—in the 1890s and the 1930s—basic changes in economic and political institutions proved necessary before a return to prosperity was possible. The paths to this economic restructuring were tangled with thickets of competing political interests, and it took years to clear the way for a decisive political resolution. This path-clearing appears to have required, in the more formal language of this section, the construction of a new SSA before accumulation could revive.

The Crisis of the Postwar SSA in the United States

We have elsewhere provided a historical account of the rise and demise of the postwar social structure of accumulation in the United States, describing its initial consolidation and its ultimate erosion under increasingly effective challenges to capitalist control (Bowles, Gordon and Weisskopf 1983: Chap. 4).

Our basic argument is that the postwar SSA rested upon four principal buttresses of United States capitalist power, each of which involved a particular set of institutionalized power relations allowing United States corporations to achieve predominant control over potential challengers in the immediate postwar period. We refer to these four institutional axes as the *capital-labor accord, Pax Americana,* the *capital-citizen accord,* and the *moderation of inter-capitalist rivalry,* respectively.[7] They remained relatively solid into the 1960s, but the success of the SSA in promoting economic growth proved ultimately contradictory. Workers, foreign suppliers of raw materials, and domestic citizens began to question and to resist the previously established structures of power. The growing strength of other capitalist nations, as well as the success of anti-capitalist movements in the Third World, further challenged the power of United States capital. Increased competition both domestically and internationally reduced capitalists' ability to protect their profitability from these incursions. The postwar capitalist system consequently began to erode; corporate capitalists found it increasingly difficult to control the terms of their interaction with the other major actors on the economic scene.

We briefly review each of these four power axes on its own institutional terms.

The Capital-Labor Accord

The first set of institutions governed relations between capital and labor in the United States after the late 1940s. This accord involved an explicit and implicit *quid pro quo,* assuring management control over enterprise decision-making (with union submission and cooperation) in exchange for the promise to workers of real compensation rising along with labor productivity, improved working conditions, and greater job security—in short, a share in capitalist prosperity. The accord also consolidated the relative advantages of the unionized over the non-unionized part of the workforce and contributed to an intensification of labor segmentation along job, gender, and racial lines (Gordon, Edwards and Reich 1982). The accord was administered, on capital's side, by an increasingly bureaucratic and hierarchical system of labor management. This system of bureaucratic control was backed up by an expanding army of management cadres devoted to supervision and discipline.

The capital-labor accord worked for a while. But it appears that the effectiveness of corporate control over labor was beginning to decline after the mid-1960s. Workers were not staging a political revolt against the capitalist system, to be sure, but, from the mid-1960s through at least the mid-1970s, many were becoming increasingly restive with bureaucratic control and many were beginning to experience—and undoubtedly to appreciate—much greater protection from insistent corporate discipline as the cost to workers of losing their jobs began to decline.[8] Corporate profits were bound to suffer.

Pax Americana

The second buttress of United States capitalist power was the postwar structure of international economic institutions and political relations that assured the United States a dominant role in the world capitalist economy. *Pax Americana* provided favorable terms for United States capitalists in their interaction with foreign suppliers of both wage goods and intermediate goods and with foreign buyers of United States produced goods. Equally important, the increasingly open world economy gave United States capital the mobility it needed to make its threats of plant closings credible in bargaining with United States workers and citizens over wages, working conditions and tax rates.

Though the United States–dominated world system conferred significant advantages on United States capital in its relations with United States workers, it affected profitability in the domestic economy most directly through its impact on the terms on which the United States could obtain goods and services from abroad. This is reflected in the United States terms of trade. The better this relative price, the more favorable the terms on which United States firms can obtain imported inputs. As one might have expected from the extent of United States power for the first couple of decades after World War II, the United States terms of trade improved substantially for a time.

But after roughly the mid-1960s, United States corporations faced growing international challenges:

— Challenges from the Third World began to undermine United States international domination in the mid-1960s. The failure of the 1961 Bay of Pigs invasion and especially the long and humiliating failure to stem the revolu-

tionary tide in South Vietnam marked a significant and escalating erosion of the United States government's capacity to "keep the world safe" for private enterprise.
— Another significant challenge in the world economy came from exporters of raw materials, primarily in Third World nations. By the early 1970s, the economic bargaining power of some of the Third World raw-material-exporting nations increased substantially; OPEC, the cartel of oil-exporting nations, was the most visible and important example.

These international challenges combined to diminish United States international power and, with it, the ability of United States corporations to profit from their powerful leverage over foreign buyers and sellers.

The Capital-Citizen Accord

The postwar SSA also included a set of political arrangements which regulated the inherent conflict between capitalists' quest for profits and people's demands for economic security and for the social accountability of business. An expanded role for the state in providing for citizens' needs was suitably circumscribed by the capitalist principle of profitability as the ultimate criterion guiding public policy.

By the mid-1960s, support for business was now being challenged. Beginning with occupational health-and-safety campaigns, a wide variety of movements emerged to challenge the hallowed identity of private greed and public virtue. With striking speed, these movements led to new government regulations affecting traffic safety, occupational health and safety, environmental protection, consumer product safety, and nuclear power generation.

In many cases these challenges arose from a wider appreciation of the importance of values like environmental protection. But in many cases, as well, they resulted much more simply from defensive and protective reactions against the rising and increasingly serious hazards of life in the postwar regime. Faced with these spreading hazards, people had no choice but to react. United States capital was able to reap substantial advantages from the corporate-citizen accord for two decades. But the contradictions of the postwar capitalist system eventually blew up in the collective capitalist face.

The Moderation of Inter-Capitalist Rivalry

For a substantial period after World War II, United States corporations were able to enjoy the fruits of substantially attenuated inter-capitalist competition. Most strikingly, the wartime devastation of the Japanese and the leading European economies left United States capitalists in the enviable position of unrivaled kings of the mountain, able effectively to dominate corporations from other advanced capitalist countries. Perhaps equally important, the rapid pace of accumulation in the domestic economy tended to provide ample room for growth for most large United States corporations within their own industries, reducing the likelihood of inter-industry merger bids or capital entry.

After the mid-1960s, however, this comfortable cushion of moderated competition began to turn into a bed of thorns. In both the international and domestic economies, intensifying competition began substantially to reduce United States capitalists' ability to maintain stability in their own ranks and deal effectively with external challengers.

— One challenge came from the increasingly intensive competition waged by corporations in Europe and Japan. Having recovered from the devastation of World War II, these corporations were able to cut into United States corporate shares of international export markets and to provide increasingly stiff import competition in the United States.

— As growth and accumulation in the United States economy slowed, further, inter-capitalist competition intensified on the domestic terrain as well (Shepherd 1982). From the merger wave of the late 1960s through the junk bond buyouts of the 1980s, firms were forced more and more to protect their rear flanks from takeovers all the while they were fighting forward battles with workers, foreign buyers and sellers, and citizens. As domestic rates of profit plunged in many industries, as well, corporations often chose to switch rather than to fight, lifting their capital out of their home industries and seeking to penetrate others; this exposed many corporations to increased exposure to market rivalry with domestic as well as foreign invaders.

Whatever the source of the challenges, United States corporations were more and more pressed after the mid-1960s by increasingly intense inter-capitalist rivalry. Their ability to organize their own ranks for battle and to pass on through higher prices the costs of their three-front war was substantially undercut.

Basic Foundations

We now have in place the essential elements for an interpretation of the stagnation of the United States economy since the mid-1960s. To recapitulate, the basic argument proceeds in four steps:

1. Long-term accumulation in a capitalist economy is fundamentally profit-led. In order to understand the pace of investment and growth, one must apprehend the determinants of capitalist profitability.
2. The rate of profit in a capitalist economy is directly affected by the power relations mediating capitalists' interactions with workers, foreign buyers and sellers, and the citizenry. The battlefield conditions in this three-front war, mediated by the degree of cohesiveness within the capitalist ranks, can potentially influence all of the major factors determining the corporate rate of profit.

Table 9.1

The Rise and Demise of the Postwar Social Structure of Accumulation

Phase	Capital-Labor Accord	Pax Americana	Capital-Citizen Accord	Inter-Capitalist Rivalry
Boom: 1948–1966	Cost of job loss rises Workers' resistance down	U.S. Military dominance Terms of trade improve	Government support for accumulation; profits main state priority	Corporations insulated from domestic & foreign competition
Erosion: 1966–1973	Cost of job loss plunges Workers' resistance spreads	Military power challenged Terms of trade hold steady	Citizen movements take hold	Foreign competition & domestic mergers begin to affect corporations
Stalemate: 1973–1979	Stagnant economy creates stalemate between capital and labor	OPEC, declining $ result in sharp deterioration in U.S. terms of trade	Citizen movements effect new fetters on business	Pressure of foreign competition & domestic rivalry intensifies

3. Capitalist power and the pace of accumulation are shaped in capitalist economies by the constituent institutions of a given social structure of accumulation. When those institutions are in place and stably effecting capitalist
domination, capital accumulation can proceed at a vigorous pace. When the
viability of those institutions begins to erode, profitability is likely to suffer
and stagnation is likely to follow.

4. This approach appears to apply closely to the case of the postwar capitalist
system in the United States. United States corporations achieved considerable
power through the construction of a new SSA after World War II, enjoying
substantial leverage through their domination of the capital-labor accord, Pax
Americana, and the capital-citizen accord as well as through the moderation
of inter-capitalist rivalry. As challenges to capitalist control developed along
all four of those institutional axes in the 1960s, United States corporations
watched their power erode and, consequently, their profitability decline.
Table 9.1 provides a brief glimpse of the dynamics of SSA consolidation and
erosion in the United States economy from 1948 through 1979.[9] Table 9.2
then summarizes the linkages flowing from the four institutional power dimensions highlighted by this historical outline to the determinants of the
profit rate outlined in the first sub-section on "Power and Profits." These

Table 9.2

Linkages Between the Postwar SSA and Components of the Profit Rate

While there is no simple (one-to-one) correspondence between each of the dimensions of capitalist power and the determinants of the profit rate, we list here the four main dimensions of capitalist power in the postwar SSA of the United States

Labor Accord	Real wage rate, labor intensity, capacity utilization
Pax Americana	Terms of trade, profit tax rate
Citizen Accord	Input-output coefficients, profit tax rate, capacity utilization
Capitalist Rivalry	Real wage rate, terms of trade, capacity utilization

linkages make possible a complete analysis of the connections running from the SSA through the profit rate to accumulation and growth.[10]

The Contradictions of Conservative Economics

That analysis extends through the 1970s. Building on that base, we can interpret the "conservative economics" reigning during the 1980s in large part as a consistent effort to restore corporate profitability by rolling back effective challenges to United States capitalist power: by raising the cost of job loss, improving the terms of trade, more vigorously flexing United States military power, reducing the intensity of government regulation, and dramatically reducing capital's share of the total government tax burden. As any observer could easily report, and as the underlying data for our quantitative indicators of the SSA also clearly confirm, the Reagan Administration made substantial progress on all of these fronts. Did it succeed in reviving the net after-tax rate of profit?

The average net after-tax rate of profit during the business cycle from 1974 to 1979 was 5.5 percent. The average net after-tax rate of profit during the not-quite-completed business cycle from 1980 through 1985 was 5.7 percent.[11] The average rate of profit in the 1960–66 cycle, by contrast, was 8.0 percent. For all of the triumphs of business interests in Washington and throughout the economy in the 1980s, the profit rate did not significantly rebound.

This appears to pose a puzzle. Conservative economics sought to roll back challenges to capital's power and succeeded in obtaining much more favorable values for many of the indicators along our four SSA power dimensions than had earlier prevailed. And yet, actual profitability did not improve.

The basic solution to this puzzle, we believe, lies in the inherent contradictions of conservative macroeconomic policy. Conservative economics relied heavily on the monetarist policies initiated in 1979 by Paul Volcker of the Fed and intensified when the Reagan Administration came to power in 1981. These policies resulted in extremely low rates of capacity utilization during the three-year recession from 1980 to 1982. Another consequence of this policy was a highly inflated value for the dollar; the resultant improvement in the United States terms of trade was similarly contradictory, in that it reduced the competitiveness of United States products on the world market and thus exacerbated the decline in capacity utilization. In sum, conservative economics won the battle for capitalist power but had apparently not yet won the war for corporate profitability, by the mid-1980s, because of the high cost of the battlefield victories imposed by the terms of the postwar SSA.

Alternative Explanations of Stagnation

Since other contributions to [the literature] elaborate a variety of alternative accounts of the stagnation of the United States economy over the past nearly two decades, we pause only briefly here to highlight some of the central differences between the account outlined in this essay and other possible explanations of the recent crisis.

Mainstream Accounts

It is common among mainstream economists to attribute the stagnation of the United States economy to a variety of "exogenous" shocks such as the oil-price jolts of 1973 and 1979 or to macroeconomic mismanagement (for presentation and critique of these views, see Bowles, Gordon and Weisskopf 1983: Chap. 3). We find, however, that these analyses are substantially incomplete and miss much of what happened in the United States economy during the rise and demise of the postwar capitalist system. Our empirical explorations suggest three principal shortcomings of conventional mainstream accounts.

— Many mainstream accounts date the crisis from the oil-price shock of 1973, but almost every salient economic indicator suggests that it began much earlier—in the mid-1960s (Bowles, Gordon and Weisskopf 1983: Chap. 2).
— Most mainstream accounts of productivity growth, profitability, and investment ignore the sorts of social determinations of macroeconomic performance which our emphasis on "challenges to capital" highlights. In a series of detailed comparisons, we find that attention to these social determinations uniformly improves our ability to explain movements in productivity growth, profitability and investment (in addition to previously cited work, see also Weisskopf, Bowles and Gordon 1983).
— Far from resulting from "exogenous shocks," the crisis of the United States economy appears to flow from the internal evolution of the postwar capitalist system. In each of our econometric investigations, we find no evidence of "structural change" in the models, suggesting that the same factors which help account for the boom also help account for the subsequent crisis.

An "Over-Investment" Crisis?

Some Marxist economists stress the importance of capitalists' collectively "irrational" decisions to "over-invest," leading to a decline in profitability from a rising organic composition of capital (see [Laibman 1987]). It is certainly true that the ratio of capital to output increased fairly steadily during the period of crisis and that, in this nominal respect, this focus on capitalist "over-investment" is potentially fruitful.

But our own analyses suggest that this kind of explanation of the postwar crisis is incomplete at best: Once one accounts for the influence of the SSA power dimensions on corporate profitability, there is no further explanatory power to be gained from adding a term to account for movements in the capital intensity of production. It does not appear, in other words, that this "over-investment" perspective offers much additional empirical insight beyond that afforded by the approach outlined here.[12]

An "Underconsumption" Crisis?

Some Marxist and post-Keynesian economists highlight problems of "underconsumption" or "effective demand" as underlying causes of the crisis of the United States economy (see [Foster 1987; Nell 1987]). These interpretations would suggest that the rate of growth of demand turned down before the rate of profit and the pace of investment, not after their inflection points; and, according to at least some accounts, that these problems of underconsumption resulted from a shift in the income distribution toward capital as a result of capital's being "too strong." We find two main problems with the empirical usefulness of this approach (see Weisskopf, Bowles and Gordon 1985:266–272):

— All of the available evidence seems to suggest that the rate of profit declined substantially *before* the downturn in the rate of growth of output or consumption.
— Despite many common assertions about the rising power of monopolies, we find that there was neither an increase in monopolistic competition nor a decisive shift in the income distribution away from labor toward capital just before or during the initial years of the crisis. Indeed, as we noted earlier, available evidence suggests that there was an intensification of inter-capitalist competition during precisely this period.

Political Implications

Capitalism is a contradictory system of power relationships that evolves in large measure through the continuing but changing forms of class struggle, international conflict and other tensions to which its structure gives rise.

To analyze the latest capitalist economic crisis we have built upon a theoretical approach to the analysis of a capitalist system which focuses on its embedded power relations and its historically contingent and inherently contradictory social structure of accumulation. We have argued that the initial decline of corporate profitability in the postwar period can be explained by a corresponding decline in the power of the United States capitalist class to deal with growing challenges from the domestic working class, the domestic citizenry, and foreign suppliers and buyers—challenges which themselves arose out of the dynamics of the postwar boom. In the last decade, in a political climate influenced by high levels of unemployment, United States capital has scored major political victories over all those groups whose challenges form the heart of our analysis of the origins of the economic crisis. But the challengers were turned back at a very high cost in economic stagnation associated with the major recessions of 1974–75 and 1980–82. Profitability has remained, on average, at a relatively low level. We attribute this outcome to the inherent contradictions of conservative macroeconomic policy under the prevailing postwar SSA.

To achieve a true victory on behalf of capital, conservative economics would have needed to alter the underlying relationship between the rate of capacity utilization and the SSA power dimensions. If it were possible to enhance capitalist power without having to depress capacity utilization to such a significant extent, this would permit much higher levels of profitability to be attained over an extended period of time and would amount eventually to a genuine alteration of the postwar SSA.

Is there any evidence that this has yet been accomplished? At the time of completion of this article, it is still too early to draw a final conclusion on the consequences of conservative economics. First, because the current business cycle did not reach its peak in 1985, our comparison of 1974–79 with 1980–85 is subject to revision. Second, and ultimately more important, it is possible that a trade-off between capacity utilization and some of the SSA variables more favorable to capital will prove to have emerged after another few years. The verdict will become far clearer when we see how heavy a dose of macroeconomic restraint will be required to keep the latest economic recovery from eroding the significant gains that capital had achieved through the monetarist "cold bath" of the early 1980s.

From a broader historical perspective, periods of economic crisis have always been periods of political conflict and institutional innovation. The nature of the political conflicts and the likely outcomes can differ radically, however, depending not only on the political organization of the contending parties and the ideological environment, but also on the nature of the economic crisis itself.

If, for example, the crisis results from the capitalist class being too strong and the demand for goods and services being insufficient as a result, a politically attractive opportunity arises for the left. In this case the short-run and the long-run interests of the working class appear to coincide: a weakening of the capitalist class will help both to end the crisis and also to increase the economic strength with which the working class can carry on the long struggle for a socialist alternative. Thus the Keynesian and social democratic policies which emerged as the dominant programs for the labor movement following the Great Depression promised to redistribute income to labor, farmers, and other non-capitalist groups and thereby stimulate demand for goods and services and end the crisis.

No such happy coincidence of short-term material interests and longer-term radical objectives is associated with the type of supply-side crisis which results initially when the capitalist class is "too weak." The most obvious exit from the crisis is that pointed to by the right: strengthen the capitalist class, restore profits and rekindle the capitalist accumulation process. In the absence of basic institutional change, any success the left may have in obstructing the restoration of unchallenged capitalist hegemony, or in further eroding capitalist power, will merely deepen the crisis. This may perhaps lay the groundwork for a more radical change, but its immediate impact on people will be a worsening of economic distress and insecurity—hardly the kind of promise upon which mass mobilizations can build.

This does not mean, of course, that there are no options for progressive forces in the face of a supply-side crisis. But it does mean that these options must be considerably more radical than those capable of resolving a demand-side crisis. If many during the Great Depression advocated a democratic and egalitarian resolution of the crisis through a redistribution of *purchasing power,* as a means of achieving a higher level of demand, an exit from today's crisis favorable to progressive forces requires the redistribution of *power itself.*

What, then, are the political implications of our analysis? If we are right that profits are central to the vitality of the United States economy as long as it remains capitalist, and that it was rising challenges from non-capitalist forces that caused the initial decline in profitability and the high costs of keeping people down that perpetuated the profitability problem, how can we confront those who contend that economic recovery hinges on capital's ability to control its challengers firmly and efficiently? How can we derive a progressive political strategy—a strategy designed to foster more popular control, more democracy, more socialism—from analysis that seems to blame progressive political forces for the economic crisis?

Two brief observations may be in order.

First, the fact that successful challenges initiated the crisis in no way assures that beating back the challenges will be an effective way to boost profits and restore the growth process. This point has been well illustrated by the high cost of United States capital's recent efforts to regain the upper hand after their setbacks in the initial stages of the current economic crisis. It is still quite unclear whether capital has yet amassed the political and economic leverage to accomplish what would amount to the construction of a new capitalist social structure of accumulation.

Second, and more important, there is a flaw in the reasoning that would seek to repress challengers as a basis for economic recovery: it presumes that there is no alternative to capitalism, and that the best we can hope for is therefore the restoration of a more efficient system of capitalist exploitation. But we believe that there *is* a socialist democratic alternative—one that offers both an alternative strategy and an alternative vision of the future.

Our analysis points to a political program based on a critique of the legitimacy of capitalist power and to an economic program highlighting the gains to be made from reducing the waste inherent in the imposition and maintenance of capitalist control. By showing that exploitation is fundamentally costly, and that its reduction is compatible with—if not necessary for—a return to economic security and opportunity, we can potentially undermine a major source of capitalist legitimacy and strength. By highlighting the problem of political power, moreover, our analysis points to popular control in both the state and the economy—that is, socialist democracy—as a progressive political alternative. Rather than legitimizing a repressive *status quo,* our theory of the crisis and declining profitability seems to us to dramatize the effectiveness of popular power and therefore to underscore its potential for social transformation.

Notes

1. We place these terms in quotation marks to suggest their relativity: "too strong" and "too weak" refer solely to the conditions for the smooth reproduction of the capitalist accumulation process, not to some other standard of political or moral desirability or behavior.

2. The concept of the social structure of accumulation was introduced in David M. Gordon (1978), and further developed and applied in Gordon (1980); and Gordon, Richard Edwards and Michael Reich (1982). This perspective is very closely related to a framework developed more or less independently in France known as the "regulation approach"; this approach builds upon the concept of a "regime of accumulation" or, alternatively, a "system of regulation." See, for example, Michel Aglietta (1979) and Alain Lipietz (1986).

3. The "rate of accumulation" is defined for the purposes of this discussion as the rate of change of the net capital stock; this measure is thus equivalent to the ratio of net investment to the lagged (net) capital stock and is highly correlated with the ratio of net investment to GNP.

4. Contrary to the distributional theory of neoclassical economics, neither profits nor wages represents the return to a scarce factor of production; capital is not a productive input (though machines are), while labor is not scarce but rather almost always in excess supply.

5. It may be useful to conclude this section on "challenges to capitalist control" by relating it to a more traditional formulation within Marxian economics called "profit squeeze" theories of crisis (see [Devine 1987] for a review of this traditional account). The two explanations share in common the perspective that crisis may occur because capitalists are "too weak." Ours expands upon the traditional formulation in three respects: First, we stress that power relationships may affect more components of the rate of profit than the profit share, as the list in this section indicates. Second, we place a greater

stress on the centrality of power relationships in the determination of the basic conditions of profitability, an emphasis which has been somewhat more implicit in traditional profit-squeeze accounts. Third, we recognize that attempts to restore capitalist power—for example, through restrictive monetary and fiscal policy—may replenish the reserve army of labor but fail to restore the profit rate as a result of their negative effects on capacity utilization.

6. This involves a more formal argument about the connection between the SSA and long economic swings. See the references in note 2 above.

7. In our earlier work we had neglected the dimension here labeled the "moderation of intercapitalist rivalry"; we introduce it in this essay in order to help overcome some inadequacies in earlier formulations.

We should also stress for the purposes of clarification that we consider these four particular institutional axes to apply concretely *only* to the postwar United States; we do not intend a more general argument that any social structure of accumulation at any time can most usefully be characterized by this specific institutional configuration.

8. This analysis builds heavily on the concept of the cost of job loss. For details on definition and measurement, see [Schor 1987].

9. This table is based on quantitative indicators defined and presented in Bowles, Gordon and Weisskopf (1986: Section 4) and some subsequent unpublished empirical work.

10. In other work we have traced the last link in this connection—from profitability to accumulation and growth. For that analysis we refer to that component of profitability which reflects the influence of underlying SSA institutional factors as the "underlying rate of profit"; we hypothesize that investment flows are especially sensitive to movements in this component of profitability. See Gordon, Weisskopf and Bowles (1986).

11. At the time of writing we could not compute a precise estimate of the rate of profit for 1986 because of the unavailability of data on the net capital stock. A rough estimate of the rate of profit for 1986 suggests that it declined from its 1985 level (from .073 to roughly .072). As a result, although another year of "recovery" improved the cycle average over that for 1980–85, there was still insufficient improvement to warrant the conclusion that corporate profitability had recovered. Based on our very approximate estimate for 1986, the estimated cycle average for 1980–86 was 6.0 percent; the difference between this value and the mean for 1974–79 was not statistically significant.

12. This exercise is presented in an unpublished appendix to Bowles, Gordon and Weisskopf (1986), available from the authors. The reverse conclusion does not hold: if the variables representing our approach are added to an equation modelling the "over-investment" perspective, the explanatory power of that equation increases substantially.

References

Aglietta, Michel. 1979. *A Theory of Capitalist Regulation: The U.S. Experience.* London: New Left Books.

Bowles, Samuel, David Gordon, and Thomas Weisskopf. 1983. *Beyond the Wasteland.* Garden City, NY: Doubleday.

Bowles, Samuel, David Gordon, and Thomas Weisskopf. 1986. "Power and Profits: The Social Structure of Accumulation and the Profitability of the Postwar U.S. Economy," *Review of Radical Political Economics* 18 (1 and 2): 132–167.

[Devine, James N. 1987. "An Introduction to Radical Theories of Economic Crises," *Macroeconomics from a Left Perspective,* Book I of *The Imperiled Economy.* New York: Union for Radical Political Economics, pp. 19–31.]

[Foster, John Bellamy. 1987. "What is Stagnation?" *Macroeconomics from a Left Per-*

spective, Book I of *The Imperiled Economy.* New York: Union for Radical Political Economics, pp. 59–70.]

Gordon, David M. 1978. "Up and Down the Long Roller Coaster." In *U.S. Capitalism in Crisis,* Union for Radical Political Economics (ed.), pp. 22–35. New York: Union for Radical Political Economics.

Gordon, David M. 1980. "Stages of Accumulation and Long Economic Cycles." In *Processes of the World-System,* T. Hopkins and I. Wallerstein (eds.), pp. 9–45. Beverly Hills: Sage Publications.

Gordon, David M., Thomas E. Weisskopf, and Samuel Bowles. 1986. "A Conflict Model of Investment: The Determinants of U.S. Capital Accumulation in a Global Context." Mimeo, New School for Social Research.

[Laibman, David. 1987. "Technical Change and the Contradictions of Capitalism," *Macroeconomics from a Left Perspective,* Book I of *The Imperiled Economy.* New York: Union for Radical Political Economics, pp. 33–42.]

Lipietz, Alain. 1986. "Beyond the Crisis," *Review of Radical Political Economics* 18 (1 and 2): 13–32.

Marx, Karl. 1967. *Capital.* 3 vols. New York: International Publishers.

[Nell, Edward. 1987. "Transformational Growth and Stagnation," *Macroeconomics from a Left Perspective,* Book I of *The Imperiled Economy,* New York: Union for Radical Political Economics, pp. 93–102.]

[Schor, Juliet B. 1987. "Class Struggle and the Macroeconomy: The Cost of Job Loss," *Macroeconomics from a Left Perspective,* Book I of *The Imperiled Economy.* New York: Union for Radical Political Economics, pp. 171–182.]

Shepherd, W.G. 1982. "Causes of Increased Competition in the U.S. Economy, 1919–1980. *Review of Economics and Statistics* 64(4): 613–626.

Weisskopf, Thomas E., Samuel Bowles, and David Gordon. 1983. "Hearts and Minds: A Social Model of U.S. Productivity Growth," *Brookings Papers on Economic Activity* (2): 381–441.

Weisskopf, Thomas E., Samuel Bowles, and David M. Gordon. 1985. "Two Views of Capitalist Stagnation, *Science and Society* 49(3): 259–286.

V

Economic Development

10

Theories of Finance and the Third World

Laurence Harris

The central economic problem faced by the Third World is how to raise the standard of living, people's income, wealth, and welfare by significant amounts. At a minimum this is necessary for both socialist and capitalist countries, in order to overcome mass poverty, hunger, and disease, but the more ambitious objective of attempting to reach or surpass the living standards of the advanced industrial countries is implicitly on the agenda for many. These questions have received ever-increasing attention in the last four decades. They were given their impetus by the breakup of the British Empire and other European colonial systems, and the challenges that national liberation wars and socialist victories in the Third World posed to the old order. The rise of new capitalist classes and new classes of industrial workers and farmers both in long independent countries (Latin America for example) and in newly industrializing former colonies (South East Asia for example) intensified the debates and conflicts over how to achieve growth. From one perspective, the increased prominence of these questions can be traced to the accelerated pace of the internationalization of capital in the modern age, the changes in its character and the transformations, contradictions and conflicts which have accompanied it.

Finance has had a major part to play in that process, an importance symbolized by the fact that the two international agencies most embroiled with development issues are now the International Monetary Fund and the World Bank—both at root financial institutions. Nevertheless, for many years the literature of "development economics" contained relatively few analyses of the role of finance. Despite its significance in reality, in academic circles it was a neglected area compared to trade, labor, and "physical" planning. Since the mid-1970s that situation has changed and a substantial body of theoretical and empirical literature now exists on aspects of finance and the Third World. Much of it has been stimulated by the large research output of the International Monetary Fund, the World Bank, and scholars associated with them, and it is firmly within either the

Keynesian or the neoclassical framework of orthodox Western economics. This paper outlines these orthodox theories, critically evaluates them, and presents an alternative approach to finance and the Third World based on the Marxist paradigm debated by radical economists in advanced capitalist countries since 1970. An aim of the paper is to show that although Marxist work on this subject is relatively rare, it does constitute a valuable basis for the study of finance and the Third World.

Keynesian and Neoclassical Perspectives

The orthodox treatments of finance and development are formally organized around one central issue: how to increase the amount of capital employed in Third World countries' production. This does not refer to capital in the Marxist sense; the problem relates to capital as a factor of production complementing labor and other inputs, to "physical capital" in the form of plant, machinery, and inventories or, in other words, to categories with similarities to (but different from) Marx's "constant capital." Moreover, by concentrating on capital in this physical sense rather than as a concept tied up with property relations and control of production, the central issue of orthodox writings is not automatically whether the increase in the amount of capital is of foreign owned or national capital, although specific theories do have a variety of implications for that question.

An early contribution to this type of analysis was the "two-gap model" developed in the early 1960s by Hollis Chenery and his collaborators (Chenery and Strout 1966; Chenery and Bruno 1962). It is a limited and simplified model formulated principally as a tool for development planners; for this reason it has been very influential in subsequent years and for a period was the foundation for much of the World Bank's development finance. The theory adopts the basic assumption of the Harrod-Domar growth model that there is a fixed relation between growth of output and growth of the capital stock; in other words, the incremental capital output ratio is constant. Similarly, aggregate saving within the economy is treated as a function of national income given by a constant average propensity to save. For the economy to grow at some target rate the required rate of growth of capital (that is, the required level of physical investment) will exceed the level of saving for many years if plausible assumptions about the size of the incremental capital output ratio and the propensity to save are made. There is, therefore, a "savings gap" that has to be filled by foreign finance if Third World economies are to grow at rates commensurate with industrialization. At the same time, there is a "foreign exchange gap" that arises because accelerated growth is directly connected to import expansion but is assumed not to generate commensurate exports in the relevant period; foreign finance also serves to bridge *this* gap. In the classic formulation of the model, these two gaps are not identical in any one period and a definite sequence is postulated under which an economy's accelerated growth involves a savings gap that is first larger and then smaller than the foreign exchange gap (Fei and Ranis 1968); foreign finance equal to the larger of the two gaps is seen as essential to growth.

The original formulation of this theory treated foreign finance as aid or, implicitly, grants to the state from abroad. Subsequent academic literature within this framework reflected the relative decline of official development aid and the rise of loans and credit as sources of Third World Finance in the 1970s; its theories of the dynamics of foreign finance in development incorporated the effects of interest payments and debt amortization on the contribution foreign finance can make to capital formation and were thereby able to relate the analysis to the debt crisis that had arisen by the 1980s (McDonald 1982). Within this class of models, differences in the initial assumptions concerning, for example, whether domestic saving is a function of Gross Domestic Product (GDP) or Gross National Product (GDP minus net foreign interest payments) yield significantly different conclusions on what level of foreign debt countries should incur and whether foreign finance is sustainable.

Even with that reformulation of the two-gap model in terms of foreign debt, its role as a theory of *finance* in development is limited, for it does not incorporate any financial institutions in its system. A related aspect is that only one role is envisaged for interest rates, acting as a channel for savings out of the country, so that, following a Keynesian tradition, interest rates are not assumed to affect the capital output ratio or the average propensity to consume by influencing the decisions of savers and investors. Therefore, mechanisms which may link finance with the processes and decisions of production and trade are absent. Two seminal works by Ronald McKinnon (1973) and Edward Shaw (1973) introduced a more neoclassical perspective that put the links between finance and those "real" processes at the center of the analysis and laid the basis for a great expansion of studies on the role of finance.

The McKinnon–Shaw approach is a theory of the role that banks, essentially indigenous national banking systems, play in enabling finance to be channeled from savers within the country to investment in profitable capital projects. Its essence is an assumption that people's saving will be higher at higher rates of interest and that, if interest rates are relatively high, enterprises only invest in highly profitable capital projects (capital with a high marginal productivity) and will therefore use relatively labor-intensive processes rather than overexpand their mechanization. High interest rates that result in increased saving and labor-intensive production are seen as appropriate for Third World countries characterized by capital shortage. These authors also argue that high interest rates stimulate the growth of financial institutions (banks), which are necessary for development, since if the rate of interest banks pay to depositors is raised, a greater proportion of (the increased) saving will be accumulated as bank deposits. As bank deposits grow, banks are able to expand their loans to enterprises (in Shaw's model), or the depositors themselves find it easier to finance their own investment in fixed capital (according to McKinnon). In emphasizing the role that banks can play in the process of development for today's Third World countries, writers in the McKinnon–Shaw school draw parallels with the historical research of Rondo Cameron (Cameron 1972; Cameron, Crisp, Patrick, and Tilly 1967), which claims to have established the importance of banks' role in the industrialization of Europe. Support from present-day experience is claimed on the basis of econometric estimates of the determinants of saving, the demand for money (including time deposits at banks), and the relation between interest rate policy and growth in Third World countries (Fry 1988).

Policies based on the McKinnon–Shaw theory promote high interest rates as one element in a package of financial liberalization which removes state ceilings from interest rates, abolishes the direction of credit and the allocation of foreign exchange by the state, and introduces flexibility to the exchange rate (for example, in the form of a controlled "crawling peg" devaluation). They have become increasingly prominent and frequent elements in the adjustment programs implemented by countries under the tutelage of the IMF and World Bank or promoted by the U.S. aid agency, USAID. Some of the greatest controversy over these policies has concerned their application to the southern cone countries of Latin America (especially Chile and Argentina) where their long-term development intentions have been combined with the use of high interest rates as a restrictive monetary policy for short-term correction of balance of payments deficits and inflation (Diaz-Alejandro 1985; Foxley 1983).

Both the two-gap model and the neoclassical model of McKinnon and Shaw place finance in the context of an economy with marked structural rigidities and constraints. In its original formulation, the former considers the effect of a structural shortage of managerial and technical skill on the rate of investment and, hence, on financial requirements (Chenery and Strout 1966); however, this is not an integral or essential feature of that model. For McKinnon, by contrast, the structural feature of Third World economies that he calls "fragmentation" is central to his analysis. Fragmentation means an absence of integrated markets so that the exchange of commodities, labor power, and finance on both a national and international basis—which enables price differences to be reduced by arbitrage—is precluded in favor of local and separated markets. The power McKinnon attributes to high interest rates and financial liberalization is based on the view that they overcome fragmentation in the financial market by channeling savings into a nationally integrated banking system and that the mobility of financial capital that results gives a strong impetus to overcoming fragmentation in other markets.

In contrast to the belief that financial policy can sweep away structural constraints, the structuralist school of economists that originated in Latin America in the 1950s and 1960s argues that the persistence of structural constraints limits the effectiveness of orthodox financial policies and makes them more likely to cause "stagflation"—slow growth, high unemployment, and inflation—than to generate accelerated development. In its modern formulation, synthesized by Lance Taylor (1983), structuralism is essentially a short-run macroeconomic model rather than an analysis of growth processes. In it the operation of policies affecting aggregate demand is shaped by persistent structural features, two of which are particularly relevant to financial policy. The first is the assumption that banks are not the only nationally integrated financial network and are, in fact, less efficient and more costly than the informal or "curb" financial markets that exist in Latin America, South East Asia, and elsewhere (van Wijnbergen 1985). The second is the assumption that because of the structural disarticulation of Third World economies, enterprises require a high level of finance for "working capital" (that is, the inventories, advances of wages, and advances of other costs necessary for the production process) so that the costs of working capital influence enterprises' selling prices, which are set on the basis of variable costs plus a percentage "markup" (Cavallo 1977). The existence of informal financial markets implies that high bank interest rates may generate an expansion of bank deposits and loans only by drawing funds away to banks from the informal market so that there is no net increase in the availability or integration of finance and there may, in fact, be a decrease. The connection of working-capital costs to the prices of finished commodities implies that increases in the interest rate that firms pay for working capital can generate inflation by causing them to raise the prices of their products.

Evaluation

Those analyses of Third World finance within the orthodox traditions of Keynesian and neoclassical economics have considerable power but substantial limitations. One weakness is that they are not able to engage fully with the dynamic processes of economic and social change that affect all Third World countries. Even many sub-Saharan African countries whose development appears blocked and stagnant in the 1980s are going through major social changes, and countries that have experienced growth, whether in Asia or Latin America, have gone through major social upheavals in the process. The orthodox theories do make an attempt to recognize the significance of these dynamic leaps, unlike most orthodox models of advanced capitalist economies, but it is necessarily a limited attempt. The two-gap model, instead of assuming that growth is a smooth linear process, sometimes employs an assumption that it requires an initial "big-push" or acceleration analogous to that postulated by the economic historian Walt Rostow (1960) as a precondition for "takeoff" to sustained growth. But the dynamics of that push are not analyzed apart from the fact that it requires foreign finance and is limited by the availability of skills. Therefore the interaction between finance and the processes of change such as changes in the labor process, the shift from agriculture to industry, the changing class structure, and changes in the legal, political, and cultural framework are not explored.

The neoclassical models—especially McKinnon's—are more directly concerned with the connection between finance and the transformation of economic relations, but, again, they have only a limited analysis. Production is seen as being in the hands of entrepreneurial households, which do not change in the process of economic growth except insofar as they choose to use greater or lesser proportions of physical capital. The only change that is considered systematically is the construction of efficient markets (particularly the market for credit), for economic change is seen as deriving from changes in exchange relations rather than production. In a different context Robert Brenner (1977) has contrasted the view that exchange relations determine economic change, a view deriving from Adam Smith, with the Marxian view that production relations are more fundamental. In the case of McKinnon and Shaw's followers, the limitation is worsened by the fact that the manner in which changes in market relations affect other economic relations is not explored in detail.

A second problem with these orthodox analyses is that they are not able to consider international finance in its own right as an influence on the Third World. This limitation arises because the national boundary is the focus of orthodox economics, which, in effect, conducts its analysis on a country-by-country basis. These writers are therefore only able to analyze international finance from the point of view of how internal developments within an individual country affect its own international trade, foreign exchange reserves, and foreign debt, and how they are mediated by the interaction between these quantities and the exchange rate and money supply. They do not generally integrate their analysis of Third World economies with a conception of international banking and finance as a multinational system with its own dynamic, which has an impact upon those economies. One aspect of this weakness is evident in the two-gap models of a country's foreign debt, for these are usually treated as debt "requirements" without any attention being paid to the international banks' willingness or reluctance to supply finance, an omission that became more obviously serious in the 1970s when multinational banks—with a dynamic of their own organized around expanding Euro-currency markets—took the initiative in pushing credit onto Third World states.

Finally, the orthodox approach has a limited perspective on the state's role in finance. Public finance, taxation, and state spending is seen only from a negative perspective. Emphasis is placed on the idea that public sector deficits can deprive private enterprises of finance needed for investment and can worsen the country's balance of payments while state regulation of banking (often induced by a desire to lower the interest cost of financing the state deficit) causes distortions and the fragmentation of financial markets. The underlying assumption is that free (private sector) markets are beneficial while state deficits and regulation prevent their potential from materializing, and this is the general basis of the liberalization policy proposed by neoclassical writers. Its faultiness on the undesirability of state regulation of finance is suggested by the fact that such writers argue that South Korea's financial reforms of 1965 were a liberalization that led to rapid industrialization and growth, but they fail to recognize that instead of producing free financial markets, the reforms involved a new system of state control of finance under which the state took responsibility for directing finance toward export-oriented industrialization and capital investment in economic infrastructure (Harris 1988c). And, on the question of whether budget deficits harm growth, it is historically the case that in many countries state borrowing has been the foundation for vigorous capital markets and private investment instead of impeding them. Moreover, public sector deficits may finance productive investment by the state itself.

Marxist Analyses

Marxist economic theory has been vigorously debated within a section of the economics profession in Western Europe, the United States, and Japan in the past two decades. The main concerns have been the theory of value, crisis theory, the labor process, and class structure in capitalist accumulation (Fine and Harris 1979; Foley 1986; Lipietz 1987). In the context of the economics of the Third World, the main disputes and advances have been in the theory of imperialism and the analysis of class formation in the transformation of modes of production. Western Marxism has had little to say directly on the role of finance in the Third World and has certainly produced nothing to compare with the writings of Preobrazhensky (1926) on the role of money and finance in a poor country's socialist development. Nevertheless, the principles applied by Western Marxists to other economic problems can yield a distinctively Marxist theory of the role of finance in the Third World. It incorporates but goes beyond traditional Marxist concepts such as imperialism, original (primitive) accumulation, and finance capital, and it does not share the limitations of the orthodox theories I have summarized above. Let me organize the presentation of this Marxist theory under the same three heads as the evaluation I presented of orthodox theories: finance and the transformation of economic relations, the role of international finance, and the relation between finance and the state.

Finance and the Transformation of Economic Relations

The prerequisite for sustained growth in any country is a far-reaching transformation of economic relations in production and associated changes in the economy's trading and commercial system. The system of money, credit, and public finance contributes significantly to these changes, either promoting or retarding them.

From a Marxist perspective the most studied transformation of this type is the birth of capitalism in Britain, which involved a historical transition from one mode of production to another; other well-studied transitions to a new, capitalist mode of production include those of the Japanese in the late nineteenth century. The role of finance in such cases of the transition to a capitalist mode of production is partly captured by Marx's concept of primitive accumulation (or original accumulation). For Marx this meant the destruction of the producers' and exploiting classes' precapitalist rights to the possession and control of land, means of production, and the conditions of labor itself. In Britain the dispossession of the peasantry created a class of "free" laborers with no property except their own labor power and it simultaneously transformed land into capital concentrated into the hands of a new exploiting class; in other words, it created the twin conditions for capitalism, capital, and the material of a proletariat. This mechanism, the land "enclosures," was complemented by financial (and other) developments further promoting the accumulation of capital that could be turned into productive capital as the new mode of production became established. Usury was one of these, and colonial plunder by merchants, backed by the financial devices of the City of London, was another. In the case of Japan, the original accumulation that helped to found the capitalist mode of production depended to a large extent on another financial mechanism to build concentrations of resources as capital; the land tax of the Meiji regime was a powerful engine that transferred resources from the countryside toward the state and toward urban classes able to initiate capitalist industrialization.

However, the role of finance in British or Japanese original accumulation cannot be applied directly to today's Third World economies, for their position is quite different from those two countries. The major difference is that the capitalist industrialization of poor countries today has to take place in the context of a world market created and dominated by already advanced capitalist countries. By contrast, capitalism in Britain was the early foundation for the modern world market, hence Britain did not have to struggle for a place within it, and Japan's transformation took place behind barriers that insulated it. Some writers, particularly Chih-Ming Ka and Mark Selden (1986), argue that, nevertheless, the concept of original accumulation is relevant to today's "late industrializing" countries and that financial mechanisms play an important role within it. Those authors use the concept fruitfully to analyze the state-led capitalist industrialization of Taiwan in its early stages during the 1950s (and socialist industrialization in China during the 1953–57 Five-Year Plan). They argue that Taiwanese original accumulation involved the state appropriating the agricultural surplus (in kind) and using it to finance the development of industrial capital in import-substitution industries initially. The two main mechanisms for this were the land tax and the state's system of bartering fertilizer for rice at rates of exchange that were unfavorable to the peasant. That system was a form of taxation that enabled the state both to profit from its exports of rice and imports of fertilizer and to accumulate foreign exchange from this trade in order to finance industry. Nevertheless, a Marxist approach to the development of capitalism in today's Newly Industrializing Countries should place it in the context of the existing capitalist world market in commodities and financial capital (as I do below) so that the concept of original accumulation cannot be applied without some amendment.

Another limitation of the concept of primitive accumulation for analyzing the transition to new modes of production in today's Third World is that the development of capitalism is not the only path forward for poor countries today; for some states, development on the basis of socialist relations of production is possible, while in many, "intermediate" systems are sustainable. However, although the concept of primitive accumulation was formulated with respect to capitalist development, in the early years of the Soviet Union Preobrazhensky (1926) developed a concept of "original socialist accumulation" from it. For him the problem of the transition to socialism was how to appropriate resources from the private, petty commodity, agricultural sector for accumulation in the state-controlled, socialist, industrial sector, and he analyzed the financial mechanisms that would effect this. Apart from the taxation of private producers, Preobrazhensky particularly emphasized the significance of state pricing policies, which act as an "invisible" but easily effective tax on private agriculture through manipulation of the terms of trade between agriculture and industry, and he argued that socialist accumulation can also be financed through the creation of money.

However, financing a transition to a socialist development path by expanding the money supply carries dangers that arise from the complex role money and finance have in mixed economies. This is illustrated by two countries that attempted development along a socialist path while retaining a large private sector: Chile under its Popular Unity government of 1970 to 1973, and Mozambique under Frelimo since 1975. Each pursued financial policies that raised the question of whether inappropriate policies toward money and finance may actively destabilize the transition to socialism and ultimately prevent it.

In a seminal book, Griffith-Jones (1981) argued that the Popular Unity government's socialist experiment failed partly because it did not take into account the active role money plays in an economy that is not completely centrally planned. In her view the strategy involved "financial disequilibrium" that focused on the state's budget deficit and at times was associated with transfers of income to state employees and private capitalists (rather than to accumulation). This led to an excessive growth of the money supply to finance the deficits and to other factors, eventually leading to a high rate of inflation. High inflation, in turn, destabilized the role of money by reducing its usefulness as a unit of account and store of value; the way that different groups experienced gains and losses in this process helped to undermine the political stability needed to carry through a transformation. Wuyts (1986) examined the financial policies of Frelimo and concluded, similarly, that state deficit financing and monetary expansion plays an active role in a society attempting to follow a socialist path. In the difficult circumstances of transition, that role may at times be positive (for example, subsidies may be necessary at crucial times to prevent a complete collapse of production) but will also have a strong ability to undermine the government's strategy. To show how the latter occurred in Mozambique, Wuyts follows a Marxist approach of examining how relations of production were affected by excess liquidity. He demonstrates that the excess money stimulated the growth of parallel markets (black markets) in commodities, and, most significantly, enabled entrepreneurs to accumulate the money as capital and employ it actively as capitalists on these markets. Excess money creation by the state facilitated the growth of capitalist trading and production for the parallel markets, changing the class structure and ultimately undermining the attempt to develop socialism. These examples illustrate the complexity of the role that money and finance can play in original socialist accumulation; their powerful effects can work to destabilize the attempts at socialist development.

Finally, the concept of original accumulation cannot be applied to all cases of financing the transformation of economic relations, for in many countries that transformation is less radical than abolishing an old mode of production and constructing a dominant new one. Developing economies are often characterized by a mixture of capitalist and "traditional" economic relations, regulation by a state that partly preserves and partly breaks up old relations, and overall domination by the global capitalist markets in commodities and finance. Under these circumstances, accumulation and development can occur as a result of some significant changes in particular relations even without any that could be called a change in the dominant mode of production. The notion of original accumulation relates to the inauguration of a new mode; it is concerned with rapid accumulation by means that are not sustainable or normal features of the new mode of production once it is established. Therefore it cannot be applied directly to this type of case. Nevertheless, even in such countries accelerated growth and the partial transformation of the economy require accumulation on a greater scale than previously, and there is no sharp dividing line in practice between the mechanisms used to finance it and those that have been used to finance the more fundamental transformations inaugurating a new mode of production.

An interesting example of the financing problems thrown up by such partial transformations is the changing character of "working capital." In capitalist accounting this category refers to the finance required for the inventories held by the firm and the trade credit advanced by it to initiate and realize a complete circuit of production. In the classical economics of David Ricardo it consists of the inventories and wages the capitalist has to advance in order to carry through the production circuit and therefore, in Marxist terms, includes variable capital and part of constant capital. Modern orthodox economists, using the accounting concept, have sometimes argued that industrialization and rural transformation lead to a reduction in the economy's need for working capital since the average level of inventories is reduced by the diminution of agriculture's relative position in the economy (Kindleberger 1958, p. 38). By contrast, Marxist theory implies that such a tendency would be counteracted by changing economic relations within agriculture. As agriculture moves from being based on the household labor of peasant farmers toward a more capitalistic system based on wage labor, it requires increased working capital in the classical economic sense since it has to finance the advance of wages before the completion and realization of production. On this basis Amartya Sen (1964) developed an interesting critique of the financing projections of India's Third Five-Year Plan.

In addition to the role finance plays in the transition to a new mode of production and in partial transformations of economic relations, it also has a role in maintaining and consolidating "backward" economic relations. Changes in class structure or preservation of class positions are at the heart of such transformation or stagnation, and finance is both an "effect" of the class structure and an instrument causing its transformation or preservation. Amit Bhaduri (1977) applies these considerations very fruitfully in his classic analysis of a dilemma long recognized as a key problem of finance in the Third World: explaining the existence of usurious interest rates charged by rural moneylenders on loans to peasants.

Previous writers, within a neoclassical orthodox framework, had emphasized the idea that such interest rates are high because the moneylenders require a premium to compensate them for the risk of default inherent in loans to peasants. Bhaduri's formal analysis, by contrast, recognizes the asymmetry in the relationship, which results from the different class positions of the moneylender and the peasant borrower. This class relationship is encapsulated in one of its effects, the unequal valuation of commodities required as collateral, and the moneylenders' ability to exploit this asymmetry through monopoly power and personal relations. High interest rates are based on these class relations in a way which reinforces and reproduces them. The unequal valuation of collateral, moneylenders' monopoly power, and personal relations with the peasants creates conditions under which the moneylenders are not faced with an exogenously determined default risk but, instead, have the power to influence the default rate by setting the interest rate. An incentive can exist to set high interest rates in order to provoke high defaults because this form of exploitation enables the moneylenders to appropriate the land, crops, or labor power pledged as collateral. In that way, high interest rates are the basis for accumulation by the landowning, merchant, or rich peasant class that acts as moneylenders and are a mechanism for consolidating the dominance of those exploiting classes within a stagnant system of backward agriculture.

The Role of International Finance

Marxist writings on the Third World give a key role to international finance that is very different from the orthodox conception. The roots of this tradition lie in the writings of Rudolf Hilferding (1910), Lenin (1916), and Nikolai Bukharin (1917–18), where a particular concept of imperialism was developed.

Despite the differences among these writers, their writings constituted a "Leninist" conception of imperialism as a new stage of capitalism. The stage was seen as characterized by a "merger" of financial capital with industrial capital in giant trusts or monopolies; the unification of these two types of capital created a new form, "finance capital." Finance capital intensified the international expansion of capital from its metropolitan centers in Europe (and the United States) into the Third World and gave it a new character, for the capital exported at this stage was seen as dominated by capital in the financial form of bonds, loans, and other financial investments. This type of capital export at this stage of capitalism constituted capitalist "imperialism," which implied an essentially parasitic relation between international capital and the Third World. Supported by colonial apparatuses, it enabled finance capital in the metropolitan countries to draw super-profits from poor countries.

Modern Marxist writings have followed two different lines regarding the implications of such imperialist relations for Third World countries themselves. The most prevalent view has been that capitalist foreign investment in Third World countries is exploitative in a way that retards their growth. A strong expression of this is located within the writings of the "dependency school" where Third World countries' foreign debt is seen as a mechanism that complements unequal exchange in trade to draw out of poor countries the surpluses that would otherwise promote accumulation within them (Frank 1964). Empirically, such writers point to long periods when interest and amortization payments from the Third World to advanced capitalist countries exceed new lending to them, a phenomenon which has become acute in the 1980s. Block (1977), Payer (1974), and other writers argue that the International Monetary Fund and the World Bank are agents of imperialism's financial system, promoting in particular U.S. capital's ability to profit from it. Alternatively, they can be seen as using financial relations to create and regulate the broad framework of global capitalist market relations thereby strengthening the internationalization of capitalist enterprises (Harris 1986, 1988a).

Another Marxist perspective, by contrast, treats imperialism's investment in Third World countries and its trade relations with them as creating the conditions for capitalism within these countries and as the source in many cases of capitalist accumulation and growth in the Third World (Warren 1980; Sender and Smith 1986). This view, associated with the work of Bill Warren, sees the export of capital as the export of capitalism, which, under certain conditions, can generate growth.

The impetus behind the financial links between the Third World and advanced capitalist countries undoubtedly lies in the outward expansionary tendencies of capital in the latter economies, and that is a key element in the theory of imperialism. But there are both theoretical and empirical grounds for doubting whether this capital necessarily has the character of finance capital, in other words, a unified form of financial and industrial capital. Historically, financial capital has been strongly linked with merchant capital instead of industrial capital in the exploitation of the Third World, and this phenomenon has persisted until recently in many areas (Kay 1975). Since the early 1970s, a different phenomenon has been still more prominent, the internationalization of financial capital separated from merchant and industrial capital, and its investment in Third World countries through media such as Eurodollar credits and bonds. This phenomenon appears to some writers to be more in line with Marx's conception of the high degree of autonomy that financial capital has (particularly in relation to his theory of fictitious capital) and to represent a general historical tendency of capitalism while the fusion of capital into finance capital exists only at particular conjunctures (Harris 1988b, Harvey 1982).

The Role of the State

Marxist writers give both the state and state power, including their role in finance, a central place in the economics of development. This has two dimensions: direct financial flows through the state by means of taxation and state spending, and state financial initiatives that strengthen the system of banks and credit markets.

In a classic essay, "Problems of Financing Economic Development in a Mixed Economy," the Polish economist Michal Kalecki (1976) related the state's taxation policy to the problem of securing the "real" resources for investment goods and basic consumption goods; the mobilization of finance by tax policy is seen as being conditioned by the real constraints on the production of food instead of being within an autonomous financial sphere. In his model the growth rate can only be raised (in the absence of foreign trade) if a transformation of economic relations in agriculture enables the supply of food to grow at a faster rate than previously. The state has to have a central role in that transformation (through land reform, rural tax policy, and other means), and, whatever rate of growth of food production is achieved, the state's fiscal policies have to be adjusted to ensure enough real resources are released to meet the required rate of growth of physical capital. Kalecki imposes the condition that increased taxation should not fall upon the poor or basic consumption goods, so fiscal policies to increase real savings involve taxation of luxury consumption or of the incomes of the wealthy. The emphasis this model places on constraints in food supply is similar to the role that the "bottleneck" in food supply plays in the Latin American "structuralist" theory of inflation (Edel 1969), but Kalecki draws the implications for public finance.

Kalecki's concern with changing production relations in agriculture to improve food supply is distinctly Marxian and so is his discussion of the problems class interest may cause for the state's attempts to concentrate taxes on the rich. Victor Lippit (1974) carries further the analysis of how class interests affect the state's ability to finance economic development. He studied the impact China's land reform of 1950 to 1952 had on the provision of finance for capital accumulation using the concepts of economic surplus and class relations as the basis of a detailed empirical study.

Lippit's study concerns the same issue as Kalecki's model—the finance of development in a *mixed* economy with a significant capitalist sector. This is so since the land reform in China did not directly inaugurate a socialist system in agriculture; the land reform program redistributed land to poor and middle peasants but it remained private land and collectivization did not occur until 1955. Lippit argues that the land reform led to a major rise in China's saving rate (in other words, the real resources to finance investment) before the collectivization of agriculture. One difference between Lippit's work and Kalecki's model is that Lippit concentrates on the ways in which, as a result of land reform, the income from agricultural output was able to be redirected toward financing development (through taxation and other means) without assuming that agricultural output itself was increased by the reform; Kalecki, in contrast, saw the rate of growth of food production as a fundamental constraint on development finance.

Lippit follows the general approach of Baran and Sweezy (1966) in referring to "surplus" as the difference between output and the amount necessary for maintaining "normal non-luxury" living standards, but in practice he equates China's agricultural rural surplus with property income in the rural sector so it is similar to the classical Marxian concept of the "surplus value" produced in agriculture. His study led to the conclusion that the "surplus," which property owners and the producers of luxury items previously received directly or indirectly from agriculture, was transferred by the land reform to poor and middle peasants; from their increased income, resources were channeled into increased saving, which financed industrialization and other capital investment. The phenomenon of redistribution from the rich to the poor leading to increased national saving is surprising since the poor have a lower propensity to save out of increases in income than the rich (they have a lower marginal propensity to save), a fact that underpins one of the key assumptions of structuralist economics. If $100 is taken from the rich, their saving is reduced by a high proportion of that sum, but when it is given to the poor they increase their consumption by a high proportion of the $100 and their saving increases by less than the saving of the rich decreases. Lippit shows that land reform overcame this problem because it enabled the state to use two instruments to channel agriculture's surplus into national saving and investment: taxation of agriculture and worsening agriculture's terms of trade by raising the relative price of manufactured goods.

The quantitative significance of these financial channels was confirmed by Ka and Selden's (1986) analysis of original accumulation during China's 1953 to 1957 Five-Year Plan. In addition to quantifying the effects, Lippit's book presents a strong analysis of social relations based on Marxist class concepts to explain why the state was able to impose these taxes and terms of trade as a result of land reform. The landlord class that existed previously resisted any increases in tax rates, and their evasion of existing taxes caused the amount yielded by rural taxes to be a low proportion of the potential. Previous governments had relied on the landlord class for political support and local administration, so government could not alienate this class by raising taxes more effectively, but land reform swept that class away from its privileged position and created the political conditions that facilitated higher tax yields. The poor and middle peasantry were able to bear the taxes and also the high relative prices of manufactured goods because land reform had substantially increased their incomes, ensuring that their standard of living was higher than previously even after payments of taxes and industry's high relative prices were taken into account.

Lippit's study is a good example of a Marxist approach that sees the interests of different classes as determining the state's ability to finance economic development. Another example is Fitzgerald (1978), who discusses the impact class interests had in Latin America during the twenty-five years following 1950; he argues that working class (and capitalist) demands for increased state spending on the one hand and specific classes' resistance to increased taxation on the other combined to generate a "fiscal crisis of the state" in Latin America. From a Marxist perspective, state taxation and expenditure is dependent on class forces; Marxist economics argues that the state is a focus of class forces and can be an instrument of class power, and that public finance is dependent on its class character. This contrasts with orthodox economic theory, which treats the state as the embodiment of a neutral rationality or the product of individual voters' choices. At most, orthodox theory sees the Third World state as supporting and supported by a set of client groups (who benefit from import licences and other monopolies conferred by the state); but the absence of a concept of social relations of production in most orthodox theories means that these client groups could come from anywhere instead of having specific class roots (Kreuger 1974). In Marxist analysis public finance is constrained by whether the state is dominated by one class or another, with each having a particular position in existing modes of production: traditional big landowners, comprador bourgeoisie or merchant capitalists, national bourgeoisie based on domestic industry, the working class, or various peasant classes.

However, the Marxist conception of the state underlying its approach to public finance has difficulties of its own. In Third World societies in particular, the class structure is not static; the balance of forces between classes changes but, more important, new class groups are in the process of formation and the state is actively involved in this. In post-colonial states where a functioning capitalist class is small (and where other classes' political power is weak), the state frequently becomes the vehicle for a new class to gain economic power by occupying positions in the state and controlling its economic levers. A related problem arises when the national state is completely dominated by the forces of international capital and is articulated only weakly with the country's classes. Under such conditions, foreign powers' aid agencies, foreign bankers, or the International Monetary Fund may play the leading role in dictating the country's public finance strategy.

The state's role with respect to banking and the credit system is subject to considerations similar to those that apply in public finance: it acts in relation to particular class interests. One dimension of this appears in the impact that state policy on interest rates and the direction of credit has on the distribution of surplus value among different class groups; for example, the direction of credit toward export industries assists accumulation by that section of the bourgeoisie. Similarly, expansion of the money supply to generate or accommodate high inflation rates can be a powerful engine to redistribute value from workers to capitalists by cutting real wages. Alternatively, the state may give financial privileges to particular classes, enabling them to build up banking capital under their control or to build conglomerate monopolies in which banks, commerce, and industry are united. This occurred, for example, in Chile (Diaz-Alejandro 1985).

The state's role in banking and credit markets is not contingent; its involvement in money and credit is necessary for their functioning. The state is necessary as the ultimate guarantor of money and the credit system; a classic conception of this is expressed in the dictum that the state's central bank has to act as lender of last resort, but the state's function as guarantor is wider than that. In addition, the national state necessarily has responsibility for regulating the boundary and connection between the national monetary system and the international system. Finally, the manner in which the state finances its own expenditure has a fundamental influence on the financial system as a whole. On the basis of its inevitable involvement in the country's money and finance, the state implements financial policies and within a Marxist framework these are seen as having particular class orientations; they promote particular class interests and they are constrained by the relative power of different class groupings. This is a strength of the Marxist conception of finance, in principle, for it provides a two-way link between financial policy and the structure and development of the economy instead of viewing the state's financial policy as autonomous. In practice, however, its main weakness is that it is difficult to identify empirically the changing class forces existing in Third World countries or the class character of Third World states.

Conclusion

The two dimensions of finance—public finance (taxation and state expenditure) and banking and credit—have been central to the processes of development and underdevelopment in the Third World. This has been reflected in recent years by financial policy being given a prominent position in development strategies. At the same time orthodox economists in the West have developed a large body of theoretical and empirical work on this subject. On the other hand, Marxist economists have written little on it although there is a significant body of Marxist writing on other aspects of economic development. Nevertheless, as this paper is intended to show, the principles of Marxist political economy can yield a scientific analysis of the role of finance in the Third World that is different from orthodox analysis. Although there are unsolved problems within the Marxist approach, these are a sign of its vitality and its openness to debate and further work.

References

Baran, P., and Sweezy, P. (1966) *Monopoly Capital.* New York: Monthly Review Press.

Bhaduri, A. (1977) "On the Formation of Usurious Interest Rates in Backward Agriculture." *Cambridge Journal of Economics.* Vol. 1.

Block, F. (1977) *The Origins of International Economic Disorder.* Berkeley: University of California Press. ·

Brenner, R. (1977) "The Origins of Capitalist Development: A Critique of Neo-Smithian Marxism." *New Left Review,* July–August 1977.

Bukharin, N.I. (1917–18) *Imperialism and World Economy.* New York: Monthly Review Press, 1973.

Cameron, R. (1972) *Banking and Economic Development: Some Lessons of History.* New York: Oxford University Press.

Cameron, R.; Crisp, O.; Patrick, H.; and Tilly, R. (1967) *Banking in the Early Stages of Industrialization: A Study in Comparative Economic History.* New York: Oxford University Press.

Cavallo, D.F. (1977) *Stagflation Effects of Monetarist Stabilization Policies.* Cambridge, Mass: Harvard University, Ph.D. thesis.

Chenery, H., and Bruno, M. (1962) "Development Alternatives in an Open Economy: The Case of Israel." *Economic Journal* 72, 79–103.

Chenery, H., and Strout, A. (1966) "Foreign Assistance and Economic Development." *American Economic Review* 56(4), 670–733.

Diaz-Alejandro, C. (1985) "Goodbye Financial Repression, Hello Financial Crash." *Journal of Development Economics,* 19(1–2), September–October 1985, 1–24.

Edel, M. (1969) *Food Supply and Inflation in Latin America.* New York: Praeger, 1969.

Fei, J., and Ranis, G. (1968) "Foreign Assistance and Economic Development: Comment." *American Economic Review.*

Fitzgerald, E.V.K. (1978) "Fiscal Crisis of the Latin American State." In J.F.J. Toye, ed., *Taxation and Economic Development.* London: F. Cass.

Fine, B., and Harris, L. (1979) *Rereading Capital.* London: Macmillan.

Foley, D.K. (1986) *Understanding Marx's Capital.* Cambridge, Mass: Harvard University Press.

Foxley, A. (1983) *Latin American Experiments in Neoconservative Economics.* Berkeley: University of California Press.

Frank, A.G. (1964) "Mechanisms of Imperialism." *Monthly Review,* reprinted in A.G. Frank, *Latin America: Underdevelopment or Revolution.* New York: Monthly Review Press, 1969.

Fry, M.J. (1988) *Money, Interest, and Banking in Economic Development.* Baltimore: Johns Hopkins University Press.

Griffith-Jones, S. (1981) *The Role of Finance in the Transition to Socialism.* London: Frances Pinter.

Harris, L. (1986) "Conceptions of the IMF's Role in Africa." In P. Lawrence, ed., *The World Recession and the Food Crisis in Africa.* London: James Currey Press.

Harris, L. (1988a) "The IMF and Mechanisms of Integration." In B. Crow, M. Thorpe, et.

al., eds., *Survival and Change in the Third World.* Cambridge: Polity Press.

Harris, L. (1988b) "Alternative Perspectives on the Financial System." In L. Harris, J. Coakley, M. Croasdale, and T. Evans, eds., *New Perspectives on the Financial System.* London: Croom Helm.

Harris, L. (1988c) "Financial Reform and Economic Growth: A New Interpretation of South Korea's Experience." In L. Harris, J. Coakley, M. Croasdale, T. Evans, eds., *New Perspectives on the Financial System.* London: Croom Helm.

Harvey, D. (1982) *The Limits to Capital.* Oxford: Basil Blackwell.

Hilferding, R. (1910) *Das Finanz Kapital.* Vienna, 1910. English translation edited by T. Bottomore, *Finance Capital.* London: Routledge and Kegan Paul, 1981.

Ka, C-M., and Selden, M. (1986) "Original Accumulation, Equity and Late Industrialisation: The Cases of Socialist China and Capitalist Japan." *World Development* 14(10/11), 1293–1310.

Kalecki, M. (1976) "Problems of Financing Economic Development in a Mixed Economy." In M. Kalecki, ed., *Essays on Developing Economies.* Brighton: Harvester Press.

Kay, G. (1975) *Development and Underdevelopment, A Marxist Analysis.* London: Macmillan.

Kindleberger, C.P. (1958) *Economic Development.* New York: McGraw-Hill.

Krueger, A. (1974) "The Political Economy of the Rent-Seeking Society." *American Economic Review,* 64(3), 291–303.

Lenin, V.I. (1916) *Imperialism: The Highest Stage of Capitalism.* In V.I. Lenin, *Collected Works,* vol. 22. Moscow: Progress Publishers.

Lipietz, A. (1987) *Mirages and Miracles.* London: Verso.

Lippit, V. (1974) *Land Reform and Economic Development in China.* White Plains, NY: International Arts and Sciences Press.

McDonald, D.C. (1982) "Debt Capacity and Developing Country Borrowing." *IMF Staff Papers,* 29(45), 603–646.

McKinnon, R.I. (1973) *Money and Capital in Economic Development.* Washington, DC: Brookings Institution.

Payer, C. (1974) *The Debt Trap: The IMF and the Third World.* London: Penguin Books.

Preobrazhensky, E. (1926) *Novaya Ekonomika.* Moscow, 1926. English translation by Brian Pearce, *The New Economics,* Oxford, 1965.

Rosenstein-Rodan, P., ed. (1964) *Pricing and Fiscal Policies: A Study in Method.* Cambridge, Mass.: MIT Press.

Rostow, W.W. (1960) *The Stages of Economic Growth.* Cambridge: Cambridge University Press.

Sen, A.K. (1964) "Working Capital in the Indian Economy: A Conceptual Framework and Some Estimates." Ch. 6 in P. Rosenstein-Rodan, ed., *Pricing and Fiscal Policies: A Study in Method.* Cambridge, Mass.: MIT Press.

Sender, J., and Smith, S. (1986) *The Development of Capitalism in Africa.* London: Methuen.

Shaw, E.S. (1973) *Financial Deepening in Economic Development.* New York: Oxford University Press.

Taylor, L. (1983) *Structuralist Macroeconomics.* New York: Basic Books, 1983.

Toye, J.F.J. (1981) *Public Expenditure and Indian Development Policy 1960–1970,* Cambridge South Asian Studies 25, Cambridge.

van Wijnbergen, S. (1985) "Macro-economic Effects of Changes in Bank Interest Rates: Simulation Results for South Korea." *Journal of Development Economics,* 18(2–3) August 1985, 541–554.

Warren, R. (1980) *Imperialism: Pioneer of Capitalism.* London: Verso.

Wuyts, M. (1986) *Money and Planning for Socialist Transition: The Mozambican Experience.* Milton Keynes, U.K.: The Open University, Ph.D. thesis.

11

The Concept of the Surplus in Economic Development

Victor D. Lippit

Introduction

In *The Political Economy of Growth,* Paul Baran developed two perspectives which were to affect deeply the radical critique of conventional development economics. According to the first, Baran writes that: "Economic development has always been propelled by classes and groups interested in a new economic and social order, has always been opposed and obstructed by those interested in the preservation of the *status quo*" (1968: 3–4). To examine concretely the manner in which a given class structure blocks or furthers development, according to Baran, it is necessary to examine its impact on the disposition of the economic surplus. Accordingly, Baran devotes an entire chapter to clarifying the concept of the economic surplus, a chapter in which he presents three different definitions of the concept. In addition, he presents a fourth definition later in the text, and a fifth in the Foreword to the 1962 printing, which appeared five years after the book was initially published. Still another definition, a sixth, was subsequently presented in *Monopoly Capital* (1966), a work which Baran wrote jointly with Paul Sweezy.

With a sure intuitive sense, Baran recognized the importance of the "surplus" concept, and the discussion which follows is meant in the fullest sense as an

I am indebted to Tom Weisskopf, Arthur MacEwan, Akmal Hussain, Harry Magdoff, Shigeru Ishikawa, Robert Pollin, Syed Hashemi, Anil Nauriya, Ahmet Tonak, John Foster, Howard Sherman and Nai-Pew Ong for their comments on and criticisms of earlier drafts of this essay. In all fairness, however, I must absolve them of responsibility for the final product, some of which remains highly controversial.

Reprinted by permission from *Review of Radical Political Economics* Vol. 17 (1/2) (1985): 1–19.

appreciation of Baran's contribution—for his work is indeed the proper starting point of development economics—as well as a critique. As I will argue below, the most useful conception of the surplus is the difference between national income and essential consumption, a conception which is based upon, but differs from, Baran's. At the heart of this way of understanding the surplus is the idea that a great deal may be revealed by examining the manner in which society disposes of what might be thought of as its "discretionary" income, the income above and beyond what is necessary to meet its socially-determined subsistence requirements.

Capital formation, like military expenditure and luxury consumption, must come out of the surplus, and by identifying the surplus as a distinct category—which has no precise counterpart in conventional national income accounting—we are able to focus on such alternative potential uses. Although low per capita incomes in underdeveloped countries (UDCs) make saving and investment appear difficult, the existence of a sizable surplus can be demonstrated for most UDCs. The problem becomes, then, why the surplus is used in the way it is and what the consequences of this may be for development.

This problem is intimately bound up with the class structure in each UDC. Thus traditional landlords who divide up their land "to let" to sharecroppers are much less likely to reinvest their income than capitalist farmers who hire labor and are constantly looking for ways to enhance their profits. It is clear that the rise of capitalist farming at the expense of landlordism will contribute to development, even though its short-term welfare consequences may be ambiguous, as former tenants are reduced to the status of farm laborers or drift into the cities as part of the marginalized population development often creates. It is not possible here for me to go into a full elaboration of the relation of surplus use to class structure, but it must be noted that the full significance of the surplus concept emerges only when this relation is considered in its entirety, i.e., only when we know which classes receive the surplus and how they dispose of it.

If capitalists use their profits in trade rather than in industrial investment, or if government officials use their access to the power of the state to direct the surplus to their personal use, then economic development is apt to suffer. By identifying which classes receive the surplus and how they dispose of it we are enabled to grasp the core dynamic of the development process, to see why development is or is not taking place, and if it is, why it takes the particular form it does. Before using the surplus in this way, however, the concept must be clarified theoretically and in a way that will make it amenable to empirical use; that is the purpose of this essay.

Although Baran's *The Political Economy of Growth* brought the concept of the surplus to the forefront of development studies, the other principal perspective Baran presents in the same work, ironically, has played a major role in inhibiting its application in development studies. According to the other perspective, underdevelopment is an historical process brought on by the expansionist thrust of the West, manifested in imperialism, colonialism and neocolonialism. The "natural" progression from precapitalist to capitalist forms of production was forestalled by this intrusion, Baran suggests, and a dependent elite created, lacking both the incentive and the ability to bring about capitalist development. Socialist revolution, in his view, sweeping away the ineffective elite classes and breaking the bonds of dependency, becomes the necessary condition for development. This perspective, subsequently elaborated and developed in the work of Andre Gunder Frank (see, for example, Frank 1972a, 1972b), came to shape the radical paradigm in development economics and, in the form of dependency theory, has even been integrated into the mainstream literature.

Recognition that underdevelopment is indeed an historical process in which the expansionist thrust of the West has played a major role is undoubtedly a great contribution to our understanding of development and underdevelopment. Pushed to an extreme form, however, it denies any relevance to economic structures within underdeveloped countries; if external forces are ultimately determinant, the investigation of class structure and surplus use within underdeveloped countries becomes quite superfluous. Thus, the widespread acceptance of Baran's second perspective undermined recognition of the first. Yet as I will argue, it is the first perspective which must provide the basis for an integrated development theory.

First of all, although the proportion of surplus flowing abroad was undoubtedly much greater during colonial days, the fact remains that at present the vast majority of the surplus is disposed of by elites within the underdeveloped countries; the share going as profits to multinational corporations or flowing abroad to foreign nationals in some other form is usually quite small.[1] Second, contrary to the analysis of the dependency school, economic development is indeed proceeding in many of the underdeveloped countries, a development which simply cannot be explained without a clear analysis of class structure and surplus use. Finally, such analysis is indispensable for understanding the significance of the far-reaching structural changes currently taking place in the economies of the underdeveloped countries. Such changes include the formation of new classes, including a bureaucratic class with its own distinct interest in certain countries, and the transformation of existing relations of production under the impact of new technology as when the Green Revolution technology leads to the replacement of traditional landlord-tenant relations by rich farmer–hired laborer relations.

My focus on the domestic class structure and surplus use within underdeveloped countries is not meant, in the least, to deny the existence or importance of the capitalist world economy. Indeed, the capitalist world economy exists and affects the processes of development and underdevelopment profoundly.[2] If the problems of underdevelopment are approached from this perspective, however, it is possible to miss the significance of the domestic class structure and surplus use. This, in fact, is what has happened in the radical development paradigm. Thus, on the one hand, a vast literature on dependency, multinational corporations and the impact of the capitalist world system on UDCs has sprung up while, on the other, there are practically no empirical studies of UDC modes of production, social formations (the combination of modes of production in a given country), or class structure and surplus use.

In one sense it is quite natural that the literature stresses external forces, since underdevelopment as a distinct phenomenon emerged only with the expansion of the European capitalist economy into the Third World. This played a central role in the structural determination of underdeveloped economies at an earlier period, and the resulting structures continue to the present to be influenced by economic and political forces emanating from the advanced countries. Yet the insight into development and underdevelopment as historical processes which this perspective affords easily leads us into error precisely because it is so powerful; it appears to offer an explanation which is self-sufficient, and to make us lose sight of the fact that institutions and the class structures associated with them, once established, have an existence which is autonomous, at least in part.

In the last analysis, development and underdevelopment are shaped by the interaction of internal and external forces. Methodologically, however, in carrying out studies of contemporary underdevelopment, the sequence in which these forces are analyzed does make a difference; it is necessary to investigate first the role of class structure and surplus use, and only when that has been done, to examine the impact of the capitalist world economy on the domestic structures of the underdeveloped countries. The reverse procedure, which until now has predominated, tends to preclude careful analysis of the domestic structures, which, as I have indicated, are ordinarily of greater significance simply because by far the greater portion of the surplus tends, at present, to be disposed of by [nationals] of the UDCs rather than by multinational corporations or other external agents. That the effect of scholarship has been significant is reflected in the contrast to which I have referred between the vast literature on dependency and the capitalist world system on the one hand, and the lack of empirical studies on modes of production, class structure and surplus use on the other. To pursue the revival of development theory, then, the domestic economic issues must be placed at the forefront. Here I propose to examine the concept of the surplus, and in a subsequent essay to take up its relation to class structure and modes of production. In examining the concept of the surplus, the [natural] starting point is the work of Paul Baran.

Baran's Concept of the Surplus

In "The Concept of the Economic Surplus," chapter two of *The Political Economy of Growth,* Baran presents three concepts of the economic surplus: actual surplus, potential economic surplus, and planned economic surplus. Through a critical examination of these concepts, and subsequently of the other definitions of surplus Baran presents elsewhere, I hope to arrive at a conception of the surplus which will be useful in economic development, providing clarification of its theory and a guide to development research.

Baran first defines the *actual surplus* as "the difference between society's actual current output and its actual current consumption. It is thus identical with current saving or accumulation" (1968: 22–23). Thus, if Y = national income, S = national saving, I = national investment, and C = national consumption, then,

$$\text{Actual surplus} = S = Y - C = I \tag{1}$$

Here surplus = investment = saving.[3] This seems to be a quite unnecessary use of the concept. Unless saving and investment are for some reason inadequate terms, which Baran never attempts to argue, it seems quite unnecessary to replace them with the term "actual surplus." Further, since the concept of the surplus is meant precisely to bring to the surface phenomena and relationships which more conventional terminology obscures, there can be no justification for using it in this context.

The second concept Baran presents is that of the *potential surplus,* which he defines as "the difference between the output that could be produced in a given natural and technological environment with the help of employable productive resources, and what might be regarded as essential consumption" (1968: 23), which is determined not in a physiological sense but by prevailing community standards. He also says that the potential surplus:

> . . . appears under four headings. *One* is society's excess consumption (predominantly on the part of the upper income groups, but in some countries, such as the United States, also on the part of the so-called middle classes), the *second* is the output lost to society through the existence of unproductive workers, the *third* is the output lost because of the irrational and wasteful organization of the existing productive apparatus, and the *fourth* is the output foregone owing to the existence of unemployment caused primarily by the anarchy of capitalist production and the deficiency of effective demand (Baran 1968: 24).

If we compare the two concepts of surplus presented thus far, letting C_{ess} = essential consumption,

$$\text{Potential surplus} \quad = \quad \text{Potential } Y - C_{ess} \tag{2}$$

$$\text{Actual surplus} \quad = \quad Y - C \tag{1}$$

then we can readily see that potential surplus exceeds actual surplus by the difference between potential and actual national income plus the difference between consumption and essential consumption. The latter difference is simply nonessential or "luxury" consumption, which, for the sake of consistency, must be defined to include such nonessential government consumption as wasteful expenditures on the military and bureaucracy. The difference between potential and actual income is meant to be clarified by the final three headings cited in the passage above.

Unproductive labor, Baran's second heading,

> . . . consists of all labor resulting in the output of goods and services, the demand for which is attributable to the specific conditions and relationships of the capitalist system, and which would be absent in a rationally ordered society (Baran 1968: 32).

Under the category irrational and wasteful organization (the third component of the potential surplus), Baran includes the underutilization of capacity that characterizes capitalist society even in prosperous times and the waste due to monopoly and monopolistic competition. The fourth and final form in which the potential surplus is hidden is the unemployment of human and material resources due principally to the insufficiency of effective demand.

We may rewrite, in equation form, Baran's presentation of the potential surplus as follows (PS = potential surplus, PY = potential national income, C_{ess} = essential consumption, and C_{non} = nonessential consumption):

$$PS = PY - C_{ess} \tag{2}$$

$$PS = Y + f + g + h - C_{ess} \tag{3}$$

where f = output lost due to unproductive labor, g = output lost due to irrational and wasteful organization, and h = output lost due to unemployment.

$$Y = C_{ess} + C_{non} + I \tag{4}$$

$$PS = C_{ess} + C_{non} + I + f + g + h - C_{ess} \tag{5}$$

$$PS = C_{non} + I + f + g + h \tag{6}$$

Thus, potential surplus must include nonessential consumption, investment, and the output foregone due to the presence of unproductive labor, waste and unemployment. Yet in explaining the four headings under which potential surplus appears, Baran fails to include investment. This is an obvious oversight on his part since his first definition of potential surplus incorporates investment implicitly. Further, investment must come out of the surplus and thus must constitute a part of the potential surplus.

A second problem with Baran's concept of potential surplus appears in his mixing of categories. In discussing unproductive workers he observes that "a

good many of these unproductive workers are engaged in manufacturing arma-
ments, luxury articles of all kinds, objects of conspicuous display and marks of
social distinction" (Baran 1968: 32). Thus luxury consumption appears twice in
his definition of potential surplus, once as the major part of C_{non} in equation (6)
above and once as part of output lost due to the existence of unproductive labor,
or f in the same equation. The value of the goods and services which could be
produced by shifting workers from unproductive activities to productive ones
already appears in the national income accounts and is included in the difference
between actual national income and essential consumption. While it is not improper to specify the products of "unproductive" labor as a part of this difference, their value cannot be added to it in calculating the potential surplus without
double counting.

Further confusion is created by Baran's treatment of workers in health, education, and so forth as being productive but supported by the surplus, like unproductive workers. Thus their income is part of the surplus but their output is not,
so that if we attempt to calculate the surplus by adding up incomes, the result
will differ from that obtained by adding up outputs.

Finally, we should note that the analytically distinctive categories in the *potential* surplus concept are those which account for the difference between potential and actual national income. It is true that Baran also emphasizes luxury
consumption and wasteful government spending, but as I will argue below, it is
possible to include these latter categories in a conception of the surplus which
avoids the pitfalls of attempting to estimate potential income. They will then still
be part of the potential surplus, but will not distinguish it from the alternative
conception of the surplus presented below. The output lost by irrational and
wasteful organization and the output lost due to unemployment remain, then, as
the distinguishing constituents of potential surplus. The implication is that an end
to monopoly, etc. and an increase in effective demand, both forestalled by the
capitalist system, would swell the national product.

This is not an unreasonable assumption for the advanced countries (although a
great many additional assumptions would have to be spelled out for a proper
assessment in specific situations), but it has limited bearing on the situation in
underdeveloped countries (UDCs). It assumes that simple reorganization and an
increase in effective demand would soon lead to increased output, whereas supply-side constraints in UDCs make such an assumption unlikely. Despite considerable waste, irrationality, unemployment and underemployment in UDCs,
increasing aggregate demand and eliminating monopoly, etc. may well have a
negligible impact on output; unlike the advanced countries (ACs), the concept of
full-employment output doesn't have much meaning in the UDCs. Even if there
is a considerable unrealized potential for greater output—and the argument presented does not discount this possibility although it does suggest it may often be
considerably smaller than it first appears and extremely difficult to estimate with
any precision—the principal uses of the concept of the surplus, as the following

discussion should make clear, do not require the estimation of potential output. Consequently, if the purpose is to develop the concept of surplus as a tool in development analysis, Baran's concept of the potential surplus would be of little value even if it were not plagued with the inconsistencies noted. To clarify the argument, three points especially are worth stressing.

First, underemployment or disguised unemployment is ordinarily considerably more significant than open unemployment in UDCs. This appears in such forms as seasonally excess labor on overcrowded family farms, excessive numbers of street vendors in urban areas, and so forth. In advanced countries, the number of unemployed can be estimated more precisely and matched against underused industrial facilities (the percentage of factory capacity being used is a figure which ordinarily is readily available). In UDCs, by contrast, the facilities and equipment which the underemployed would potentially use—and even the enterprises in which they would work—commonly do not even exist. Since the potential surplus would incorporate, moreover, not their total output but their net output, we are faced with the impossibly conjectural task of estimating costs as well as gross products for nonexistent enterprises. Further, we must assume that the requisite financing, managerial skills, technical skills and other complementary factors would somehow be forthcoming, and again make the most conjectural estimates of what the real costs of these would be. To the extent, moreover, that a particular supply-side constraint cannot be removed with the given productive forces at the disposal of the economy—due to the absence of critical managerial or technical skills, for example, or because the foreign exchange needed to import essential equipment is unavailable—then even the existence of underutilized resources may not be a clue to potentially greater output.

Second, a principal reason for estimating the surplus is to examine the implications of systemic change. Thus, for example, if a capitalist economic system with its various features pushing national income down below its potential level were to be replaced by a more "rational" socialist system, the potential national income would be realized; that is to say, what appears under capitalism as a potential surplus would appear after a revolutionary transformation of society and the establishment of socialism as a real surplus. If valid, this argument would lend validity to the attempt to estimate potential surplus.

This argument, however, is unacceptable because it requires comparing a "perfect" socialist economic system with a real existing capitalist one. Thus the systemic factors which push economic output below the full potential of a capitalist economy with a given development of the productive forces are taken into account, but the systemic factors which push real socialist economies with the same productive forces below their potential are excluded. The comparison between a real capitalist society and an ideal socialist one creates an illusion that socialist revolutions can bring about an enormous jump in national income in and of themselves. If this were true, we should have witnessed enormous jumps in the national incomes of such countries as the Soviet Union, Cuba, China and

Vietnam immediately after their revolutionary transformations took place. Needless to say, no such jump in national incomes has occurred—at least nothing sustainable—since above and beyond the problems of transition the socialist economies also have systemic factors operating to push their incomes below their theoretical potential, factors which include among others, the well-known efficiency problems of centrally-planned economies (see, for example, Nove 1977) and the rise in bureaucratic-administrative expenditures.

Finally, perhaps the single most important reason for analyzing the surplus—including especially its extent, the classes which receive it and the manner in which they dispose of it—is to grasp the dynamic underlying the process of development or underdevelopment in existing economies. Even the comparative analysis between domestic and foreign disposition of the surplus falls within this area. To understand the real workings of existing economies it is essential to have some conception of the surplus, but the conception of potential surplus, which moves the analysis to some ideal socialist economy with no systemic restraints on its productive potential, is quite beside the point. For all of these reasons, then, although the concept of the potential surplus may have limited usefulness in particular instances, it cannot be made a core concept in the analysis of economic development and underdevelopment.

The third concept of the surplus Baran presents is the *planned economic surplus;* it is relevant only to socialism. According to Baran (1968: 41–42), the planned economic surplus is equal to the "optimum" (planned) output minus the "optimum" (planned) consumption. This simply reduces the concept to optimum or planned investment or saving under socialism.[4] The critique of Baran's concept of actual surplus is once again applicable: there is nothing wrong with the term "planned investment," so why should a new term be substituted for it? To do so is to empty the concept of surplus of its distinctive content.

Later in the text, Baran (1968: 60) introduces a fourth definition of surplus, the largest possible surplus, which he defines as the "difference between full employment output and some physiological subsistence minimum level of mass consumption." It is not really clear why this concept is useful or why, after devoting an entire chapter to an exposition of three concepts of the surplus, Baran chose casually to throw a fourth into the stew. Even the terminology is suspect, for it can readily be seen that as Baran has defined the terms, the potential surplus may well be larger than "the largest possible surplus."

In March 1958, Nicholas Kaldor reviewed *The Political Economy of Growth* in *The American Economic Review.* Quite understandably, he had some difficulty with the concept of the surplus. In the Foreword to the 1962 printing of the book, Baran takes him to task for this, accusing Kaldor of confusing the surplus with statistically observable profits. Baran's criticism is legitimate in part, for the two concepts must be distinguished, but in clarifying the difference between them, Baran ends up presenting a fifth conception of the surplus. According to this, the surplus is composed of profits, rent, interest, and the rising share of output going to sustain unproductive workers in advertising, public relations, administration, the legal profession, and so forth. This latter part of the surplus has its counterpart in the "ever-widening gap between the productivity of the *necessary productive workers* and the share of national income accruing to them as wages" (Baran 1968: xx).

Just as national income can be found either by summing the final values of the goods and services produced or by summing the incomes generated in producing them, the surplus can be found by examining either the output or the income side of national income. Thus, there can be no objection to Baran's presenting the surplus concept from the income side, but it is fair to note that in doing so he jumps from his consistent presentation from the output side in the text itself. Since the new definition has no direct counterpart in the first four, it will be useful to consider the relation between his initial definitions and his new one, as well as to consider the merits of the new definition in itself.

The concept of essential consumption, which Baran presents in discussing the potential surplus, covers the entire population; the potential surplus is found by subtracting the entire population's essential consumption from the potential national income. However, in the fifth definition of the surplus (introduced in the Foreword to the 1962 printing), the essential consumption of profit, rent and interest recipients, and the essential consumption of unproductive workers are included in the surplus. If people belonging to these "unproductive" groups are regarded as having the same right to subsistence as the rest of the population, then treating their essential consumption as part of the surplus is incorrect. The concept of the surplus is meant, in part, to help identify funds potentially available for development expenditure, and funds which provide basic subsistence for any part of the population are simply not available for this purpose. Thus, Baran's inclusion of the subsistence income of the "unproductive" groups in the surplus—that is, in his fifth definition of the concept—is improper.

Further, Baran excludes from the surplus the entire income of the necessary productive workers. This approach is satisfactory only to the extent that such incomes afford only a subsistence living standard, that is, only to the extent that they support essential consumption. Surely, however, this condition is widely violated in practice as monopoly elements in labor markets enable some productive workers, at least, to earn quasi-rents or incomes higher than competitive market forces would allow them. For example, physicians, engineers and other skilled workers, or workers who are members of strong unions, may be able to attain earnings well above what is needed to sustain their essential consumption. Even certain government workers—in UDCs especially—may enjoy incomes substantially higher than those which competitive markets would allow. Where such earnings permit a lifestyle which is far in excess of the community standard of essential consumption, they must be included in the surplus, but in Baran's formulation they are not.

Finally, we must take into account the possibility that substantial numbers of labor income recipients do not receive enough income to sustain essential consumption; widespread manifestations of malnutrition and other indicators of poverty in UDCs suggest that this is often a significant phenomenon. If the concept of the surplus is to be linked to essential consumption, then the amount necessary to raise labor incomes to the subsistence level must be subtracted from property incomes when calculating the surplus. This Baran fails to do in his fifth definition of the concept.

Redefining the Surplus

In defining the surplus, it is important to keep in mind the function it is meant to serve. If we assume that the first claim on a society's output is to meet the essential consumption needs, public as well as private, of all its citizens, then the remainder of its output, the surplus, may be thought of as representing a kind of discretionary fund that the society may choose to utilize in a variety of ways. It is from this "discretionary fund" or surplus that the capital accumulation needed to sustain development must be drawn. In order to grasp precisely the dimensions of the accumulation problem in underdeveloped countries, it is necessary to know the size and composition of the surplus, which will clarify the issue in a way that conventional national income accounting cannot. Thus, whereas conventional approaches would indeed seem to legitimize "vicious circles of poverty" theories according to which UDCs remain poor because they cannot afford to save and invest, Paul Baran pointedly asks which countries have been too poor to build monuments and fight wars, activities which can be sustained only by a substantial surplus.

Besides its evident significance in aggregate economic studies, the concept of the surplus provides the key to analyzing the structural relationships underlying the dynamic forces responsible for bringing about social change or for blocking it. Whereas the capitalist mode of production is overwhelmingly dominant in the advanced capitalist countries, the UDCs are characterized by a mixture of modes of production, each with its characteristic development of the forces of production (capital, technology, labor skills, etc.) and its own particular relations of production.[5] In capitalist and precapitalist societies, these relations are exploitative in the sense that the owners of property or the controllers of social coercion live off the surplus created by the direct producers. Analyzing the process of surplus generation and disposition can thus provide the key to grasping the entire social structure. In UDCs, this includes the forces sustaining underdevelopment and those promoting development.

The notion of the disposition of a surplus above subsistence determining whether or not a nation will experience economic development is not an unfamiliar one in the classical economics literature. Thus David Ricardo argued, in effect, that English landlords were given to luxury consumption expenditure while capitalists were driven to invest. Since workers in the long run would receive only subsistence wages, national economic development depended on the capitalists receiving the surplus. In precisely parallel fashion, in Third World countries today, an agrarian sector characterized by rich peasants or capitalist farmers actively investing and introducing new technology is much more apt to promote development than one characterized by absentee landlords who divide up their land to rent out in small plots and who have nothing to do with the process of production itself.

The concept of the surplus is potentially of considerable importance in development analysis, then, so that redefining the concept based on the above critique of Baran's presentation appears to be more reasonable than abandoning it. In Baran's presentation of the potential surplus, he introduces the concept of essential consumption. Since, as I have argued, we can regard such consumption as bearing a prior claim on society's output of goods and services, his deducting it from output in order to determine the size of the surplus is quite in order. On the other hand, distinguishing between potential and actual output introduces an element of considerable conjecture in the calculation and, as I have argued, one that is of dubious validity in UDCs. The most straightforward and useful conception of the surplus, therefore, is simply the difference between actual national income (Y) and essential consumption. To distinguish it from Baran's various definitions, this conception of the surplus can be referred to simply as "the surplus." Y can be found conveniently in conventional national income accounts. The concept of essential consumption, however, requires some further clarification if it is to be used in empirical research.

First, I might stress that the use of the term essential consumption here, like Baran's usage, is not meant to imply a physiological subsistence minimum. Rather, it is the standard at which people regard their basic needs as being met and thus is culturally determined and changes over time. It includes social as well as private consumption insofar as the social consumption—such as a certain level of educational services, public transportation, and so forth—is part of the accepted minimum standard. Thus, essential government expenditure is included in essential consumption. Excessive government expenditures on the military, bureaucracy and the like, by contrast, would constitute part of the surplus.[6]

While the fact that essential consumption is culturally determined creates some ambiguity, there are many aids to determining it and the ambiguity should create no insurmountable problems as long as the assumptions are carefully spelled out. Thus, for the United States the Bureau of Labor Statistics describes a minimum budget for a family of four to maintain a socially decent living, assuming it rents an inexpensive five-room apartment, drives an eight-year-old car, and so forth. In some underdeveloped countries, rich peasants can be distinguished on the basis on hiring one or more full-time laborers to work for them, poor peasants must hire themselves out to others for much of their time, and middle peasants have about enough land to keep themselves fully occupied and enough income to meet their basic needs. Their income can often be used as the essential consumption standard for the entire countryside, the essential consumption for which can then be calculated as the average per capita income in middle peasant households, including the value of government services consumed, times the rural population.[7]

Meeting essential consumption needs requires greater income in urban areas than in rural ones, but these too are amenable to empirical analysis. In many cases studies which have attempted to define poverty lines (see, for example, International Labour Office 1977) can be used; in others field study may be necessary, but in either case the same procedure of multiplying the urban population by the per capita essential consumption requirements can be followed. Various refinements of this procedure—such as modifying essential consumption requirements to take into account the age and occupational structures of the population—are possible, but the most important distinction is that between the differing subsistence requirements in urban and rural areas.

The surplus can also be calculated by examining the income flows of the population, as has been discussed above. Although the procedure will be somewhat more complicated, it has the advantage of clarifying the class structure even as the surplus is calculated. Based on the criticisms of Baran's fifth definition of the surplus presented above, we can define the surplus from the income side as equal to unearned income (profit, rent and interest) plus the quasi-rent or monopoly component in labor incomes minus the essential consumption requirements of the recipients of unearned income minus the income required to raise below-subsistence labor incomes to the subsistence level; these relationships appear below in equation (8). In practice, it is sometimes possible to simplify this and merely use the property share (profit, rent and interest) as a reasonable approximation of the surplus in UDCs. If the monopoly component in labor incomes is not very great, as may often be the case in UDCs—the nonagricultural population is smaller than in ACs, there are fewer skilled and professional workers, there are no professional athletes earning a million dollars a year, and so forth—neglecting it should not prove too consequential. Moreover, the other elements omitted—the subsistence requirements of property-share recipients and the additional subsistence income requirements of low-income labor-share recipients—work in the opposite direction, so to some extent the omissions will be offsetting. Further, if we were to add in an assumption that the confiscation of private property would force profit recipients into the labor market like everyone else, and that there they would be able to earn their subsistence requirements, then we needn't subtract those requirements from the available surplus. Institutional change in the form of expropriation would then swell the national income by the product of their labor, leaving the surplus formerly constituted by the income flows to property owners undiminished.[8]

The factor that is most likely to make the property share of national income diverge from the surplus is the existence of below-subsistence incomes among a sizable proportion of the labor-share income recipients. This "labor-income deficit," that is, that portion of essential labor consumption not provided for by labor incomes (because the income flows instead to the owners of property in the form of profit, rent and interest) is reflected as noted above in the widespread evidence of malnutrition and other indicators of poverty in UDCs. If the surplus is that portion of national income in excess of subsistence or essential consumption, the labor-income deficit must be subtracted from property income to obtain the surplus.

Whether or not the surplus can reasonably be approximated by the property share of national income (profit + rent + interest) depends in each case on the extent to which the remaining elements in the equation (8) (see below) are minor or offsetting. Thus, for example, if the above-subsistence incomes flowing to senior government officials and other recipients of labor income in excess of that amount needed to secure essential consumption were sufficient to raise poor peasants and others below the essential consumption level to that level, and if the property owners constitute a small share of the total population (so that their essential consumption requirements constitute a small share of the nation's total), then the property share of national income will represent a reasonable approximation of the surplus. Even if this is not the case, the surplus can be estimated from the income side of national income if the adjustments to the property share income noted above (and reproduced in equation 8) are taken into account.

To demonstrate the consistency of the two approaches to calculating the surplus I have presented, one from the output side of national income and one from the income side, I can put the two equations together. Recalling that C_{ess} = essential consumption and that the labor-income deficit stands for the income required to raise the income of labor-share recipients to a level sufficient to support essential consumption, I can write:

$$\text{Surplus} = Y - C_{ess} \tag{7}$$

$$\text{Surplus} = \text{profit + rent + interest + that part of labor income which} \tag{8}$$
supports nonessential consumption – the essential consumption of unearned income recipients – the labor income deficit

$$Y - C_{ess} = \text{profit + rent + interest + that part of labor income which} \tag{9}$$
supports nonessential consumption – the essential consumption of unearned income recipients – the labor income deficit

Since $C_{ess} = C_{ess}$ of unearned income recipients + C_{ess} of labor and C_{ess} of labor = that part of labor income which supports essential consumption + the labor-income deficit.

C_{ess} = C_{ess} of unearned income recipients + that part of labor income which supports essential consumption + the labor-income deficit

Then:

$Y =$ profit + rent + interest + that part of labor income (10)
which supports nonessential consumption + that part
of labor income which supports essential consumption

and:

$Y =$ profit + rent + interest + labor income (11)

Since (11) is the definition of national income (from the income side), the compatibility of the two approaches to the surplus presented is clear. Thus, we have been able to present two basic approaches to calculating the surplus: either subtract essential consumption from national income or add together the property-share components of national income, subject to the adjustments noted above. The latter, as we have noted, can under appropriate circumstances be approximated by the property share. Where this is not feasible, the product-side approach has the advantage of simplicity, but either method is theoretically correct and the two concepts are consistent. While some of the data required to estimate the surplus must be tailored to the definitions presented, some of the data generated for national income accounts can be adapted to the surplus framework.

At this point it may be useful to consider two additional definitions of the surplus, the one Baran presents with Sweezy in *Monopoly Capital*, and another presented by Ron Stanfield in his 1974 essay, "A Revision of the Economic Surplus Concept." In *Monopoly Capital*, Baran and Sweezy define the surplus rather ambiguously as "the difference between what a society produces and the costs of producing it" (1966: 9). "What a society produces" is, of course, the national income, so this part of the concept raises no difficulty. The costs of producing it, however, reduce essentially to the wages of productive workers. Thus, as in the case of Baran's fifth definition, the subsistence requirements of the unproductive workers and the property-share recipients are included in the surplus, while the "monopoly" component in wage and salary incomes is excluded; as we have seen this treatment is unsatisfactory.

Further, Stanfield points out that whereas in *The Political Economy of Growth*, Baran groups essential public consumption (government expenditure) with essential private consumption, thus excluding it from the surplus, in *Monop-*

oly Capital he and Sweezy treat all government expenditure as part of the surplus. Since essential government expenditure is indeed a necessary cost of production—drinking water, public transport and so forth are necessary if production is to be maintained—including it in the surplus is inconsistent with Sweezy and Baran's own definition. Including essential public consumption with essential private consumption as part of subsistence income, as Baran initially did, seems to be a more satisfactory approach to specifying the surplus. In other respects, his *Monopoly Capital* definition reduces to that in the 1962 Foreword, and thus suffers from the same defects.

In his essay, Ron Stanfield defines the economic surplus as the difference between potential output and essential consumption, where potential output is treated as full employment (of material resources as well as of people) output and essential consumption is "that consumption necessary to reproduce the extant productive capacity" (1974: 70). Since this latter definition is somewhat ambiguous, it would seem more reasonable to stay with community standards of subsistence requirements as the guide to essential consumption. Further, as I have argued, the Keynesian framework underlying the notion of full employment output has limited relevance in UDCs, making actual income a far more satisfactory benchmark than potential income in calculating the surplus. Again we are brought back to a definition of the surplus as the difference between actual income and essential consumption.

Using the Concept of the Surplus

I have argued that the concept of the surplus is a central one in economic development, especially when used in conjunction with an examination of class structure. Having clarified the concept of the surplus, I would like to turn next to the manner in which the concept may be used. I would like to argue that by ascertaining the size of the surplus and who receives it, we can identify potential sources of development finance which more conventional national income accounting techniques obscure. More broadly, an examination of the disposition of the surplus in conjunction with an analysis of class structure can make it possible to grasp the dynamics of development or the factors blocking it, depending on which case is applicable. Finally, by comparing the surplus which flows to nationals of UDCs with that which flows abroad and by analyzing the relation between the two, it will be possible to see how incorporation in the world capitalist system affects development. By their very nature, these propositions do not admit unambiguous "proofs." What I hope to do through the use of examples, however, is to indicate the usefulness of the surplus concept, both to vindicate the lengthy clarification of its meaning presented here and to serve as a research guide in the development field.

If we compare the Chinese economy in 1933 to the Chinese economy in 1953, we can observe that although per capita income in the two years was similar, the savings rate in the former year was only 1.7 percent of net domestic product, whereas by the latter year it had increased to 20 percent of net domestic product (Lippit 1974: 151). In an economy with a per capita income approximating (in 1957 prices) U.S. $60 per year (Perkins 1975: 134), this appears to be a quite extraordinary feat, and from the vicious circle of poverty perspective would appear to have been made possible only through intolerable pressure on the living standards of the masses. Yet in 1953 the health, education and living standards of the masses were substantially superior to what they had been twenty years earlier. How could both investment and consumption increase simultaneously?

This question has no solution in the conventional development paradigm. From the standpoint of the surplus, however, the answer is readily apparent. According to the evidence I have presented in two earlier works (Lippit 1974, 1978), using the most conservative assumptions the surplus in the Chinese economy of the 1930s, and indeed in prerevolutionary China generally, cannot have amounted to less than 30 percent of national income. Thus, out of a per capita income of $60, a *maximum* of $42 (= 70 percent) went to sustain essential consumption, with the actual figure more likely to have been in the $35–$39 range. A 20 percent investment rate in 1953 implies per capita investment of about $12 and a consumption level of about $48. Thus, despite the higher investment, popular consumption increased by a minimum of 14 percent, with the actual figure likely to have been more than 20 percent.

In Bangladesh, per capita income in 1979 was estimated at U.S. $90 (World Bank 1981: 134), placing it among the very poorest countries in the world. There appears on the surface to be no room for substantially raising the accumulation rate from domestic resources. Yet consider the following account relayed to the author by an acquaintance of the principal. An industrialist in Bangladesh pays a substantial bribe to Ministry of Industry officials to approve a factory to process agricultural products for export and a $2 million loan for imported machinery the factory will require. In fact, $1.2 million worth of machinery is imported but invoices totaling $2 million are presented to the Ministry officials whose cooperation has been assured. Pocketing the $800,000 difference, the industrialist sets out on a world tour, pausing long enough in Europe to deposit the balance in a Swiss bank.

On his return to Bangladesh, he withdraws funds from the enterprise for reasons which have little or nothing to do with its business activity. Consequently, its financial condition deteriorates and loan repayment schedules cannot be met; the time has come to approach the Ministry for a new loan. This actual case suggests that even in a country as poor as Bangladesh, the conventionally aggregated national income data may conceal a substantial surplus. In fact, according to an unpublished study by Syed Hashemi (1984), a substantial surplus does exist, amounting to approximately 25 percent of national income. The greater portion of the surplus currently flows to the merchant and bureaucratic classes, which dispose of it in ways that are not conducive to development, ranging from nonessential consumption to capital flight.

The particular classes which receive the surplus have a great bearing on its disposition. If these are indeed capitalists or, in the countryside, rich peasants, there is a good chance that they will invest a portion of it. If, however, they are not directly involved in production processes themselves, the chance is small. Thus in accounting for the fact that the Green Revolution technology has taken hold in India's Punjab but not in its West Bengal province, we must take note of the difference in production relations in the two regions.

In the Punjabi economy, rich peasants play a leading role. Rich peasants, possessing more land than they can till themselves, usually hire some labor. Since they themselves take part in farming activities and management, they have an eye open for practices which will raise productivity and profits. At the same time, they are ready to branch out into other profitable activities, including agricultural processing industries. In Meiji Japan (1868–1912), for example, practically every village had a rich peasant who had branched out into sake-brewing (Hirschmeier 1954: 102). Indeed, rich peasants have often constituted a dynamic class of rural entrepreneurs and played a major role in early capitalist development.

The economic behavior of the rich peasant class is guided by its profit opportunities. Thus there is no assurance that its activities will contribute to development; they probably will not if the greatest profit opportunities lie in moneylending or purchasing poor-peasant crops at times of distress for resale later. Further, even if profit opportunities are greatest in agricultural production, they may result in such practices as increasing greatly the use of tractors and other labor-displacing machinery, causing considerable rural distress. The point to be stressed is that the development impact of this class can be determined precisely only by ascertaining the share of the surplus it receives and the manner in which it disposes of it.

Traditional landlords of the Asian type are much less likely to engage in activities which contribute to development. The typical practice, common in prerevolutionary China and still in much of South and Southeast Asia today, is for the landlord to provide the land for a share of the crop, often about 50 percent, or sometimes for a fixed rent which is adjusted to reflect the going norms of what constitutes the appropriate landlord's share. The landlord typically has nothing to do with the actual farm practice—and prefers to keep his hands clean. The surplus flowing to landlords is likely to wind up in luxury consumption, the accumulation of more land, jewelry or other assets, and so forth; it is rarely invested.

In West Bengal, where traditional-type landlords play a much greater role than they do in the Punjab, the Green Revolution has not taken place. The difference between the Punjab and West Bengal in this regard must be understood, at least in part, as a reflection of the differing class structures in the two regions and the differing use of the surplus associated with them. To understand precisely to what extent this is true must await more detailed studies of class structure and surplus use in the two regions than are presently available. It should be noted, concurrently, that class structures are not immutable; they may well shift in response to exogenous factors or class struggles or both. If rich peasants can acquire new technology and use land more profitably than land-lords, the landlords may find themselves under pressure to take an active part in farm management themselves so that they can adopt the new techniques, or sell out to rich peasants who can. This phenomenon has been observed to some extent in India, Pakistan and the Philippines.[9]

The public welfare consequences of development are also deeply affected by the pattern of surplus use. The tenant is among the disadvantaged in rural Asia, but far less so than the landless laborer. Basing rural development on the invest-ment activities of rich peasants implies a great increase in the number of landless laborers, people condemned to a precarious existence when times are good, misery and death when they are not. Contrary to some widely held opinions, increases in poverty and other social maladies do not necessarily suggest that development is not taking place. Rather, they often reflect the patterns of devel-opment produced by a given class structure and its attendant surplus use.

Conclusion

At the outset of the essay, I suggested that the perspective which emphasizes the role of the capitalist world system in sustaining underdevelopment has had un-fortunate consequences in shifting attention away from the domestic sources of underdevelopment and development, away from class structure and surplus use. Once the internal factors influencing development have been investigated prop-erly, however, analysis of the interactions between the domestic economy and the world capitalist system is entirely in order. Contrary to the dominant world system paradigm, however, such interactions do not uniformly block develop-ment, and in most instances where they are unfavorable—in the post-colonial period—the negative impact of the domestic class structure and its attendant pattern of surplus use can be shown to be substantially greater.

To demonstrate these propositions would carry me well beyond the scope of this essay. My point is simply that while development and underdevelopment are ultimately historical processes, the principal factors shaping these processes *today* lie primarily within the Third World countries. An important part is played, however, by the capitalist world economy interacting with their domestic class structures and affecting thereby their patterns of surplus use. Such interac-tions must be investigated after the internal class structures and patterns of sur-plus use have been clarified. This methodology is necessary to forestall the neglect of what is in fact primary, an unfortunate consequence of the widespread influence of world-system theory.

I have argued that both the world-system theory and the emphasis on class structure and surplus use have their roots in the work of Paul Baran. Baran correctly perceived the significance of the surplus concept, and its basic nature as constituting on the one hand society's "discretionary" income, a potential source of development finance, and on the other the specific fruits of class domination, as those who command property, power or both extract their income from the immediate producers. Unfortunately, however, Baran failed to present the concept in a clear and consistent fashion, one which would make it readily usable in empirical research.[10] Furthermore, the predominance of world-system theory, also with its roots in Baran's work, has tended to obscure the critical role the concept of the surplus must play in the analysis of economic development. The intention of this essay has been to confront these two problems by clarifying the concept of the surplus and by indicating its central role, in conjunction with the analysis of class structure, in the analysis of development and underdevelopment.

Notes

1. Some authors have attempted to argue that a substantial surplus outflow takes place via the mechanism of unequal exchange (Emmanuel 1972; Amin 1974). According to this thesis, which assumes that the value (but not the price) of goods is determined by their embodied labor content, goods produced in underdeveloped countries with a given labor content—reflecting not just the number of hours of labor but its level of skill and the capital and technology which accompany it—have a lower exchange value internationally than goods with a comparable labor content produced in advanced countries. Thus, when exchange takes place between the two, additional goods must be provided by the underdeveloped countries, representing an outflow of surplus. Although the concept of unequal exchange is deficient theoretically, I cannot here present a full-scale critique. Let it suffice to note that even if the theory were correct, the surplus which it claims flows abroad through differential pricing would not even exist in the absence of trade, which gives rise to a portion of the surplus by changing the composition of production within underdeveloped countries. Thus it can hardly be claimed that trade draws off a pre-existing surplus, and at most the theory reduces to one of unequal division of the gains of trade.

2. The fullest exposition of the concept of the capitalist world economy appears in the works of Immanuel Wallerstein; see especially *The Capitalist World Economy* (1979).

3. The national income accounting here, and subsequently, ignores net exports (X - M). Government expenditure is not treated as a separate item, but government consumption is included in C and government investment is included in I.

4. The terms "planned investment" and "planned saving" differ from the common Western meaning of "intended investment" and "intended saving"; here they simply mean the investment and saving levels determined by a central planning board.

5. There has been a considerable debate in the literature as to whether the coexistence of capitalist and "precapitalist" relations in UDCs does indeed imply the coexistence of different modes of production. Although I believe it does, there are some who argue that precapitalist relations in the periphery have been restructured into capitalism to serve the needs of capital, and that they reflect therefore the specific form capitalism assumes in the periphery. For a discussion of the relations among modes of production in UDCs see Jairus Banaji (1977), Aiden Foster-Carter (1978), Ashok Rudra, Utsa Patnaik, et al. (1978), and Harold Wolpe (1980).

6. Clearly, some level of public administrative expenditure can be regarded as neces-

sary, as can some level of military expenditure as long as nations exist in a competitive world system. Although some degree of conjecture is inevitable in distinguishing between essential and nonessential government expenditure, reasonable criteria for the distinction can be advanced, and the problem can be minimized by making these explicit.

7. Tenants who operate substantial farms may also be regarded as middle peasants if their incomes are commensurate with those of smallholders who do not hire in or out a great deal of labor. The point here is not to specify a standard class structure for underdeveloped countries, but to indicate the way in which class analysis may be used in estimating essential consumption.

8. To the extent that surplus labor hinders the productive absorption of the former property-income recipients, of course, that is to the extent the marginal product of labor equals or approaches zero, this part of the argument is rendered inapplicable.

9. For Pakistan, the resumption of land from tenants and the conversion of (some) landlords to large-scale capitalist farmers is documented by the Ph.D. dissertation of S. Akmal Hussain (1978). For the Philippines, some comparable examples are provided in Shigeru Ishikawa (1970: 25–31).

10. Technical shortcomings are probably inevitable in the work of anyone who, like Baran, is forced by the tenor of the age to pursue his studies largely in isolation. In Baran's case, they do not diminish the power or relevance of the analysis, but do necessitate such follow-up studies as this one to clarify the conceptual framework and pave the way for empirical research.

References

Amin, Samir. 1974. *Accumulation on a World Scale,* Vol. 1. New York: Monthly Review Press.

Banaji, Jairus. 1977. Modes of Production in a Materialist Conception of History. *Capital & Class* No. 3: 1–44.

Baran, Paul. 1968. *The Political Economy of Growth.* New York: Monthly Review Press.

Baran, Paul and Paul Sweezy. 1966. *Monopoly Capital.* New York: Monthly Review Press.

Emmanuel, Arghiri. 1972. *Unequal Exchange.* New York: Monthly Review Press.

Foster-Carter, Aiden. 1978. The Modes of Production Controversy. *New Left Review* No. 107: 47–77.

Frank, Andre Gunder. 1972a. The Development of Underdevelopment. In, *Dependence and Underdevelopment,* James D. Cockcroft, Andre Gunder Frank and Dale L. Johnson (eds.), pp. 3–17. Garden City, New York: Anchor Books.

————. 1972b. Economic Dependence, Class Structure, and Underdevelopment Policy. In, *Dependence and Underdevelopment,* James D. Cockcroft, et al. (eds.), pp. 19–45. Garden City, New York: Anchor Books.

Hashemi, Syed. 1984. *Class Structure and Surplus Flows in the Economy of Bangladesh.* Unpublished Ph.D. dissertation, University of California, Riverside.

Hirschmeier, Johannes. 1954. *The Origins of Entrepreneurship in Meiji Japan.* Cambridge, MA.: Harvard University Press.

Hussain, Syed Akmal. 1978. *The Impact of Agricultural Growth on the Agrarian Structure of Pakistan.* Unpublished Ph.D. dissertation, University of Sussex.

International Labour Office. 1977. *Poverty and Landlessness in Rural Asia.* Geneva: International Labour Office.

Ishikawa, Shigeru. 1970. *Agricultural Development Strategies in Asia: Case Studies of the Philippines and Thailand.* Tokyo: Asian Development Bank.

Kaldor, Nicholas. 1958. Review of, *The Political Economy of Growth. American Eco-*

nomic Review XLVIII(1): 164–170.

Lippit, Victor D. 1974. *Land Reform and Economic Development in China.* White Plains, NY: International Arts and Sciences Press.

———. 1978. The Development of Underdevelopment in China. *Modern China* 4(3): 251–328.

Nove, Alec. 1977. *The Soviet Economic System.* London: George Allen & Unwin.

Perkins, Dwight. 1975. Growth and Changing Structure of China's Economy. In, *China's Modern Economy in Historical Perspective,* Dwight Perkins (ed.), pp. 115–165. Stanford: Stanford University Press.

Riskin, Carl. 1975. Surplus and Stagnation in Modern China. In, *China's Modern Economy in Historical Perspective.* Dwight Perkins (ed.), pp. 49–84. Stanford: Stanford University Press.

Rudra, Ashok, Utsa Patnaik, et al. 1978. *Studies in the Development of Capitalism in India.* Lahore: Vanguard Books.

Stanfield, Ron. 1973. *The Economic Surplus and Neo-Marxism.* Lexington, Massachusetts: Heath Books.

———. 1974. A Revision of the Economic Surplus Concept. *Review of Radical Political Economics* 6(3): 69–74.

Wallerstein, Immanuel. 1979. *The Capitalist World-Economy.* Cambridge: Cambridge University Press.

Wolpe, Harold (ed.). 1980. *The Articulation of Modes of Production.* London: Routledge & Kegan Paul.

World Bank. 1981. *World Development Report 1981.* New York: Oxford University Press.

12

Institutional and Organizational Framework for Egalitarian Agricultural Growth

Azizur Rahman Khan

Introduction: The Problem

In Asia, as in much of the developing world elsewhere, few countries have evolved an appropriate institutional framework for equitable growth of the agricultural sector of the economy. Much of the South Asian experience in recent decades can be characterized as relative stagnation with inequality while the typical South-East Asian experience is perhaps not too inaccurately characterized as growth with inequality.[1] Certain East Asian experiences have been claimed as solitary examples of growth with equality. The Taiwan area and South Korea are often cited as examples of non-socialist institutional reform leading to egalitarian growth of agriculture. Closer analysis, however, has made it increasingly clear that these are very much in the nature of special cases not likely to be easily replicated elsewhere. For quite some time it was believed that China held out an alternative, socialist example of reasonably rapid growth with a very high degree of equality. While the achievement of China must still be regarded as remarkable, recent official indictments raise serious questions about the effectiveness of the institutional-organizational framework of the commune system in generating an acceptably high rate of growth.

Institutional constraints on growth and equality in the agrarian societies have been a major concern of development theories. Such theories have frequently argued that existing institutions prevent both the attainment of higher output and its better distribution. To give an example, one of the widely held views among

Reprinted by permission from *Growth and Equity in Agricultural Development: Proceedings, Eighteenth International Conference of Agricultural Economists,* eds. Allen Maunder and Kazushi Ohkawa (Oxford, England: Gower, 1983), pp. 229–237.

development economists is that the existing inequality in the distribution of land and the consequent prevalence of widespread labour-hiring in the countries of Asia not only perpetuate inequality but also limit output below the potential level by restricting the use of labour below the level that would obtain under egalitar- ian peasant farming based on family labour (because the market wage that dic- tates the quantity of labour hired for use is higher than the "cost" of family labour). The implication is that an institutional change such as land reform, ushering in peasant farming based on family labour to replace currently wide- spread labour-hiring by larger farms, would promote both higher outputs and its better distribution.

This paper will argue that the above position represents an overly optimistic view. It neglects the important aspect of the cost of institutional change. Such cost arises out of a number of factors. First, there is the cost of transition which is often critical for those poor Asian countries which cannot absorb such cost, in the form of lower output during the transition phase, without going through large-scale starvation. Second, every institution has its own systems of infra- structure and incentives which break down when the institution is overthrown. The new institution has to be provided with its alternative infrastructure and incentive systems. This entails cost in terms of the necessary time for adjustment and resources. The lack of these considerations makes the attraction of institu- tional change as the supposed sufficient vehicle for spearheading the process of egalitarian growth deceptively appealing. In reality the above costs almost al- ways force a trade-off between growth and equality thereby robbing such institu- tional reforms of the attraction of appearing to promote both these objectives. The purpose of the paper is not to preach that one should abandon the path of promoting egalitarian growth through institutional change but to argue that the policymakers must be adequately aware of the costs involved and try to limit them as far as possible by avoiding over-optimism.

Institutional Change through Egalitarian Land Reform

An institutional change that is often recommended for those agrarian societies which are unprepared for or unwilling to make a basic change in their social systems is an egalitarian land reform of the Japanese-South Korean-Taiwanese type. It is argued that equality will be promoted by the egalitarian distribution of ownership of land to which, due to its scarcity, accrues a very high proportion of net output and that production will increase due to the much greater application of labour and effort as a result of the replacement of hired labour by family labour. The highly plausible theoretical argument is reinforced by the practical experiences of South Korea, the Taiwan area and Japan.

The fact that the experience has not been replicated elsewhere has generally been attributed by analysts to the lack of political will on the part of the political leadership and the power of those who own much of the land. It is frequently argued that in the above cases the problem of political will was solved by the presence of an occupation army and the power of the landowning classes had been eroded by the fact that they were (or were the collaborators of) the militarily defeated parties. The problems presented by the lack of political will on the part of the government and the political power of the landowning classes are real obstacles to land reform. However, to attribute the success in these East Asian cases entirely to the solution of these problems appears misleading.

In these East Asian cases, even in the pre land reform days, the operational landholdings were by and large small family farms, without much inequality in their size distribution, although the ownership units were distributed unequally. This is in rather sharp contrast to the phenomenon obtaining in contemporary developing Asia (particularly, South Asia) where the distribution of operational holdings is very unequal. In most cases the degree of inequality is greater in ownership distribution than in the distribution of operational holdings but the absolute inequality in the latter is very high.

The causes of this very different pattern of tenancy between East Asia and the contemporary developing Asia are not clear and is a priority area for interdisciplinary research. However, it is quite clear that the task of carrying out a highly egalitarian land reform was rendered a great deal easier in East Asia by the special characteristics of tenancy prevalent before land reform. The redistribution of ownership units could not have created much disorganization in so far as the operators of landholdings—the actual farmers—did not have to be disturbed significantly. Nor was it necessary for the new owner-operators to acquire entrepreneurial and technical knowledge which they, as tenant-operators, already possessed.

In much of the contemporary developing Asia the circumstances are vastly different in so far as the size of the operational landholdings—the farms—is highly unequally distributed. An egalitarian land reform of the East Asian type must bring about extensive redistribution among operational landholdings. Thus, some kind of a social upheaval is inevitable in carrying out land reform in these countries. This means that in order to face up to the task a much greater political will and organizational power will be required under these circumstances than was necessary in the East Asian cases.

Secondly, even in the unlikely event of finding the political will and organizational power, a good deal of time and resources would be required to replace entrepreneurship, knowledge, and the overall infrastructural network. Those becoming farmers as a result of redistribution will need time to acquire entrepreneurial ability and technological and marketing know-how. More importantly, new channels of credit and investible resources will have to be established. All these will require time and resources. Although some of it will probably be offset by the greater labour use promoted by the institution of peasant farming based on family labour it is highly likely that aggregate output will fall in the short run. The extent of such fall and the length of the time period over which it takes place may be limited if the political will of the reforming government is adequately backed by a strong organization and sensible policies to improve the skills, entrepreneurial abilities and command over resources of the new peasant owners. It is, however, unrealistic to think that such a major social change can be brought about at no cost to society.

On balance, the problem of adequate political will would appear to be the decisive factor. It should, however, be recognized that the need for greater political will derives from the greater obstacle arising out of the more highly unequal distribution of operational landholdings in these countries as compared to the successful East Asian cases.

Collective Agriculture

The presence of political will, so rare a phenomenon in the contemporary non-socialist countries of Asia, is a frequent characteristic of revolutionary socialism. This has often led to thoroughgoing land reforms under its banner. However, revolutionary socialism looks upon egalitarian land reform as nothing more than a brief interregnum marking the transition towards the collective organization of agriculture. An outstanding example is the case of the People's Republic of China which completed a land reform by 1952. According to all available evidence it resulted in a very egalitarian redistribution of rural income and the generation of a high rate of surplus for national investment.[2] And yet within 5 years—by the end of 1957—private farming and land ownership as the partial basis of income distribution were virtually abolished. By then 96 percent of the peasant families had been organized into advanced cooperatives under which land and other means of production ceased to be privately owned and the collective product came to be distributed entirely on the basis of work performed.

The arguments in favor of such rapid transition towards collectivization can be divided into two broad categories: those based on considerations of efficiency and those claiming that it would facilitate greater egalitarianism and quicker transition to socialism and, ultimately, communism. The first set of arguments emphasize the economies of scale, the greater ease in generating high rates of investable and marketable surplus to facilitate industrialization and the mobilization of labour to undertake capital construction. In the Soviet case these considerations—indeed the narrower ones pragmatically contributing to the needs of rapid industrialization—were decisive. Even in the Chinese case many of the arguments were based on considerations of efficiency and the technical transformation of agriculture. Thus Mao Zedong, in his famous report "On the Question of Agricultural Cooperation" in July 1955, argued that socialist industrialization was incompatible with peasant agriculture which would neither generate the required surplus nor create sufficient demand for the output of industry. But Mao also argued the case for collectivization on grounds of equity:

> As is clear to everyone, the spontaneous forces of capitalism have been steadily growing in the countryside in recent years, with new rich peasants spring-

ing up everywhere and many well-to-do middle peasants striving to become rich peasants. On the other hand, many poor peasants are still living in poverty for lack of sufficient means of production, with some in debt and others selling or renting out their land. If this tendency goes unchecked, the polarization in the countryside will inevitably be aggravated day by day. Those peasants who lose their land and those who remain in poverty will complain that we are doing nothing to save them from ruin or to help them overcome their difficulties. Nor will the well-to-do middle peasants who are heading in the capitalist direction be pleased with us, for we shall never be able to satisfy their demands unless we intend to take the capitalist road (Mao Zedong, 1972).

The argument that egalitarian peasant farming after land reform is an obstacle to the distributional goals of revolutionary socialism needs to be understood more clearly. At first, it would appear puzzling. A sufficiently egalitarian peasant farming could do away with wage labour so as to eliminate exploitation in the Marxist sense of the appropriation of surplus value. By continued enforcement of a land ceiling it should be possible to ensure this particular objective.

However, the two kinds of bourgeois rights that Marx talked about in the *Critique of the Gotha Programme* are preserved under this kind of peasant farming as sources of inequality. The first of these rights refers to the inequality in the distribution of rental income among peasant households due to unequal land and resource endowment. In a vast country like China anything remotely resembling strict equality in the distribution of land and assets would be impossible to ensure however thorough the land reforms may be. To curtail this right one must begin by collectivizing land and other assets and then gradually transfer their ownership from lower levels of collectives (for example teams) to higher levels (for example brigades and communes) until the level of ownership by all the people is reached.

The second type of bourgeois right arises out of the principle of relating earning to ability in so far as the latter is not proportionate to need. On this Marx was quite explicit in the *Critique of the Gotha Programme:*

> one man is superior to another physically or mentally and so supplies more labour in the same time, or can labour for a longer time. . . . Further, one worker is married, another is not; one has more children than another, and so on and so forth. Thus with an equal performance of labour, and hence an equal share in the social consumption fund, one will in fact receive more than another, one will be richer than another, and so on. To avoid all these defects, right instead of being equal would have to be unequal (Karl Marx, 1972).

Let us now examine these efficiency and equity arguments against the continuation of the post land reform egalitarian peasant agriculture in the context of achieving the goals of revolutionary socialism. The economies of scale argument is exaggerated in the context of a typical Asian agriculture characterized by a low degree of mechanization. Indeed, it is doubtful if there is any significant economy of scale in farming activities (excluding capital construction). In the mobilization of labour for capital construction there are significant economies of scale that can be taken advantage of under collective institutions. However, such advantage is at best a practical one: in principle, it should be possible to organize such activities by promoting co-operation among equal peasants. In terms of the mobilization of investable and marketable surpluses, again, there are clear practical advantages of collective institutions. It is far easier to collect marketable surplus from a few collective enterprises than from a vast number of peasants. A collective organization, like that of the Chinese communes, provides a framework for a simple system of concealed tax on lower collective units (for example teams) through the drafting of labour (who are given work points by their teams) for work at the higher collective units (for example communes).

While the substitution of peasant farming by collective farming provides some of the advantages of a practical nature noted above from the standpoint of efficiency, it has to face up to a very basic problem of efficiency in the organization of production, namely, the setting up of an incentive system. The nature of agricultural work is such that, as one moves out of the organizational framework of a peasant family into that of a collective, the evaluation of performance, the institution of a system of payments, the organization of management decisions and related matters become exceedingly difficult. If the basic accounting unit is small, as in the case of the *teams* of the Chinese communes, the problem of organizing an efficient system of incentives can still be approached. As the size of the basic accounting unit increases, the supervision and evaluation of work become very difficult and the cleavage between payments and performance becomes large. The organization of incentives on a conventional basis becomes impossible.

From the standpoint of equity, collective agriculture has little advantage over egalitarian peasant farming. The two kinds of bourgeois rights that are the sources of inequality under private peasant farming are also preserved under collective agriculture. The bourgeois right arising out of unequal access to land and productive assets need not be any greater under private farming than under a system of collectives in which the basic accounting unit is relatively small (for example an average team in the Chinese communes consisting of about thirty households). For such a small community in a homogeneous location it should always be possible to make land reform so egalitarian as to provide each household with roughly equal amounts of land and assets per person. The second type of bourgeois right is preserved under collective agriculture in so far as payments are based on the work performed (that is the socialist principle of "to each according to his work").

Indeed, both in the Chinese communes and in the Soviet *kolkhozy* evidence has been found that the income from personal plots is more equitably distributed than the collective income.[3] The present writer has tried to explain this phenomenon as follows:

The distribution of income in the socialized sector, *in principle,* is proportional to the individual members' capacity to work. Individuals differ in terms of such capacity. In the socialized sector such differences in capacity result in larger income differentials because individuals work with relatively large amounts of capital and other resources. Thus the resulting distribution can be as unequal as individuals are in terms of ability. In the non-socialized sector there are such severe limitations on the volume of means of production per person that the differences among individuals' capacity to work cannot be fully translated into differential results of work. As a consequence, the distribution of income can be less unequal than that of the ability to work (Khan and Ghai, 1979).

For a sufficiently egalitarian peasant farming, under the usual kind of land and capital constraint observed in a typical Asian country, the same result would obtain in comparing the outcome of egalitarian peasant farming with the alternative of collective agriculture. The present writer has argued that in China the main gain in terms of improved rural income distribution was achieved by land reform and that since then further gain during successive phases of collectivization has been minimal (Khan, 1977).

Bourgeois rights can be restricted under the system of collective agriculture by raising the level of the basic accounting unit and by the gradual replacement of work done by need as the principle of payment. These, indeed, were tried in some advanced communes in China. It is, however, clear that these practices directly conflict with the conventional principles of organizing an efficient system of incentives. Both these restrictions on bourgeois rights result in the deviation of compensation from effort to such a degree that the material basis for efficient production breaks down unless the human agents of production cease to respond to the usual assumptions of being actuated by self interest (including the interest of the family and, perhaps, the immediate clan). Marx himself was so keenly aware of this problem as to realize that "right can never be higher than the economic structure of society and its cultural development conditioned thereby."[4] The precondition of successfully curbing the bourgeois rights is to bring about such a basic change in the attitudes and responses of the members of the labour force as to make them cease to behave in accordance with the standard assumption of orthodox economics that individuals, households and groups work for higher material consumption. In spite of the brief periods of experimentation in China this is by and large an uncharted path. No human society has yet succeeded in organizing itself on this basis for a substantial length of time and/or on a sufficiently wide scale.

For collective agriculture to provide significantly greater equality than a highly egalitarian, post land reform, peasant agriculture, bourgeois rights will have to be curtailed to such an extent as to make it impossible to set up an efficient system of incentives (in the absence of sufficient preparatory work in effecting basic change in human behavior of proportions not experienced by any human society to date). This will render the collective system a far less efficient organization for productive efficiency in comparison with peasant agriculture. Attempts at hastening the path towards higher levels of collectivization, prompted either by considerations of expediency or by doctrinaire belief in the urgency or feasibility of curbing bourgeois rights, could easily create such great problems of productive efficiency as to require a backward step in the direction of restoring much of the elements of egalitarian peasant farming as the only available method of ensuring efficiency. Recent experiments in China with the so-called responsibility system indicate evidence of this. The lesson seems to be that revolutionary socialism should look upon egalitarian peasant farming, ushered in by post-revolution land reform, as a less temporary stage of agricultural organization and begin transition towards collective agriculture only after the subjective conditions have been fulfilled. As already indicated, a sufficiently egalitarian peasant farming is non-exploitative in the Marxist sense of eliminating the appropriation of surplus value. The bourgeois rights preserved under it can be modified significantly by using the instrument of fiscal policy. In any case, the existing forms of collectives are not able to curb these rights much more significantly.

Some Conclusions

1. Stagnation and growth with inequality in the rural economies of the contemporary developing Asia can be attributed, in substantial degree, to the prevalence of inappropriate institutions that are characterized by a high degree of inequality in the distribution of land and assets.

2. The change in these institutions—in particular, in the unequal distribution of land and assets—is highly desirable from the standpoint of the promotion of equality.

3. The hope that an appropriate institutional reorganization would *automatically promote egalitarian growth* is unrealistic.

4. Much of the hope of a non-revolutionary solution of the institutional problem of agriculture is based on the experience of East Asia. This hope is unlikely to be realized in contemporary developing Asia. Historical difference between East Asia and the contemporary developing Asia makes the cost of such reform in the latter a great deal higher in terms of the necessary political will, organizational ability and resources for an alternative infrastructure.

5. At least from the standpoint of the necessary political will revolutionary socialism appears to be a superior medium [for] instituting successful land reform. Such movements have, however, seen land reform as a short-lived transitional phase on the way to collective agriculture. The rapid transition to collectivization has by and large been promoted by [considerations of] expediency and [the] pragmatic need to generate high enough rates of investable and marketable surplus. The arguments of greater equity and efficiency have rarely

been valid. The generation of greater equity without a loss of efficiency would require fundamental changes on the "subjective" side by way of changing the responses of the human agents. Little preparatory work has ever gone into this. The problem is on the very frontier of human experience. But without some idea as to whether and how it can be resolved the transition to collective agriculture would appear to be premature.

Notes

1. These are broad generalizations to which exceptions can be found. Growth of agricultural production in India during the 1960s and 1970s was about 2¼ per cent per year or just a shade higher than that in population. This was typical of [the] South Asian growth rate. Agricultural growth in Pakistan and Sri Lanka was a little higher while that in Bangladesh and Nepal was a little lower. In South-East Asia agriculture in the Philippines and Thailand grew at annual rates of over 4½ and 5½ per cent respectively. Indonesian growth rate was about 3¼ per cent over the two decades but higher during the 1970s. In both the South and South-East Asian countries inequality continued to be very high. This has been widely documented. For example, see ILO (1977) and Griffin and Ghose (1979).

2. See Charles R. Roll, Jr. (1974) and Khan (1977).

3. See Khan and Ghai (1979) for similar evidence in the Soviet Central Asian Republic and Griffin and Saith (1981) for that in the Chinese communes.

4. The quotation is from Karl Marx (1972). Many Marxists suggest that a higher level of material well-being will automatically make it possible to de-emphasize material incentives. According to this view it will become easy to organize the distribution on the basis of the principle of "to each according to need" once the economy attains a high level of material production. This, to the present writer, sounds like naive optimism which de-emphasizes the need to organize changes on the subjective front.

References

Griffin, Keith, and Ghose, Ajit, "Growth and Impoverishment in the Rural Areas of Asia," *World Development*, Vol. 7, 1979.

Griffin, Keith, and Saith, Ashwani, *Growth and Equality in Rural China*, ARTEP, Bangkok, 1981.

ILO, *Poverty and Landlessness in Rural Asia*, Geneva, 1977.

Khan, A.R., "The Distribution of Income in Rural China," 1977.

Khan, A.R., and Ghai, D.P., *Collective Agriculture and Rural Development in Soviet Central Asia*, Macmillan, 1979.

Mao Zedong, "On the Question of Agricultural Co-operation," in *Selected Readings from the Works of Mao Zedong*, Beijing, Foreign Languages Press, 1971.

Marx, Karl, *Critique of the Gotha Programme*, Beijing, Foreign Languages Press, 1972.

Roll, Charles R., Jr., *The Distribution of Rural Incomes in China: A Comparison of the 1930s and the 1950s*, Harvard Ph.D. Dissertation, 1974.

13

"Market Socialism" and Its Critics

Alec Nove

This paper examines the attack on "market socialism" from the left, i.e., from those who believe that the very term "market socialism" is a contradiction in terms, that the East European reformers are in process of retreat from socialist aims, if not actually restoring capitalism.

This view commands considerable support from the "New Left" both in the West and in parts of the Third World. This species of criticism should be distinguished from the resistance to reform on the part of the party and planning machinery, which, though it sometimes cites similar ideological arguments, is powerfully motivated by bureaucratic habits and self-interest; certainly the New Left critics think that this is so. It is perhaps less easy to distinguish the "left" critique from one sometimes heard from another quarter: that, whether good or bad, market socialism is inconsistent with the vision of Marx and Engels. For Paul Craig Roberts, for instance, it is clear that Marx saw commodity production and markets as characteristic of capitalism, bringing alienation in their wake, and therefore the reformers are un-Marxist, indeed the prewar Lange was also un-Marxist (Roberts, 1971).

This type of Western critic is presumably little interested in the existence or non-existence of viable alternatives to a centralised non-market economy, or in the relative inefficiency of this or that model of a planned economy. If, indeed, it could be proved that market-type reforms were necessary and inescapable in Eastern Europe, Paul Craig Roberts would probably say: well, so be it, but it simply proves that Marx's economic vision was wrong!

This, of course, cannot be the argument of Bettelheim, Sweezy and others like them, who sympathise with Mao's position and, therefore, while opposing both the Soviet leadership (for bureaucracy and conservatism) and the "liberal" re-

Reprinted by permission from *Political Economy and Soviet Socialism,* Alec Nove (London: George Allen and Unwin, 1979), pp. 112–132.

formers (for revisionism), must assert that they have a viable socialist economic model. The present paper will examine in detail the ideas of Bettelheim, as these are expressed in his recent work (Bettelheim, 1970a). His arguments are clear and succinct, and it seems to me that it is useful to consider them seriously. I am not in sympathy with their ideas, but who better than Bettelheim to compel one to develop systematic counter-arguments? In first analyzing and then criticising Bettelheim's ideas, I am trying to see them from a standpoint which, for want of a better phrase, I would call "feasible socialist economics." That is to say, I try to see what form of organisation of production and distribution *could* work, given nationalisation or socialisation of the means of production. To put the same thing in another way: I am seeking for possible ways in which a Soviet-type economy *could* function. I realise that this approach begs an important question: feasibility is hard to define, and the impossible can, given time, become possible. Technical progress, social engineering, the impact of collectivism on human psychology, could alter many of the parameters which affect the discussion. This is doubtless so. However, such changes, if assumed, must be spelled out by the analyst, and not brought in as silent assumptions. Nor can one get round them by facile assumptions about human nature. It is sometimes said that critics of the New Left are prisoners of an outlook formed under acquisitive capitalism, that under socialism men will try to do good. Maybe they will, who knows, though a little scepticism would not be out of place: men have a remarkable capacity for equating the good of society with their own self-interest, a capacity which may have little to do with private ownership of factories and mines. But, in any case, men cannot be expected to do "good" in economic affairs unless it is shown that what *is* good can be identified.

Let me set out Bettelheim's ideas, as I understand them. He begins by noting the "gap which separates the theoretical propositions of Marx and Engels, concerning the socialist mode of production, and the reality of 'socialist countries' " (Bettelheim, 1970a, p. 9). (The words "socialist countries," when used to describe Eastern Europe or the USSR, are always placed in inverted commas.) This, he maintains, is linked with a double misunderstanding: a failure to distinguish between fully developed social systems and those in transition, and a tendency to treat as socialist those systems in transition which have in fact left the socialist road. We shall see that Bettelheim is deeply concerned with problems of transition, and indeed he realises that too rapid a move towards what he would call socialism could be counter-productive. However, he bitterly opposes the "pseudo-decentralisation which is today attempted in the countries of Eastern Europe," which is "none other than the restoration of the 'market mechanism,' implying thereby the abandonment of socialist planning." He concedes that the virtues of socialist planning have been "obscured" by excessive centralisation, a "hypertrophy of the state apparatus" which stands in the way of social control over production and ends up by reinforcing the role of money and market (ibid., pp. 10–11).

Bettelheim has no trouble in establishing that Marx and Engels defined socialism as excluding commodity and market relations. This is most vividly stated in a familiar passage in Engels's *Anti-Dühring*. "Direct social production" will exclude commodity exchange, therefore also the transformation of products into commodities and into values. The quantity of social labour will also be measured directly, in hours. Production plans will be made in the knowledge of the *utility* of various products, compared with one another and with the quantity of labour necessary for their production. "People will decide all this quite simply, without the use of so-called 'value.' "

None of this is the case in "socialist countries" today. In practice, Eastern Europe has an uneasy combination of monetary measures (prices, value categories, etc.) and socially and politically determined priorities, representing two different species of economic calculation. We shall see that Bettelheim finds good reasons to expect their coexistence in the transition period.

To make progress towards socialist economic calculation, it is necessary to begin by identifying the "social utility" (*effet social utile*) of various products. How? "Here is a problem which has not yet been fully solved [*sic*]" (Bettelheim, 1970a, p. 10). All products have in common the fact that they enter into socially organised production and consumption. Bettelheim proceeds to distinguish very carefully between *economic* calculation and *monetary* calculation: the latter uses "not measured magnitudes but *given* multitudes," in the sense that prices are given, without (in capitalism) their level being meaningfully defined or determined. "Economic" calculation in Bettelheim's sense requires taking into account the "substitutability" both of labour and of products, which would seem to admit, indeed require, the concept of opportunity cost. Under capitalism the object of production is the appropriation of surplus value, for which the satisfaction of needs is but a means, hence the link between socially necessary labour and the rationality of profitability as a criterion. But under socialism the theoretical context should be "not one related to values and prices, but *social utility*," and the distribution of productive efforts should be related to *this* measure.

Why, then, has this not happened? Bettelheim advances a number of reasons, among them the inadequate development of productive forces, and also the continued existence of a capitalist world. But he devotes most space to other causes. Thus the inadequacy and contradictory nature of prices in the USSR, Poland, etc., led to a search for better economic calculation, by combining plan and market. He mentions Novozhilov and Nemchinov, but remarks: "These economists' attempts are ambiguous, since they fail to distinguish between economic calculation and monetary calculation," and while they have made an important contribution to the discussion they are none the less "contaminated" by "unscientific ideology" and by the growth of commodity and market relations.

Prices, he insists, conceal rather than bring out the real economic magnitudes. Computations designed to minimise costs or maximise returns are logical enough for capitalists, but they teach us nothing directly about the needs of development of socialist production, or the improvement of conditions of production and of the toilers' existence.... At best they could identify those productive combinations which, within a given structure of prices, wages and techniques, would maximise the total surplus value which capital can extract from the exploitation of labour-power. (Ibid., p. 25.)

(So much for the whole Soviet discussion about optimal programming!)

According to him, socialist economic calculation has also made such slow progress because many Marxist economists have neglected use-value, and have also resisted marginal calculation, although it follows from the differential calculus. Then, he claims, Engels's reference to the "simplicity" of socialist computation has been misunderstood. In fact, he points out,

a product is often the result of the work of all of society, and not only of that labourer or group of labourers who have made it.... Their work involves very large amounts of the work of others, to provide tools and objects of labour and auxiliary means, which are combined within a highly complex social organisation.... Most are made by groupings of workers which also produce simultaneously a great variety of products, so that their contribution to each product cannot be directly measured and requires a highly complex series of analytical operations. (Ibid., p. 30.)

(It does indeed! And how does one go about it?)

So Engels's "simplicity" seems to mean something other than simplicity, merely directness, i.e., identifying need and cost without the interposition of commodity-money relations. But neither the labour input in time nor social utility can yet be measured. So computations using commodity-money categories are in fact made in Eastern Europe. This is inevitable, argues Bettelheim, but can lead to error, and also to illusions.

Bettelheim does not agree with Bukharin's view that economics disappears under socialism. For him, unlike Bukharin, it is *not* concerned exclusively with commodity exchange. Under socialism, economic phenomena would be directly observable, instead of being hidden. Under socialism, there would be not only productive forces to be organised but also relations of production, a complex structure which can be the subject of Marxist economic analysis.

In the transition period, in which value and commodity categories persist, there must be a set of social relations which require such categories. These exist when relations between producers are "duplicated" by relations between proprietors, and when the producers and proprietors are relatively independent and enter into purchase-and-sale relations with one another. These relations are, in Marxist terms, a form of *dissimulation,* i.e., the relations between men take on a "phantasmagoric form of relations between things." Bettelheim remarks, justly, that socialist planned relations can also "dissimulate," because of the great complexity of inter-relations within a plan, which can give rise to "plan fetishism."

This line of thought could lead, however, to stressing the *identity* of opposites, of plan and market, and thus to an identity between perfect market and perfect planning. This would mean accepting the ideas of Pareto and Barone, but he insists that this would be to confuse the different *functions* of plan and market, the confusion being similar to that between (real) economic calculation and monetary calculation.

Under socialism, insists Bettelheim, products will not be made for exchange but for use. There will be no more contradiction between private and social labour. But what about transitional society? The existence of value categories, alongside plan, must mean that "the phantasmagoric forms of relations between things" persist, *and* that lack of information and imperfect organisation limit the action of politics (and of the state planners) upon economics.

But has not private property in means of production been eliminated? Yes, but, said Marx, "useful objects become commodities because they are the products of private work carried on independently of one another." Bettelheim considers, rightly in my view, that the formal ownership is a good deal less important than independence, or autonomy. That is to say, it follows from his argument that any management, whether appointed or elected by the workers, will produce "commodities" (i.e., goods for *exchange*) if its work is organised separately from other groups with other managements. The central plan leaves many gaps, and combines administrative orders with a variety of monetary measures (profit-and-loss account, bonuses for cost reduction, etc., etc.) which are only explicable in terms of an autonomous field of action for management in production and in relations with other managers. This is so even under Soviet centralisation, and is even more obviously so in Yugoslavia or Hungary.

Property is not the point. Preobrazhensky and Stalin thought that value categories survive because of the survival of non-socialist sectors. This is not good enough, writes Bettelheim. One must face up to the survival of "commodity fetishism" within the state sector. The principal reason, he insists, is the fragmentation, the fact that relations have to be established between work which, "though carried out independently, depends more or less on the work of others." The process of co-ordination by plan reduces the area within which commodity relations manifest themselves, imposes constraints on exchanges. But a plan can effectively co-ordinate only on conditions, political ("effective participation of the masses") and economic ("scientific economic and social analysis") which are not yet present (ibid., pp. 53, 54).

But how is one to achieve what Bettelheim calls "the effective participation of the masses in the elaboration and execution of plans," so as to achieve "the effective domination of the producers over the means of production and the product," which for him are the essential features of socialist production relations? He is well aware that all this can be distorted by bureaucracy, privilege, indifference. In some cases the rot has gone so far as to require revolutionary changes. But he refuses to be precise on how a real socialist plan should operate.

All depends on circumstances, the degree of development of production forces. There could be many combinations of central plan and the "superposition of mutually co-ordinated plans" below the central level.

Within these conceptions, it is obvious that reforms designed to increase the influence and range of action of market forces are highly offensive to Bettelheim.

During the transition period, "ownership" by the state could be more juridical than real. Power over property, possessions, can belong in some degree to the management. This would be analogous to the ownership by shareholders of property with a degree of *de facto* control of managers under modern capitalism. The state, if it is a workers' state, by imposing limits on enterprise autonomy, should be enforcing "the domination of the toilers" over production, over "the means and results of their labour." It therefore follows that, while the existing state or planning mechanism may have many defects, in principle Bettelheim opposes the idea of enterprise autonomy, insofar as it is precisely by (correct) intervention that the interests of the whole toiling masses are given priority over the monetary computations of the enterprise. But he recognises that, even in a workers' state, there could be a "separation of the workers from their means of production," since the state, by reason of its remoteness, may not be the best means of ensuring the domination of labour. Possibly, the Chinese communes provide a suitable model, a higher form than that of "state property pure and simple," because they are also *political* organs, within which social-political desiderata take priority over the economic. However, it does not seem that Bettelheim is well acquainted with the Chinese model.

The word "enterprise" requires definition, and Bettelheim finds it inapplicable to socialism, preferring "production unit." An "enterprise" operates with money, pays wages, administers sub-units, possesses a profit and loss account. It is thus capitalist in its very nature, even if it is "self-managed" in the Yugoslav manner. For, "in the absence of socialist planning, the enterprise, whether or not 'self-managed,' is dominated by capitalist production relations, and must work for the return on its capital (*mise en valeur de son capital*)." Even when the enterprises are subject to control and intervention from the planners they remain an institution within which capitalist relations reproduce themselves. "Only a revolutionarisation of the production units can put an end to this capitalist apparatus and replace it by a new apparatus" (ibid., pp. 70–71). (But which?) Enterprises by their existence separate workers from their means of production and separate productive units from each other (*"double séparation"*).

In passing, Bettelheim makes the interesting point that economies of scale under capitalism could be the result of capitalist economic relations rather than of techniques as such. This is certainly a valid observation with regard to the size of firms, and perhaps also to the size of some equipment, since both could give *organisational* economies, which by no means follow if the mode of production is radically altered. However, his corollary is a more questionable one: that the

Chinese have avoided the burdens of primitive socialist accumulation by not copying Western capitalist techniques, thus providing a model superior to that of the USSR.

The "enterprise," then, is appropriate to capitalist ideology: hiring and firing, hierarchy, discipline are its features, which go naturally with production for sale. He advocates "the ideological revolutionarisation of the workers, which causes them to affirm themselves as the real masters of production," leading to "the elimination of money in the relations between productive units . . . the domination of the plan over productive units." How? "In the form of the domination of the workers over the means of production" (ibid., pp. 76, 77), a domination which the plan must express.

Bettelheim builds on. the idea of state capitalism, a system of state-owned enterprises associated with the era of imperialism. He sees it as an unstable, transitional phase, which could slide into capitalism, through the growth of market relations. Surplus value under state capitalism can be used for socialist purposes by a workers' state, but it can be misappropriated by a "ruling class" consisting of an alliance of managers and their (state) controllers.

In one of his recent articles, Bettelheim stressed the importance, from the point of view of socialism, of "the nature of the class in power." He notes that "to identify 'plan' with socialism and 'market' with capitalism (which is true tendentially) aids the bourgeoisie (and notably the Soviet bourgeoisie), to exercise its domination under cover of a 'plan' in the name of which it withdraws all rights of expression from the exploited classes" (Bettelheim, 1970b, p. 8). In other words, for him the plan can be "an instrument of the domination of the direct producers over the conditions and results of their activity" only under certain political-social conditions. Only then the plan becomes "a 'concentrate' of the will and aspirations of the masses, of their correct ideas." (Ibid., p. 9. Shades of Rousseau's *volonté générale!*)

He returns several times to the need for a *calcul économique social.* "Commodity relations link production units through their products, not through their work. The work is done in each unit separately, and *they are thus not directly related [confrontés]*. This is precisely the characteristic of commodity production . . . which renders impossible a real economic calculation, a direct measure of socially necessary labour" (Bettelheim, 1970a, p. 81). Yugoslav enterprises serve merely to divide the workers, who only have the illusion of self-management, since "they cannot really dominate the use of either their means of production or of their products, since this is itself dominated by commodity (i.e., market) relations" (ibid., p. 82).

Bettelheim admits that, "in the transition period," the (workers') state's exercise of power over property separates the direct producers from "their" means of production, of which "they are owners only through the intermediary of the state." This would be acceptable if "the state apparatus is genuinely dominated by the toilers." Otherwise, the state officials become "the effective owners."

They dispose of the surplus as they think best, and are "compelled to grant a dominant role to the market and to profitability criteria" (ibid., p. 87). This can be shown from "the history of the USSR during the past ten years" (!!). The alternative is that state property and state capitalism should be replaced "by social appropriation"(?). Instead of this, one sees in Eastern Europe unstable combinations of commodity relations and administrative orders, the latter being sometimes obeyed by enterprise managers, and this is not a real plan. It is then a short step for revisionist critics to see the need for a strengthening of market relations in the interests of "efficiency."

How, then, should relations between productive units be organised? Bettelheim (rightly) stresses the need for diversity. If relations between given units are continuous and close, they could become larger "complex units" with some species of joint management. These larger units could be inter-related "either by the plan, or by the joint management, or by one of the units which dominates others," or finally there could be "direct relations" between productive units.

The contradictions in the transition period between plan and market are in some respects analogous to the contrasts within a capitalist corporation between the profit of the whole corporation and that of its parts. The general social interest, embodied in the plan, must (for Bettelheim) represent *politics* expressing the domination of "direct producers." Otherwise, the plan is a "phoney" (*simulacre*).

"The means of establishing socially useful links between economic units and techniques can be increasingly concentrated at the level of the planning organs, closely connected with the various workers' collectives, corresponding to a real social appropriation" (ibid., p. 111). (I must admit that for me this is peroration and not economics.)

Politics dominates economics, says Bettelheim, yet the economic factor is dominant. How can this be? The answer: "The economic is the determinant through the intermediary of politics." But some cannot see this, and proclaim the interference of the political organs to be arbitrary. This could only be so if it is "subjectivist and voluntarist," unscientific, etc. In the USSR this is indeed often so. Ineffective forms of state intervention cause conflict and confusion. An apt phrase: the top planners "face a screen between themselves and reality, which also acts as a mirror which transmits back to the planners an image of their own wishes." Plans are thereby "fulfilled" formally, but only formally.

How can one achieve the subordination of state institutions to the "direct producers"? Only through struggle against a constant "tendency to *separate* the functions of control and direction and those of carrying out the work. This tendency is itself inscribed in the ideological relationships produced by *institutions* . . . inherited from societies dominated by non-workers." The fundamental law of developed socialism is the "law of the social direction of the economy," under which one has a direct economic and social calculation, which does not proceed by the detour of the law of value, as Engels said (ibid., pp. 124, 125).

Since in the transition period there must be prices, these should (according to Bettelheim) be plan prices, which reflect economic policy and not "the exigencies of the law of value." Then the allocation of labour will be subordinated to the construction of socialism, i.e., to achieving "the direct control of the immediate producers over production ... therefore for the present and future needs of the producers," politically evaluated. In particular, "the planning and investment should no longer be subordinated to the criterion of rate of return, whether financial or monetary." Instead, we should have the criterion of *"social and political efficacy"* (his emphasis) (ibid., p. 125). This he equates with Stalin's 1952 formulation about "profitability from the standpoint of the whole national economy."

In his discussion with Sweezy, Bettelheim elicited from the latter the following statement of a common position:

> When the bureaucratically administered economy runs into difficulties, as it certainly must, there are two politically opposite ways in which a solution must be sought. One is to weaken the bureaucracy, politicise the masses and ensure increasing initiative and responsibility to the workers themselves. This is the road towards socialist relations of production. The other way is to put increasing reliance on the market, not as a temporary retreat (like Lenin's NEP) but as an ostensible step towards a more efficient "socialist" economy. . . . It is, I submit, the road back to class domination and ultimately the restoration of capitalism. (Bettelheim, 1970a, p. 21.)

Bettelheim warns against too rapid an elimination of prices and money. Their use follows from the relative autonomy of production units, from the unavoidable incompleteness of planning in the "period of transition." Planned prices should encourage productive units to behave in line with the plan, to minimise cost, and so on. Premature abandonment of this is likely to lead to confusion, as it has done (he maintains) in Cuba. It is too early to reconcile efficient use of means of production with purely quantitative allocation. Prices are real, sums of money are paid, and this is necessary, though this means imperfect, "indirect" calculation and requires limitations on the role of money. (All this seems to be a case against ultra-ultra-leftism.)

Bettelheim speculates about a possible "multi-level social unit of calculation," perhaps an international one, and promises to examine this question in a subsequent work.

He says, rightly, that rationing of scarce resources can be a consequence not of socialist planning as such, but of imbalance, of failure to co-ordinate. It is silly "to blame money for disequilibria which it merely brings to light," and which cannot be abolished merely by eliminating money (Bettelheim, 1970b, p. 135).

At the end of the transition period? Well, then we would have "ideological socialist relations," which will be constituted by the co-operation of production units with the object of the realisation of a socially optimal totality (*un ensemble*) of economic and political purposes. Such co-operation will assure the socialist independence of production units, achieved by "the extension of the field of action of direct producers (*producteurs immédiats*), their domination over the conditions of production and reproduction" (ibid., p. 134). (Once again, to me this is eloquent rather than informative.)

So ends my summary of Bettelheim's case. What comment or critique can and should be made?

The first point that occurs to me is to be astonished at the omission of any mention of scarcity and abundance. True, Bettelheim refers to the insufficient development of productive forces as one of the factors responsible for the survival of "commodity" relations, but he nowhere even begins to define what he regards as "sufficient." His repeated statements about choice leave one to infer that he means choices between alternative ends and means, that by doing or making A one is not doing (or doing less of) B. Were it otherwise, it would be his duty to say so. We must therefore assume that the needs of all the members of society are greater than the means available to satisfy them, certainly in the transition period, and presumably also when "socialism" in his definition comes about. His definition says much about the producers' control over production and the product, and about the direct measurement of social utility without the interposition of money. The word "abundance" does not occur. We must therefore assume that many citizens wish to obtain more of certain things than can at that time be produced, that inputs are limited, so that opportunity-cost is a reality. It is in *this* sort of situation that Bettelheim calls for his complex of socialist measures, not an imaginary utopia in which all is available in plenty to all. In any case, his critique of East European reformers can only make any sense in the context of an economy coping with relative scarcities.

Let us now tackle a fundamental Bettelheimian proposition: that the *producers* should control the instruments of production and the product. What does this mean? If the proposition affirms the right of the members of a producers' collective to decide among themselves the conditions of their work, this represents a comprehensible plea for industrial democracy and self-management. But surely Bettelheim means more than this. If he does, then he must be wrong. Suppose a group of workers are operating some physical plant which produces sulfuric acid, or bread, it does not matter which for the present purpose. It is *at least* as reasonable to assert that the product, and therefore the use to which the instruments of production are put, should be determined by the *user*, the *consumer*, as by the producer. Bettelheim criticises the Yugoslav "self-management" model because "the workers *cannot really dominate* the use of their means of production or of the product, because their use is itself dominated by market relations." *But why should they do so?* If a market does not indicate what the customers (users, consumers) want, then some other person or institution must. Bettelheim might reply: "Oh, but the collectivity of workers discuss the needs of their customers in a comradely way." Then one must ask him: "Yes, but under conditions of relative scarcity there will be more potential customers (at zero prices) than productive capacity. On what basis will the workers decide which need it is best—from the standpoint of society—to supply?" It is not a question of good will or bad will, but one of knowledge. This is quite unclear in Bettelheim's model. He implies that the central planners and various intermediate bodies will co-ordinate everything. But if a central planner *tells* the producers of bread and sulfuric acid what they ought to produce, then are they "really dominating" their own equipment and products?

Choices are to be made about end-products based upon units of social utility. Presumably, these choices must be made by central planners? I cannot see how a collectivity, a group of workers, engaged in making buttons, sulfuric acid, thread, skirts, internal combustion engines or whatever, can compare alternative social utilities. At that level, this is simply not possible. How would planners carry out their vital function? Let us abstract from such possibilities as inertia, laziness, indifference. The planners, and the political leaders, are hereby assumed to be the nearest approach to angels conceivable in an irreligious world: they wish to do good by their fellow-men. How do they go about discovering men's needs, at zero price, and arranging them in order upon a scale of social utility? In what units is social utility to be measured? We are dealing here with a country, numbering millions of people, not a couple of hundred *kibbutz* members who can meet together, argue, vote (and then purchase their needs in a market economy). We are dealing with a range of consumer goods which, fully disaggregated by type, run into millions of variants. It is true, of course, that some goods or services can be, often are, produced or supplied by political decision which is not derived from a market: water, for instance, or education. One could decide on a free ration of bread, milk, toilet paper. Museums could be free, and so could babies' diapers or medicines. The possibility or desirability of having a segment of the economy where goods or services are supplied without payment is hardly in dispute in principle. But we may be sure that Bettelheim has much more than this in mind, his vision is all-inclusive. Can he then not even hint *how*, along what lines, the measurement of social utility is to take place, and *who is to do the measuring*?

While I do not suggest that Bettelheim does or should follow the doctrines of Trotsky, it is not irrelevant at this point to quote Trotsky's ideas, because they at least grapple with the problem of scarcity, and, it seems to me, have a much more realistic view of its consequences.

Firstly, Trotsky ascribed "the basis of bureaucratic rule" to shortages of consumer goods.

> When there are enough goods in a store, purchasers can come whenever they want to. When there are few goods, the purchasers are compelled to stand in line. When the lines are very long, it is necessary to appoint a policeman to keep order. Such is the starting-point of the power of the Soviet bureaucracy. It

"knows" who is to get something and who is to wait. . . . Nobody who has wealth to distribute ever omits himself. (Trotsky, 1964, pp. 159, 160.)

Bettelheim may object that Trotsky was writing about a poor society at a difficult moment. True. But if demand exceeds supply, at any price or at zero price, there will be queues, for bread at primitive levels, for spare parts for motor vehicles (or for motorcycles) at higher standards of life. It is Bettelheim's duty to take this point seriously.

Trotsky again:

> Cast-iron can be measured in tons, electricity in kilowatts. But it is impossible to create a universal plan without reducing all branches to one and the same value denominator. If the denominator is itself fictitious, if it is a product of bureaucratic discretion, then it eliminates the possibility of testing and correcting the plan in the process of its implementation. (Trotsky archives, cited in R.B. Day, 1973.)

Of course, Trotsky is talking about the transition period, and still envisages some sort of moneyless communism ahead. But quite clearly he would be unhappy about Bettelheim's notion of plan prices, because "they open up unlimited room for bureaucratic subjectivism in the area of planning," to add another phrase from the same Trotsky source. Nor did Trotsky see the coexistence of plan and "commodity" elements in the same spirit as Bettelheim. For the latter, conflict between plan and market forces is almost synonymous with the struggle between the workers' state and the law of value. Trotsky, it would seem, was concerned with a reconciliation or balance between them. "Only the interaction of three elements, of state planning, of the market, and of Soviet democracy can provide the country with proper leadership in the transitional epoch." (*Byulleten' oppozitsii,* 1932, no. 5, also cited in Day, 1973.) Bettelheim may reply that he admits the survival of money-commodity categories in the transition period. But surely he does so most grudgingly, in a highly theoretical sense, and in much more abbreviated time scale, unrelated (almost) to the abundance within which full communism is alone conceivable in pure theory. (Abundance and queues cannot coexist.)

Sweezy wrote:

> It is obvious that what is needed is, in Bettelheim's words, "domination by the immediate producers over their conditions of existence, and therefore in the first instance over their means of production and their products." *The question, however, is what this means* and, perhaps equally important, what it does *not* mean. *There are no ready-made answers to this question* and (to the best of my knowledge) *very few studies bearing upon it.* (Sweezy, 1972, p. 9. Emphases mine.)

One might think that such studies might antedate attacks on the East European reformers for not doing what perhaps cannot in fact be done. Furthermore, there is a basic unclarity about the meaning both of "socialism" and of the "transition period." Sweezy at least distinguishes between both these terms and the more advanced state of "full communism" (e.g., see ibid., p. 9, "a viable socialism . . . capable of moving forward on the second leg of the journey to communism"). Sweezy also discusses equality, and is willing to contemplate "a high price in terms of immediate output and efficiency for achieving and maintaining it." (Undeniably, market relations do carry with them dangers of excessive inequality, though experience suggests that a state-operated non-market economy is not free of this danger either.) He also shows a proper concern for the relationship between needs and resources. "The absurd and ultimately disastrous bourgeois notion of insatiable wants must be decisively repudiated," he writes (ibid., p. 12). One can repudiate all one pleases, but the economic and social fact of relative scarcity is not thereby eliminated.

And what about choice of means? How does one compare costs? In hours, perhaps modified to take care of unequal skills? This would be totally unsatisfactory. Firstly, as Bettelheim himself said, to measure the number of hours devoted to each product is a very complex affair indeed. Secondly, it ignores altogether the relative scarcity of different means. Novozhilov once pointed out that the latest machine is bound to be in short supply, even under full communism, unless it be assumed that technological progress ceases. How does opportunity-cost enter into cost measurement in hours? Over fifty years ago, there were many "moneyless" schemes. In 1920 Strumilin had imagined "the utility of products" as the criterion for output decisions, but choice of means, and indeed transactions between enterprises, were left undefined. Yurovsky's critique is worth quoting: "Karl Marx analysed social relations in capitalist society from the standpoint of expenditure of labour on production of commodities, but this cannot of itself serve as a basis for making this capitalist principle [i.e., labour as a basic of value] a feature of socialist practice." Strumilin and his ilk wrongly ignore gifts of nature. Has land in the centre of cities not an especially high scarcity-value? How, without money, can one compare investment alternatives? How can the organ responsible for production and investment even begin to identify economic effectiveness? At best it can achieve an input-output balance (in Yurovsky's words, *svesti kontsy s kontsami*), but is this the best way to satisfy social needs? It would make more sense if the planners could allocate resources towards those items for which people are willing to pay more, "since the willingness to pay more is itself evidence that the given product is more wanted." But of course this requires a market for consumer goods. The state would invest in the indicated directions, earning a surplus, "a kind of interest rate on capital" and thereby finance accumulation. "Only the memory of the fact that interest on capital forms a class income in capitalist society can serve as a psychological basis for a refusal to make calculations of this type. No rational basis for such a refusal exists." (Yurovsky, 1928, pp. 115–19.)

Yurovsky's argument is the stronger because he knows (and I also know!)

that the price system is imperfect, that frequently "monetary computation and social welfare do not coincide" (ibid., p. 94). There are externalities, uncertainties, fluctuations, which distort in some degree every price system. This is not in dispute. Nor can anyone doubt that the *indirect* identification of wants and of means, through the medium of money and exchange, can in itself cause disequilibria: this was said long ago by Tugan-Baranovsky, and indeed underlies Keynes's analysis. It is the main reason why Say's law fails to work. But surely it behooves a critic to be aware of the function of money. It has existed for some millennia, in a variety of forms, because it fulfills a number of purposes: it facilitates choice, it is a medium of calculation, it helps to identify need, it serves in the search for the best means to satisfy needs. That it does all these things imperfectly is no reason for denouncing it unless some better method is found. Economists in Moscow's TsEMI told me that the only way in which planners could identify what people wanted was to let them "vote with the ruble." Otherwise, they would not know what advice to give to the political leadership concerning the needs of society. They added, rightly, that some of society's needs manifest themselves other than through the market (e.g., the need for leisure, public parks, education, etc., etc.), and some that do manifest themselves ought to be discouraged (e.g., vodka).

Bettelheim repeatedly asserts the need for politics to dominate economics. What does this mean? Can he define his terms? If, with an acceptable distribution of income, *economic* forces imply an unsatisfied demand for cuddly toys, crusty white rolls, books by Dostoevsky, decorated chinaware or dining tables, on what "political" ground should such "economic" forces be resisted? Is not all Soviet experience a warning against *not* insisting that the planners have a *duty* to respond to such economic forces as these? Indifference to people's needs is a danger to be guarded against, is it not, rather than strengthened by doctrines about the primacy of politics? The same is true of choices of means. If a given machine, location, design, fulfills requirements most economically, then it releases more resources utilisable for the satisfaction of other wants. This sets up the presumption that it is the best choice to make. True, this presumption can be shown to be mistaken. Kalecki once said: "The worst thing to do is not to calculate; the second worst thing is to follow blindly the results of your calculation." There may be reasons, known to *all* economies, for taking a different decision: external effects, regional policies, and so on. This was known even to the tsar's ministers when they decided to build railways, and it is known to the East European reformers.

It is simply not good enough to quote approvingly Stalin's 1952 dictum about profitability from the standpoint of the whole economy. To consider *each* decision from such a standpoint is totally impracticable, because the size of resultant bureaucracy would be counter-productive and self-defeating. In all economies, decision making incurs costs. One *cannot* take all the consequences of everything into account, though ideally no doubt one should. It is necessary to identify those *kinds* of decisions which do have external effects so considerable that intervention of central authority is called for. But even granted that this happens frequently, this does not necessarily justify the emphasis on "politics" versus "economics." Thus, the railway line to Odessa was of immense *economic* benefit to Russia, even though most of this benefit did not show up in the accounts of the railway itself. The Yugoslav government's successful measures to stimulate tourism on the Adriatic coast was not the triumph of politics *over* economics, but the carrying out by the state of sound economic measures. If the state is the principal investor, as must be the case if private capital does not exist, investment decisions are in a formal sense "political," i.e., they are taken by ministers. But ministers are super-managers. The government must combine its function as board of directors of "USSR Ltd." with its political function. Why advise it, as Bettelheim seems to do, to put political considerations first? What political considerations? What about Trotsky's "unlimited room for bureaucratic subjectivism?" Would it not have been better for him to speak of the *merging* of the political and economic, in the sort of sense in which the head of the government *is* the head of the economy, *ex officio* chief planner?

Of course, Bettelheim is for responsiveness and rationality, and he hates "bureaucratic subjectivism" as much as anyone. But *by what criteria,* under his pattern of thinking, can a bureaucratically subjectivist decision on resource allocation or investment be identified as such, and contrasted with the "correct" decision? One of the most astonishing of his assertions is that "the domination of the state bourgeoisie" leads to the growth of monetary and market relations, and that this is apparent from the history of the Soviet Union in the past ten years (Bettelheim, 1970a, p. 87). Not only is the "state bourgeoisie" resisting the economic reforms with fair success, but it is somehow implied that the Stalin period was in some undefined respect superior, either because the state was to a greater extent a workers' state, and/or because it was able to a greater extent to impose social-political priorities against commodity-and-market forms. Bettelheim was rather uncritical of Stalin, but surely he knows that bureaucratic indifference to the needs of ordinary people became very deeply ingrained precisely under Stalin's rule, *and* that arbitrary irrationalities in economic decision making were exceedingly common. With all its imperfections, the Soviet system under Brezhnev is surely somewhat more alive to people's needs, more conscious of the duty to study and provide for them than it was in Stalin's day. True, what Bettelheim calls the "state bourgeoisie" feel more secure from arbitrary arrest, and their individual needs may be better catered for. This must be taken into account in any serious "class" analysis of the present-day Soviet system. But it would be far-fetched, would it not, to ignore the reduction in wage differentials, the housing program and a few other features of "the past ten years," and to imply that somehow the working-class or socialist principles were in better shape in 1952 than in 1972.

Perhaps by the priority of politics Bettelheim has in mind the priority of the struggle to achieve socialism, as against a "pure" economic rationality. But he continues to insist on this even under socialism, even under conditions where it is by no means clear who is struggling with whom for what. He should clarify.

Bettelheim himself admits an evolution in his thinking: he now realises that state ownership plus planning is not of itself enough, indeed does not prevent the emergence of a new ruling class, the "state bourgeoisie" (Bettelheim, 1970b, pp. 8–9). Good. One wishes he were clearer about the connection between central planning (i.e., the systematic replacement of market relations) and the power of the political-planning-managerial machine. In the name of what Marxist-analytical principle should one expect them *not* to take advantage of their social situation? Is this not idealism? Is it sensible to compare an imaginary perfect harmony in a moneyless economy with imperfect markets? This is like a Western right-wing scholar comparing perfect competition and optimal resource allocation *à la* Chicago with the messy reality of the USSR, a procedure I once defined as "comparing model with muddle."

Finally, let us get down to a key point of the entire argument. Bettelheim *rightly* relates "commodity production" not to property but to fragmentation, division. It follows that he must face a contradiction. If *"les producteurs immédiats"* are to feel that their means of production are under their control, then clearly they must be in a position to decide what is done with them. In Yugoslavia, the elected management committee decides by reference to the market. In his scheme, the decisions *must* logically be subordinate to the planning apparatus. A factory making sulfuric acid or machine tools is a segment of a closely inter-related whole, as Bettelheim knows, indeed insists. In the absence of market-type links with the rest of the economy, the workers can no more be allowed to decide on their own what they should do than the railwaymen at Crewe can decide what trains should run through Crewe. When, in a market economy, systematic links are very tight-knit, they are often of a non-market type. The use of Crewe station is such an example. Not the invisible but the visible hand governs its operations. Of course, a "socialist" Crewe would also be in this position, taking *instructions* about its operations. Bettelheim's marketless world of collectivities must also be subject to the visible hand. How can they decide for themselves? Every decision about what to produce, whom to supply, whence to draw inputs, has external effects, in the sense that it calls for economic decisions and has consequences in places for which the given collectivity is not responsible; it has consequences which it cannot even estimate. It is *not* a question of pessimistic assumptions about the goodness of Man. We are discussing the identification of what is the right thing for Men (or a given group of men) to do, what Man *must* know to be able to take decisions.

To operate such a system requires a large body of officials. At the very least it must lead to the danger of bureaucratic deformation. Appeals to democracy are of little relevance, not because democracy is unimportant, but because it is hard indeed to apply it to the complex task of managing and planning a moneyless economy. A simple example will suffice. The phrase "voting with the ruble" has some operational meaning as a guide to what people might prefer, though the mechanism does work imperfectly in the real world and cannot be expected to be perfect. But "voting through the ballot-box" *cannot* be an operational means for ascertaining people's wants, save in the form of very broad priorities which are at best general indications to planners (e.g., more housing and schools). The ballot-box is even less relevant to decisions about the use of plastics, alternative ways of power generation or other questions to do with means.

Of course, one could envisage upward and downward communications, involving citizens as consumers, production units, local authorities, industrial associations, planners, political leaders. But the existence of information flows cannot, with the best will in the world, be more than the first precondition for correct choice between alternatives. It can quite easily multiply the number of possible courses of action between which choices must be made.

Bettelheim seems silently to ignore the question of conflicts of interest, apparently believing that in a socialist society everyone is in some sort of mystic communion with everyone else. This seems to me to be either Rousseau's "*volonté générale,*" or idealism, or both. Of course, class differences can lead to conflict. But are there not other contradictions too? Call them non-antagonistic if you must, but they must go on existing, if only because, to a Marxist, a world without contradictions is a world without movement.

Let us look at a few contradictions relevant to our theme. They all arise from the fact of scarcity in relation to possible or potential desires of people—for beautiful houses, bridges, roads, television sets, clothes, holiday trips, pictures, etc., etc. In a world context, even simpler desires are unlikely to be fulfilled for the bulk of the people for many generations, and we must meanwhile organise an economy which is capable of meeting as many needs as possible (subject to constraints imposed by ecology as well as productive capacity). The word "equality" figures in this book of Bettelheim's as little as does scarcity, but let us assume that he desires a considerable degree of equality. It remains the case that differences of opinion will arise even on what constitutes equality. (Per family or per capita? What compensations for unpleasant nature of job, heavy responsibility, etc.; how much interchangeability of occupations? How much higher education should be provided and for whom?) Inhabitants in a given area will strive for improvements which inhabitants elsewhere might prefer to have in *their* area. Producers of a given product might prefer not to make the effort needed to give greater pleasure to the users of the product, claiming (and how will it be disproved?) that the effort is greater than the extra satisfaction which it yields. Professor Bettelheim's wish to extend library holdings in Paris on his subject may come into conflict with the wishes of his confrères in the University of Rennes (or of Calcutta). My desire for a new theatre in Glasgow is not necessarily shared by those who wish to build more houses or schools instead.

All these examples are unrelated to class conflict. They must occur if resources are insufficient to meet needs. Some of these conflicts have to be reconciled by a political process in all systems. My point is that Bettelheim *puts into this process the whole economy,* even while he withdraws such objective guidelines (via the hated "law of value" and price mechanism) as can be available to the decision makers.

The whole complex issue of centralisation-decentralisation is complex precisely because people see things differently at different levels. This is so partly because of their situation (i.e., what they know, what they are responsible for), partly because of interest. ("Nobody who has wealth to distribute ever omits himself," wrote Trotsky. Please note the word *"ever."*) One cannot assert that the right action will always be discerned either at the centre, or the periphery, or at some intermediate level. Bettelheim does agree that a variety of organisational forms would be necessary. What he seems unable to grasp is that, in a modern integrated economy, the lower levels will have nothing to guide them except instruction from the higher levels, *unless* they base their activities on some objective criteria such as might be provided (though imperfectly) by price-and-market signals. The invisible hand *might* be consistent with workers' self-management. The visible hand *must* imply a vastly complicated system of instructions and administrative allocation, operated by a large and complex group of people whose role and functions incline them to bureaucratism. The "struggle" against bureaucratism could not be carried on by fine phraseology (to which the French language well lends itself) about the toiling masses, or even by denouncing bureaucracy. One must devise ways in which *objective* measurement becomes both a check on bureaucratic distortion and a guideline to the conscientious official anxious to do his job well. Alternatively, one must find means to remove from the "bureaucrats" responsibility for various decisions, which compels one to seek alternative *criteria,* which enables one to dispense with over-centralisation. How is all this to be done? In Bettelheim's transition period it cannot be done at all if economists advise the government that they should alter prices so as to facilitate the achievement of the plan. If they do this, they cannot discover a basis of determining what the plan should be. It is by no means clear to me how they determine it when "socialism" in Bettelheim's sense is reached.

I wish that Bettelheim, or those who think like him, would criticise the Hungarian or Soviet reformers from a standpoint which bears some relation to what in fact could be *done,* within a reasonable time-span, in the countries concerned. Might he not at least contemplate the possibility that the attempt to replace "the law of value" with central resource allocation is itself partly responsible for the bureaucratic deformation that he denounces? How can a "workers' state" be one, or remain one for long, if a multitude of officials control the productive apparatus of the economy? They *are* the substitute for the market, a substitute also, surely, for meaningful "self-management." To fulminate about the bureaucratic behaviour of bureaucrats is satisfying to the psyche, but is not very useful. The *zamglavmetalsnab* in Moscow acts as he does because of the whole logic of his functions, not through ideological backsliding or hostility to "the working class" from which he has himself probably sprung. In Mao's China he might have to spend a period hoeing cabbages in a village, but I doubt if this will affect his behaviour as a *zam.*

This is not an attack on socialism, or a disguised glorification of the market mechanism in any form: only a plea for some hard thinking and for avoiding question-begging generalities. It is unreasonable to ask Bettelheim for any *precise* blueprint of his future world, but it is not unreasonable to request him to indicate in the most general form how his economy *might* function. Quotations from Marx and Engels are not enough. In his speech following the death of Lenin, Bukharin listed a number of phenomena which had arisen since the death of Marx and could not have been known to him. He asked: "What do we mean by Marxism? It is a methodology—a system of investigating social phenomena . . . is it a certain set of ideas . . . and in addition a set of concrete guidelines (*polozhenii*)?" He then went on to assert, rightly, that Leninism, while consistent with Marxist methodology, went beyond "the sum of ideas that Marx actually had" about the reality which he knew. (Heitman, 1967, pp. 223–224. *Lenin kak marksist,* 1924.) Marx and Engels, especially the Engels of *Anti-Dühring,* could simply have been mistaken about how a modern industrial socialist economy could be run, just as they might well have been astonished had they seen Russia as the first country with a "Marxist" regime. Other things which they could not have foreseen could have modified their views. They did several times insist, did they not, that the shape of a future socialism was not known to them?

Counter-attack invited. *Messieurs, c'est à vous de tirer.*

References [excerpts]

C. Bettelheim (1970a): *Calcul économique et formes de propriété,* Paris.
C. Bettelheim (1970b): *Monthly Review,* vol. 22, no. 7.
R.B. Day (1973): *Leon Trotsky and the Politics of Economic Isolation,* Cambridge.
I. Deutscher (1964): *The Age of Permanent Revolution: A Trotsky Anthology,* New York.
S. Heitman (ed.) (1967): *Put' k sotsializmu v Rossii* (a selection of Bukharin's works), New York.
S. Heitman (1969): *Bukharin, A Bibliography with Annotations,* Stanford, Calif.
P. Sweezy (1972): *Monthly Review,* vol. 23, no. 9, 1972.
L. Trotsky (1964), see Deutscher (1964).
L.N. Yurovsky (1928): *Denezhnaya politika sovetskoi vlasti,* Moscow.

14

Toward a Socialism for the Future, in the Wake of the Demise of the Socialism of the Past

Thomas E. Weisskopf

Introduction

What is socialism really all about? The revolutionary events of 1989 in Eastern Europe, and the enormous changes that have been taking place in the Soviet Union since then, have raised this question with renewed acuity.

The idea of socialism developed historically out of opposition to the reality of capitalism. The basic goals of the movement for socialism have thus been formulated in reaction to the perceived ills of capitalism. To condense an enormous literature on the subject of socialist goals, I would suggest that socialism has been committed most fundamentally to the following objectives:

(1) *Equity:* as against the capitalist reality of great inequalities of income and wealth, socialism calls for a much more egalitarian distribution of economic outcomes and opportunities by class, race, gender, region, etc.
(2) *Democracy:* as against the institutional framework of liberal democracy in the political sphere, which has characterized the most democratic of capitalist societies, socialism calls for a much truer and deeper democracy—

This paper grew out of my involvement in lively and wide-ranging discussions of Marxism and socialism over the Progressive Economists' Network (PEN) for electronic computer correspondence. I am grateful to countless PEN participants for their engagement in these discussions; and I would like to mention in particular my indebtedness to Michael Lebowitz for his role in a series of stimulating debates. I am also grateful to Sam Bowles, Michael Goldfield, Fred Moseley, David Kotz and Victor Lippit [for constructive comments on earlier drafts of this paper. I remain, of course, solely responsible for the views expressed here]. Reprinted with permission from *Review of Radical Political Economics,* Vol. 24, Nos. 3/4 (Fall/Winter 1992), pp. 1–28.

one that enables people more fully to exercise control over their own economic fate.

(3) *Solidarity:* as against the celebration of the individual under capitalism, socialism calls for the promotion of solidarity among members of communities extending from the neighborhood to the whole of society—encouraging people to develop the sense and the reality of themselves as social rather than simply individual beings.

In addition to its commitment to these goals that distinguish it from capitalism, socialism has historically been committed to the improvement of people's material standards of living. Indeed, in earlier days many socialists saw the promotion of improving material living standards as the primary basis for socialism's claim to superiority over capitalism, for socialism was to overcome the irrationality and inefficiency seen as endemic to a capitalist system of economic organization. In the present time—at least in the more affluent parts of the world, where capitalism has brought substantial improvements in living standards and where problems of ecological balance loom more important than problems of starvation or malnutrition—this growth objective has receded in importance for socialists. However, the extent to which any resource-using economic or social objective can be achieved—whether it be improving the environment or eliminating hunger—remains dependent on the degree of efficiency with which the system of economic organization operates. I will therefore articulate—as do most socialists, explicitly or implicitly—one additional important socialist objective:

(4) *Efficiency*: socialism requires that resources be used wisely and nonwastefully in order that resource-using economic and social goals can be more successfully achieved.

In this paper I seek to explore what kind of socialist system can promise to make good on the socialist commitment to these goals, in light of the manifest failure of the political-economic systems of the USSR and Eastern Europe to do so. I will begin in section I by discussing the implications of the events of 1989; this leads me to identify two potentially fruitful models for socialism in the future—market socialism and participatory socialism. Sections II and III explore in turn each of these two forms of socialism; I pose and seek to answer questions with which critics have challenged the advocates of each. I conclude in section IV by articulating the kind of socialism that seems to me to hold the greatest promise of living up to time-honored socialist ideals.

I. The Implications of 1989

There can be no doubt that 1989 marks a watershed in the history of socialism. Although, as we now know, the disintegration of the political-economic systems of the USSR and Eastern Europe had already been under way for at least a decade, 1989 was the year in which the failure of these systems became visible to one and all. As people took to the streets in Eastern Europe, rulers scrambled to dissociate themselves from the old order. After the failed coup against Mikhail Gorbachev in August 1991, it has become perfectly clear that even in the successor states of the Soviet Union itself there can be no return to the political-economic system of Lenin, Stalin or Brezhnev.

The events of 1989 are clearly the main reason why we (and many others) are now discussing the future of socialism. Of course, the conventional wisdom is that socialism has no future—only a past. As Robert Heilbroner (1989: 4) put it: "Less than 75 years after the contest between capitalism and socialism officially began, it is over: capitalism has won." We on the Western Left reject that conventional wisdom, because we argue that where there has been economic failure—in Eastern Europe, in the Soviet Union, if not in all of the Communist-Party-directed socialist economies—it has not been a failure of true socialism, but of something very different.

Is there anything, then, for us to learn from 1989? Indeed, I believe there are several important lessons.

First of all, we must recognize that Communist-Party-directed socialism—the type characteristic of all actually existing socialist systems the world has known[1]—was a worse economic failure than most of us had previously been willing to admit. In the Soviet Union and Eastern Europe, at least, it not only failed to provide much growth and efficiency in its last decade or two; it also failed to achieve real equity, and it was ecologically disastrous.[2] In these respects the accomplishments of CP-directed socialism have been somewhat more impressive in less developed economies such as those of China and Cuba, especially as compared with their own past experience; but even in these more favorable instances there have been many disappointments. And, of course, all these societies have been extremely undemocratic, and almost always deeply alienating to their workers and citizens.

Second, we cannot simply dismiss this dismal record as having nothing to do with socialism. Of course CP-directed socialism is a far cry from the democratic, egalitarian and solidaristic society that most of us on the Left have advocated. There are even some Western Leftists who have consistently refused to apply the label "socialist" to the societies at issue. Nonetheless, most Western Leftists are to some extent tainted by the record of the CP-directed state socialist countries.

For one thing, these countries have exhibited certain characteristics that have been associated with socialism, not just by CP officials and old-fashioned socialists, but by many contemporary Western Leftists—e.g., society-wide control of capital formation, strict limitation of the role of private ownership, strong curbs on the operation of markets, guarantees of employment and basic social services to all citizens. Moreover, many on the Left have compared aspects of the performance of the CP-directed socialist economies—e.g., their long-term growth record, their egalitarianism, their social services—favorably with that of capitalist economies. Even when such a favorable comparison is justified by the evidence (e.g., in comparing many of Cuba's social achievements with those of other Latin American countries), to claim that it represents any kind of victory for socialism is to accept that what has been constructed in countries like Cuba is indeed a form of socialism.

Confronted with such concerns, many of us have held out hope that at least some of the CP-directed socialist systems—however distorted and unsatisfactory their current structure—might evolve toward a truer form of socialism.[3] This again lends credence to the notion that the CP-directed socialist systems do have something to do with the socialism that we advocate.

Perhaps, then, 1989 represents the vindication of a small minority of Western Leftists—those who have always sharply criticized the CP-directed socialist systems and who have consistently refused to consider them as having anything whatsoever to do with socialism. There are two main schools of socialist thought on the Western Left that have been "pure" in this respect; I believe that they can usefully be characterized as *liberal-democratic* and *communitarian,* respectively.[4]

Liberal-democratic socialists have stressed the general socialist goal of democracy, arguing in particular that liberal democracy—a political system including constitutionally protected civil rights and liberties, democratic elections, etc.—is an absolute prerequisite for a socialist society worthy of the name. This implies that socialist economic institutions, designed to promote such other socialist goals as equity and solidarity, must be built upon a liberal-democratic political foundation. The construction of socialist society is seen not as the replacement of "bourgeois democratic institutions" by some entirely different and superior form of democracy, but as deepening the democratic nature of these institutions and extending them from the political through the social to the economic arena. From this perspective, the authoritarian character of political rule in all of the CP-directed socialist societies has disqualified them from the very start as exemplars of socialism.[5]

Communitarian socialists are also committed to democracy, but democracy of a less liberal and more participatory kind. In the communitarian vision it is the socialist goal of solidarity which receives the greatest emphasis—people are to develop and sustain solidarity as active participating members of communities ranging from the neighborhood and the workplace to the society as a whole. The political and economic institutions of liberal democratic capitalism are to be discarded; what is envisaged is a revolutionary transformation to an egalitarian participatory society in which people jointly and directly control their own fate. From this perspective, the CP-directed socialist societies are rejected because of their retention of many of the individualistic patterns and hierarchical structures of capitalist societies, as well as for their betrayal of democratic ideals.[6]

Liberal-democratic socialists generally advocate a form of democratic *market socialism,* in which liberal democracy is combined with an economic system characterized by predominantly collective forms of ownership of the means of production and by the use of markets as the predominant means of resource allocation and distribution—subject to some government planning, intervention and regulation. Collective ownership is designed to promote egalitarianism in both economic and political spheres; markets are seen as indispensible both to individual freedom of choice and to efficient resource allocation; and government regulation is seen as necessary to assure that the general interest prevails over particular interests and to limit the development of substantial inequities.

Communitarian socialists generally advocate a form of democratic *participatory socialism,* in which there is collective social control of the means of production and in which decentralized participatory planning institutions replace the market as a mechanism for resource allocation and distribution. This is a vision of socialism in which, to put it in Marxist terms, both exploitation and alienation are overcome; thus not only private property but also markets must be abolished. Instead of responding as independent self-interested individuals to market signals in the economic arena, people are to develop and sustain themselves as interdependent social beings as they participate together in making consumption and production decisions.

Both the market socialist model envisaged by the liberal-democratic socialists and the participatory socialist model envisaged by the communitarian socialists are sharply differentiated from the CP-directed socialism of the past. In the following two sections of this paper I will consider market socialism and participatory socialism in more detail [by posing and attempting to respond to questions that each of them must face from skeptical critics. In the final section I will offer my own conclusions about the kind of system that offers the best promise of a socialism for the future].

II. Market Socialism

The idea of a market-based form of socialism was first given serious attention in the 1920s, when it was promoted by people within the social-democratic wing of Marxism as a desirable alternative to the marketless form of socialism identified with Marx's vision of full communism and embraced by the Bolshevik wing of Marxism. The first systematic theoretical exposition of the functioning of a market socialist economy was undertaken by Oskar Lange in the 1930s, who has ever since been recognized as the pioneer of market socialism.[7] Lange's original model involved both actual markets (in consumer goods and labor), simulated markets (in producer goods), and a limited but critical role for central planning (e.g., in determining the rate of investment and the distribution of income). All enterprises were to be owned by the government, but run according to profit-maximizing rules by independent managers. Since Lange's exposition of his original model of market socialism, a great deal of work has been done by advocates of market socialism—many of them economists from and/or interested in the post–World War II Eastern European countries—seeking to improve upon Lange's model while dealing with various problems raised by critics.[8]

Out of this continuing literature on the conceptualization of market socialism has emerged a variety of different models, but they all share the same central defining purpose. Market socialism seeks to promote socialist goals of equity, democracy, and solidarity while largely retaining one major feature of capitalist economies—the market—but largely replacing another major feature of capitalism—private ownership of the means of production. For at least the major sectors and/or the most important enterprises in the economy, market socialists propose some form of *social* ownership of enterprises.

"Ownership" is a complex concept encompassing a variety of rights, which can potentially be assigned to a variety of different people. For our purposes it will be useful to identify and distinguish two such rights in particular: (1) the right to enterprise *control* and (2) the right to enterprise *income.* The right to control confers the prerogatives and responsibilities of management: those who control the enterprise (or their representatives) make the decisions about how the enterprise will be operated, who will work in it and under what conditions, whether or not any aspects of the enterprise are to be expanded, contracted, sold or liquidated, etc. The right to income confers a claim to the surplus generated by the enterprise—i.e., the net (or residual) income after fixed obligations have been paid.[9]

The standard capitalist enterprise is owned by private individuals or shareholders who have (ultimate) control over management according to the nature and the amount of their ownership shares; a small number of individuals or shareholders may have predominant control. Under market socialism enterprise control is social rather than private. Control of a market socialist enterprise is held by a community of people, each of whom—in principle—has an equal say in the management of the enterprise; as a practical matter, this (ultimate) control is usually exercised via appointment of managerial staff. There are two principal variants of such social control, depending on the nature of the community in whom control rights are vested:

(1) *Public management:* enterprises are run by managers who are appointed by and accountable to an agency of government (at the national, regional, or local level), which agency represents a corresponding politically-constituted community of citizens.[10]

(2) *Worker self-management:* enterprises are run by managers who are appointed by and accountable to those who work in them (or their elected representatives), with control rights resting ultimately with the community of enterprise workers (on a one-person one-vote basis).[11]

In the standard capitalist enterprise, ownership by private individuals or shareholders conveys not only control rights but also income rights—again according to the nature and the amount of their ownership shares. Under market socialism income rights are held socially rather than privately. The surplus of the market socialist enterprise accrues to a community of people in a relatively egalitarian manner. Here again there are two principal variants of such social claims to income, depending on the nature of the community holding the claim:

(1) *Public surplus appropriation:* the surplus of the enterprise is distributed to an agency of government (at the national, regional, or local level), representing a corresponding community of citizens.[12]

(2) *Worker surplus appropriation:* the surplus of the enterprise is distributed to enterprise workers.[13]

These two different ways of assigning control rights and income rights under market socialism can generate a matrix of four different possible market socialist models, since there is no *a priori* reason why each set of rights must be assigned in the same way. As it happens, however, most contemporary advocates of market socialism lean primarily in one direction or the other: there is one school favoring what I will label the "public enterprise model," characterized by public management and public surplus appropriation, and a second school favoring the "worker enterprise model," characterized by worker self-management and worker surplus appropriation.[14]

Although the replacement of private with social control and income rights at the enterprise level is what most clearly distinguishes market socialism from (market) capitalism, advocates of market socialism also generally call for a greater degree of government intervention into markets than is the norm in capitalist economies. Such intervention does not primarily take the form of quantitative controls, of the kind associated with the discredited system of centrally planned socialism. Instead, it involves more extensive government provision of public goods and services, more extensive public capital formation, more extensive government regulation of enterprises, and more extensive use of taxes and subsidies to internalize external effects that would otherwise be neglected by individual consumers and producers in the market environment. The objective here is to shape the environment in which the market operates, and to use the market rather than replace it, so that market price and cost valuations will approximate true social benefits and costs.[15] The difference between market socialism and capitalism in this respect is essentially one of degree rather than kind; apart from public control and income rights in enterprises, the economic role of government in a market socialist system differs little from that of government in the more regulated (e.g., social-democratic) capitalist systems.

Market socialism has been challenged both by those who question the ability of markets to function efficiently in the absence of capitalist private property rights, and by those who question the ability of social ownership forms to meet socialist goals in the context of markets. I have discussed elsewhere (Weisskopf

1992) the former line of criticism; here I will focus on the concern that market socialism is not really socialist enough. This latter concern tends to revolve around the following kinds of questions.

1. Don't market systems systematically undermine efforts to serve general public interests?

Markets provide an environment in which people are encouraged to find ways to better themselves at the expense of others—through individual rent-seeking behavior, the formation of self-aggrandizing coalitions, etc. As a result, there would appear to be a systematic tendency for the general social interest to be undermined by the pursuit of particular private interests.

This line of argument is theoretically plausible; yet it is not decisive. Rent-seeking behavior and self-aggrandizing coalitions of one kind or another can and will occur under any conceivable system of economic organization that permits some people to live better than others. Virtually every system will therefore require institutions that limit anti-social behavior. The only way in which an economic system of organization *per se* could eradicate the problem would be if that system, by virtue of its controls on individual patterns of living, precluded any individual from enjoying the gains from self-interested behavior.

Thus a solution to the problem of such behavior could come only at the price of strict limits on privacy and freedom of choice—a price that market socialists are unwilling to pay.

2. Don't market systems unfairly reward good luck?

In market capitalist economies people are rewarded for productive contributions due to the property they own (in the form of capital income); such rewards to property ownership not only have very unequal distributional consequences, but they are generally not necessary to assure deployment of the property in production. In market socialist economies people are rewarded primarily for productive contributions due to their own labor.[16] Yet market socialism, like capitalism, maintains rewards to people's natural abilities (in the form of labor income), even though such rewards may not really be necessary to elicit the deployment of those abilities in production. Moreover, worker self-managed forms of market socialism are likely to favor those people who happen to work in prosperous areas or enterprises but do not necessarily work any harder or longer than other people who work in less prosperous areas or enterprises.

A more just system of economic remuneration would arguably link payment solely to differential personal effort and personal sacrifice, not to the luck of the genetic or economic draw. While market socialist systems do not achieve this ideal, they do not depart from it anywhere near as much as do capitalist systems. Moreover, to the extent that unwarranted returns to [people] due to their luck in the genetic lottery or in economic circumstances remain, the resulting differentials can be diminished by a progressive system of income taxation.[17]

3. Won't any kind of market system lead to inequalities that contradict the socialist goals of equity and democracy?

Critics of the "market" within market socialism suggest that it will generate an elite minority of "coordinators"[18]—e.g., public investment bankers, public enterprise directors, self-managed firm managers, even government planners— who end up gaining disproportionate economic and political power, much as do capitalists within a capitalist system.

It is certainly true that under market socialism there must be some people occupying positions of key decision-making responsibility, and in all likelihood such people will have higher incomes as well as greater power than most of the rest of the population. Thus inequalities of income and power would surely develop under market socialism. But they would just as surely be much smaller than under capitalism—because market socialism eliminates most returns to property ownership, which is the predominant source of inequalities under capitalism. While there would still be ample scope for inequalities associated with differential skills, talents, and responsibilities, it is hard to see how the equivalent of a propertied capitalist class could emerge from the more privileged strata of a market socialist society.

Although a market system could not assure anything close to full equality of income and power for all participants, neither could any economic system in a complex society. Such societies require sophisticated decision-making institutions of one kind or another; and there are bound to be great differences among people in their ability (or desire) to participate effectively in decision-making processes.

4. Won't markets undermine solidarity and community?

Critics of market socialism also argue that markets of any kind tend to breed selfish motives and competitive behavior on the part of producers and consumers, dividing people instead of uniting them, encouraging indifference to rather than empathy for others, and discouraging the development of public-spirited community consciousness and solidarity.

To transact effectively in markets people do have to think mainly in terms of their own individual (or family) welfare, while setting aside consideration for others; markets encourage anonymity, autonomy and mobility rather than community, empathy and solidarity.[19] Market socialism thus admittedly does not provide direct support for a culture of community, empathy and solidarity. Yet it surely does provide a less hostile environment for the development of such characteristics than (market) capitalism because it attenuates, via greater egalitarianism and stronger democracy, the consequences of unfettered markets and unrestricted private property ownership. Although economic institutions are powerful social and cultural forces, they are neither monolithic nor omnipotent; hence community, empathy and solidarity may be fostered in other spheres of life even in a market system.

5. Will market socialism be any more successful than social-democratic variants of capitalism in achieving socialist goals?

Advocates of social democracy share the socialist objectives of advocates of market socialism, but they differ as to the best means to achieve them. Where market socialism seeks to promote the public interest, greater equity, democracy and solidarity primarily by transferring capitalist ownership rights to communities of citizens and/or workers, social democracy seeks to do so by government policy measures designed to constrain the behavior of capitalist owners and to empower other market participants. Thus social democrats do not try to do away with either the market or private property ownership; instead, they attempt to create conditions in which the operation of a capitalist market economy will lead to more egalitarian outcomes and encourage more democratic and more solidaristic practices than would a more conventional capitalist system.

Market socialists have traditionally been highly suspicious of social democracy, on the ground that its failure to attack head-on the source of capitalist power—private ownership of the means of production—would ultimately prevent it from attaining socialist objectives. But as models of market socialism have been refined over the years, the distinction between market socialism and social democracy has been somewhat blurred. Partly because of the problematic experience of East European CP-directed socialist economies with limited market-oriented economic reforms, advocates of market socialism have come to support an increasingly wide scope for markets and increasing autonomy for public and/or worker enterprises operating within the market environment.[20] While such proposals do not amount to the restoration of full capitalist private property rights, it does open up opportunities for individuals to receive some forms of capital income.

The elimination of large-scale private property ownership under market socialism certainly leads to a much more equal distribution of income than obtains under conventional capitalism. Both theory and the actual experience of social democracy, however, suggest that government taxation and spending programs can substantially reduce the extent of income and wealth inequalities within a capitalist economy. As far as the pattern of enterprise management is concerned, there is also good reason to question how far market socialism really differs from social democracy. Market socialist enterprise managers, whether accountable to government agencies or to enterprise workers, are expected to operate their enterprises in such a way as to maintain profitability in a market environment; this means that they will typically have only limited leeway to steer the enterprises in a direction much different than would managers accountable to [private] shareholders.[21] And, indeed, to prevent autonomous public enterprises or worker self-managed firms from acting in their own particular interest, as against the general social interest, it would in all likelihood be necessary for government to regulate them or their markets just as is done by social-democratic governments in a capitalist economy.

At a more fundamental level, market socialism does not dispense with individual gain incentives and the necessarily associated inequalities. Instead, it seeks:

    (a) to link differences in rewards more closely to corresponding differentials in the actual productive effort contributed by people to the economy; and

    (b) to reduce the extent of differences in rewards associated with differentials in productive effort, so as to reduce (greatly) the resultant distributional inequity without reducing (much) the incentives they generate.[22]

Again, this is precisely what social democracy tries to do—albeit in a different way than market socialism. Social democracy achieves greater egalitarianism via *ex post* government taxes and subsidies, where market socialism does so via *ex ante* changes in patterns of enterprise ownership. As for serving the general social interest, market socialists and social democrats agree that, where the unfettered market will not achieve important social goals, the first option is to try to guide the market toward socially optimal behavior (via appropriate taxes, subsidies, etc., to internalize externalities by "planning with the market"); where this is not adequate, the second option is to replace price-and-market mechanisms by quantitative controls and/or direct state operation of enterprises.

On further reflection, one might well ask of market socialists: what compelling reason is there to restrict forms of enterprise ownership to types in which control and income rights accrue to (citizen or worker) communities rather than to private shareholders? Why not simply provide a level market playing field in which all types of enterprises can compete on a truly equal basis? Most contemporary market socialist models in any case allow for individual or small-scale private enterprise. Could not the problems of excessive wealth and power associated with large-scale private enterprise be addressed as easily and successfully via taxation and regulation as via restrictions on private ownership?

To sustain the superiority of the market socialist over the social democratic approach to achieving socialist objectives, I would argue as follows. In redefining and reassigning (to workers and/or communities) rights that form the point of departure for markets, market socialism intervenes into the market system before markets operate—while social democracy intervenes (mainly) after markets operate. This makes social democracy much more vulnerable to weakening or disintegration under political challenge, since tax-and-subsidy schemes and government regulation are much easier to reverse than changes in property rights.[23] Moreover, the maintenance of property-owning capitalists under social democracy assures the presence of a disproportionately powerful class with a continuing interest in challenging social democratic government policies. Under market socialism there may well emerge a kind of managerial class with disproportionate power; but its power is likely to be less disproportionate because enterprise control rights and personal wealth will not be so highly concentrated.

III. Participatory Socialism

Although market socialism has become relatively popular on the Left in recent years, there is a much older socialist tradition that has always rejected the idea of including markets in anything other than a transitional phase following capitalism. Karl Marx wanted to rid the world not only of the inequalities associated with private property, but of the alienation and commodity fetishism associated with the operation of market systems. This was the Marxist tradition embraced by the Russian Bolshevik revolutionaries, and it remained an important part of the ideology—though not the practice—of Soviet socialism for decades after the Revolution of 1917. In point of fact, none of the "actually existing" CP-directed socialist economies of the USSR, Eastern Europe, China, Cuba, etc., came close to dispensing with markets[24]—even though they limited the operation of markets in many ways.

Contemporary participatory socialists seek to revive this marketless Marxist ideal, but in a manner very different from that of the Bolshevik tradition. First of all, they reject the authoritarian rule associated with the CP-directed socialist economies and insist instead on a democratic political framework. Second, they reject the hierarchical central planning apparatus that has hitherto been utilized as the main alternative to market exchange and insist instead on a process of decentralized planning in which people participate as equals.

Just as in the case of market socialism, ideas and conceptions of a marketless participatory socialism have been developed in various ways by various authors—starting with utopian socialists even before Marx and continuing through anarcho-syndicalists down to present-day advocates of democratic and participatory planning. Most recently, important contributions to the literature on participatory socialism—providing unusual and laudable detail on the actual institutions and functioning of decentralized democratic planning systems—have been published by Pat Devine and by Michael Albert and Robin Hahnel.[25] These and other conceptions of participatory socialism differ in many respects, but they are all based on the replacement of market forces (which allocate resources by generating material incentives for individual economic agents acting in their own best interest)[26] by a system of decentralized and coordinated planning (designed to allocate resources via negotiation among and between appropriately constituted groups of workers, consumers, community residents, and citizens in general).

The basic decision-making units of the participatory system are typically workplace workers' councils and neighborhood consumers' councils, in which production and consumption decisions are made collectively by workplace and neighborhood communities, respectively. But these basic decision-making units are embedded in a larger network of related politically-constituted bodies, designed to bring to bear relevant considerations and concerns that transcend the scope of individual workplaces and neighborhoods. A critical role in the network of non-market decision-making institutions is played by various planning boards, which are responsible for collecting and dispensing information and for coordinating the decisions of separate councils and entities in such a way that decentralized production and consumption plans emanating from all the workplaces and neighborhoods ultimately converge to a feasible overall pattern of production and consumption. The relevant information to be considered in decision-making includes both quantitative data about production and consumption processes and qualitative evidence about the ramifications of each production and consumption activity.

Advocates of this kind of participatory economic system assert that it can attain far more successfully than market socialism the socialist goals of egalitarianism, democracy and solidarity—*because* of the absence of markets—while performing at least as efficiently as a market system—*in spite of* the absence of markets. Advocates of market socialism, on the other hand, find this effort to do without market forces highly quixotic and thoroughly problematical; they question the feasibility of a participatory socialist system, and sometimes also its desirability. Some of the main concerns raised by critics of participatory socialism are reflected in the following questions.

1. Wouldn't the allocation of resources in a complex economy by means of participatory decision-making institutions place impossible demands on information processing and inordinate demands on people's time?

Since Adam Smith's original exposition of the mechanism of the "invisible hand," advocates of the market have celebrated its ability to process the enormous amount of information necessary for coordinated economic decision-making in a complex economy and to convey it in a simple way to individual economic actors, so that they have both the information and the incentive to act in an economically efficient manner. Most economists believe that the only other way that resources can be allocated in a complex economy is via a centralized, hierarchical system of administrative commands[27]—the system that has been so deeply discredited by the experience of the CP-directed socialist economies. Participatory socialists take up directly the challenge to develop a third resource allocational mechanism that avoids both the use of markets and the hierarchy of an administrative command system.

To replace the market without using administrative commands, they propose an enormous number and a vast network of decision-making bodies on which individuals will sit, process information, deliberate, and arrive at decisions. Precisely because they don't trust the information summarized in and conveyed by market prices, they require these decision-making bodies to consider in detail both the qualitative and the quantitative implications of alternative ways of allocating resources. This places some staggering requirements on the system as a whole:

    (a) to involve every virtually everyone in the society in group decision-making processes;

    (b) to compile an enormous amount of information about the economy and to make that information available in a timely and accessible way to individuals engaged in economic decision-making at one level or another;

(c)   to develop a system of accounting—as a supplement if not an alternative to conventional market prices—that enables the social value of different production and consumption activities to be measured and compared, so that individual decision-makers can understand the aggregate social consequences of any given set of decisions;

(d)   to find a way for the group of people involved in any given decision-making body to arrive in a reasonably harmonious and timely fashion at agreement on decisions; and

(e)   to develop a system to assure that the myriad plans developed at the ground level of the decision-making network, when aggregated, converge to a consistent pattern of resource allocation for the economy as a whole.

The mere listing of these requirements is enough to generate skepticism about whether and how they can possibly be met. Even if, in principle, institutions and processes can be developed to accomplish the necessary tasks (and Albert & Hahnel and Devine have advanced some ingenious ideas to do so), one is bound to wonder whether the whole system would actually function in practice. Assuming that computer technology could be relied upon to process and disseminate the enormous amount of information needed to make the system work, how would people be persuaded to provide the needed information in an unbiased and disinterested manner? And even if all the needed information could be accurately compiled, wouldn't participatory planning require each individual to dedicate so much time, interest and energy to assessing the information and participating in decision-making meetings that most people would get sick and tired of doing it?

2. Isn't the process of democratic decision-making sufficiently complex and problematic that it should be applied only to a limited range of critical decision-making areas?

Advocates of decentralized participatory planning to replace market forces generally place great weight on democracy—both as a desirable goal in itself and as the best means to arrive at decisions that truly reflect people's interests. In so doing, however, they tend to ignore the myriad problems involved in establishing fair and efficient democratic decision-making processes. First of all, choice among alternative voting conventions is complex and critical: when should decisions be made by simple majority, by a super-majority, or by consensus? What will distinguish constitutionally protected rights from those subject to democratic voting? If in principle people's votes on any particular issue should vary according to the extent to which they are affected by a decision, how should the weighting actually be determined in practice?

Explicitly political forms of economic decision-making are favored by advocates of participatory planning over impersonal and individual market processes, on the grounds that people should take explicitly into account the larger social context and the interdependence of their decisions. But won't the politicization of all kinds of decisions lead to excessive conflict, strife and anger, and/or to the formation of political blocs and parties which tend to compress the great variety of individual views and preferences into lowest-common-denominator platforms and programs? Direct participatory democracy is generally favored over indirect representative democracy, on the grounds that people should be required to listen to and confront one another as directly as possible in arriving at decisions. But isn't the practice of participatory democracy sufficiently difficult, time-consuming and emotionally draining that it would in practice have to be limited to a relatively small range of decisions?

A system of decentralized and negotiated planning is expected by advocates of participatory socialism to assure egalitarianism in economic decision-making, yet in practice such a system might well enable some people to exercise much greater influence over decisions than others. Disproportionate influence would not arise from disproportionate wealth or income, but from disproportionate interest in and aptitude for the relevant decision-making processes. People are likely to vary greatly in terms of their ability to access and process information, to negotiate with others, and to influence group decision-making; so political and economic inequalities can easily emerge in marketless as well as in market societies.

These kinds of concerns about the operation of democratic decision-making processes should not of course be read as a condemnation of democracy, much less as a plea for a purely free-market economic system or an authoritarian political system. Rather, such concerns suggest that democratic political institutions ought to focus on a critical and manageable range of decision-making arenas, rather than be used for all kinds of economic as well as political decisions. Direct voice in economic decision-making through negotiating and/or voting procedures is surely not the only, nor necessarily always the best, way for people to have their interests represented in the societal resource allocation process. People's individual and collective interests can often best be served by a combination of the opportunities for choice and exit provided by markets and the economic policy measures undertaken by democratically elected governments.

3. Wouldn't it be very wasteful to try to allocate labor without an incentive system that rewards individuals according to the market-determined value of their work contributions?

Albert and Hahnel (1991a and 1991b) have argued that their participatory planning model actually has an important efficiency (as well as equity) advantage over market systems in its ability to reward people for work according to effort rather than according to result. They propose that the consumption opportunities available to individuals be linked to an individual's *input* into the production process—in the form of personal effort made or personal sacrifice endured. They criticize the market principle of linking individuals' rewards for work to the market-determined value of their *output,* because the latter depends on variables over which individuals have little or no personal control—e.g., natural talent, job location, the vagaries of market demand.

Albert's and Hahnel's proposal would surely lead to greater equity in the reward for labor than the market-based alternative,[28] but their claim of greater efficiency is misguided. They argue that it is most efficient for people to be rewarded according to their personal input because individuals would then be best motivated to supply the one factor which they actually control. Albert and Hahnel suggest that the alternative of a market-determined-output reward system is wasteful and misdirected because it rewards performance due in considerable part to factors beyond the individual's control. But the case for a personal-input reward system is flawed on two counts.

First of all, it is very difficult to observe and measure an individual's sacrifice or work effort and to determine how much of a work result was due to such personal input rather than to other aspects of the work. Measurable indexes of personal input would surely have to be quantitative in nature (e.g., time at work), for how could the quality of a person's effort be adequately measured? Any input-oriented incentive scheme would thus tend to encourage the substitution of quantity for quality of effort. Moreover, people would have an interest in understating their natural talents and abilities and in encouraging the perception that good performance had much more to do with their personal input than other factors, while bad performance was mainly the result of bad luck.[29]

Second, even in the absence of any measurement problems, an incentive structure geared to reward individuals according to their personal input would be quite inefficient. Although it would presumably elicit greater work effort and sacrifice on the part of individuals, it would do nothing to assure that such effort and sacrifice were expended in a desirable way. The social good is best served by encouraging activities the results of which are highly valued relative to the cost of undertaking those activities. In order to motivate people to expend their efforts in a desirable way, it is therefore necessary to reward activities according to the value of work output rather than according to the quantity of work input. If market valuations of output do not adequately reflect the general social interest, then it follows that those output valuations ought to be modified accordingly—not that work should be rewarded according to an input measure instead. If one insists on ethical grounds that work be rewarded according to personal input, then one must be prepared to allocate resources by means that do not depend on the motivation of work via individual material reward.

4. Wouldn't a participatory economic system be viable only if there were a prior transformation of people's basic consciousness from one that is individually oriented to one that is socially oriented?

Advocates of market socialism assume that people will tend to behave as *homo economicus* and seek to attain the greatest possible individual rewards; they seek to achieve socialist goals by structuring the market environment in which self-interested individuals make their decisions, in such a way that people will choose to undertake economic actions in a socially desirable way. Advocates of participatory socialism are highly critical of such a market-oriented motivational scheme and seek to diminish the role of individual material incentives. But what alternative incentives are available? There are a number of possibilities. On the positive motivational side, people could derive satisfaction (a) from the intrinsic interest of the more enjoyable parts of their work, (b) from the social esteem that might accrue to them for a job well done and/or a social duty performed; (c) from the knowledge that they had met their responsibilities to others in the society, and/or (d) from a vicarious sharing in the enjoyment derived by others from consumption and production activities to which they contributed. On the negative motivational side, people could be discouraged from antisocial behavior by (e) the watchfulness and peer pressure of fellow consumers and workers, and/or (f) the practical inability of getting away with such behavior (whether it is excessively high consumption or excessively low production) in a society committed to egalitarianism.

In order for such mechanisms to add up to a workable system of motivation which could substitute for individual material incentives, there would surely have to be a wholesale conversion of human behavior patterns from *homo economicus* to what might best be characterized as *homo socialis*—i.e., a person whose very consciousness was socially rather than individually oriented. It is a fundamental premise of Marxism that people are strongly influenced by their socio-economic environment—that people's values and behavior can and will become different as historical and socio-economic conditions change. Accepting this premise, one can envisage that in a participatory economic environment people might develop the solidaristic attitudes and cooperative capabilities which would make a participatory socialist system work. What remains to be examined, however, is the process whereby both the needed institutions and the needed values and behavior patterns would emerge. I will return to this question in the final section of the paper.

5. Wouldn't a participatory economic system tend to be too intrusive in restricting individuality, privacy and freedom of choice?[30]

Critics of participatory socialism question whether it can adequately protect the legitimate interests of those who hold and wish to act on minority views. True democracy requires not only that people have more or less equal influence over decisions that affect them to the same degree, but that minorities be protected from majority decisions—however equally and fairly they are arrived at—which disadvantage them in important ways. Under participatory socialism there are many important decision-making bodies that are expected to operate by majority vote. Citizens are expected to exercise a great deal of voice in participating in these decision-making bodies. If a decision doesn't go the way of a particular individual or group, however, the opportunities for exit are limited: changing workplaces or neighborhoods in order to enter new decision-making groups remains possible, but one cannot be confident that this would be easy to do in practice.[31]

Although not a goal that is usually voiced explicitly by socialists, freedom of choice—in how to live, what to consume, what kind of work to do, how to express oneself, how to define one's social identity, etc.—is an important value. A participatory system is likely to require people to justify many of their choices along these lines to some kind of collective decision-making body, which in turn is bound to limit the extent to which people can really get their choices accepted—no matter how democratically decision-making bodies are constituted.[32] By enabling individuals to make most choices without reference to what others think about their decisions, a market system provides much greater freedom of this kind. Of course it does so only for people who have the wherewithal to afford alternative choices; thus for a market system to promote meaningful freedom of choice for all, the distribution of income must be reasonably equitable.

In order to avoid the hierarchy of power, income and prestige that tends to develop when people specialize in particular jobs, Albert and Hahnel (1991a and 1991b) have proposed that "balanced job complexes" be established in participatory socialist societies. Under this plan each individual would engage in a variety of work tasks with varying degrees of desirability, combined into a job complex that would be characterized by an average degree of pleasantness comparable to that of every other individual's job complex. But many people are likely to prefer doing more specialized work activities than would be permitted under such a balanced-job-complex requirement, which means that enforcement of the requirement might well involve implicit or explicit coercion. Moreover, many people might well prefer to have certain activities carried out by other specialists rather than by participants rotating through from the rest of their balanced job complexes; not just brain surgery and airplane piloting come to mind here, but also such everyday activities as teaching, writing and the performance of music, art and sports. Apart from their inhibition of personal freedom, balanced job complexes designed to avoid specialization seem likely to deprive society of the benefits of activities performed well only by people who have devoted a disproportionate amount of time and effort to them.[33]

These kinds of questions about the desirability of participatory socialism stem from the attribution of fundamental value to a significant degree of individuality, privacy, and freedom of choice—in addition to and alongside the more traditional socialist goals of equity, democracy and solidarity. The more weight one places on the former kind of objectives, the more skeptical one will be about the desirability of participatory socialism.

IV. Conclusion

Having raised many of the arguments both for and against the variants of socialism with the strongest claims to a future, I turn now to an attempt to decide on the one that offers the most promise to achieve the basic goals of socialism. The most important choice to be made is between market socialism and participatory socialism. Before turning to that choice, however, it will be useful to consider what kind of market socialism provides the best alternative to participatory socialism.

A. Public Enterprise vs. Worker Enterprise Market Socialism

Market socialism calls for the replacement of private by social control and income rights within a (government-guided) market environment. An important question for advocates of market socialism is whether to base the social rights on communities of *citizens* or *workers*. Should control rights—the rights to manage the enterprise—be vested in governmental agencies (democratically accountable to electorates of citizens) or in workers' councils (democratically accountable to electorates of enterprise workers)? Should income rights—the rights to the surplus generated by the enterprise—accrue to the general public (via government agencies) or to enterprise workers?

Advocates of *public management* stress its advantages vis-à-vis worker self-management with respect to "capital efficiency"—access to capital funds, encouragement of risk-taking, technological progress, etc. Advocates of *public surplus appropriation* stress its advantages with respect to equity at the societal level: channeling the residual income of enterprises into an aggregate "social dividend" recognizes the interdependence of all production activities, protects workers and citizens against the potential risk and inequity of having their capital income tied to the performance of a particular enterprise (which may do well or do badly for reasons of luck rather than merit), and can distribute society's surplus much more equitably than when individual enterprises retain much of their own surplus.

Advocates of *worker self-management* stress its advantages vis-à-vis public management in several different respects: (1) "labor efficiency"—motivation of work effort and quality, disciplining of management, organizational improvement, etc.; (2) democracy: worker self-management at the enterprise level is in and of itself democratic, and may well reinforce democracy at the political level; and (3) solidarity: through greater participation in workplace and enterprise decision-making, workers may gain a stronger sense of solidarity with their fellow workers. Advocates of *worker surplus appropriation* stress its advantages with respect to labor efficiency and solidarity, as workers' incomes are linked collectively to the performance of their enterprises.

Clearly there are significant trade-offs here. Different kinds of social control rights are advantageous with respect to different kinds of efficiency considerations, and different kinds of social income rights are advantageous with respect to different socialist objectives of equity, democracy and solidarity. A reasonable solution to the dilemma of choice—consistent with the overall spirit of compromise inherent in market socialism—would be to encourage a mixture of public and worker control and income rights, emphasizing each in the particular circumstances in which it would do the most good. Such a compromise could take the form of promoting public management in those industries and enterprises characterized by relatively large economies of scale and/or relatively extensive externalities, and promoting worker self-management in industries and enterprises with smaller economies of scale and/or less significant externalities. Since income, unlike control, can easily be shared, it might well be best to promote patterns of enterprise income rights in which there is both a social dividend claim and an enterprise worker claim.

B. Market Socialism vs. Participatory Socialism

To make this choice, socialists must confront two major, separable issues. The first issue is whether and how people could be expected to change from *homo economicus,* as we know him/her in contemporary capitalist societies, to *homo socialis,* as he/she is depicted in the operation of participatory socialist societies. The second issue is how much value we should attach to the opportunity for individuals to exercise such libertarian rights as freedom of choice, privacy and the development of one's own specialized talents and abilities—as compared to the more traditional socialist goals of equity, democracy and solidarity.

In the effort to build a socialist society, market socialists take the terrain of *homo economicus* to be the relevant one—at least for the present and the foreseeable future. If people act essentially as *homo economicus,* it follows that a significant amount of inequality, hierarchy, competition, etc., are necessary ingredients of an efficient economic system; and this is one important reason for the market socialist acceptance of markets. Participatory socialists, on the other hand, believe that for the construction of socialism within the foreseeable future *homo economicus* need not be an unalterable fact. They argue (with Marx) that *homo economicus* is the result of a particular pattern of historical development (and a related pattern of unequal power), which can be changed if people decide to do so and act collectively on that desire. The struggle for *homo socialis* can itself help to bring about the desired change in human values and behavior, which would then permit the socialist goals of equity, democracy, and solidarity to be achieved with reasonable efficiency under a system dependent on participation and cooperation rather than autonomy and competition.

Many market socialists—for example, Alec Nove (1991: Part 1)—dismiss the idea of *homo socialis* as utopian, and on that basis reject participatory socialism as utterly irrelevant to the fashioning of a "feasible" socialism for the foreseeable future. In the previous section I raised many of the arguments with which skeptics question the feasibility of a participatory economy, and these arguments have made a skeptic of me. I believe, however, that even if we skeptics are wrong about the potential viability of *homo socialis,* there remains a solid reason for turning away from the communitarian vision of socialism.

Consider what it would take to move from here to there. The same Marxist reasoning which suggests that *homo socialis* is perfectly possible, within an appropriately symbiotic institutional context, suggests that people who have been living in a capitalist institutional environment will be deeply imprinted with the characteristics of *homo economicus*.[34] To transform *homo economicus* into *homo socialis* would thus involve a massive change in people's mind-sets. Such a transformation might conceivably be imposed on a society by an authoritarian elite, but it is virtually impossible to imagine it being generated by a democratic process that respected the current attitudes and preferences of the general public.

This reasoning does not rule out the possibility of any kind of democratic social change from contemporary conditions. It does suggest, however, that such change must be gradual enough so that it is realistic to expect that people—as they are, in their current socio-economic environment—can be persuaded of the desirability of the change. This seems to me a compelling reason for pursuing socialism in terms of the more modest ambitions of market socialists. Even if one's ultimate hope is to progress to a participatory form of socialist society, a gradual move to some form of market socialism—which would begin to change people's actual socio-economic environment in a more socialist direction—would appear to be a necessary first step in achieving a democratic transition.

Whether a subsequent transition from market socialism to participatory socialism would in fact be desirable remains an open question. In my discussion of participatory socialism in the previous section I suggested that certain libertarian objectives associated with personal freedom of choice can best be satisfied only if individuals have the kind of opportunities for choice (and for exit) that a market system alone can provide. While the replacement of markets with a participatory economic system—if feasible—would arguably contribute to a more egalitarian, democratic and solidaristic society, the point is that it would appear to do so at a cost in terms of libertarian objectives.

It is undeniable that such libertarian objectives smack of "bourgeois rights," while the objectives of equality, democracy and solidarity have traditionally been the most strongly associated with socialism. I submit, however, that both kinds of objectives are important ingredients of a good society, and that the task for socialists is to assure the attainment of both in significant measure. I therefore believe that market socialists are right to opt for a significant role for markets, recognizing that this involves a sacrifice of some degree of equality, democracy and solidarity, but expecting that it will deliver more respect for individuality and privacy and more freedom of choice.

C. Democratic Self-Managed Market Socialism

I have thus concluded with an endorsement of market socialism. To emphasize that democracy should be the essential cornerstone of the socialist project—in the process of transition as well as in the organization of institutions—I include the word "democratic" in my characterization of market socialism. And to emphasize that democracy must be extended from the political to the social to the economic sphere of life, I include also the word "self-managed."

A democratic self-managed market socialism combines:

(1) *A liberal democratic political framework,* under which government (at all levels) is accountable to citizens via regular democratic elections in a context of civil rights and civil liberties, and participatory democratic mechanisms are promoted at local levels where direct participation is feasible.

(2) *Social rights to the control and the income of enterprises* (above a modest size), with these rights to be divided between communities of citizens and communities of workers according to pragmatic criteria.

(3) *Markets as the predominant mechanism for resource allocation,* providing informational and incentive benefits as well as freedom of choice, with the opportunities for exit afforded by markets complementing the opportunities for voice afforded by participatory democracy in local politics and enterprise self-management.

(4) *A significant economic and social policy role for the state,* whereby the market is rendered the servant rather than the master of society: the national government formulates and implements overall macroeconomic policy, influencing but not controlling the rate and pattern of investment, and also undertakes microeconomic intervention as needed to achieve important goals—not only via taxes and subsidies but also by directly providing certain goods and services (e.g., capital or consumption goods with strong public good characteristics), by assuring general social security (to maintain economic welfare for all), and by pursuing active labor market policies (to keep unemployment down).

However attractive and convincing this vision of socialism may be to its advocates, we must recognize that its general appeal is still very limited. On the Right, it confronts powerful political forces and a powerful ideology favoring capitalism over socialism. On the Left, it faces obstacles even among people upset with the present system, convinced of the need for fundamental change and ready to embrace some form of socialism.

The problem is that the call for market socialism is simply not the kind of clarion call that is emotionally satisfying or politically inspirational; the case for market socialism is all too reasoned, too balanced, too moderate. This is its virtue, but also its Achilles' heel. Who will rally behind its banner? If it is ever to get anywhere, it will need the backing of a strong political movement; and a political movement needs powerful rallying cries and effective popular mobilization to get off the ground. Democratic self-managed market socialism needs to resonate more fully and more clearly with public hopes and aspirations, or it is likely to remain a socialism *for* the future but not *of* the future.

Notes

1. I will consistently use the term "Communist-Party-directed" (or the abbreviated "CP-directed") to describe the kind of socialism that has actually existed in the Soviet Union, Eastern Europe, China, Cuba, Vietnam and North Korea. There are of course many other

adjectives that have been used to characterize this type of socialism—"actually existing," "bureaucratic state," "centrally planned," etc.—and some have even called it a form of (state) capitalism. I prefer "CP-directed" because it underlines in a compact way the authoritarian, hierarchical, bureaucratic nature of both the political and the economic system.

2. A complete balance sheet on CP-directed socialism in Eastern Europe and the Soviet Union would have to include also such positive achievements as the public provision of free education and health care (among other social services), the availability of low-cost transportation and housing, and greater public access to culture—however modest and restricted some of these benefits may have been. For an insightful attempt to draw such a balance sheet, see Peter Marcuse's (1991) account of his experience in East Germany when the old system was crumbling in 1989–90.

3. This is the implication of a quotation from Serge Mallet that I and my co-authors endorsed in the introductions to all three editions of Edwards, Reich and Weisskopf (1972, 1978, 1986). Mallet (1970: 45) asserts that the societies of the Soviet Union and Eastern Europe are to true socialism "what the monsters of the paleolithic era are to present animal species: clumsy, abortive prototypes."

4. I do not include Trotskyist Marxists among those who have consistently rejected CP-directed socialist systems because—although they have been among the most acerbic critics of Stalinism and of the Soviet Union for at least half a century—they do not reject all forms of communist party control over socialism.

5. Liberal-democratic socialists are for the most part not closely associated with Marxism; however, some do consider themselves Marxist and see Communist Parties as having betrayed the principles of Marxism. The most prominent liberal-democratic socialists in the United States are associated with Dissent magazine, notably the late Michael Harrington; see, for example, Harrington (1989).

6. Communitarian socialists include Marxists who identify with Marx's long-run vision of a truly communist society as well as "new Leftists" who reject many elements of the Marxist tradition. One of the best known exponents of this school of thought in the United States is Noam Chomsky; for a detailed discussion of what a communitarian socialist society would look like, see Albert and Hahnel (1991).

7. See Lange (1936–37) and Lange and Taylor (1938). Abba Lerner also made seminal contributions to the early literature on market socialism; see Lerner (1934) and (1936).

8. For a brief survey of the history of the idea of market socialism, see Brus (1987); for a recent contribution to the literature on conceptualizing market socialism, see Nove (1991).

9. In this context the enterprise surplus should be defined to include also any capital gains or losses.

10. Examples of recent models of market socialism characterized by public management include those of John Roemer (1991) and Leland Stauber (1977).

11. Examples of recent models of market socialism featuring worker self-management include those of David Schweickart (1980) and David Ellerman (1990)—though in Schweickart's model the national government retains control over net capital formation, and Ellerman does not explicitly use the term "market socialism".

12. For example, in Roemer's model of market socialism, (most of the) enterprise surpluses flow back to the national government to be distributed (in large part) to the general public in an equitable manner as a "social dividend;" in Stauber's model, local government agencies receive enterprise capital income *qua* shareholders and either use it for local public purposes or redistribute it to local citizens.

13. For example, in both Schweickart's and Ellerman's models of worker self-management, the enterprise surplus accrues strictly to its workers—though there are taxes and/or other charges which must first be paid to government.

14. Roemer's and Stauber's models of market socialism represent different kinds of public enterprise models, while Ellerman's is a worker enterprise model; Schweickart's is predominantly a worker enterprise model, but includes some characteristics of a public enterprise model—e.g., government control over net capital formation.

15. Market valuations are expected to reflect "true" social benefits and costs to a much greater extent under market socialism than under capitalism not only because of the greater degree of internalization of externalities, but also because of the more equal distribution of income that results from the socialization of enterprise income rights; thus overall market demand will not disproportionately reflect the demands of a minority of wealthy individuals.

16. The elimination of rewards to property ownership under market socialism is not complete because most market socialist proposals allow for some private ownership of small businesses and for some payment of interest-type returns on individual savings.

17. Progressive taxation is of course also possible in market capitalist systems, but it is surely more likely to be successfully instituted in a market socialist system because of its greater overall economic and hence political equity.

18. This term "coordinator" has been introduced by Albert and Hahnel (1981) to characterize the managers and beneficiaries of the CP-directed socialist economies, but it would seem equally appropriate as a term to characterize any small group of people who are able to parlay critical decision-making roles in a social system into disproportionate political and economic power.

19. See Bowles (1991) for a very suggestive analysis of the impact of markets, as cultural institutions, on the process of human development.

20. This evolution in the thinking of advocates of market socialism toward an increasing role for markets can be seen very clearly in differences between Brus (1972) and Brus and Laski (1989).

21. Some critics of market socialism have argued that a market socialist system is fundamentally unstable, bound to veer back to a form of capitalism under the pressures on enterprises imposed by competition in a market environment. Certainly market competition restricts the scope of viable options for any kind of producing enterprise; but the argument that it obliterates distinctions among enterprise types is based on a very unrealistic economic model of capitalism—one in which "black-box" firms face no problems of contract enforcement, worker motivation, etc.; only under such restrictive assumptions is there no room at all for discretionary decision-making by firm management and is the market all-determining. For a stimulating debate on these issues, see the exchange between Arnold (1987) and Schweickart (1987).

22. As Miller (1989: 30) has put it: "for markets to operate effectively, individuals and enterprises must receive primary profits, but the proportion of those profits that they need to keep as private income depends on how far they require material (as opposed to moral) incentives."

23. The experience of Sweden since the mid-1970s is often cited to show the vulnerability of social democracy to pressures to move toward a more traditional form of capitalism. For informative analyses of the trials of the Swedish model of social democracy in recent years, see Lundberg (1985) and Pontusson (1987).

24. The period of "War Communism" in the Soviet Union during the civil war years immediately after the Bolshevik Revolution constitutes an exception to this assertion, but of course one associated with exceptional circumstances.

25. See Devine (1988) and Albert and Hahnel (1991a) and (1991b); of the Albert and Hahnel works, the former is a highly accessible popular presentation of their model, while the latter provides a more rigorous and technical presentation of their ideas.

26. Devine (1988) takes pains to distinguish between "market exchange" and "market

forces;" the latter is distinguished from the former as the process whereby "change [in the economy] occurs . . . as a result of atomized decisions, independently taken, motivated solely by the individual decision-makers' perceptions of their individual self-interest" (p. 23).

27. I refrain deliberately from using the term "central planning" to describe this system, since the literature on such systems demonstrates clearly that their planning mechanisms have been unable to bring about the coordinated fulfillment of any kind of consistent central plan; see, for example, Wilhelm (1985).

28. On the other hand, if equity were really the primary concern, why not reward people according to their need instead of their work input—in other words, why not replace Albert's and Hahnel's version of the socialist distributional principle with Marx's communist principle?

29. It is of course often difficult to measure the result or output of an individual's work, but the difficulties in measuring work output are qualitatively less significant than the difficulties associated with measuring an individual's work input. The former difficulties have mainly to do with distinguishing the contributions of different workers to a joint output, while the latter have to do with disentangling an individual's personal effort from the person's natural abilities.

30. Many of the issues raised here about the desirability of participatory socialism have already been discussed in a persuasive critique of Albert and Hahnel (1991a) by Folbre (1991: 67–70).

31. Of course, changing workplaces or neighborhoods is not that easy to do in practice for many people in market economies either; but the point is that market economies offer individuals or minorities other kinds of opportunities for exit when they make choices that differ from those of the relevant majority.

32. Even the option of switching workplaces and neighborhoods, or forming new ones, does not completely overcome this problem; aside from any difficulties in effecting such switches, there will be societal rules in a participatory economy which every workplace and neighborhood must adhere to, and no doubt many issues of interpretation of those rules which will call for socially determined decisions. Of course, even the most individualistic society must adhere to some rules if it is to survive at all; but the point is that societal rules loom more important in a communitarian society in which people's responsibility to one another is elevated to a guiding principle.

33. As Moore (1980) has argued forcefully in a critique of Marx's vision of full communism, the material basis of cultural complexity is precisely the division of labor.

34. The same surely holds true for people who have been living in a CP-directed socialist institutional environment, where the motivational system remained rooted in individual material incentives.

References

Albert, Michael and Robin Hahnel. 1981. *Socialism Today and Tomorrow*. Boston: South End Press.
———. 1991a. *Looking Forward: Participatory Economics for the Twenty First Century*. Boston: South End Press.
———. 1991b. *The Political Economy of Participatory Economics*. Princeton, NJ: Princeton University Press.
Arnold, N. Scott. "Marx and Disequilibrium in Market Socialist Relations of Production." *Economics and Philosophy* 3 (1).
Bowles, Samuel. 1991. "What Markets Can—and Cannot—Do." *Challenge* (July–August).
Brus, Wlodzimierz. 1972. *The Market in a Socialist Economy*. London: Routledge & Kegan Paul.

————. 1987. "Market Socialism." In John Eatwell, Murray Milgate and Peter Newman (eds.), *The New Palgrave: A Dictionary Of Economics*. London: Macmillan.

Brus, Wlodzimierz and Kazimierz Laski. 1989. *From Marx to the Market*. London: Oxford University Press.

Devine, Pat. 1988. *Democracy and Economic Planning*. Boulder, CO: Westview Press.

Edwards, Richard C., Michael Reich and Thomas E. Weisskopf. 1972, 1978, 1986. *The Capitalist System*. Garden City, NJ: Prentice-Hall.

Ellerman, David. 1990. *The Democratic Worker-owned Firm*. Winchester, MA: Unwin Hyman.

Folbre, Nancy. 1991. Contribution to "Looking Forward: A Roundtable on Participatory Economics," *Z Magazine* (July–August).

Harrington, Michael. 1989. *Socialism, Past and Future*. Boston: Little Brown.

Heilbroner, Robert. 1989. Interview under the heading "No Alternatives to Capitalism." *New Perspectives Quarterly* (Fall).

Lange, Oskar. 1936–37. "On the Economic Theory of Socialism." Part 1 and 2, *Review of Economic Studies* 4.

Lange, Oskar and Fred Taylor. 1938. *On the Economic Theory of Socialism*. Minneapolis: University of Minnesota Press.

Lerner, Abba. 1934. "Economic Theory and Socialist Economy." *Review of Economic Studies* 2.

————. 1936. "A Note on Socialist Economics." *Review of Economic Studies* (4).

Lundberg, Erik. 1985. "The Rise and Fall of the Swedish Model." *Journal of Economic Literature* 23 (1).

Mallet, Serge. 1970. "Bureaucracy and Technology in the Socialist Countries." *Socialist Revolution* 1 (2).

Marcuse, Peter. 1991. *Missing Marx: A Personal and Political Journal of a Year in East Germany, 1989–90*. New York: Monthly Review Press.

Miller, David. 1989. "Why Markets?" In Julian Le Grand and Saul Estrin, *Market Socialism*. London: Oxford University Press.

Moore, Stanley. 1980. *Marx on the Choice between Socialism and Communism*. Cambridge, MA: Harvard University Press.

Nove, Alec. 1991. *The Economics Of Feasible Socialism Revisited*. London: Harper-Collins Academic.

Pontusson, Jonas. 1987. "Radicalization and Retreat in Swedish Social Democracy." *New Left Review* #165.

Roemer, John. 1991. "The Possibility of Market Socialism." Working Paper No. 357, Department of Economics, University of California, Davis.

Schweickart, David. 1980. *Capitalism or Worker Control?* New York: Praeger.

————. 1987. "Market Socialist Capitalist Roaders." *Economics and Philosophy* 3 (3).

Stauber, Leland. 1977. "A Proposal for a Democratic Market Economy." *Journal of Comparative Economics* 1 (3).

Weisskopf, Thomas E. 1991. "The Drive Toward Capitalism in East Central Europe: Is There No Other Way?" Working Paper, Department of Economics, University of Michigan.

————. 1992. "Challenges to Market Socialism: A Response to Critics." *Dissent* (Spring).

Wilhelm, John. 1985. "The Soviet Union Has an Administered, Not a Planned, Economy." *Soviet Studies* 37.

15

Socialist Economic Development
in the Post-Soviet Era

Victor D. Lippit

Less than seventy-five years after it officially began, the contest between capitalism and socialism is over: capitalism has won. The Soviet Union, China and Eastern Europe have given us the clearest
possible proof that capitalism organizes the material affairs of humankind more satisfactorily than socialism: that however inequita-
bly or irresponsibly the marketplace may distribute goods, it does so
better than the queues of a planned economy; however mindless the
culture of commercialism, it is more attractive than state moralism;
and however deceptive the ideology of a business civilization, it is
more believable than that of a socialist one. Indeed, it is difficult to
observe the changes taking place in the world today and not conclude that the nose of the capitalist camel has been pushed so far
under the socialist tent that the great question now seems how rapid
will be the transformation of socialism into capitalism, and not the
other way around, as things looked only a half century ago.
                                        —Robert Heilbroner (1989)

In the more than six years that have passed since Robert Heilbroner penned the
passage above, events certainly seem to have confirmed his verdict. Communism
has collapsed or entered a stage of radical reform, while privatization and extension of the market system have enhanced the vitality of capitalism, which now
appears everywhere ascendant. Yet in the very same essay, Heilbroner casts
doubt on his own conclusions from two perspectives. The first concerns the
source of the primary threat to the capitalist system; the second concerns the
relation between communism and socialism. Following the lead paragraph cited

above, Heilbroner observes that "the economic enemy of capitalism has always been its own self generated dynamics," and goes on to argue that socialism, above and beyond being a system of economic organization, "has stood for a commitment to social goals that have seemed incompatible with, or at least unattainable under, capitalism—above all the moral, not just the material, elevation of humankind" (p. 109). In thinking about the transformation of economic systems, these two qualifications bear further consideration. This is especially true with regard to the future of the less developed countries, where institutional flexibility is generally far greater than it is in the industrialized capitalist economies.

Throughout the Third World, the appeal of socialism has been founded on two central planks, both of which Heilbroner alludes to in his article. First, the ability of the Soviet Union to industrialize in the span of two or three five-year plans seemed to demonstrate the economic feasibility of its approach to "instant" industrialization. Second, the moral framework of socialist development, a path that appeared to promise development without the extremes of inequality and poverty that have normally accompanied its capitalist counterpart, held great appeal to those who sought a development path marked by social justice. Since the second appeared to be anchored in the first, the collapse of the Soviet model poses an essential challenge to the advocates of socialist development. This challenge is heightened by the increasingly apparent inadequacy of the parastatal (state-owned) corporation as an agent of development in Third World countries; such corporations, it had been hoped, might reconcile pursuit of the public interest with decentralized, efficient management.

To address this challenge, it is necessary first to clarify the essential characteristics of socialism. Contrary to the commonplace definition, used widely in books on comparative economic systems, socialism is not simply an economic system characterized by widespread public ownership of the means of production. In this regard, two points especially are worth noting. First, capitalists as a class clearly may benefit from widespread public ownership if such ownership provides goods and services from which they benefit as producers (e.g., public transport), reduces their own costs of production, or absorbs costs they would otherwise have to bear. Second, in Third World countries with "mixed" economies, state enterprises may be (and typically have been) run in such a way that they benefit primarily those in the state bureaucracy or others who have privileged access to them, rather than working people as a class.

In the light of these two considerations especially, it appears most reasonable to distinguish among economic systems on the basis of the dominant class interests they express rather than to elevate the ownership system to the place of defining characteristic. If this is done, a taxonomy of development paths can be presented as follows (Lippit 1988, p. 22):

(1) capitalist development
(2) statist development

(3) socialist development
(4) nondevelopmental statism.

This taxonomy is not meant to describe the paths of particular countries, which usually involve a mix of two or more paths, but to present pure forms for use as benchmarks in analyzing particular cases. It differs from Heilbroner's analysis—and indeed from most conventional analysis—in explicitly recognizing "statism" as a form of social organization distinct from both capitalism and socialism. In the statist social formation, the bureaucracy (those with privileged access to the power and resources of the state) constitutes the dominant class and pursues economic activities in such a way as to further its own interests primarily. Since the bureaucracy often cannot be reduced to an expression of the "more fundamental" or essential class interests of workers or capitalists, conceptualizing economic systems in the form of a capitalist-socialist duality is clearly inappropriate.

Perhaps the clearest example of a statist social formation and statist development model is that provided by the former Soviet economy. The system of central planning, which characterized the Soviet economy, is inevitably hierarchical in the extreme, concentrating authority in the hands of a bureaucracy. Even in those Third World countries that avoided central planning but attempted to give socialist ideals expression in the form of widespread public ownership, elements of statism became widespread. Most typically, the parastatal corporations established there absorb resources provided by the rest of the society, and/or are operated in a manner that affords extensive privilege to the bureaucracy and the fortunate few (relative to the size of the labor force) who gain employment in them. In "nondevelopmental statism," the corruption and drain on public resources become so great that developmental possibilities are foreclosed altogether; the most obvious examples include the Philippines under Marcos, Haiti under the Duvaliers, and Mobutu's Zaire.

This analytical framework makes it possible to consider Heilbroner's thesis in a new light. It suggests that economic systems be distinguished primarily on the basis of the dominant classes that characterize each rather than on the basis of ownership patterns alone. If the issue is reconceptualized in this way, then it will be apparent that what we are witnessing in the current era is the collapse not of socialism and the socialist mode of production, but of statism and the statist mode of production. Further, if only two modes of production or two social formations are postulated, then the collapse of one necessarily implies the "triumph" of the other. If, however, three or more modes of production or social formation can be identified, the collapse of any one carries no such implication.

Whatever terminology we choose, however, a collapse definitely has taken place, and it does have profound implications for our understanding of socialist development in the Third World. In addition to the collapse of the statist social formation in the Soviet-type economies, the failure of the statist mode of production (primarily parastatal corporations) in Third World countries has become increasingly evident. As a consequence, throughout the Third World—and in Latin America especially— privatization has become the order of the day. To understand the significance of these changes, we must consider further the meaning of socialism—of a socialist social formation.

A particular social formation is defined by its particular mix of modes of production (MsOP) and of the activities (exchange, public taxation and expenditure, and so forth) that tie them together. A socialist social formation is one that expresses primarily the class interests of people who work for a living, as opposed to those of the owners of property (capitalists) or people with privileged access to the power and resources of the state (bureaucrats). If socialism is thought of in this way, then it will immediately become evident that it must be characterized by a mixture of various modes of production, even if the socialist MOP is predominant. For example, ordinary people can obviously benefit from privately owned restaurants, laundries, bicycle repair shops, and so forth. And if the individual owners of such establishments can improve their service by hiring several employees to assist them, that in no way diminishes the fact that they serve predominantly working-class interests.

What MsOP are appropriate for a socialist society? Perhaps the best thought-out array is that proposed by Alec Nove in *The Economics of Feasible Socialism Revisited* (1991, p. 213):

1. State enterprises, centrally controlled and administered.
2. State-owned (or socially-owned) enterprises with full autonomy and a management responsible to the workforce.
3. Cooperative enterprises.
4. Small-scale private enterprises, subject to clearly defined limits.
5. Individuals (e.g., freelance journalists, plumbers, artists).

The state enterprises would include public utilities, as well as very large units whose activities are integrated (especially vertically) and/or have a monopoly position. A rail network or oil and petrochemical complex are typically hierarchical and even in a capitalist economy are administered by large corporations. To minimize bureaucracy and enhance worker participation and control, small size should be preferred wherever possible. When the efficiencies dictated by large units outweigh the adverse effects of bureaucracy, however, large enterprises will have a role to play. Using the terminology I have employed, such enterprises constitute the statist MOP.

In a socialist society, an ongoing contradiction exists between the interests of the employees at a particular institution and the broader class interests of working people. Employee "ownership" in the former Yugoslavia, for example, mandated minimizing new hires (to maximize profit shares for the existing labor force) even when national unemployment rates were extremely high. In the state enterprises described above, management would be responsible to the state (representing the broad public interest), and of course to the users, as well as to the workforce. Even so, such enterprises would perforce remain relatively hierarchical. Thus, for example, railroad workers might prefer to avoid night and weekend work, but that preference cannot be allowed to dictate train schedules.

In the second MOP Nove indicates—the socially owned enterprises—a great deal more autonomy for the workforce would be possible, especially since the enterprise itself is fully autonomous; we might call this a socialist MOP. As in the case of the state enterprises, ownership rights would remain with the state, and this would distinguish both from the cooperative enterprises (cooperative MOP), in which the means of production would belong to the workers. In both the socially owned and cooperative enterprises, however, managers would be appointed by the workforce, either directly or through representatives. The principle in each case would be to allow as much autonomy to the workforce as possible, consistent with the enterprises meeting their broader social obligations.

Small-scale private enterprises, Nove's fourth category, correspond to the capitalist MOP. "If any activity (not actually a 'social bad' in itself) can be fruitfully and profitably undertaken by any individual, this sets up the presumption of its legitimacy" (p. 219). Restrictions would be established as to the number of workers hired and capital employed—an enterprise exceeding these restrictions could be converted to a socially owned or cooperative enterprise, with proper compensation to the owner. The entrepreneur-organizer would have to work in the enterprise him/herself—there would be "no *unearned* income, arising simply from *ownership* of capital or land" (p. 220). Those private activities carried out purely by individuals (the petty commodity MOP), Nove's fifth and final category, is self explanatory.

A socialist social formation might well be characterized by a mix of the five MsOP Nove identifies; a *feasible* socialism, as Nove argues, would have to be market-based. It is worth keeping in mind that every social formation, including capitalism, is composed of a mix of MsOP. Any effort to create a unitary MOP, such as that undertaken in the former Soviet Union or in China under Mao, must result in great inefficiency and ultimately defeat the very ends it is intended to serve. This would be as true of capitalism if its ideologues succeeded in privatizing everything, as it has been with "socialism" in China, the former Soviet Union, and elsewhere.

If we think about socialism in this way, then we depart dramatically from the historical experience of efforts to construct socialism, both in Soviet-type economies and in the Third World generally. In both, socialism has been pursued via a focus on the role of state ownership and limits on the role of the market, which reached extremes in the cases of China and the Soviet Union. In these two countries, moreover, the forcible collectivization of agriculture enabled the state to extract the rural surplus to finance industrialization, depriving the largest proportion of the working population of control over their own labor and the surplus it generated (Nolan 1988).

If we think of socialism in terms of the class interests of working people, then a democratic system embodying varied MsOP such as that outlined by Nove appears appropriate; the hierarchical, bureaucratic societies of pre-reform China and the Soviet Union clearly belong to another category—what we have termed "statism." In considering the reasons for which efforts to construct socialism have taken such a wrong turn historically, we must certainly assign a prominent role to conceptual flaws in the history of socialist thought.

Perhaps most significant among these is the conception—which can be traced back to Marx and Lenin—of economic activity as something that can be reduced to administration; Lenin indeed believed that the entire economy could be planned and run like the post office (Nove 1991, p. 36). Much as the manager of an office can discharge his/her duties by identifying the space requirements, furnishings, supplies, numbers of secretaries required, and so forth, and by then proceeding to acquire them, socialism has been conceived as a system that can be rationally planned in like fashion. This conception of economic activity, however, fails to perceive the critical role played by initiative, incentives, and innovation. Herein lies a major element underlying the collapse of the Soviet-type economy.

Even in those parts of the Third World where communist parties have not prevailed, socialist ideals of development have often been present in the early stages of institution-building. These have been reflected most often in the establishment of an array of parastatal enterprises, and in reserving large sectors of the economy for the state. The operation of state enterprises, however, has generally been marked by corruption and inefficiency, with staff members and others enjoying privileged access often the primary beneficiaries. Indeed, rather than generating significant resources for the state to use for public purposes, they often absorb the surplus generated elsewhere in the economy.

Consider Pemex, for example, Mexico's state-owned oil company. Overstaffed by at least one-third, Pemex employed about five times as many workers per dollar of revenue as Royal Dutch/Shell did in 1986. On $13 billion of total revenues in 1987, profits reached just $2 million (*Wall Street Journal* 1988, p. 3). Inefficient operations combined with corrupt union and management officials to limit the benefits that might have accrued to the national treasury. Since Mexico's budget deficit was a major factor generating inflation, the inefficient operation of the giant oil company played an important role in the nation's downward economic spiral in the 1980s.

The point to be emphasized here is the importance of breaking with the conception of socialism that identifies it with exclusive state ownership and/or central planning, and that sees the extension of state ownership *in itself* as constituting a move toward socialism. As I have suggested, these arrangements can more appropriately be termed "statism" and the "statist MOP." The collapse of the Soviet-type economy that has taken place, as well as the widespread movement to privatize parastatal corporations in Third World nations, represents, contrary to Heilbroner, a defeat of statism and the statist MOP, not of socialism.

The immediate consequence of this defeat, however, has indeed been the promotion of capitalism. The potential alternative posed by Nove of a market socialism composed of various modes of production has not been implemented anywhere. When Nove talks of a "feasible socialism," he is addressing the possibility of creating such a system within fifty years in the already-industrialized nations. Although his focus is not on the special circumstances of the less developed countries, the theoretical framework he provides can be used to examine the ideas of socialist transition in the Third World. Those issues remain of concern because capitalist development proceeds today, as it always has, amid massive human suffering, and because, as I will argue below, the destruction of the environment associated with the capitalist system mandates the search for an alternative. In the remainder of this essay, therefore, I would like to extend Nove's consideration of the economics of feasible socialism to the issues of socialist transition in the Third World. My intention is simply to sketch in a framework for analysis and debate.

Socialist Transition in the Third World

In parts of the Third World, efforts to construct socialism must first of all come to grips with the contradiction between the expanded political power of the state, especially in post-colonial Asia and Africa, and its weak economic capacity. The expanded political power of the state, reflected in what Hamza Alavi (1972) refers to as the "relative autonomy" of the bureaucratic-military oligarchy in post-colonial societies, results above all from the social distortions created by colonialism. The colonial power replaces the dominant class in the colony in that it controls the disposition of the economic surplus generated. At the same time, it typically creates an institutional framework for capitalist development. Since the metropolitan capitalists are displaced by independence and the Third World capitalists remain weak and underdeveloped in the aftermath of colonial rule, civil society cannot provide classes with sufficient power to challenge the authority of the bureaucratic-military groups.

At the same time, however, and despite the state's command over resources, its ability to use them efficiently and effectively is sharply constrained. This reflects to some extent a lack of experience in and qualifications for economic management, but primarily it reflects pervasive corruption and difficulties inherent in state-managed enterprises that are insulated from market forces. These difficulties have been broadly misconceived in the socialist tradition, which treats economic activity as something that can be "rationally" administered from the center without giving due regard to the critical role of incentives, initiative, and innovation.

The result of the contradiction between the political power of the state and its economic weakness was the widespread establishment of inefficient, surplus-absorbing parastatal enterprises, the same enterprises that are today being rapidly privatized. As I have indicated, the major lacuna in the conception of the parastatal corporation is the neglect of the critical role that must be played by individual motivation in carrying out economic activity—by the microeconomic actors. Incentives to work hard and effectively, to develop new products and methods of production, and to exercise initiative in confronting the innumerable problems encountered in carrying out production remain relatively weak.

The foregoing argument suggests that the direct role of the state in economic activity must be limited, even in any socialist development process. Both experience and logic have revealed unambiguously the negative impact that direct participation tends to bring in the form of corruption; inefficiency; and disincentives to work, innovate, and assume initiative. Since we have argued, however, that socialism should be understood not as a system of state ownership and control, but rather as a system in which the working classes determine the disposition of the surplus and stand as the system's primary beneficiary, this does not preclude the possibility of a socialist development process or of a development process that at least incorporates socialist elements. The challenge, essentially, is to establish institutions that will allow market mechanisms to work and permit a variety of ownership systems, minimizing the direct role of the state but preserving for it a critical role in macroeconomic regulation, one that would go beyond that of the capitalist system in assuring the protection of social needs as well as orderly markets.

The implication of this for socialist organization in the Third World is the need for a sharply reduced role for the state in the direct management of affairs at the enterprise level, the encouragement of cooperatives and small-scale private activity, and the establishment of jointly owned state-private enterprises. At the same time, in the interest of efficiency, markets must remain as unhindered as possible. This in turn requires an initial distribution of productive resources that is as equal as possible. Without this, the free action of markets tends to exaggerate initial inequalities sharply; as economic reform in Mexico took hold, for example, the number of billionaires rose from two to thirteen in the two years to 1993 (*Forbes* 1993, pp. 66–67), bringing Mexico to fourth place in the world in its number of billionaires while poverty and unemployment remained widespread.

The need to minimize the inefficiency and corruption associated with state-owned enterprises, as well as to maximize incentives, also suggests that the design of socialism in the Third World must allow a greater role for the private sector than it would in more developed countries. This makes it all the more important for public policy to ensure that as development proceeds, meeting the basic needs of the entire population receives priority; adequate savings/investment rates are maintained; and gross inequalities in the distribution of income, wealth, and power are forestalled. Several practical measures can be adopted to pursue these objectives.

First, to enable society as a whole to benefit from the characteristically disproportionate increase in the value of land as development proceeds, land should be retained in public hands as much as possible or acquired through eminent domain. Housing plots in the city of Islamabad, for example, established as the capital of Pakistan in 1961, have increased in value many times since then. The increase in value depended not on any productive contribution by the owners, but on the development activity going on around them. To the extent that such unearned gains can be captured for public purposes, provisions for health, education, and other pressing social needs can be facilitated.

In industry, enterprise forms must be consciously designed to minimize the corruption and inefficiency that have come to characterize state-owned corporations. One way to achieve this would be to mandate state ownership of perhaps 40 percent of any enterprise above a certain size, enabling the state to share directly in profits as well as to receive revenue from corporate taxes. This would leave primary control in private hands, hopefully assuring efficient operation while giving the state some leverage over corporate decision making through its sizable minority stake. Other measures of influence could of course be exerted through state bank loan restrictions or other public policies to encourage or discourage particular types of investment (such policies have been widely used in South Korea and Japan).

It would also be appropriate for the state to mandate that a certain proportion of the privately held shares be owned by the employees, giving them a direct stake in the performance of the enterprise. To improve the management and incentive structure of the existing parastatal corporations, they too could be converted into state-private enterprises through a 60 percent privatization, with a portion of the privatized shares sold to employees under extended payment terms or perhaps in part through a profit-sharing plan that distributes shares. Of course the logic of state-private joint enterprise requires competition and the absence of protection. Where natural monopolies prevail, as in the case of utilities or railroads, for example, full state ownership *may* remain desirable if an incentive structure can be established that will ensure efficient and effective performance.

With regard to small-scale enterprise, whether rural or urban, private activity should remain the norm. Paralleling Nove's suggestion, when such enterprises reach a certain size, conversion to a cooperative or state-private form with compensation would be appropriate. Cooperatives could be encouraged via preferential tax rates or other means. In general, markets should be as free as possible, including financial and foreign-exchange markets, with state interventions limited mainly to instances where important externalities exist.

In Third World socialism the state must retain a critical role in defining the macroeconomic parameters. Moreover, from industrial policy to assuring a satisfactory national savings/investment rate and the provision of basic needs, the state's economic role would be a major one. The main withdrawal I am suggesting is from direct enterprise management, with a concomitant opening of markets.

In thinking about socialism, it is important to get away from the conception of public ownership of the means of production as its defining characteristic. Rather, economic systems are characterized by the class interests they represent. A socialist social formation is one that best serves the interests of working people—whether in industry, agriculture, or services. According to the framework I have presented here, Heilbroner's article errs in its conception of socialism, and in positing as possible social formations a capitalism/socialism duality to the neglect of statism. As the statist social formation has crumbled in Soviet-type societies, and as the parastatal corporation rapidly gives way to privatization, it is important to remain aware that capitalism is not the only alternative, and that actual social formations can incorporate elements from different pure forms.

Is Third World Socialism Feasible?

Marx once wrote that no mode of production disappears from the face of the earth until all the possibilities for developing the forces of production it affords have been realized. Clearly, capitalism is now entering a new stage of enhanced vitality as the world market becomes increasingly integrated, the former communist countries begin to participate, and Third World countries open their economies to international trade and investment. Under these circumstances, it is legitimate to question the relevance of any discussion of Third World socialism.

The case for maintaining such a discussion ultimately rests on three planks. First, actual economic systems or social formations are never "pure"; they always entail some elements of other systems—a mixture of modes of production even when one is clearly dominant. Thus even in the United States, where the capitalist mode of production is dominant, the statist mode of production (the Tennessee Valley Authority, Amtrak) and small-scale communes can be found. Laying out the basis for pure alternatives helps to clarify the nature of actually existing systems and the possibilities for their modification.

Second, capitalist development continues to be characterized by child labor, insecure employment, persisting poverty, and other ills. This legitimizes an ongoing search for alternatives, even following the failure of one such effort with the collapse of the centrally planned statist system. Moreover, the prevalence of the central planning alternative resulted in inadequate attention to market-based alternatives, which only now can be explored properly. Further, just as the capitalist system in the industrialized nations varies from the intensely free market systems of the Anglo-American variety to the social democratic welfare states of northern Europe, the latter of which approach socialist goals in a variety of areas, so too one can envision amelioration of some of the harshest features of capitalist development in the Third World. Clarifying theoretical alternatives may help to bring this about.

Finally, as Kenneth Boulding argues in "The Economics of the Coming Spaceship Earth" (chapter 16 in this volume), a fixed environment is ultimately inconsistent with the unlimited growth of economic activity. Since capitalism is driven by the accumulation process, which results in unlimited growth, another system will eventually have to replace it as a condition for human survival. A great deal of damage has been done to the environment since capitalism became dominant in the sixteenth century, and much more will doubtless be done before capitalism disappears a few centuries hence. As Third World countries introduce new institutions to facilitate their development, however, they can do so in a way that will both ameliorate the environmental destructiveness of the capitalist system and ease the transition to a post-capitalist society when the time is ripe.

Capitalism is an enormously dynamic system, strongly geared to the growth of material production when institutional barriers are minimized. It may well be that a market socialism for developing countries will not be practical, given their overriding material concerns. Perhaps a market socialism will become feasible only when concerns with the quality of life replace the present preoccupation with the quantity of material possessions. This is more apt to happen first in the more developed countries than in the less developed ones.

To the extent that these observations hold, the search for a feasible socialism in Third World countries may appear quixotic. For the reasons advanced at the start of this section, however, the quest remains worthwhile.

References

Alavi, Hamza. 1972. "The State in Post-Colonial Societies." *New New Left Review,* no. 74 (July/August), pp. 59–82.

Forbes, July 5, 1993, pp. 66–67.

Heilbronner, Robert. 1989. "Reflections: The Triumph of Capitalism."

Lippit, Victor D. 1988. "Class Structure, Modes of Production and Economic Development." *Review of Radical Political Economics,* vol. 20, nos. 2 & 3, pp. 18–24.

The New Yorker, January 23, p. 98.

Nolan, Peter. 1988. *The Political Economy of Collective Farms.* Boulder, CO: Westview Press.

Nove, Alec. 1991. *The Economics of Feasible Socialism Revisited.* London: Harper Collins Academic.

Wall Street Journal, September 27, 1988, pp. 1–3.

VII

The Environment

16

The Economics of the
Coming Spaceship Earth

Kenneth E. Boulding

We are now in the middle of a long process of transition in the nature of the image which man has of himself and his environment. Primitive men, and to a large extent also men of the early civilizations, imagined themselves to be living on a virtually illimitable plane. There was almost always somewhere beyond the known limits of human habitation, and over a very large part of the time that man has been on earth, there has been something like a frontier. That is, there was always some place else to go when things got too difficult, either by reason of the deterioration of the natural environment or a deterioration of the social structure in places where people happened to live. The image of the frontier is probably one of the oldest images of mankind, and it is not surprising that we find it hard to get rid of.

Gradually, however, man has been accustoming himself to the notion of the spherical earth and a closed sphere of human activity. A few unusual spirits among the ancient Greeks perceived that the earth was a sphere. It was only with the circumnavigations and the geographical explorations of the fifteenth and sixteenth centuries, however, that the fact that the earth was a sphere became at all widely known and accepted. Even in the nineteenth century, the commonest map was Mercator's projection, which visualizes the earth as an illimitable cylinder, essentially a plane wrapped around the globe, and it was not until the Second World War and the development of the air age that the global nature of the planet really entered the popular imagination. Even now we are very far from having made the moral, political, and psychological adjustments which are implied in this transition from the illimitable plane to the closed sphere.

Reprinted with permission from Kenneth E. Boulding, "The Economics of the Coming Spaceship Earth" in *Environmental Quality in a Growing Economy*, ed. Henry Jarrett (Baltimore, MD: The Johns Hopkins Press for Resources for the Future, 1966) © 1966 by Resources for the Future, Washington, D.C.

Economists in particular, for the most part, have failed to come to grips with the ultimate consequences of the transition from the open to the closed earth. One hesitates to use the terms "open" and "closed" in this connection, as they have been used with so many different shades of meaning. Nevertheless, it is hard to find equivalents. The open system, indeed, has some similarities to the open system of von Bertalanffy,[1] in that it implies that some kind of structure is maintained in the midst of a throughput from inputs to outputs. In a closed system, the outputs of all parts of the system are linked to the inputs of other parts. There are no inputs from outside and no outputs to the outside; indeed, there is no outside at all. Closed systems, in fact, are very rare in human experience, in fact almost by definition unknowable, for if there are genuinely closed systems around us, we have no way of getting information into them or out of them; and hence if they are really closed, we would be quite unaware of their existence. We can only find out about a closed system if we participate in it. Some isolated primitive societies may have approximated to this, but even these had to take inputs from the environment and give outputs to it. All living organisms, including man himself, are open systems. They have to receive inputs in the shape of air, food, water, and give off outputs in the form of effluvia and excrement. Deprivation of input of air, even for a few minutes, is fatal. Deprivation of the ability to obtain any input or to dispose of any output is fatal in a relatively short time. All human societies have likewise been open systems. They receive inputs from the earth, the atmosphere, and the waters, and they give outputs into these reservoirs; they also produce inputs internally in the shape of babies and outputs in the shape of corpses. Given a capacity to draw upon inputs and to get rid of outputs, an open system of this kind can persist indefinitely.

There are some systems—such as the biological phenotype, for instance the human body—which cannot maintain themselves indefinitely by inputs and outputs because of the phenomenon of aging. This process is very little understood. It occurs, evidently, because there are some outputs which cannot be replaced by any known input. There is not the same necessity for aging in organizations and in societies, although an analogous phenomenon may take place. The structure and composition of an organization or society, however, can be maintained by inputs of fresh personnel from birth and education as the existing personnel ages and eventually dies. Here we have an interesting example of a system which seems to maintain itself by the self-generation of inputs, and in this sense is moving toward closure. The input of people (that is, babies) is also an output of people (that is, parents).

Systems may be open or closed in respect to a number of classes of inputs and outputs. Three important classes are matter, energy, and information. The present world economy is open in regard to all three. We can think of the world economy or "econosphere" as a subset of the "world set," which is the set of all objects of possible discourse in the world. We then think of the state of the econosphere at any one moment as being the total capital stock, that is, the set of all objects, people, organizations, and so on, which are interesting from the point of view of the system of exchange. This total stock of capital is clearly an open system in the sense that it has inputs and outputs, inputs being production which adds to the capital stock, outputs being consumption which subtracts from it. From a material point of view, we see objects passing from the noneconomic into the economic set in the process of production, and we similarly see products passing out of the economic set as their value becomes zero. Thus we see the econosphere as a material process involving the discovery and mining of fossil fuels, ores, etc., and at the other end a process by which the effluents of the system are passed out into noneconomic reservoirs—for instance, the atmosphere and the oceans—which are not appropriated and do not enter into the exchange system.

From the point of view of the energy system, the econosphere involves inputs of available energy in the form, say, of water power, fossil fuels, or sunlight, which are necessary in order to create the material throughput and to move matter from the noneconomic set into the economic set or even out of it again; and energy itself is given off by the system in a less available form, mostly in the form of heat. These inputs of available energy must come either from the sun (the energy supplied by other stars being assumed to be negligible) or it may come from the earth itself, either through its internal heat or through its energy of rotation or other motions, which generate, for instance, the energy of the tides. Agriculture, a few solar machines, and water power use the current available energy income. In advanced societies this is supplemented very extensively by the use of fossil fuels, which represent, as it were, a capital stock of stored-up sunshine. Because of this capital stock of energy, we have been able to maintain an energy input into the system, particularly over the last two centuries, much larger than we would have been able to do with existing techniques if we had had to rely on the current input of available energy from the sun or the earth itself. This supplementary input, however, is by its very nature exhaustible.

The inputs and outputs of information are more subtle and harder to trace, but also represent an open system, related to, but not wholly dependent on, the transformations of matter and energy. By far the larger amount of information and knowledge is self-generated by the human society, though a certain amount of information comes into the sociosphere in the form of light from the universe outside. The information that comes from the universe has certainly affected man's image of himself and of his environment, as we can easily visualize if we suppose that we lived on a planet with a total cloud-cover that kept out all information from the exterior universe. It is only in very recent times, of course, that the information coming in from the universe has been captured and coded into the form of a complex image of what the universe is like outside the earth; but even in primitive times, a man's perception of the heavenly bodies has always profoundly affected his image of earth and of himself. It is the information generated within the planet, however, and particularly that generated by man himself, which forms by far the larger part of the information system. We can think of the stock of knowledge, or as Teilhard de Chardin called it, the "noosphere," and consider this as an open system, losing knowledge through aging and death and gaining it through birth and education and the ordinary experience of life.

From the human point of view, knowledge, or information, is by far the most important of the three systems. Matter only acquires significance and only enters the sociosphere or the econosphere insofar as it becomes an object of human knowledge. We can think of capital, indeed, as frozen knowledge or knowledge imposed on the material world in the form of improbable arrangements. A machine, for instance, originates in the mind of man, and both its construction and its use involve information processes imposed on the material world by man himself. The cumulation of knowledge, that is, the excess of its production over its consumption, is the key to human development of all kinds, especially to economic development. We can see this preeminence of knowledge very clearly in the experiences of countries where the material capital has been destroyed by a war, as in Japan and Germany. The knowledge of the people was not destroyed, and it did not take long, therefore, certainly not more than ten years, for most of the material capital to be reestablished again. In a country such as Indonesia, however, where the knowledge did not exist, the material capital did not come into being either. By "knowledge" here I mean, of course, the whole cognitive structure, which includes valuations and motivations as well as images of the factual world.

The concept of entropy, used in a somewhat loose sense, can be applied to all three of these open systems. In material systems, we can distinguish between entropic processes, which take concentrated materials and diffuse them through the oceans or over the earth's surface or into the atmosphere, and antientropic processes, which take diffuse materials and concentrate them. Material entropy can be taken as a measure of the uniformity of the distribution of elements and, more uncertainly, compounds and other structures on the earth's surface. There is, fortunately, no law of increasing material entropy, as there is in the corresponding case of energy, as it is quite possible to concentrate diffused materials if energy inputs are allowed. Thus the processes for fixation of nitrogen from the air, processes for the extraction of magnesium or other elements from the sea, and processes for the desalinization of sea water are antientropic in the material sense, though the reduction of material entropy has to be paid for by inputs of energy and also inputs of information, or at least a stock of information in the system. In regard to matter, therefore, a closed system is conceivable, that is, a system in which there is neither increase nor decrease in material entropy. In such a system all outputs from consumption would constantly be recycled to become inputs for production, as for instance, nitrogen in the nitrogen cycle of the natural ecosystem.

In the energy system there is, unfortunately, no escape from the grim second law of thermodynamics; and if there were no energy inputs into the earth, any evolutionary or developmental process would be impossible. The large energy inputs which we have obtained from fossil fuels are strictly temporary. Even the most optimistic predictions expect the easily available supply of fossil fuels to be exhausted in a mere matter of centuries at present rates of use. If the rest of the world were to rise to American standards of power consumption, and still more if world population continues to increase, the exhaustion of fossil fuels would be even more rapid. The development of nuclear energy has improved this picture, but has fundamentally altered it, at least in present technologies, for fissionable material is still relatively scarce. If we should achieve the economic use of energy through fusion, of course, a much larger source of energy materials would be available, which would expand the time horizons of supplementary energy input into an open social system by perhaps tens to hundreds of thousands of years. Failing this, however, the time is not very far distant, historically speaking, when man will once more have to retreat to his current energy input from the sun, even though with increased knowledge this could be used much more effectively than in the past. Up to now, certainly, we have not gotten very far with the technology of using current solar energy, but the possibility of substantial improvements in the future is certainly high. It may be, indeed, that the biological revolution which is just beginning will produce a solution to this problem, as we develop artificial organisms which are capable of much more efficient transformation of solar energy into easily available forms than any that we now have. As Richard Meier has suggested, we may run our machines in the future with methane-producing algae.[2]

The question of whether there is anything corresponding to entropy in the information system is a puzzling one, though of great interest. There are certainly many examples of social systems and cultures which have lost knowledge, especially in transition from one generation to the next, and in which the culture has therefore degenerated. One only has to look at the folk culture of Appalachian migrants to American cities to see a culture which started out as a fairly rich European folk culture in Elizabethan times and which seems to have lost skills, adaptability, folk tales, songs, and almost everything that goes up to make richness and complexity in a culture, in the course of about ten generations. The American Indians on reservations provide another example of such degradation of the information and knowledge system. On the other hand, over a great part of human history, the growth of knowledge in the earth as a whole seems to have been almost continuous, even though there have been times of relatively slow growth and times of rapid growth. As it is knowledge of certain kinds that produces the growth of knowledge in general, we have here a very subtle and complicated system, and it is hard to put one's finger on the particular elements in a culture which make knowledge grow more or less rapidly, or even which make it decline. One of the great puzzles in this connection, for instance, is why the takeoff into science, which represents an "acceleration," or an increase in the rate of growth of knowledge in European society in the sixteenth century, did not take place in China, which at that time (about 1600) was unquestionably ahead of Europe, and one would think even more ready for the breakthrough. This is perhaps the most crucial question in the theory of social development, yet we must confess that it is very little understood. Perhaps the most significant factor in this connection is the existence of "slack" in the culture, which permits a divergence from established patterns and activity which is not merely devoted to reproducing the existing society but is devoted to changing it. China was perhaps too well organized and had too little slack in its society to produce the kind of acceleration which we find in the somewhat poorer and less well organized but more diverse societies of Europe.

The closed earth of the future requires economic principles which are somewhat different from those of the open earth of the past. For the sake of picturesqueness, I am tempted to call the open economy the "cowboy economy," the cowboy being symbolic of the illimitable plains and also associated with reckless, exploitative, romantic, and violent behavior, which is characteristic of open societies. The closed economy of the future might similarly be called the "spaceman" economy, in which the earth has become a single spaceship, without unlimited reservoirs of anything, either for extraction or for pollution, and in which, therefore, man must find his place in a cyclical ecological system which is capable of continuous reproduction of material form even though it cannot escape having inputs of energy. The difference between the two types of economy becomes most apparent in the attitude toward consumption. In the cowboy economy, consumption is regarded as a good thing and production likewise; and the success of the economy is measured by the amount of the throughput from the "factors of production," a part of which, at any rate, is extracted from the reservoirs of raw materials and noneconomic objects, and another part of which is output into the reservoirs of pollution. If there are infinite reservoirs from which material can be obtained and into which effluvia can be deposited, then the throughput is at least a plausible measure of the success of the economy. The Gross National Product is a rough measure of this total throughput. It should be possible, however, to distinguish that part of the GNP which is derived from exhaustible and that which is derived from reproducible resources, as well as that part of consumption which represents effluvia and that which represents input into the productive system again. Nobody, as far as I know, has ever attempted to break down the GNP in this way, although it would be an interesting and extremely important exercise, which is unfortunately beyond the scope of this paper.

By contrast, in the spaceman economy, throughput is by no means a desideratum, and is indeed to be regarded as something to be minimized rather than maximized. The essential measure of the success of the economy is not production and consumption at all, but the nature, extent, quality, and complexity of the total capital stock, including in this the state of the human bodies and minds included in the system. In the spaceman economy, what we are primarily concerned with is stock maintenance, and any technological change which results in the maintenance of a given total stock with a lessened throughput (that is, less production and consumption) is clearly a gain. This idea that both production and consumption are bad things rather than good things is very strange to economists, who have been obsessed with the income-flow concepts to the exclusion, almost, of capital-stock concepts.

There are actually some very tricky and unsolved problems involved in the questions as to whether human welfare or well-being is to be regarded as a stock or a flow. Something of both these elements seems actually to be involved in it, and as far as I know there have been practically no studies directed toward identifying these two dimensions of human satisfaction. Is it, for instance, eating that is a good thing, or is it being well fed? Does economic welfare involve having nice clothes, fine houses, good equipment, and so on, or is it to be measured by the depreciation and the wearing out of these things? I am inclined myself to regard the stock concept as most fundamental, that is, to think of being well fed as more important than eating, and to think even of so-called services as essentially involving the restoration of a depleting psychic capital. Thus I have argued that we go to a concert in order to restore a psychic condition which might be called "just having gone to a concert," which, once established, tends to depreciate. When it depreciates beyond a certain point, we go to another concert in order to restore it. If it depreciates rapidly, we go to a lot of concerts; if it depreciates slowly, we go to a few. On this view, similarly, we eat primarily to restore bodily homeostasis, that is, to maintain a condition of being well fed, and so on. On this view, there is nothing desirable in consumption at all. The less consumption we can maintain a given state with, the better off we are. If we had clothes that did not wear out, houses that did not depreciate, and even if we could maintain our bodily condition without eating, we would clearly be much better off.

It is this last consideration, perhaps, which makes one pause. Would we, for instance, really want an operation that would enable us to restore all our bodily tissues by intravenous feeding while we slept? Is there not, that is to say, a certain virtue in throughput itself, in activity itself, in production and consumption itself, in raising food and in eating it? It would certainly be rash to exclude this possibility. Further interesting problems are raised by the demand for variety. We certainly do not want a constant state to be maintained; we want fluctuations in the state. Otherwise there would be no demand for variety in food, for variety in scene, as in travel, for variety in social contact, and so on. The demand for variety can, of course, be costly, and sometimes it seems to be too costly to be tolerated or at least legitimated, as in the case of marital partners, where the maintenance of a homeostatic state in the family is usually regarded as much more desirable than the variety and excessive throughput of the libertine. There are problems here which the economics profession has neglected with astonishing singlemindedness. My own attempts to call attention to some of them, for instance, in two articles, as far as I can judge, produced no response whatever; and economists continue to think and act as if production, consumption, throughput, and the GNP were the sufficient and adequate measure of economic success.[3]

It may be said, of course, why worry about all this when the spaceman economy is still a good way off (at least beyond the lifetimes of any now living), so let us eat, drink, spend, extract and pollute, and be as merry as we can, and let posterity worry about the spaceship earth. It is always a little hard to find a convincing answer to the man who says, "What has posterity ever done for me?" and the conservationist has always had to fall back on rather vague ethical principles postulating identity of the individual with some human community or society which extends not only back into the past but forward into the future. Unless the individual identifies with some community of this kind, conservation is obviously "irrational." Why should we not maximize the welfare of this generation at the cost of posterity? *"Après nous, le déluge"* has been the motto of not insignificant numbers of human societies. The only answer to this, as far as I can see, is to point out that the welfare of the individual depends on the extent to which he can identify himself with others, and that the most satisfactory individual identity is that which identifies not only with a community in space but also with a community extending over time from the past into the future. If this kind of identity is recognized as desirable, then posterity has a voice, even if it does not have a vote; and in a sense, if its voice can influence votes, it has votes too. This whole problem is linked up with the much larger one of the determinants of the morale, legitimacy, and "nerve" of a society, and there is a great deal of historical evidence to suggest that a society which loses its identity with posterity and which loses its positive image of the future loses also its capacity to deal with present problems, and soon falls apart.[4]

Even if we concede that posterity is relevant to our present problems, we still face the question of time-discounting and the closely related question of uncertainty-discounting. It is a well-known phenomenon that individuals discount the future, even in their own lives. The very existence of a positive rate of interest may be taken as at least strong supporting evidence of this hypothesis. If we discount our own future, it is certainly not unreasonable to discount posterity's future even more, even if we do give posterity a vote. If we discount this at five percent per annum, posterity's vote or dollar halves every fourteen years as we look into the future, and after even a mere hundred years it is pretty small—only about one-and-a-half cents on the dollar. If we add another five percent for uncertainty, even the vote of our grandchildren reduces almost to insignificance. We can argue, of course, that the ethical thing to do is not to discount the future at all, that time-discounting is mainly the result of myopia and perspective, and hence is an illusion which the moral man should not tolerate. It is a very popular illusion, however, and one that must certainly be taken into consideration in the formulation of policies. It explains, perhaps, why conservationist policies almost have to be sold under some other excuse which seems more urgent, and why, indeed, necessities which are visualized as urgent, such as defense, always seem to hold priority over those which involve the future.

All these considerations add some credence to the point of view which says that we should not worry about the spaceman economy at all, and that we should just go on increasing the GNP and indeed the Gross World Product, or GWP, in the expectation that the problems of the future can be left to the future, that when scarcities arise, whether this is of raw materials or of pollutable reservoirs, the needs of the then present will determine the solutions of the then present, and there is no use giving ourselves ulcers by worrying about problems that we really do not have to solve. There is even high ethical authority for this point of view in the New Testament, which advocates that we should take no thought for tomorrow and let the dead bury their dead. There has always been something rather refreshing in the view that we should live like the birds, and perhaps posterity is for the birds in more senses than one; so perhaps we should all call it a day and go out and pollute something cheerfully. As an old taker of thought for the morrow, however, I cannot quite accept this solution; and I would argue, furthermore, that tomorrow is not only very close, but in many respects it is already here. The shadow of the future spaceship, indeed, is already falling over our spendthrift merriment. Oddly enough, it seems to be in pollution rather than in exhaustion that the problem is first becoming salient. Los Angeles has run out of air, Lake Erie has become a cesspool, the oceans are getting full of lead and DDT, and the atmosphere may become man's major problem in another generation, at the rate at which we are filling it up with gunk. It is, of course, true that at least on a microscale, things have been worse at times in the past. The cities of today, with all their foul air and polluted waterways, are probably not as bad as the filthy cities of the pretechnical age. Nevertheless, that fouling of the nest which has been typical of man's activity in the past on a local scale now seems to be extending to the whole world society; and one certainly cannot view with equanimity the present rate of pollution of any of the natural reservoirs, whether the atmosphere, the lakes, or even the oceans.

I would argue strongly also that our obsession with production and consumption to the exclusion of the "state" aspects of human welfare distorts the process of technological change in a most undesirable way. We are all familiar, of course, with the wastes involved in planned obsolescence, in competitive advertising, and in poor quality of consumer goods. These problems may not be so important as the "view with alarm" school indicates, and indeed the evidence at many points is conflicting. New materials especially seem to edge toward the side of improved durability, such as, for instance, neolite soles for footwear, nylon socks, wash and wear shirts, and so on. The case of household equipment and automobiles is a little less clear. Housing and building construction generally almost certainly has declined in durability since the Middle Ages, but this decline also reflects a change in tastes toward flexibility and fashion and a need for novelty, so that it is not easy to assess. What is clear is that no serious attempt has been made to assess the impact over the whole of economic life of changes in durability, that is, in the ratio of capital in the widest possible sense to income. I suspect that we have underestimated, even in our spendthrift society, the gains from increased durability, and that this might very well be one of the places where the price system needs correction through government-sponsored research and development. The problems which the spaceship earth is going to present, therefore, are not all in the future by any means, and a strong case can be made for paying much more attention to them in the present than we now do.

It may be complained that the considerations I have been putting forth relate only to the very long run, and they do not much concern our immediate problems. There may be some justice in this criticism, and my main excuse is that other writers have dealt adequately with the more immediate problems of deterioration in the quality of the environment. It is true, for instance, that many of the immediate problems of pollution of the atmosphere or of bodies of water arise because of the failure of the price system, and many of them could be solved by corrective taxation. If people had to pay the losses due to the nuisances which they create, a good deal more resources would go into the prevention of nuisances. These arguments involving external economies and diseconomies are familiar to economists and there is no need to recapitulate them. The law of torts is quite inadequate to provide for the correction of the price system which is required, simply because where damages are widespread and their incidence on any particular person is small, the ordinary remedies of the civil law are quite inadequate and inappropriate. There needs, therefore, to be special legislation to cover these cases, and though such legislation seems hard to get in practice, mainly because of the widespread and small personal incidence of the injuries, the technical problems involved are not insuperable. If we were to adopt in principle a law for tax penalties for social damages, with an apparatus for making assessments under it, a very large proportion of current pollution and deterioration of the environment would be prevented. There are tricky problems of equity involved, particularly where old established nuisances create a kind of "right by purchase" to perpetuate themselves, but these are problems again which a few rather arbitrary decisions can bring to some kind of solution.

The problems which I have been raising in this paper are of larger scale and perhaps much harder to solve than the more practical and immediate problems of the above paragraph. Our success in dealing with the larger problems, however, is not unrelated to the development of skill in the solution of the more immediate and perhaps less difficult problems. One can hope, therefore, that as a succession of mounting crises, especially in pollution, arouse public opinion and mobilize support for the solution of the immediate problems, a learning process will be set in motion which will eventually lead to an appreciation of and perhaps solutions for the larger ones. My neglect of the immediate problems, therefore, is in no way intended to deny their importance, for unless we make at least a beginning on a process for solving the immediate problems we will not have much chance of solving the larger ones. On the other hand, it may also be true that a long-run vision, as it were, of the deep crisis which faces mankind may predispose people to taking more interest in the immediate problems and to devote more effort for their solution. This may sound like a rather modest optimism, but perhaps a modest optimism is better than no optimism at all.

Notes

1. Ludwig von Bertalanffy, *Problems of Life* (New York: John Wiley and Sons, 1952).

2. Richard L. Meier, *Science and Economic Development* (New York: John Wiley and Sons, 1956).

3. Kenneth E. Boulding, "The Consumption Concept in Economic Theory," *American Economic Review,* 35:2 (May 1945), pp. 1–14; and "Income or Welfare?" *Review of Economic Studies,* 17 (1949–50), pp. 77–86.

4. Fred L. Polak, *The Image of the Future,* Vols. I and II, translated by Elise Boulding (New York: Sythoff, Leyden and Oceana, 1961).

17

Marxian Crisis Theory and the Contradictions of Late Twentieth-Century Capitalism

Thomas E. Weisskopf

In this paper I raise the following question: does Marxian crisis theory provide a useful framework within which to analyze late twentieth-century capitalism? My answer, baldly put, is *no*. Not that contemporary capitalism is free of any crisis tendencies; quite the contrary. But the kind of crisis tendencies on which Marxian crisis theory has focused attention are, I believe, becoming less and less relevant to contemporary capitalist societies, while different sources of capitalist crisis are becoming increasingly significant. Indeed, I will argue that to gain an understanding of the type of generalized crisis to which the advanced capitalist nations are likely to become increasingly vulnerable in the future, we must look not to Karl Marx but to David Ricardo and to Karl Polanyi.

I begin in section 1 with a review of Marxian crisis theory in its various formulations, drawing both on Marx's own writings and on the writings of contemporary Marxian scholars. In section 2, I address two key questions: is late twentieth-century capitalism significantly different than the capitalism that developed in the early decades following World War II, and is it possible that the world capitalist system is now emerging from the generalized economic crisis which plagued it in the 1970s and at least the early 1980s? Tentatively affirmative answers to these questions lead me in section 3 to suggest that changes in the internal character and external environment of the capitalist system have rendered Marxian crisis theory increasingly irrelevant as a basis for analyzing the

This paper was originally presented at the conference "Marxism Now: Traditions and Difference," 30 November–2 December 1989, at the University of Massachusetts-Amherst. I am grateful to Sam Bowles, David Gordon, Ron Caplan, and Bruce Norton for their constructive comments on an earlier draft, but I remain solely responsible for this final version. Reprinted with permission from *Rethinking Marxism,* Vol. 4, No. 4 (Winter 1991).

evolution and potential contradictions of contemporary capitalism. In sections 4 and 5, I seek to analyze what I believe to be the two most important potential sources of contradictions in contemporary capitalism: the deterioration of the natural environment and the deterioration of the social environment, respectively. I conclude in section 6 with some more speculative observations about the nature of the crisis tendencies of late twentieth-century capitalism and the kind of structural transformation that might be necessary to overcome them.

A Brief Review of Marxian Crisis Theory[1]

Marx's Own Writings

Capitalism, for Karl Marx, was a mode of production that would foster a historically unprecedented rate of capital accumulation and a consequently rapid development of the forces of production. Yet Marx also argued that capitalism would subject itself periodically to serious structural crises—crises that would disrupt the process of accumulation and ultimately threaten the viability of the mode of production itself. The possibility of such structural crises he attributed to the use of money in exchange and the anarchy of capitalist production. But the mechanism generating crises, according to Marx, was the internally contradictory nature of the accumulation process under the capitalist mode of production: as he expressed it in *Capital,* volume 3, "the *true barrier* to capitalist production is *capital itself*" (1967, 250).

The theory of capitalist economic crisis that Marx developed most fully in *Capital* was linked to his "law of the tendency of the rate of profit to fall." According to this law, the capitalist accumulation process generates a rise in the organic composition of capital (usually interpreted as the ratio of constant capital to variable capital, a measure of the capital-intensity of production). The rise in this ratio is contradictory in that it tends to erode the basis (variable capital) on which surplus value is created, thus reducing the rate of profit (the ratio of surplus value to total—constant plus variable—capital). Marx identified five possible counteracting tendencies to this logic, but he believed that in the long run an inexorable rise in the organic composition of capital (ROCC) would force down the rate of profit and thereby ultimately arrest the accumulation process itself.

Elsewhere in *Capital,* Marx alluded to different kinds of internal contradictions that could lead to capitalist crisis. One of these was the tendency of the capitalist accumulation process to restrict the purchasing power of the masses (i.e., workers, as distinct from capitalists). Since workers generally need to spend most or all of their income in purchasing the necessities of life, while capitalists need not do so, a shift in the distribution of income against wages and in favor of profits would tend to depress the total demand for commodities. If and when this occurred, capitalists would not be able to sell (at full value) all of the commodities they had produced, and a crisis of failure to "realize" surplus value would ensue. Although Marx himself did not explicitly draw such a conclusion, the logic of this realization failure (RF) argument points to a long-run secular tendency toward economic stagnation in capitalist economies.

Yet another possible source of crisis identified by Marx was the tendency for the capitalist accumulation process to deplete the excess supply of labor represented by the "industrial reserve army." Depletion of the industrial reserve army is contradictory for the accumulation process because it makes it more problematical for capitalists to fire workers and thus it tends to strengthen the bargaining power of the working class. A stronger bargaining position enables workers to claim a higher share of income in wages, which in turn is likely to result in a fall in the rate of profit and a fall in the rate of accumulation. Because the slowdown in accumulation would itself tend to replenish the reserve army, Marx viewed this depletion of the reserve army (DRA) crisis scenario as one that could explain a cyclical pattern of boom and crisis but not a long-run secular tendency toward a major structural crisis.

Each of the three variants of Marxian crisis theory highlighted by this brief review points to a different possible source of capitalist economic crisis. In the language of contemporary economics, the potential sources of crisis can be described as follows: (1) accumulation-induced changes in the development and application of technology, which reduce the rate of profit by reducing the output generated by a unit of capital; (2) accumulation-induced changes in the pattern of spending, which lead to a deficiency in aggregate demand relative to aggregate supply; and (3) accumulation-induced changes in the relative power of workers and capitalists, which reduce the rate of profit by reducing the share of output going to capital. These three alternative variants of Marxian crisis theory are based on putative contradictions of accumulation arising in the spheres of production, circulation, and distribution, respectively.

The Work of Contemporary Marxian Political Economists

Since Marx's time many Marxian scholars have sought to develop and extend his analysis of capitalist economic crises in such a way as to shed light on the actual experience of industrialized capitalist economies. A variety of different crisis theories has been advanced to explain periods of capitalist crisis; but almost all of these theories can be associated in their general approach with one of the three variants—ROCC, RF, or DRA—of Marx's own crisis analysis described above.

The essence of Marx's ROCC theory of crisis is that the development of technology and/or the choice of techniques of production by individual competing capitalist firms, each seeking to improve its own competitive position through profit-making and capital accumulation, results at the aggregate level in a decline in the ratio of output to capital stock and a consequent decline in the rate of profit. This argument has generated an extensive debate among modern

Marxian economists as to the conditions under which it could possibly be valid. Okishio (1961) and others (Steedman 1977; Roemer 1979; Bowles 1981) have shown that if the real wage is held constant, there is no way in which the introduction of new techniques of production by competitive profit-maximizing capitalist firms could lead to a decline in the aggregate rate of profit. But proponents of the ROCC theory have questioned whether the real wage should be held constant, and they have formulated several more or less plausible scenarios under which a process of technological change by competitive capitalist firms could (but need not necessarily) end up lowering the aggregate rate of profit (see Shaikh 1982; Foley 1986, ch. 8; Laibman 1987).[2]

The essence of Marx's RF theory of crisis is that the capitalist accumulation process operates to distribute purchasing power in such a way that aggregate demand does not keep pace with the aggregate supply of commodities. This argument has been most fully developed by Sweezy (1942) and Baran and Sweezy (1966), and it has an obvious affinity with Keynesian macroeconomic theory. In distinguishing sharply between capitalists and workers and their respective incomes and spending patterns, however, it is more Marxian (and Kaleckian) in spirit. Most modern proponents of an RF theory of long-run capitalist stagnation link its relevance to the rise of giant corporations in the twentieth-century "monopoly" phase of capitalist development (see Steindl 1952; Baran and Sweezy 1966; Foster 1987). It is argued that the real purchasing power of the working class will be more restricted by monopolistic than by competitive firms, and/or that incentives to invest will be restrained by monopolistic competition.

Marx's DRA theory of crisis is grounded in conflict between capitalists and workers over the distribution of income, and the relative ability of each class to exercise power on behalf of its own distributive claim. Although intended by Marx to serve as an explanation of the cyclical downturns (and upturns) associated with the short-run capitalist business cycle, its basic logic can also be applied to deeper and longer economic crises (and booms)—such as those associated with long waves in capitalist development. The DRA approach has been extended by contemporary Marxian scholars (Rowthorn 1976; Bowles, Gordon, and Weisskopf 1983, 1990; Weisskopf, Bowles, and Gordon 1985) to include additional sources of distributive claims conflicting with the capitalist claim of profits, such as the income claims advanced by foreigners (via the terms of international trade) and domestic citizens (via state taxation). The scope of the theory has also been extended beyond conflict over distributive shares to conflict over other factors that affect the profit rate—for example, the output-capital ratio, which depends *inter alia* on technological choices made by capitalists seeking to maintain effective control over workers, and on government regulation of business in response to popular demands to protect citizen interests (see Bowles, Gordon, and Weisskopf 1986). With such extensions the DRA theory becomes a more general "challenges to capitalist power" (CCP) theory of capitalist economic crisis, and the relevant sources of power are broadened from the size of the reserve army of labor to a variety of social, political, and economic forces that affect the ability of different classes to attain their economic goals in conflict with one another.

The Application of Marxian Crisis Theory to Long Waves

Marxian crisis theory may be applied to the cyclical downturns of a capitalist economy associated with the short-run business cycle, but it is of greatest interest in its application to the longer periods of deep and generalized economic crisis associated with the long-wave behavior of capitalist economies. The history of modern capitalism suggests that there have been at least three periods during which most of the industrialized capitalist economies have experienced such a structural crisis. The first (and least certain) is the period of relatively deep recession in the last decade of the nineteenth century, referred to at the time as the "Great Depression." The second (and most certain) is the period of the 1930s, when most of the capitalist economies of the world were mired in what is now known as the "Great Depression." The third and most recent is the period of stagflation beginning in the early 1970s and lasting at least through the early 1980s, in which the entire world capitalist economy suffered simultaneously from slow growth, high unemployment, and high inflation.

Proponents of different variants of Marxian crisis theory have sought to apply them to some or all of the major capitalist structural crises identified above. Most of the literature on the ROCC theory has been theoretical in nature, but some contemporary Marxian scholars have suggested that a version of this theory can help explain the crisis of the late nineteenth century or the most recent economic crisis (see Wright 1979, ch. 3; Michl 1989). The RF type of Marxian crisis theory has often been applied to explain the economic crisis of the 1930s, although its application in this instance is not without controversy (see Devine 1983; Dumenil, Glick, and Rangel 1987); some scholars have also sought to explain the most recent economic crisis in RF terms (see Szymanski 1984; Foster 1987). Versions of the CCP variant of Marxian crisis theory have most often been applied to the most recent economic crisis (see Glyn and Sutcliffe 1972; Bowles, Gordon, and Weisskopf 1987).

My own view is that the crisis of the Great Depression lends itself most readily to an RF analysis (since inadequate aggregate demand was so obviously the major problem of the time), and that the most recent crisis of the "Great Stagflation" lends itself most readily to a CCP interpretation (since there is strong evidence of a profit squeeze before the end of the postwar growth boom). But my purpose here is not to argue the relative merits of different variants of Marxian crisis theory as applied to past capitalist crises. Rather, it is to examine the relevance of Marxian crisis theory—in any form—to contemporary capitalism as it is developing in the last two decades of the twentieth century.

Is Late Twentieth-Century Capitalism Still in Crisis?

Characterization of Late Twentieth-Century Capitalism

From the end of World War II up to the early 1970s the world capitalist economy experienced a period of rapid economic growth and capital accumulation which was unprecedented in scope. This long-wave boom—sometimes labelled the postwar "golden age" of world capitalism—was followed by a period of generalized economic crisis extending into the early 1980s. Whether this crisis is continuing up to the present time, or, alternatively, whether a new period of boom has begun in the 1980s, remains a matter of some controversy. What is clear, however, is that—partly as a consequence of the economic crisis in the 1970s—the institutional structure of the capitalist mode of production has undergone some important changes in recent years.

The institutional structure of the advanced capitalist economies in the first three decades following World War II could aptly be described as "welfare state capitalism." During this period, for the first time, all of the major features of the welfare state were in place (to different degrees, of course, in different countries). These welfare state features included a government commitment to maintain relatively high employment by means of Keynesian demand management, an extensive public system of social security, public provision for unemployment compensation, and in general an important role for the state both as purchaser and allocator of goods and services and as regulator of private businesses and labor markets.

With the growing economic crisis of the 1970s, however, pressures began to mount to change some of the basic structural characteristics of the post–World War II advanced capitalist economies. Right-wing political forces were successful in attributing much of the blame for the crisis to the "excesses" of the welfare state, and by the late 1970s and early 1980s right-wing parties desirous of cutting back the economic role of the state had scored significant political successes in national elections in many of the advanced capitalist countries. Especially notable were the electoral victories of Margaret Thatcher in the United Kingdom in 1979 and Ronald Reagan in the United States in 1980; their parties and ideological positions have remained dominant up to the present time. Most centrist and left-wing parties, feeling the pressure from the Right, have also modified their own economic policy positions in directions that would curb the extent and impact of the welfare state.

Contributing significantly to these changes has been the growing international economic integration of the world capitalist system. Active international markets for capital as well as goods and services have put increasing competitive pressure on business firms everywhere, and—most important—they have made it more difficult for individual governments to maintain national policies of any kind. In this context political coalitions supporting the major elements of welfare state capitalism have lost much ground to their neoconservative rivals, who favor further integration into the global market and the unleashing of market forces everywhere.

In view of all these developments, I think it is fair to conclude that the post–World War II system of welfare state capitalism has given way in the 1980s to a new type of system in the advanced capitalist nations.[3] The new system does not dispense with the welfare state, but it reduces significantly the economic role of the nation-state and it gives pride of place to market forces on a world scale. To characterize this new system, I will use the label "global market capitalism."

Performance by Conventional Quantitative Criteria

Does global market capitalism show any signs of generating a new long-wave economic boom in the wake of the crisis of the 1970s and early 1980s? In the decade following 1973 conventional macroeconomic performance indicators—such as the rate of GNP growth, the rate of labor productivity growth, the rate of unemployment, and the rate of inflation—painted an incontrovertible picture of growing stagflation in the capitalist world, culminating in the deep worldwide recession of the early 1980s. Since then, however, the picture has been rather more mixed. Across the advanced capitalist economies there have been signs both of improvement and of continuing stagnation in aggregate macroeconomic performance.[4]

In a few of the advanced capitalist economies—most notably the United States—there was a strong recovery of both output and employment after the nadir of the early 1980s. The Japanese economy, which suffered less in the hard times than most other capitalist economies, continued to record relatively high output growth throughout the 1980s—albeit with slowly rising unemployment rates. Most of the Western European economies showed faster output and productivity growth in the 1980s than in the 1970s, although unemployment has remained well above the levels achieved in the golden years before 1973. In all of these economies the rate of inflation has declined considerably from its level in the 1970s. Overall, in terms of such aggregate macroeconomic performance indicators, the 1980s were still closer to the stagnation of the 1970s than to the boom conditions of the "golden age"; but there is little question that the trend through the last decade has been upward.

The same mixed pattern is displayed by the two indicators of capitalist vitality most strongly highlighted by Marxian crisis theory—the rate of profit and the rate of capital accumulation. Profit and accumulation rates across the advanced capitalist economies were generally buoyant in the 1950s and 1960s, then dropped sharply in the late 1960s or early 1970s and remained very low into the early 1980s. Since then, however, they have risen again—though not to levels comparable with those of the 1960s.

It is surely too early to declare that the most recent generalized capitalist economic crisis is over; but with each year that passes without a major downturn, such a conclusion appears more warranted.[5] Indeed, I believe that if one confines attention to the kind of aggregate macroeconomic performance indicators I have mentioned here, the decade beginning around 1983 may well be seen as one in which the major capitalist economies rebounded from the doldrums of the 1970s and early 1980s to generate considerably more satisfactory macroeconomic performance.

Would this kind of macroeconomic recovery suggest that global market capitalism has been successful in rescuing a faltering capitalist system from its earlier crisis condition? In a limited sense, I think the answer is *yes*. Capitalism has proved itself historically to be a resilient economic system, capable of regenerating its economic dynamism after each major economic crisis in the past. Throughout the capitalist world today there are new signs of economic dynamism, although these are by no means ubiquitous across the economic landscape.

Still, in terms of its ability to deliver the goods, modern capitalism appears to have a great deal of life left in it. Anyone waiting for a terminal collapse in the capacity of capitalist economies to generate profits, capital accumulation, and economic growth is likely to have to wait a great deal longer.[6]

Performance by Increasingly Relevant Qualitative Criteria

Even if capitalism does continue to deliver the goods by conventional performance criteria, however, it does not follow that the capitalist system can be expected to grow smoothly and without contradictions for the foreseeable future, much less that it is a system that is capable of meeting real human needs. On the contrary, there is increasing evidence that the present direction of the advanced capitalist economies—however successful it may become in terms of conventional indicators of profitability, capital accumulation, and economic growth—is giving rise to increasingly serious problems.

To analyze capitalism in general, and contemporary global market capitalism in particular, in terms of conventional indicators of macroeconomic performance is to do so on the most favorable possible terms. In order to gain an understanding of the contradictions most likely to disrupt capitalist economic performance in the late twentieth century, one has to look first at several aspects of the current performance of the advanced capitalist economies that are obscured by conventional macroeconomic indicators.

The danger signals for the world capitalist system in the early 1990s are numerous. Economic stagnation and high unemployment still characterize many regions; major trade imbalances abound; the international debt situation is routinely described as one of crisis; and the burden of financing public programs and transfers is proving onerous to many governments, both national and local. But the single development that looms as most threatening in the long run is the *deterioration of the natural environment.*

In the late 1980s and early 1990s reports of the growing depletion of the atmospheric ozone layer, the gradual warming of the earth's temperature, the destruction of tropical rainforests, the salinization and desertification of crop lands, and so on, have underlined an ecological crisis of increasing proportions. The capacity of the earth to support life, to provide natural resource inputs, and to absorb waste products has been increasingly tested with each passing year. Capitalism has historically been highly successful at delivering a rapid rate of growth of material production and consumption; but now rapid economic growth, far from being a solution to the problems generated by capitalist development, is increasingly contributing to the magnitude of those problems via its impact on the natural environment.

Of course the capitalist economies are not the only ones that contribute to and are threatened by an ecological crisis. This is a global phenomenon and a global problem. But capitalism is clearly the dominant mode of production in the world, responsible for the lion's share of resource use, production, consumption, and waste disposal. And capitalist economies, especially when operating under market-oriented policies, are especially prone to generate ecologically unhealthy effects. This is both because environmental costs of production are largely external to the profit-maximizing calculus of individual firms, and because the kind of comprehensive planning necessary to assure ecologically sound resource use is anathema to capitalist free marketeers. Thus there is every reason to believe that under global market capitalism the deterioration of the natural environment will become increasingly serious in the 1990s.

It is not only the natural environment that is threatened by the contemporary pattern of capitalist development; the same can be said of the "social environment." Under global market capitalism the capitalist economies of the world are generating *increasing inequalities*—by region, race, class, and gender—and *increasing insecurity and instability* for a large fraction of their populations. Economic divisions and economic insecurity lead to political and social tensions that can bring about a decline in the quality of life for everyone, as the social environment loses its capacity to sustain civil peace and harmony.

Evidence of the unusual degree of inequality fostered by capitalist growth under global market capitalism is provided by the very uneven pattern of recovery from the depths of the economic crisis in the early 1980s. Most of the advanced capitalist countries were characterized by rapid growth in certain favored regions (e.g., the two coasts in the United States, the south in the United Kingdom and Germany) and continuing stagnation in other regions (the Midwest and the farm states in the United States, the northern regions of the United Kingdom and Germany). Within the advanced capitalist nations service sectors have boomed while manufacturing sectors have generally languished. Of the "developing" capitalist economies some are booming (e.g., South Korea, Taiwan), while many are stagnating; and in all cases there are substantial internal regional differentials. In general, the dividing line between areas of prosperity and areas of stagnation in the capitalist world is now as often to be found *within* capitalist nations as *between* the advanced and the less developed nations. Apart from growing regional differentials, inequalities by sex, race, and ethnicity have tended to increase in most of the advanced capitalist nations as labor markets have become increasingly polarized between good jobs and bad jobs, and as previously secure and well-paid industrial working-class jobs have become scarcer.

Economic growth under capitalist relations of production has always tended to be highly uneven. Some regions do much better than others, depending on the match between current patterns of demand and regional resource endowments; regions that were initially advantaged tend to be able to build on those advantages, while initially disadvantaged regions fall further behind, in a dynamic of cumulative disequilibrium. Income distribution by class, race, and gender is subject to the same kind of disequalizing forces: initial advantages and disadvantages tend to cumulate over time as resources and opportunities flow disproportionately to those already in the strongest economic position.

As in the case of environmental deterioration, however, there is good reason to believe that in recent years the disequalizing tendencies of capitalist economic growth have become especially pronounced. First of all, the increasing degree of internationalization of the capitalist world economy has opened up much wider channels for the flow of resources from disadvantaged to advantaged regions. Under welfare state capitalism national governments had limited the disequalizing effects of unfettered capitalist economic activity by adopting policies designed to redistribute income and opportunity to the less advantaged sectors of the population, or at least to curb the gains flowing to the most advantaged. But under global market capitalism both the willingness and the ability of national governments to do so has been greatly diminished. These factors have combined to make the 1980s—and in all likelihood the 1990s—a period in which the naturally disequalizing tendencies of capitalist growth have been given unusually free rein.

In addition to its disequalizing tendencies, capitalism has always been an economic system in which considerations of security, stability, and community are subordinated to considerations of competition, change, and mobility. The history of capitalist development is marked by confrontation of the capitalist logic of the free market, and its attendant process of creative destruction and renewal, with popular demands for a more secure and fulfilling social and economic environment. Indeed, the rise of the capitalist state as an economic actor, culminating in the development of the welfare state, can be interpreted in considerable part as a response to popular resistance to the unfettered operation of free markets.

Once again, however, there is reason to believe that recent developments in the capitalist world have led to the exacerbation of insecurity of a kind that has long been characteristic of the capitalist growth process. The growth of international economic integration and competition has made economic activity in any given part of the world economic system much more vulnerable to developments elsewhere in the system. And the global market capitalism of the 1980s and 1990s has been characterized by a retreat from welfare state activities designed to promote economic security and community stability, and a consequent growth in the degree of insecurity and instability experienced by many people living within the capitalist countries. It is not unreasonable to attribute the recent growth of racism in the Western world, and the resurgence of neofascist political movements in countries like France and West Germany, to social tensions fostered by an economic system that no longer provides a modicum of stability and security to a large disadvantaged part of the population.

The deterioration of the natural and social environments of contemporary capitalist economies is clearly of major importance in any effort to examine the possibility of future structural crises. Yet these trends simply do not show up in the kind of aggregate macroeconomic indicators—such as the rate of output growth and the rate of profit—by which capitalist economic performance is conventionally measured.

The Increasing Irrelevance of Traditional Marxian Crisis Theory to Contemporary Capitalism

All of the variants of Marxian crisis theory discussed in section 1 share certain general features. First of all, they are concerned with *conventional* indicators of macroeconomic performance—such as the rate of growth of GNP, the rate of profit, the rate of capital accumulation, and the real wage rate. Even those Marxian ROCC theorists who work within the framework of the labor theory of value, utilizing value magnitudes such as the organic composition of capital and the rate of exploitation, are concerned to use their value analysis as a basis for explaining ultimately trends in the kinds of conventional macroeconomic indicators listed above.

Second, Marxian crisis theorists usually analyze *aggregate* macroeconomies—either national economies, or the capitalist sectors thereof, or entire sectors such as manufacturing. Finally, Marxian crisis theorists focus on *quantitative* (or at least quantifiable) macroeconomic variables, such as GNP, profit rates, distributive shares, capital stock, aggregate demand, capacity utilization rates, and so on. Even those Marxian CCP theorists who reason in terms of social and political factors affecting class conflict and power have sought to develop quantitative measures of the power wielded by different classes, in order to integrate this approach into quantitative analyses of the behavior of conventional performance indicators such as the profit rate and the accumulation rate (see, e.g., Bowles, Gordon, and Weisskopf 1986).

Thus it is fair to say that Marxian crisis theorists in general betray an economistic bias in their analysis. Theoretical models are formulated, and empirical analysis is carried out, in terms not too dissimilar from conventional macroeconomics. To be sure, Marxian crisis theorists pay much more attention than do orthodox macroeconomists to the profit rate as an object of analysis. Moreover, in seeking to explain the behavior of the profit rate, Marxian crisis theorists are much more likely to stress the role of class divisions (e.g., between capitalists and workers) in explaining patterns of consumption or the distribution of income. Some Marxian crisis theorists employ a value-theoretic framework foreign to orthodox macroeconomics; and those Marxian theorists concerned with class conflict and class power bring social and political elements into their analysis in a much more significant way than do conventional macroeconomists. But in the final analysis contemporary Marxist crisis theory presents itself as a somewhat wayward branch of modern macroeconomics rather than as a distinctively different way of assessing and analyzing macroeconomic trends in capitalist economies.

These observations about the economistic bias of Marxian crisis theory do not necessarily invalidate it as a source of insight into the behavior of the advanced capitalist economies. Indeed, I believe that the CCP theory provides a persuasive analysis of the decline in profitability experienced by virtually all of the advanced capitalist economies in the late 1960s and/or early 1970s, and this is a critical part of the story of the most recent economic crisis. However, I believe that actual developments in the 1980s—and prospective developments in the 1990s—are rendering Marxian crisis theory in any variant increasingly irrelevant as a basis for analyzing future crisis tendencies in the advanced capitalist economies.

First, as I have noted already in section 2, it is no longer clear that these economies are in fact in the kind of structural economic crisis to which Marxian crisis theory has generally been applied. Conventional macroeconomic performance indicators paint a rather ambiguous picture in the late 1980s and early 1990s, with most advanced capitalist economies doing better than in the 1970s although nowhere near as well as in the 1960s. Almost all the capitalist economies show economic dynamism in some regions and sectors—along with continuing economic stagnation in other regions and sectors. Such mixed evidence can be used either to claim that the capitalist world is still in a major structural economic crisis, or that it has begun to emerge from the most recent such crisis.

Second, the specific kinds of problems on which Marxian crisis theories focus attention no longer appear to pose major obstacles to the maintenance of profitability or capital accumulation in the capitalist world. There is little evidence that the current pattern of technological change is unusually or excessively biased toward labor-saving, capital-using techniques of production in such a way as to exert downward pressure on the rate of profit (as per the ROCC variant). Nor is there much evidence that distributive shifts in favor of capital in the 1980s have caused significant problems of realization (as per the RF variant). Although world demand has yet to regain the buoyancy of the 1960s and early 1970s, some markets are experiencing boom conditions while others are slowly emerging from the doldrums of the early 1980s. It has become increasingly apparent that capitalism can thrive on markets catering to the rich and to the military, without necessarily having to depend on the purchasing power of the masses. Finally, there is also little evidence that capitalists as a class have seen their profit shares or profit rates squeezed by the successful exercise of class power on the part of contending classes (as per the CCP variant). On the contrary, throughout most of the world capitalist system political developments in the 1980s have strengthened the power of capitalists relative to that of workers and other potential challengers.

In order to understand better the forces that might generate crisis conditions in the coming decades, we must be prepared to move beyond the conventional indicators of macroeconomic performance and the traditional variants of Marxian crisis theory.

The standard indicators of macroeconomic performance used by Marxist crisis theorists and conventional macrotheorists alike—rates of GNP growth, rates of capital accumulation, rates of profit, rates of real wage growth, and so on—have the virtue and the limitation that they are quantitative measures of economic activity associated with the production and consumption of goods and services. They fail to capture, however, the kind of qualitative elements of macroeconomic performance—in particular, changes in the quality of the natural environment and the quality of the social environment—which loom as increasingly important to the evolution of late twentieth-century capitalism.

Potential Contradictions of the Deteriorating Natural Environment

The Depletion of Environmental Assets

The evaluation of trends in the quality of the natural environment is important to an assessment of trends in the overall welfare of a society. An economy in which rapid growth in GNP is accompanied by rapid deterioration of the natural environment may not be performing as well as an economy in which GNP growth is much slower but whose natural environment is being maintained or enhanced. This suggests that conventional measures of aggregate economic welfare—such as the level of GNP in any given year—should be augmented by a commensurate estimate of the net change in the quality of the natural environment. The underlying principle is that measures of income or output should represent *sustainable* levels thereof—that is, levels of income or output generated by an economy *after* allowance has been made for the maintenance of the stock of (natural) "environmental assets" with which the economy began the year.[7]

This accounting principle is recognized in the case of physical capital assets: thus net national income/output is in principle a better measure of the current production of an economy than gross national income/output, because the former deducts from the latter an estimate of that part of current output that is needed to maintain the initial stock of capital assets. One should try to do the same with environmental assets, that is, deduct from measures of net national income/output an estimate of the amount of current output that would be necessary to maintain the quality of the natural environment at its beginning-of-the-year level. Societies that maintained their natural environment—either by pursuing development patterns that did not compromise its quality, or by undertaking activities designed to improve it—would be recognized as having performed correspondingly better, *ceteris paribus,* than societies whose development patterns put great stress on the environment and that did not undertake activities to offset this stress.

In practice, of course, it is extremely difficult to quantify changes in the quality of the natural environment. The quality of the natural environment depends on the cleanliness of air and water, and on the availability and quality of land, forests, animals, and mineral resources; more generally it depends on the maintenance of the earth's ecological balance. It is enhanced by measures that reduce pollution and acid rain, that purify the water in lakes and rivers, that increase the availability of parks and outdoor recreational facilities, and that nourish agricultural land. It is reduced by depletion of the ozone layer, by the warming of the earth's atmosphere, by the destruction of forests, by congestion of parks and wilderness areas and by the use of land as waste disposal sites.

Although it is currently still impossible to get even rough quantitative estimates of the net depletion of environmental assets in a given society, it is not so difficult to evaluate the general direction of change. The kind of evidence cited in section 2 leaves little doubt that in much of the capitalist world today (and no doubt in much of the noncapitalist world as well) the trend in the quality of the natural environment is downward. The last decade has witnessed increasing depletion of the atmospheric ozone layer, gradual warming of the earth's temperature, increasing destruction of tropical rainforests, major oil spills, contaminated beaches, polluted harbors and acid-rain-impacted forests and lakes, the depletion of fossil fuel reserves, the loss of arable land and green belts to urban and industrial expansion and waste disposal sites.

All of these trends cast increasing doubt on the validity of conventional measures of macroeconomic performance as indicators of the true prosperity of contemporary economies, because—for the most part—the depletion of environmental assets is simply not registered in the form of lower output or productivity growth rates, or lower profit rates and real wage rates. But the problem is greater than the neglect of environmental asset depletion by conventional performance measures. More than that, economic activities undertaken to limit the extent of depletion of such assets are often treated just like productive activities that increase the final output of goods and services available to a society, rather than as "environmental maintenance activities" that make no net contribution to the society's well-being.

Examples of environmental maintenance activities include the production and installation of pollution-control devices, the detoxification of rivers and lakes, the desalinization and reforestation of land, and programs to protect wild life and wilderness areas, all of which are designed to maintain the quality of the natural environment. Quite apart from the failure to take account of the depletion of societies' environmental assets, the treatment of such environmental maintenance activities as final-output-producing activities leads to overestimation of the true rate of growth of real income/output and of the true rate of profit and real wage.

The growing pressure of the pattern of contemporary capitalist development on the quality of the natural environment can thus show up either in the form of deterioration in the quality of that environment, or in the form of an increasing amount of economic activity devoted to efforts to maintain that quality. The evidence from recent years suggests that both of these outcomes are generally observed: the natural environment has been deteriorating in the 1980s and 1990s, at the same time as environmental maintenance expenditures have risen to limit the rate of deterioration.

Potential Contradictions

However seriously the trends in environmental quality and in environmental maintenance expenditure noted above may be detracting from the overall performance of contemporary capitalist economies and the overall welfare of contemporary capitalist societies, it remains to analyze how and why such trends should generate major structural crises. I have already suggested that the relevant trends are not generally registered in the form of lower rates of growth of conventional macroeconomic performance indicators such as the level or rate of growth of GNP. Nor do they necessarily show up in the form of reduced profit rates or reduced accumulation rates; so there might not be any symptoms of structural crisis in terms of traditional Marxian crisis theory. How then might the deterioration of the natural environment be contradictory for capitalism, that is, how might it interfere with the normal functioning of a capitalist system in such a way as to threaten the continuing viability of the system? Several possible scenarios come to mind.

First, it is possible that growing pressures on the natural environment might reach a point at which the capacity of the natural environment to support continuing production might become severely impaired. For example, warming of the earth's atmosphere might lead to climatic changes that would render a substantial amount of previously arable land unfit for further agricultural production; or depletion/exhaustion of a key mineral resource might make important lines of industrial production infeasible or prohibitively expensive. Such examples can be represented as cases of substantial technological regress: in an inversion of the usual pattern of technological progress, natural environmental conditions change in such a way as to *reduce* the real output that can be produced with given inputs of labor and capital.

Adjustment to technological regress would be difficult in any society. It is arguably especially difficult for a capitalist society because long-run growth of material production and consumption has traditionally been an especially important vehicle for managing the social and economic tensions that would otherwise arise from the uneven and unstable pattern of economic development so characteristic of capitalism. Without the lubrication of long-run material growth, the potential tensions could easily get out of hand.

A second possible contradiction scenario is one in which growing pressures on the natural environment are met by increasing expenditure on environmental maintenance activities designed to prevent an intolerable decline in the quality of the environment—for example, expenditure on land and forest replenishment and pollution control to limit the deterioration of the natural environment. Such expenditures would require that a growing proportion of the real output generated by productive economic activity be withdrawn from activities contributing to an enhancement of people's welfare and directed instead to activities preventing a decline in their welfare. The true net output of the economy would grow more slowly, or possibly even decline, and the distribution of the burden of that decline would become a contentious issue.

Just as in the previous case of effective technological regress, one would expect tensions to escalate over the way in which the burden of slow or negative real economic growth would be shared among different segments of the society. For the reasons suggested above, such a burden of economic sacrifice would likely be especially difficult for a capitalist society to manage. Issues of relative power might well arise around the distribution of the burden, much as in the class conflict and power analysis of the CCP variant of Marxist crisis theory. However, the present context is fundamentally different in that the claim competing with that of the capitalist class emanates originally not from the efforts of any other class or group to improve their economic position, but from a decline in the availability of real economic benefits to be shared among the competing claimants.

Either of these first two scenarios would sooner or later turn into a crisis of accumulation recognizable to Marxian crisis theorists; for some of the burden of technological regress would be likely to fall eventually on profits, and, even failing this, the investment climate would surely deteriorate. But note that such a scenario would not conform to any one of the three major variants of Marxian crisis theory, for the crisis would not involve the pattern of technological change, the inadequacy of aggregate demand, or a decrease in the power of the capitalist class relative to that of other contending classes.

Instead, the underlying problem could be described as a secular increase in the "real cost of social reproduction," resulting from the growing extent to which the carrying on of production and consumption activities draws on ultimately limited environmental resources (which should be accounted for at the effective cost of replacing them). It is not that some finite limit on the supply of any given resource may be reached at a certain time. It is rather that, as ever greater levels of production, consumption, and waste disposal are carried out, more and more stress is put upon the available land, water, and air, and it becomes increasingly difficult to gain access to new supplies of resources.

A final possible contradiction scenario is one in which growing pressures on the natural environment do not lead to serious constraints on continued production or to any significant increase in the burden of environmental maintenance expenditures; instead, in this scenario, they are allowed simply to take their toll on the quality of the environment. Although measured rates of growth of GNP and real wages and rates of accumulation and profit would be unaffected, people would begin to perceive that their welfare was deteriorating in an important respect. The decline in the quality of the natural environment could lead to such a decline in the perceived welfare of major segments of the society that a crisis not of accumulation but of the *legitimacy* of the existing economic system would develop. Reacting against the increasingly manifest inability of the existing system to provide for people's real needs—whatever the conventionally measured rate of growth of production and consumption—popular movements could conceivably arise to force a change to a new system less harmful to the quality of the natural environment.

This final scenario also involves an increasing real cost of social reproduction; but in this case the cost is borne not in the form of lower real incomes to some or all classes within the economic system, but in the form of a depletion of environmental assets (that would begin to impinge on real incomes in future years). Although the phrase "increasing real cost of social reproduction" is Marxian in terminology, my argument in this section of the paper is really more Ricardian than Marxian—Ricardian in its concern about the limits on economic activity imposed by an ultimately finite environment.[8]

Potential Contradictions of the Deteriorating Social Environment

The Augmentation of Social Tensions

Many of the points made in the previous section with respect to the quality of the natural environment apply in principle also to the quality of the social environment. Just as one should take into account changes in the natural environment in assessing a society's overall macroeconomic performance, so one would like to consider changes in the social environment in evaluating overall welfare.[9]

In practice, however, the quality of the social environment is even more difficult to conceptualize and even less quantifiable than the quality of the natural environment. The social environment is enhanced by the extent to which people feel secure in their homes, their neighborhoods, and their communities; by the amount of stability in their lives; and by the degree of peace and harmony in which they are able to live with and relate to one another. It is reduced by crime, strife, instability, war, and other such forms of social pathology affecting individuals, communities, and nations.

It would probably stretch the imagination too far to conceive of social environmental assets (peace? harmony?) that could be depleted like natural environmental assets. A preferable alternative may be to think of deterioration of the social environment in terms of the augmentation of social tensions. Societies whose pattern of development serves to reduce (or at least maintain) the current level of social tensions should be recognized as having performed correspondingly better, *ceteris paribus,* than societies whose pattern of development exacerbates social tensions.

Even in the absence of comprehensive quantitative indicators of trends in the extent of social tensions in the advanced capitalist countries, it is not difficult to evaluate the general direction of change in recent years. The kind of evidence cited in section 2 points to deterioration in the quality of the social as well as the natural environment. The 1980s and early 1990s have been characterized by growing inequalities of all kinds, as well as growing insecurity for large numbers of people. Most of the advanced capitalist world has experienced an increasing incidence of drug use and drug-related crime, heightened racial and ethnic tensions, and a declining sense of social and community responsibility.

These kinds of negative developments are of course not reflected in conventional macroeconomic performance indicators (except possibly the rate of unemployment, with which many indicators of social pathology are correlated). Yet, as in the case of the natural environment, the scope of the problem of a deteriorating social environment is understated by the extent to which social tensions have actually increased. This is because economic activities undertaken to limit or counteract the augmentation of social tensions are generally treated in the national accounts like final-output-producing activities, rather than as "social maintenance activities" that make no net contribution to society's well-being. Examples of social maintenance activities include the provision of police and security services, the operation of the judicial system, the building and operation of prisons, drug control programs and other public health activities, all of which are designed to maintain the quality of the social environment.

The increasingly adverse impact of the pattern of contemporary capitalist development on the quality of the social environment can thus show up either in the form of an augmentation of social tensions, or in the form of an increasing amount of economic activity devoted to efforts to contain those tensions. The evidence from recent years suggests that both of these outcomes are generally observed: the social environment has been deteriorating at the same time as social maintenance expenditures have risen to limit or counteract that deterioration.

Potential Contradictions

The more complex and interrelated the social and economic system becomes, the more stress is put on social relations among people and the greater the difficulty of maintaining the social environment. This trend is surely intensified by market-oriented forms of capitalism, as compared with welfare-state systems. But deterioration of the social environment need not necessarily prove contradictory for a capitalist society—particularly if it is occurring in the context of relatively good economic performance by conventional criteria. Indeed, the experience of countries like the United States and the United Kingdom in the last decade seems to suggest that capitalism (in its global market form) can thrive in spite of a very considerable augmentation of social tensions. There is reason to believe, however, that a continuing deterioration in the social environment will ultimately impair the process of capitalist development.

How might the deterioration of the social environment interfere with the normal functioning of a capitalist system in such a way as to threaten its continuing viability? Unlike the case of the natural environment, it does not seem possible that changes in the social environment could generate the equivalent of substantial technical regress. But each of the remaining two contradiction scenarios envisaged as a possible consequence of depletion of environmental assets has its counterpart in a scenario that could arise from growing social tensions.

Growing pressures on the social environment might well be met by increasing expenditure on social maintenance activities designed to prevent or counteract an intolerable augmentation of social tensions. For example, a surge in the incidence of crime might elicit major new expenditures on crime prevention, or the burgeoning of a poverty-related disease (such as AIDS) might require major new expenditures on public health programs. To finance such expenditures a growing proportion of the real output generated by productive economic activity would have to be withdrawn from activities contributing to an enhancement of people's welfare and directed instead to activities preventing a decline in their welfare. The true net output of the economy would grow more slowly, and the distribution of the burden of that decline would become a contentious issue.

In the other possible contradiction scenario, growing pressures on the social environment would not lead to any significant increase in the burden of social maintenance expenditures; instead, they would simply take their toll on the quality of the social environment. Although quantitative macroeconomic performance indicators would not necessarily be affected, people would surely perceive that their welfare was deteriorating in an important respect. The augmentation of social tensions could conceivably lead to such a decline in the perceived welfare of major segments of the society that a crisis of legitimacy of the existing economic system would develop.

Neither of these two contradiction scenarios would conform to any of the three major variants of Marxian crisis theory. Instead, the underlying problem could again be described as a secular increase in the real cost of social reproduction, referring in this case to the growing extent to which production and consumption activities generate social tensions. Whether the increase in social tensions is contained by social maintenance expenditures, or is allowed to proceed unchecked, it amounts to a real social loss and thus a "real cost of social reproduction." Here the Marxian phrase reflects an argument that is fundamentally Polanyian in its concern about the destructive social consequences of an unfettered market system.[10]

Toward a Crisis of Late Twentieth-Century Capitalism?

In analyzing the crisis tendencies of capitalism there is a natural tendency on the part of Marxian scholars to conflate normative critique of the capitalist system with positive analysis of capitalist contradictions. As a normative matter we deplore the deterioration of the natural environment and the poisoning of the social environment that accompanies the spread of global market capitalism. In our positive analysis we look for potential contradictions in such developments that could enhance the potential for transforming global market capitalism into a more rational and humane system.

It is tempting to assume that increasing irrationality (as in contemporary capitalist treatment of the natural environment) and increasing inhumanity (as in contemporary capitalist treatment of the social environment) will necessarily generate contradictions that render the system not only irrational and inhumane but also unviable. This is most likely to be the case if the potential contradictions impinge directly upon the process of capital accumulation—by causing the profit rate to fall and/or the investment climate to deteriorate to the point where a full-fledged crisis of accumulation is at hand. Such a consequence is envisaged in the first two contradiction scenarios involving the deterioration of the natural environment (in which the capacity of the natural environment to support production is impaired, and in which increasing environmental maintenance expenditures are undertaken) and in the first contradiction involving the deterioration of the social environment (in which increasing social maintenance expenditures are undertaken).

Yet if the potential contradictions do not impinge directly upon the accumulation process—as under the contradiction scenarios in which the natural or social environment is simply allowed to continue to deteriorate, without any expensive remedial action—then they may not render the capitalist system unviable. I have suggested that under these conditions a legitimacy crisis, rather than an accumulation crisis, may arise. But it is by no means clear that the tensions generated by a deteriorating natural or social environment would necessarily cause a legitimacy crisis of a magnitude that would really threaten the viability of the system.

In the case of an accumulation crisis the economic structure of the capitalist system is directly affected; in the case of a legitimacy crisis it is the political structure of the system that is directly affected. A capitalist society *could* be rendered unviable because of tensions generated in its political structure; but it *must* be rendered unviable if its economic structure is no longer capable of sustaining a positive rate of profit or a positive rate of accumulation. Thus an accumulation crisis is more certainly threatening to a capitalist society than a legitimacy crisis.

To be sure, pressure on the political structure arising from a legitimacy crisis could be translated into pressure on the economic structure. It would be if the political tensions had the consequence of seriously impairing the investment climate. And it might be if the political authorities were ultimately obliged to undertake environmental or social maintenance activities to stem the deterioration of the natural or social environment, and if a significant part of these maintenance expenditures were financed at the expense of profits. In either of these two cases, what began as a legitimacy crisis could end up becoming an accumulation crisis. Nonetheless, contradiction scenarios that lead initially to a legitimacy rather than an accumulation crisis appear somewhat less likely to threaten the viability of a capitalist system.

From this perspective it would appear that the deterioration of the natural environment poses a greater threat to the viability of contemporary global market capitalism than the augmentation of social tensions. For, as the Thatcher-Major and Reagan-Bush experiences have demonstrated so clearly, social tensions can be allowed to grow to a very considerable extent without necessarily undermining the perceived legitimacy of the capitalist system and the political strength of its strongest supporters and ideologues. But it is not at all so clear that environmental deterioration can be allowed to continue without generating insoluble political and economic problems for capitalism.

What would it take to prevent or overcome a crisis of the natural and/or the social environment? Now that it has become clear that in centrally administered socialist societies there was a deterioration in the natural and social environments at least as serious as those being generated under global market capitalism, one must address the question of whether there is any reason to expect that some form of socialism would be more capable of dealing with the potential problems that I have suggested will threaten the viability of capitalism. I believe the answer is definitely *yes;* but the case for this answer is necessarily rather general and abstract, for the requisite socialist alternative would have to be very different from the type of socialist societies that the world has known to date.

To restrain and ultimately reverse the ongoing deterioration of the natural environment it will be necessary to develop methods of coordinating the management of environmental assets in an ecologically sound manner. Some improvement could be expected from ecologically judicious state intervention into markets involving natural resource use and waste product disposal, so that negative externalities arising from the use of depleting assets and the abuse of the environment are internalized (requiring resource users and polluters to bear the true social costs of their activities). But the problem goes much deeper than this. To stem the powerful forces generating the deterioration of the natural environment it will be essential to reshape the whole contemporary pattern of production and consumption in such a way as to promote resource-nurturing rather than resource-using and resource-wasting activities.

To reverse the current deterioration of the social environment—the increasing inequality, insecurity, and instability associated with contemporary capitalism—it will be necessary to develop the capacity to impose politically determined social priorities on the market system, rather than letting unregulated markets govern the larger system. Some progress could undoubtedly be made by restoring and strengthening the kind of government welfare-state provisions that in the first few decades after World War II protected many individuals, groups, and communities from the worst ravages of the unfettered market. But the traditional means of rendering capitalist societies more humane are not likely to be sufficient to overcome the powerful global market forces that are currently shaping the social environment. Greater egalitarianism, community, and stability can only be achieved and preserved if the scope for play of the individualistic and competitive logic of the market is restricted and replaced in some important spheres by social and cooperative methods of decision making and resource allocation.

It is possible that a comprehensive structural reform of the global market capitalist system, with a view to guiding the market and intervening to counteract its most damaging effects, could succeed in significantly slowing the deterioration of both the natural and social environments while maintaining the capitalist foundations of the system. Such structural reform, to be successful, would surely have to be at least on the scale of the kind of political and economic restructuring of capitalism that has hitherto been possible only in the wake of a generalized economic crisis (e.g., the establishment of welfare-state capitalism following the devastation of the Great Depression).

To bring about a significant improvement in the natural and social environments, however, the socioeconomic system would have to be restructured to the point where its fundamental logic was transformed. The systemic need for continual growth in the production and consumption of material goods and services would have to be replaced by a systemic emphasis on redistribution and conservation. The sovereignty of the individual would have to yield much ground to the interests of the community, and effective mechanisms for making collective decisions democratically would need to be developed as viable alternatives to individual choice.

In short, many of the democratic and egalitarian ideals of socialism would have to be put into practice—as they have not been heretofore. But where Marx originally saw socialism as a system that would arise from the contradictions of a capitalist system that had produced the foundations for material abundance, it now appears that socialism will most likely be needed to overcome the contradictions of a capitalist system that is increasingly undermining those foundations.

Notes

1. Under the general heading of "Marxian crisis theory" I include the kind of crisis theories in the Marxian tradition that have received the most attention in the literature and

that have been most often applied to explain concrete periods of capitalist economic crisis. I recognize that Marx's work on accumulation and crisis has been and may be interpreted in many different ways; my brief survey is intended not to be exhaustive but to focus on the most prominent interpretations of Marxian crisis theory.

2. A somewhat different kind of theory in which a rising organic composition of capital is associated with a falling rate of profit has been developed by Moseley (1987), who emphasizes the Marxian distinction between productive and unproductive labor.

3. David Gordon (1988) has argued forcefully to the contrary that "recent changes in the global economy [amount to] the decay of the older order and not yet the inauguration of a new [order]" (p. 25). The wealth of statistical information on which Gordon bases his conclusion, however, extends only through the year 1984; I believe that subsequent developments justify my own conclusion.

4. The performance trends cited in the following paragraphs are based on standard national macroeconomic statistics compiled by the Organisation for Economic Cooperation and Development (OECD) and the U.S. Bureau of Labor Statistics (BLS).

5. The U.S. economy entered into a cyclical recession in mid 1990, and most of the capitalist economies have displayed sluggish growth at best in recent years; but this performance hardly amounts to a major downturn or a generalized economic crisis.

6. In a stimulating earlier critique of theories of capitalist crisis, John Willoughby (1989) has argued not only that global capitalism is not currently in crisis but that even the 1970s and the early 1980s did not constitute a period of generalized capitalist crisis.

7. The need to systematically incorporate trends in the quality of the natural environment into national income and product accounts has been recognized in a recently growing literature on integrated environmental and economic accounting; see, inter alia, Bartelmus (1987); Repetto et al. (1989); and Ahmad, El Serafy, and Lutz (1989).

8. Although Marxian crisis theory has not traditionally addressed concerns of environmental sustainability, Marxist theory in its broader dimensions may have much to contribute to the analysis of an ecologically finite world. For a persuasive argument to this effect, see Raskin and Bernow (1991).

9. Unlike the case of the natural environment, I am aware of no systematic effort to incorporate trends in the social environment into a national income accounting framework.

10. In a very interesting article that has stimulated my own thinking along these lines, Bienefeld (1989) draws attention to the way in which recent trends in world capitalism amount to "unlearning the lessons of history" drawn by Karl Polanyi—in particular, the lesson that a socioeconomic order in which the self-regulating market serves as the basic organizing principle cannot possibly be stable and viable in the long run.

References

Ahmad, Y.J.; El Serafy, S.; and Lutz, E., eds. 1989. *Environmental Accounting for Sustainable Development.* Washington, D.C.: The World Bank.

Baran, P. and Sweezy, P. 1966. *Monopoly Capital.* New York: Monthly Review Press.

Bartelmus, P. 1987. "Accounting for Sustainable Development," United Nations Department of International Economic and Social Affairs, Working Paper #8, New York.

Bienefeld, M. 1989. "The Lessons of History and the Developing World." *Monthly Review* 43 (July–August): 9–41.

Bowles, S. 1981. "Technical Change and the Profit Rate: A Simple Proof of the Okishio Theorem." *Cambridge Journal of Economics* 5 (June): 183–86.

Bowles, S.; Gordon, D.; and Weisskopf, T. 1983. *Beyond the Waste Land.* Garden City, NY: Anchor-Doubleday.

————. "Power and Profits: The Social Structure of Accumulation and the Profitability of the Postwar U.S. Economy." *Review of Radical Political Economics* 18 (Spring–Summer): 132–67.

————. 1987. "Power, Accumulation and Crisis: The Rise and Demise of the Postwar Social Structure of Accumulation." In *The Imperiled Economy*, book I, ed. R. Cherry et al. New York: Union for Radical Political Economics.

————. 1990. *After the Waste Land.* Armonk, NY: M.E. Sharpe.

Devine, J. 1983. "Underconsumption, Over-investment and the Origins of the Great Depression." *Review of Radical Political Economics* 15 (Summer): 1–28.

Dumenil, G.; Glick, M.; and Rangel, J. 1987. "Theories of the Great Depression: Why Did Profitability Matter?" *Review of Radical Political Economics* 19 (Summer): 16–42.

Foley, D. 1986. *Understanding Capital.* Cambridge, MA: Harvard University Press.

Foster, J. 1987. "What Is Stagnation?" In *The Imperiled Economy*, book I, ed. R. Cherry et al. New York: Union for Radical Political Economics.

Glyn, A. and Sutcliffe, B. 1972. *Capitalism in Crisis.* New York: Pantheon Books.

Gordon, D. 1988. "The Global Economy: New Edifice or Crumbling Foundations?" *New Left Review*, no. 168 (March–April): 24–65.

Laibman, D. 1987. "Technical Change and the Contradictions of Capitalism." In *The Imperiled Economy*, book I, ed. R. Cherry et al. New York: Union for Radical Political Economics.

Marx, K. 1967. *Capital.* Volume 3. New York: International Publishers.

Michl, T. 1989. "The Wage-Profit Function and US Manufacturing." *Review of Radical Political Economics* 20 (Summer–Fall): 80–86.

Moseley, F. 1987. "Marx's Crisis Theory and the Postwar U.S. Economy." In *The Imperiled Economy*, book I, ed. R. Cherry et al. New York: Union for Radical Political Economics.

Okishio, N. 1961. "Technical Change and The Rate of Profit." *Kobe Economic Review* 7: 86–97.

Raskin, P. and Bernow, S. 1991. "Ecology and Marxism: Are Green and Red Complementary?" *Rethinking Marxism* 4 (Spring): 87–103.

Repetto, R. et al., 1989. *Wasting Assets: Natural Resources in the National Income Accounts.* Washington, D.C.: World Resources Institute.

Roemer, J. 1979. "Continuing Controversies on the Falling Rate of Profit: Fixed Capital and Other Issues." *Cambridge Journal of Economics* 3 (December): 379–98.

Rowthorn, B. 1976. "Late Capitalism." *New Left Review*, no. 98 (July–August): 59–83.

Shaikh, A. 1982. "Neo-Ricardian Economics: A Wealth of Algebra, A Poverty of Theory." *Review of Radical Political Economics* 14 (Summer): 67–84.

Steedman, I. 1977. *Marx After Sraffa.* London: New Left Books.

Steindl, J. 1952. *Maturity and Stagnation in American Capitalism.* New York: Monthly Review Press.

Sweezy, P. 1942. *The Theory of Capitalist Development.* New York: Monthly Review Press.

Szymanski, A. 1984. "Productivity Growth and Capitalist Stagnation." *Science and Society* 48 (Fall): 295–322.

Weisskopf, T.; Bowles, S.; and Gordon, D. 1985. "Two Views of Capitalist Stagnation." *Science and Society* 49 (Fall): 259–86.

Willoughby, John. 1989. "Is Global Capitalism in Crisis? A Critique of Postwar Theories." *Rethinking Marxism* 2 (Summer): 83–104.

Wright, E. 1979. *Class, Crisis and the State.* London: Verso Press.